The Underground Railroad –
A Movement That Changed America

Book design by James Russell
Indexing and proofreading by Clive Pyne Book Indexing

Manufactured by CreateSpace

Registration with the US Government Copyright Office,
Washington, DC, applied for April, 2011.

Published in the United States of America by
St. Clair Press

Manufactured in the United States

First Edition

2018 2017 2016 2015 4 3 2 1

ISBN 978-1511569958

THE UNDERGROUND RAILROAD

A Movement That Changed America

Evelyn Millstein

ST. CLAIR
PRESS

This book is dedicated to three people:

My husband Al Millstein
who told me I must write this book,
then spent ten years helping me
turn my rough draft into a readable
manuscript.

Bob McGowan,
my wonderful publisher,
who first told me how much he
loved the book.

Ron Aronson
who took time out of his busy life
to edit the entire work.

PREFACE

The Underground Railroad was a movement that changed the course of our Nation's history, a story that, until now, had never fully been told. A well-organized movement, the Railroad was unique in that it was created and led by African Americans, the first interracial movement in American history. The Railroad was the only national antislavery organization with branches both in the North and South. Its members risked their lives by helping thousands of slaves find freedom in the North or Canada. These heroic men and women refused to obey the Fugitive Slave Law which defined slaves as property rather than persons, and made assisting a runaway a federal crime. The Underground Railroad organized such powerful civil disobedience struggles against officials trying to enforce the Fugitive Slave Law that the South felt that the very existence of their slave society was at risk. During the Civil War the Underground Railroad grew even stronger. President Lincoln stated that the thousands of fugitives who joined the Union army were crucial in bringing about the defeat of the Confederacy.

TABLE OF CONTENTS

Preface
Introduction

INTRODUCTION

When Jim Daniels, a Missouri slave, slipped across the border into the Kansas territories to find John Brown, he was a desperate man. In only two days, he, his wife and babies were going to be separated forever because they had all been sold to different slaveholders. Brown had become famous as the leader of an armed band of abolitionist men battling against the gangs of invading Missouri slaveholders determined to make Kansas a slave state. Daniels also knew that Brown was a conductor on the Underground Railroad. Daniels pleaded with Brown to help rescue his family and a group of other slaves whose families were also about to be torn apart. The fugitives knew that they would have to travel 1,000 miles to reach safety in Canada.

The rescue of a group of Missouri slaves should have been just another one of the thousands of secret rescues organized by the Underground Railroad. Then something happened that made this rescue unique. At one of the plantations, one of John Brown's rescuers, Aaron Stevens, had slipped into slaveholder David Cruise's house to bring out a young woman when Cruise suddenly appeared. Stevens believed that Cruise was about to shoot him, so he pulled out his own gun and opened fire. Cruise was killed instantly.

The escape of eleven slaves became front-page news all over the nation. John Brown became one of the most wanted men in America with a price of $3,000 on his head. Even the president of the United States, James Buchanan, offered a personal reward of $250 for Brown's capture. Teams of state posses and mobs of slave hunters set off to apprehend John Brown and the fugitives, and to collect the reward.

John Brown brilliantly turned this potential disaster into one of the great triumphs of the Underground Railroad. Brown called on William Hutchinson, the Kansas correspondent for the *New York Times* and asked him to meet the fugitives. Hutchinson was deeply touched when he heard their stories, and realized the suffering they were willing to endure for freedom. Hutchinson filled the New York Times with stories about the heroism of the fugitives. The winter of 1859 was bitterly cold, and his articles described in vivid detail how the runaways, many of them women and children, were forced to plow through deep snow drifts before they reached the next station on the Underground Railroad. One of Hutchinson's articles told the story of how John Brown and his men fought off a posse of seventy-five men. The entire North was mesmerized by this great escape.

Finally, on February 4, 1859, the fugitives reached the free state of Iowa. The entire town of Grinnell turned out to greet the exhausted fugitives with gifts of money and supplies. When the people of Springfield heard that several posses were still pursuing the fugitives, the town's citizens made a public statement that they would fight to the death against anyone who tried to seize the runaways.

On March 9 when the refreshed fugitives were ready to move on, they were escorted to the train station by an honor guard. The fugitives were hidden in a boxcar for their trip to Chicago. John Brown was worried about this last part of the escape because Chicago was teeming with posses and slave hunters eager to collect the many rewards that had been posted for the capture of the fugitives as well as his own arrest. Brown had traveled ahead of the fugitives so he could meet with the head of Chicago's Underground Railroad, black businessman John Jones and his white friend, Alan Pinkerton. Pinkerton, who two years later would be responsible for protecting President Elect Abraham Lincoln from a series of dangerous assassination plots, just laughed at Brown's worries. "Your fugitives are perfectly safe here in the city. If you are worried about the Fugitive Slave Law (which made it a federal crime for anyone to help a runaway slave), people here are so enraged over the law that it cannot be enforced in Chicago." And, Pinkerton continued, "You, John Brown, have become such a hero over this rescue that no official in the city dare arrest you." To prove his point, Pinkerton first approached a group of prominent citizens and quickly raised $600 for the fugitives. Then Pinkerton went to the home of Colonel O.C. Hammond, General Superintendent of the Michigan Central Railroad. Hammond immediately offered Brown a private car stocked with plenty of food and water which would travel non-stop to Detroit. Detroit's Underground Railroad had a ferry waiting that whisked the fugitives across the Detroit River to freedom in Canada.

This dramatic escape is only one example of the kind of power wielded by the Underground Railroad, a movement that helped change the course of American history, a movement whose real history has never before been told.

The Underground Railroad was the first interracial organization led by African Americans in our nation's history. Black people had been fleeing slavery ever since the first captured Africans were dragged off a sailing ship to be sold to Virginia planters in 1619. When the first Congress passed a Fugitive Slave Law in 1787 making it legal to pursue the slave owners' human property in every state or territory in the nation, African Americans responded by setting up a series of safe houses and networks to protect fugitives and guide them to freedom. Antislavery whites were part of the Railroad from the very beginning. By the 1830's, the Underground Railroad had well-organized networks that stretched from deep in the South all the way to Canada. Even in the slavery South, these secret networks had dedicated white rescuers. It was a comradeship that had never been seen before in America. But this does not explain how a minority of antislavery men and women, willing to risk their lives to aid fugitives, turned into the kind of powerful movement that would help change the course of American history. This book tells the way in which the struggles by Railroad members to challenge the Fugitive Slave Laws helped turn northerners from indifference to slavery to opposition to the South's "peculiar institution".

By 1830 cotton was the single most valuable commodity produced in the United States. Plantation owners were some of the wealthiest men in America; New England textile manufacturers were growing rich producing cotton cloth; northern merchants were flourishing on the sale of cotton products. Half the cargo in all of the ships traveling from American ports to Europe was cotton.

Slaveholders insisted that only slave labor could grow cotton, and these Americans who had succeeded beyond their dreams aggressively opposed anything that might upset the plantation system that was growing the golden crop. Outside of land itself, the major source of a Southerner's wealth was in his slave property. By 1860 the value of the four million men women and children held in bondage was close to three billion dollars in today's money. No wonder these rescuers were seen by southerners as criminals out to steal their valuable property. In 1787, Southern leaders convinced their local assemblies to vote in favor of the new Constitution by promising them that the Fugitive Slave Clause, backed by the power of the new Federal government, would stem the flow of fugitive slaves.

Instead, individual antislavery rescuers responded to the Fugitive Slave Clause of the Constitution by creating a new organization, the Underground Railroad. The first great heroes of the Railroad were the fugitive slaves themselves. What great courage it took to leave the only world they had ever known, beloved family members and friends, and strike out into the unknown with only the north star to guide them. The risks were enormous. If you failed, as so many fugitives did, the punishment was brutal. Severe beatings and other forms of torture were common. Some runaway slaves were permanently maimed with ears or limbs amputated. Other recaptured fugitives were hanged as an example to any other slave thinking of running away. Any southern rescuer, black or white, caught aiding a fugitive, was sure to face a long jail sentence. For some white rescuers, their fate was a mystery; they simply disappeared forever. Yet in spite of the danger, the southern Railroad's networks continued to grow. Its operations were so secret that it remained a puzzle that Southerners never solved. This book only begins to tell the story about its range and complexity.

Every man, woman or child who succeeded in escaping was a threat to the whole system of slavery. Not only did every escape mean that the slaveholder had lost a piece of valuable property, but it challenged the whole excuse for slavery itself. Black people, slaveholders were telling the world, were incapable of living independent lives outside the benevolent care of their masters. Since slaves were "incapable of making their own plans or even thinking for themselves," it had to be some outside force that was seducing their contented and docile slaves into running away. They quickly decided it must be those "dammed northern abolitionists" sneaking into their peaceful southland and inducing their slaves to flee.

By the 1830's the South's paranoia about the North began to escalate. The American Constitution was a compromise document; in it slave states had won some significant concessions from the North which led them to believe that the institution of slavery was going to be even more protected under the new Constitution than it had been under the old Articles of Confederation. One of the most important compromises came during the debate over elections to the House of Representatives. When the delegates decided that the number of representatives allotted to each state would be based on population, the South fought and won the right to have their slaves counted as 3/5th of a man. This victory was important because it increased the number of representatives their region would have in the new congress.

The Fugitive Slave Clause was another victory for the South. Southern delegates declared that slavery was more protected within the new federal government than ever before.

In 1836, Elijah Lovejoy, the white publisher of an antislavery newspaper, was murdered in Illinois by a pro-slavery mob. Northerners were horrified. A white man was killed simply because he dared publish an antislavery newspaper. Northerners began to speak out against a new danger to their liberties: they called it "slave power."

Southerners never understood how every discussion of slavery in Congress and in Northern newspapers managed to reach slave cabins in the South so quickly, even though it was a criminal offence to teach a slave to read. The slave grapevine operated so effectively because slave servants were everywhere and totally ignored by slaveholders. While waiting on tables, cleaning, cooking, and driving carriages, they were also listening to the conversations of their masters. These household servants carried the news of events to everyone in the slave quarters. Later during the Civil War, Union soldiers were surprised to find a cherished picture of John Brown, torn from some local newspaper and hidden for years, now hanging in a place of honor in so many slave cabins.

Baffled by the slave grapevine and desperate to keep their slaves isolated and ignorant, Southern politicians began a campaign to keep the entire nation from talking about slavery. They insisted that Congress reject any discussion of slavery. They forced Congress to pass the Gag Rule that forbade Congress from accepting any antislavery petitions. Northerners were furious. How dare Southerners tell a citizen of the North that he was forbidden to send a petition on slavery to his own congressional representative? Angry protests poured into Congress until, in 1844, the House of Representatives was forced to repeal the Gag Rule.

In the 1840's fugitive slaves had become some of the most popular speakers on the northern lecture circuit. This celebrity status was destroying the rosy picture of plantation life that slaveholders had been promoting for years. The whip lashes on Frederick Douglass's back; the agony displayed by Henry (Box) Brown when he talked about watching his wife and babies shackled to a slave trader to be taken away from him forever; the painful experience of the beautiful Ellen Craft, a woman as white as their own wives or daughters describing her life as a slave, changed the way many northerners felt about slavery. As more and more slaves fled north, they were followed by bands of slave hunters invading northern communities. As a result slavery was no longer a distant evil as northerners were forced to watch black people being dragged away in chains.

During the 1840's the South began to believe that the North was turning against slavery. How else could one explain that a slew of new organizations known as Vigilance Committees had set up shop in several northern cities? These Vigilance Committees' public mission was to protect the rights of free black citizens, but everyone understood that most of the Committees were really terminal stations of the Underground Railroad. City governments ignored their existence. As slave hunters invaded more and more northern communities in search of runaways, people demanded that their government do something to control this invasion. Many of the states responded by passing a series of Personal Liberty Laws that made it illegal for any state or local government officials to aid an owner or slave hunter when they tried to recapture their "human property." The Fugitive Slave Law was publically defied in several northern communities in Iowa, Wisconsin and Michigan. Slave hunters in those communities discovered that, when they tried to recapture a fugitive, they themselves were arrested on kidnapping charges. Southern paranoia grew increasingly strong, and some of their more radical politicians began talking openly about secession.

The Mexican-American war was over; the peace treaty gave America a vast new territory reaching from the Rio Grande to the Pacific Ocean. A new war was just beginning, a war within the nation itself. The question that was dividing the country was the demand by southerners for the legal right to bring their slaves into all of these new territories, since they lay below the Mason Dixon line. While northerners seemed resigned to allow slavery to continue in the South where it had always been legal, they were adamant that slavery must never be introduced into these new lands.

In 1849 the political battle between North and South became so bitter that the United States Government was paralyzed. For almost a year it was impossible to pass any piece of legislation, no matter how vital. Then in 1850, Senator Henry Clay, the great compromiser, came up with a solution. In his plan, each side would get one of their major demands and, at the same time, give up another demand. The North demanded that California enter the Union as a free state. The South had demanded that they be allowed to bring their slaves into California. For months the battle raged on; then Clay offered the South something they wanted even more than California – the most far-reaching, comprehensive new Fugitive Slave Law that Congress could write. This draconian law gave complete power to slaveholders or their representatives (slave hunters) to capture any black man they suspected of being a fugitive. They no longer had to go into a court of law to prove that their suspect was indeed a fugitive slave; instead, all they had to do was obtain the signature of a single magistrate, appointed by the federal government. This magistrate would receive $5.00 if he freed the suspect, but $10.00 if he allowed the suspected fugitive to be returned to slavery. The law made it a crime to aid a fugitive, and an even more draconian section of the law required that every citizen must help a slaveholder or slave hunter recapture a suspected runaway slave. This new law turned every northerner into a slave hunter. The South believed that passing a powerful Fugitive Slave Law would help stem the flood of slaves fleeing north. They also believed that this new law would destroy the Underground Railroad. For this they were willing to give up California. Thus the Great Compromise of 1850 was passed, and the United States government began to function normally again.

Northerners were furious at the new law, and many people vowed that they would resist it. There were whole communities, like the citizens of Syracuse, New York, who publically vowed to resist the Fugitive Slave Law. On October 21, 1850, the City of Chicago adopted a series of resolutions releasing city officials from obeying any provisions of the law. An additional resolution set up a special branch of Chicago's police force made up only of black policemen whose only job was to patrol the city's streets, monitoring every known slave hunter, to make sure they did not seize any suspected fugitive.

Southerners watched angrily in 1851 as fugitive Shadrack Minkins was rescued right out of a Boston courtroom by a well-organized band of Underground Railroad activists and sent on to safety in Canada. When the Federal government tried the leader of this group of rescuers, Lewis Hayden, a Boston jury refused to convict him. Later that year, in Christiana, Pennsylvania, there was a bloody confrontation between a slave owner leading a federal posse and a group of black men and women determined to protect the fugitive slaves hiding in the home of local black leader, John Parker. When the slaveholder was killed, Parker and many of the other blacks managed to escape. Federal officials were so infuriated when they were unable to capture a single one of the rescuers, they instead arrested two white Quakers who had been at the scene. These two men had rushed to the Parker house hoping to help end the confrontation. The government charged the peace-loving Quakers with treason. Federal government officials explained the extreme charge by insisting that, under the Fugitive Slave Law, it was treasonous to refuse to join a slave hunting posse. The entire nation was outraged that two Quakers, whose religion forbade them from any form of violence, would be charged with such a serious crime. It did not take long for a jury to acquit the two men. The level of anger against the Fugitive Slave Law continued to rise. It was no wonder that, by the time John Brown led his band of fugitives from Missouri to Detroit, many communities very publicly welcomed the fleeing slaves. By 1859, the State Supreme Courts of Wisconsin and Ohio were ready to declare the Fugitive Slave Law unconstitutional in their states.

Many Southerners grew increasingly concerned over the North's growing antislavery actions. As they watched northerners' escalating public defiance of the Fugitive Slave Law, they felt that this was only the first step in the abolition of slavery itself. When Abraham Lincoln was elected president in 1860, the South decided against any further compromises to save the Union. In 1861, eleven states seceded from the Union.

In 1861 when the war began, Abraham Lincoln insisted that the Civil War was a war whose only goal was to preserve the Union. The Abolition Movement almost immediately began to challenge the significance of the war. In the beginning, Lincoln was eager to reassure slaveholders that he had no intention of interfering with slavery. He promised that the Fugitive Slave Law would still be enforced even for Confederate slaveholders. But in May 1861, at Fortress Monroe, Virginia, a Union military installation, three fugitive slaves hoped that this fort could be the newest station on the Underground Railroad. They told the commander of Fort Monroe, General Butler, that they had run away from the Confederate front where they had been ordered to help build a series of new fortifications. The General was happy to have a few extra hands to work on his own fortifications. When their angry owner showed up under a flag of truce demanding the return of his slaves, Butler refused, announcing that these ex-slaves were now contraband of war. The news spread swiftly throughout the local slave quarters that General Butler was protecting fugitives. Within three months, hundreds of slaves showed up at Fortress Monroe. Soon Union installations all over northern Virginia were flooded with runaway slaves. Since the Union army was always short of workers, these "contrabands" were quickly put to work, and Lincoln's policy of enforcing the Fugitive Slave Law was in tatters.

In 1862 Lincoln could not decide what to do with the thousands of "contrabands." On one hand the President was still trying to convince slaveholders in the border states of Maryland, Kentucky, and Missouri that he was not out to liberate their slaves. Sometimes a Union officer would still be ordered to return a fugitive to a slaveholder. Most of the time, however, the Union army was so short of workers, needed for digging trenches and building forts, that they ignored the Fugitive Slave Law completely.

When the war began, the Confederate government was smugly confidant that they had the manpower to win the war. Their secret weapon was slavery. "Our slaves," they boasted, "would be happy to labor in the trenches to support our army, while all of our soldiers will be free to fight on the battlefield." To the government's amazement, their loyal slaves began to flee to the Federal forces the moment the Union army appeared. The Confederate army was forced to assign soldiers to guard duty to prevent their slave workers from escaping, soldiers that were badly needed on the battlefield.

As soon as the war began, African Americans began pleading with the Federal government to let them fight. For the first two years of the war, the answer they got was a resounding no. This war, they were told, was not about slavery, and there was no place for black men in the Union army. Besides which, Lincoln had been told that black men were incapable of fighting in a war. If you gave a black man a gun, not only would he flee in terror from the battlefield, but his weapon would quickly fall into the hands of the Confederate Army. Of course the reality was that African Americans had been fighting against the Confederacy since the war began because they had already set up a widespread spy network throughout the South. This network had become the most important spy operation for the Union army. Black men were soon recruited as army scouts and, by 1862, many of these scouts were mounting guerrilla raids deep into Confederate territory.

Stories of the courage and skill of these black Union supporters changed the President's mind about the ability of African Americans to fight. As part of the Emancipation Proclamation in 1863, Lincoln invited black men of the North and South to enlist in the Union army. The courage of these black troops at Port Hudson, Fort Wagner and Chaffin Farm and many other battlefields proved conclusively that African Americans were formidable soldiers.

The leaders of the Confederacy were also impressed by the fighting ability of their ex-slaves. In the late fall of 1864, the war was going badly for the Confederate army. Casualties were high; they desperately needed to find new troops to fight on the battlefield, but there was no place left to find them. Jefferson Davis reluctantly told Congress that, if the Confederacy was going to survive, it would have to recruit their own slaves to fight on the side of the South. The only way that we can convince our slaves to fight for us, Davis argued, was to offer them freedom if they joined our army.

A torrent of outrage and rejection greeted this announcement. After all, his many critics shouted, the South created the Confederacy in order to protect slavery. Now Jefferson Davis proposed to destroy slavery. Most southerners refused to even consider such a proposal. Davis explained only to his closest confidants that slavery was already dead, and that the survival of the Confederacy depended on the fighting power of their own slaves. Only when General Robert E. Lee joined Davis in supporting the proposal to enlist slaves in the army did the Confederate Congress agree to allow blacks into their army. Before the recruitment campaign could be implemented the war ended.

On January 31, 1865 Congress voted to pass the 13th Amendment to the Constitution which abolished slavery in the United

States. While there were many reasons for this great triumph of democracy, the Amendment would never have been passed were it not for the determination of thousands of African Americans who chose to flee slavery. Their flight inspired a group of black and white crusaders to create a new organization, the Underground Railroad. The infrastructure of this organization was a vast network of safe houses and rescuers that made a successful escape from slavery possible. Even more important, the Railroad created a powerful movement of people who were willing to defy an unpopular law to protect the rights of runaway slaves to be free. During the Civil War, black southerners overwhelmingly supported the North which helped make the Union victory possible.

It was the men and women of the Underground Railroad who helped destroy slavery in America. This book tells the story of this remarkable movement.

CHAPTER
1
PRELUDE – THE AMERICAN REVOLUTION

Slave deck on the *Bark Wildfire*, 1860. Source:
Library of Congress Prints and Photographs Division

The American Revolution was one of the great turning points in human history, an event that would inspire people all over the world. Yet our revolution had a fatal flaw, slavery, which existed in every colony in America. It would take ninety years of political struggle and the bloodiest war in the nation's history before America could claim to be a free nation.

The Underground Railroad, the first racially integrated movement in American history, became one of the most powerful weapons in the destruction of slavery.

Slavery began in the American colonies in August, 1619 when a Dutch ship arrived in Jamestown, Virginia carrying 20 Africans. Almost immediately, slaveholders began complaining about how many of their slaves were running away. Because colonial America was still a vast wilderness, many slaves found that freedom was as close as the nearest forest or swamp, so there was no need for highly organized escapes. Many slaves found sanctuary among the local Indian tribes. Other fugitives simply fled to another colony and insisted that they were freedmen.

By 1700 slaves who sought freedom found it more difficult to find safe havens when they escaped. A loose network, mostly black, was developing to help them seek liberty. Because the American colonies were a trading nation, the most important part of this network was the sea and the ships that sailed the Atlantic Ocean. Ships sailed up and down the American coast, and from every port to England, Europe. And since whaling and fishing were among the colonies' most vital industries., fugitive slaves could easily find jobs aboard fishing vessels.. The officers were white; but when the American Revolution began, 25% of the seamen who worked on these ocean going vessels were black men; many of these sailors, like the revolutionary martyr, Crispus Attucks, were fugitive slaves.

Once aboard ship, nobody cared if you were a free man or a fugitive slave, as long as you were able to endure the harsh life of a seaman. Men from Europe and the British colonies mingled with black men from America, the Caribbean, and even Africa. Aboard ocean going vessels, the entire crew lived and worked together. There was very little privacy or individual freedom aboard ship. The seamen were often united in ongoing struggles against the captains and officers for decent food, and against the brutal working conditions and barbarous punishment they frequently received.

For decades, England had been kidnapping colonial men to serve in the British navy. If most sailors considered conditions on merchant ships to be harsh, they were luxurious compared to life in the Royal Navy. The food was typically rotten and unfit to eat, and the wages were abysmally low. Often, even these pitifully small wages might be withheld for years. Not surprisingly the British found it almost impossible to recruit sailors, so they were forced to use press gangs, men who were authorized by the navy to kidnap as many men as they needed to fill their ship's quota. They called it impressment. Those men who resisted impressment could be charged with treason and executed. Once aboard a ship of the British navy, the kidnapped men might be shunted from ship to ship without being allowed to leave the vessel, because naval captains always worried that, once ashore, the seaman would escape. No wonder seafarers looked at impressment as a form of slavery. This impressment policy affected not just seamen but the people in every coastal community in America. In 1757 in a single nighttime raid in the city of New York, 800 men were kidnapped off the streets; this was 1/4 the city's adult male population. American seamen, both black and white, led colonists in major struggles against impressment. This brotherhood of seamen had been battling Great Britain for years, well before Parliament passed the Stamp Act in 1765 precipitating the colonists' revolt against England,

One of the most famous battles against impressment took place in Boston in 1747. Fifty kidnapped sailors had just fled the *H.M.S. Lark* and were hidden by sympathetic Bostonians. Commander Knowles, captain of the ship, immediately sent out a press gang to sweep the Boston harbor. Three hundred sailors immediately spread the news throughout the city, then led thousands of Bostonians on a march to the harbor to confront the press gang. Colonists kidnapped the Lark officers and held them as hostages; then they seized the sheriff and put him into the town stocks. Next, thousands of people marched into the Provincial Council Chambers to prevent the Council from lending support to the naval ship. As a final act of defiance, the mob invaded the home of Massachusetts Governor William Shirley and informed him that if he allowed these officers to impress any Massachusetts citizens he would receive the same kind of physical abuse that kidnapped sailors routinely received from British Naval officers. As they left Governor Shirley's home their leaders shouted that if he did not remain neutral in the pitched battle going on in the streets of Boston, angry citizens might decide to hang him. The

Governor quickly retreated to his summer home outside the city.

This struggle against impressment was fought in every coastal town in the colonies. British officers were finally instructed to send out press gangs only when they were sure seamen were not around to organize community resistance. Crispus Attucks was just following the seaman's traditional struggle against the English government when he led a group of sailors and other Bostonians against British troops in 1770 in the first skirmish of the American revolution; Attucks was killed in the ensuing events. Thomas Jefferson listed impressment as one of the important indictments against England in the Declaration of Independence

Sam Adams, who in 1765 would lead the colonists in their successful struggle against the Stamp Act, was just a young man when he watched American sailors fight off an attempt by a Royal Navy's press gang to force a group of young men onto a British naval ship. It was a battle he never forgot.

In 1765 England passed the Stamp Act. The French and Indian War was over, and the cost of that war was threatening to bankrupt the British government. It was time, members of Parliament believed, that the American colonists help pay the cost of that war. The Stamp Act required that a special stamp be purchased and attached to every document circulated in the colonies. Stamps would now be required for every legal document, newspaper, or bill of sale. Parliament never imagined the ferocious reaction that the Stamp Act would produce in America.

The Stamp Act was a tremendous blow to most Americans who believed that they were British citizens. Ever since the American colonies had received their royal charters, they had enjoyed a kind of benign neglect from England. Parliament had been content to impose taxes only on international trade. The colonies themselves made most of the decisions on internal matters. For over one hundred years this system had worked well; now, suddenly, Parliament had changed this basic agreement.

The issue was not simply the tax itself; it was the basic question of who was going to govern the colonies – England or the colonists. Leaders of every colony believed that their royal charters were sacred covenants between the king and the colony. According to these charters, only the king had the right to tax the colonies. Nowhere in these charters was Parliament given any power to legislate on the internal affairs of an American colony. For generations Englishmen had fought for the right not to be taxed without representation, yet no colonist had the right to vote for any member of Parliament. Colonists would passionately fight for their right to be treated as British citizens. From every colony, streams of letters and petitions were soon crossing the Atlantic demanding that Parliament repeal the Stamp Act. When the news came back to the colonies that Parliament had ignored every one of their pleas and simply announced that the Stamp Act would become law on November 1, 1765, Americans were outraged.

Boston led the colonies in their revolt against the Stamp Act. Sam Adams knew that gentlemanly letters and petitions alone would never defeat the Stamp Act. Something more radical was needed, something that would make the Stamp Act unenforceable.

Adams had learned an important lesson watching the seamen who had successfully battled British impressment gangs. England had been forced to pay more attention to battling sailors than to floods of written protests. In 1765 Sam Adams became the leader of the first Sons of Liberty organization. One of his first steps was to recruit the leader of Boston's South End gang, the shoemaker Ebenezer McIntosh. Together they planned to create chaos in the streets of the city. McIntosh was a master of this kind of guerrilla theater. He had led many battles against press gangs, and many of his members were unemployed seamen, dock workers, shop keepers and mechanics, most of whom were potential targets of British impressment. The new Stamp Act would be another attack on the rights of his members. McIntosh hated the Stamp Act so much that he arranged for a truce between his gang and his rivals, the North End gang, so they could join together in the attack on the Stamp Act.

On the morning of August 14, 1765, Bostonians awoke to the sight of an effigy of Andrew Oliver, the newly appointed Stamp Collector, hanging from a tree. Angry mobs were roaming the streets. When Lieutenant Governor Thomas Hutchinson ordered Sheriff Greenleaf and his deputies to cut down the effigy, the sheriff discovered that hundreds of McIntosh's men had gathered around the tree (later known as the liberty tree) daring him to touch the effigy. Greenleaf retreated. At sundown thousands of people marched toward the wharf carrying Oliver's effigy, built a huge bonfire, beheaded the effigy and tossed it into the flames. Mobs destroyed Oliver's warehouse which had been built to house the detested stamps. As a final touch, hundreds of men marched to Oliver's home, smashed open the doors and demolished most of its elegant furnishings. The next day the shocked Oliver resigned his commission as stamp revenue collector and sailed back to England.

For days mobs rampaged throughout the city, and nervous leaders of Boston's protest movement, like Sam Adams, wondered what they had unleashed. The council issued a warrant for McIntosh's arrest, but mob leaders threatened more violence if McIntosh were arrested, so he remained free. Some of the more traditional leaders of the Sons of Liberty worried that the mob had gotten out of control. Nonetheless, during the three days of violent demonstrations there had been no deaths, and the only property that had been damaged was the property of officials involved in the operations of the Stamp Act. The goal of these so called "out of control mobs" was to frighten the Stamp officials into resigning. In Boston they certainly succeeded. Sons of Liberty were quickly organized throughout the colonies. Revolutionary mobs followed Boston's example and attacked stamp collectors in most of the other cities and towns in the American colonies.

Even leaders like Sam Adams, who had been leading the struggle against the Stamp Act, were surprised and worried about this revolutionary mob that had suddenly exploded into political action. According to British General Thomas Gage, American seamen, both black and white, had become important leaders of this "mob." Common people had never had any political power in colonial governments. Only men of property could hold office or even vote. Now, for the first time, these common people had discovered that they, too, had power, and they decided to use that power to advance some of their own demands. Common folk, whom both England and many colonial leaders nervously called the "mob," would help turn the struggle to repeal an objectionable law into a movement to create the first democratic republic in modern history.

On November 1, 1765, British ships sailed into colonial harbors carrying the detested stamps. The second round of the Stamp Act battle was about to begin. In Boston, acting governor Thomas Hutchinson was nervously considering his options. The stamps had been placed temporarily in Fort Castle Williams, guarded by 130 armed British soldiers. The governor had been told that hundreds of people were already collecting artillery for an attack on the fort. Hutchinson hastily decided to take the stamps out of the fort and place them aboard a British Man of War.

British officials in other port cities also discovered that it was difficult, if not impossible to bring any of these stamps into their cities or towns because of the surveilance of members of the Sons of Liberty. If some stamps managed to get past the vigilance committees, the stamps remained unusable because the Sons of Liberty had launched a national movement to boycott any merchant that used the hated stamps. To enforce this boycott, they turned again to the same association of seamen, mechanics, shop keepers and working men who had organized such effective political riots in the past. These men patrolled the streets of American cities and towns to make sure that no merchant dare place a stamp on any product. Newspapers obeyed the ban and refused to publish. Courts closed, which delighted most common people because they could not be thrown into debtors prison or have their small farms foreclosed. Only criminal courts continued to operate since they were exempt from the stamp requirement.

In New York City two merchants who had been discovered using stamps were confronted by members of the Sons of Liberty. A meeting was hastily called to discuss the issue with the merchants. Five thousand angry citizens faced off against the businessmen who quickly apologized to the crowd. Soon the stamps were piled in the street and burned.

The Stamp Act was unenforceable and, in April, the news reached America that parliament had repealed the act. There was wild rejoicing throughout the Colonies. The people believed that they had won the battle to preserve their rights as Englishmen. They were wrong. A new battle was just over the horizon. Parliament announced that they were activating an old law that required the Colonies to house and support British troops. Parliament also imposed a new set of taxes. The Townshend Acts, as they were known, convinced the Colonists that Parliament was still determined to treat the colonists as second class citizens. The Sons of Liberty launched a new, more complex struggle against Parliament, a boycott against all English goods. "Non-Importation," the Sons of Liberty believed, was a much more powerful weapon because it was sure to hurt the entire British economy. In order for the non-importation movement to be successful, it had to be organized in every colony in America.

This new patriot movement was spreading throughout the colonies. The "Non Importation" pact was signed by thousands of merchants all over the country, and those businessmen who refused to sign were soon visited by local members of the Sons of Liberty.

The mostly peaceful struggle against the Townshend Act went on for four years, due to the tight control that the Sons of Liberty wielded over their members. Yet there were still enough violent protests to worry England. One incident took place in Boston Harbor when the British warship, *Romney* sent a press gang into the city to find sailors to fill out its depleted crew. Three hundred people collected at the wharf, and a riot nearly broke out. British officials hastily ordered the Romney to release the kidnapped seamen and to leave the port as soon as possible.

Since the beginning of Stamp Act struggles, America's 480,000 slaves had been listening intently to the patriots' outcries against England They too wanted liberty and equality. But in 1765, slavery was legal in every colony in America. Black men and women hoped that these revolutionaries would end American slavery along with British tyranny. In the north, slaves had good reason to support the revolutionary struggle. The prevailing mood in Boston was antislavery. James Otis announced in his great pamphlet, "The Rights of the British Colonies," that all men including black men are born free. In 1765 Boston's town meeting passed a resolution instructing their delegates to the State Legislature to introduce a bill to outlaw the importation and purchase of slaves.

Crispus Attucks, a fugitive slave from Massachusetts, who had a family tradition of fighting for freedom, believed in the promise of the resolution. One of his ancestors was John Attucks, a Wampanoag Indian. Attucks fought beside chief King Philip, the Wampanoag Indians' greatest hero. In 1675 King Philip had led his people in a series of battles against British settlers who were invading Wampanoag lands. John Attucks was was captured and executed by the British in 1676.

In 1750 Crispus Attucks escaped from his master, deacon William Brown of Framingham, and took refuge in Boston. Determined to recapture his property, Brown placed an advertisement in the Boston gazette offering a reward of ten pounds for information on the whereabouts of his slave. The 27-year-old Attucks found safety as a crew member on one of hundreds of whaling ships that regularly sailed in and out of Boston.

We do not know just when Attucks joined the Sons of Liberty. The only piece of evidence we have about Crispus Attucks' leadership within the Sons of Liberty was found by John Adams. In 1773. Adams was searching through some British archives when he found an undated letter addressed to Lieutenant Governor Thomas Hutchinson. This letter warned the governor that if he persisted in allowing British troops to harass the people of Boston there would be bloodshed. The letter stated that if violence erupted it would not be the fault of the British soldiers "who were but passive Instruments, were Machines, neither moral nor voluntary." The blame belonged to Hutchinson alone. "You was a free Agent You acted, cooly, deliberately, with all that premeditated Malice, not against Us in Particular but against the People in general." The letter was signed, Crispus Attucks.[1]

Crispus Attucks, Source: *Wikipedia Images*

British merchants had been complaining bitterly about the damage that America's non- importation movement was doing to their business, and Parliament was finally beginning to listen. While they reluctantly decided to repeal most of the Townshend Acts, leaders of Parliament also decided that they must do something about the fact that the British government seemed to be losing control of Boston. In 1770 they announced that two regiments of British redcoats were being dispatched to the city of Boston.

---

[1]Kaplan, Sidney and Emma Kaplan. *The Black Presence in the Era of the American Revolution*. Amherst: University of Massachusetts Press, 1989. (Pg. 9-10)

On the night of March 5, 1770, tensions in Boston between the British and the colonists were escalating. Parliament had sent hundreds of soldiers to be quartered in the city, and the Sons of Liberty had responded by mounting a major campaign to harass these unwelcome troops. Now, rumors were flying throughout the city that the British army was planning an attack against the people of Boston. All day long bands of men led by the Sons of Liberty patrolled the streets and watched for any sign that the rumors were true. The leader of one of these bands was Crispus Attucks. All night long hostile throngs crowded around the English troops taunting them. British soldiers nervously gripped their guns trying not to panic. Finally, Private White, who was guarding the Custom House, broke. When a teenager began to jeer at him, White struck the boy several times. White called for help and a troop of British soldiers marched into the street to deal with the mob. The soldiers pointed their guns at the crowd and ordered them to disperse. The fire bell sounded.

Crispus Attucks at The Boston Massacre 1770. Source: *Wikimedia*

Hundreds of people hurried to the Custom House believing that the British soldiers were firing on the demonstrators. Crispus Attucks and his men were patrolling the area near the Custom House when Attucks heard the bell tolling. He rushed towards the Custom House holding a long cordwood stick in his hand. He threw himself in front of an officer, grasping the officer's bayonet with one hand while attacking another officer with his stick. Shots rang out. Two bullets struck Attucks in the chest and he fell dead in the street. Four other Americans were killed while six other demonstrators were wounded.

10

The funeral for the slain men took place on March 8. Twelve thousand Bostonians marched in the procession. The memory of Crispus Attucks was cherished throughout the nation as the first martyr of the American Revolution.

American seamen were always the most vocal supporters of independence. Most of them never wavered in their support for the American Revolution. Many thousands of American sailors were charged with being pirates and traitors rather than considered prisoners of war. George Washington never exchanged British soldiers for these sailors. Whenever he had the opportunity to exchange prisoners, Washington always picked experienced soldiers because he was always so short of fighting men. American sailors were thrown into British prisons and prison ships for the duration of the war. They were trapped in a desperate situation. Conditions were abominable. Thousands were dying of disease. These men were offered a very tempting choice. They could leave their dreadful prisons by joining the Royal Navy. Most of these seamen refused the British offer. Instead of defecting, they decided to resist. On the prison ship *Jersey*, the men organized themselves within their prisons into what they called a republic, and established their own laws with penalties for prisoners who disobeyed these laws. Some of these imprisoned American seamen actually celebrated the 4th of July under the noses of their British jailors. Others even managed to escape.

The struggle against England continued and in May, 1775, the conflict became a shooting war when British soldiers and Massachusetts militia fired on each other in the battles of Lexington and Concord.

In spite of the fact that black men had fought and died in the early battles of Lexington, Concord, and Bunker Hill, George Washington refused to allow any men of color, even freedmen, to enlist in his new Continental Army. He was, after all, a slaveholder, and he believed that the liberty he was fighting for was for white men only. There was no question in his mind that the new American nation must remain a slaveholding republic. How could he allow black men to fight for America if their reward was not to be freedom? But two things happened to change George Washington's mind. The first event was triggered by the British governor of Virginia, Lord Dunmore. The governor was a desperate man. He had, in the South, no real army to fight the American rebels, as the loyalists were not rushing to enlist. Finally, in November, 1775 Lord Dunmore issued an invitation to the slaves of the American patriots fighting against the British. This proclamation stated that any slave of a rebel master who would enlist in the British army would be granted his freedom. Almost overnight a movement developed to help black men fighting men find their way to Dunmore's headquarters. Slaves as far away as Georgia heard about the proclamation and took off to find the British army.

George Washington instantly understood that Dunmore's proclamation posed a grave danger to the revolution, even in the North. Washington was also worried that northern slaves, if the Patriots did not offer them some hope of freedom, would rush to enlist soldiers in the British army. So, he hastily withdrew his ban on black troops.

There was a second more compelling reason why Washington quietly dropped his objections to recruiting black soldiers his urgent need for fighting men. The British army in America had 79,000 seasoned troops and were able to defeat Washington's raw recruits on battlefields all over New York. Finally, Washington rallied his battered troops and retreated across the Delaware River. By December of 1776, when the British army settled into winter quarters in Trenton, Washington had lost 3,000 men. Only Washington's brilliant Christmas Eve raid on the British army at Trenton saved the American cause from complete demoralization.

Most of Washington's Continental Army was made up of local militiamen who had enthusiastically enlisted for a term of three months. Only a small percentage of soldiers had signed up for a year's service. Now that the three month enlistment term was over, these militiamen expected to go home. The Continental Army was about to collapse. The Continental Congress tried to assign quotas to each state but most states could not fill their quotas. Reluctantly Washington announced that states could begin recruiting slaves with their masters' permission. Northern states eagerly began filling their quotas by offering freedom to any slave who would enlist for the duration of the war.

In the terrible winter of 1777-1778, when Washington retreated to Valley Forge, the Continental Army shrank from 17,000 to a meager 5,000. Rhode Island had been devastated by the revolution; two thirds of the state including its major city, Newport, was occupied by the British. The governor had no way of meeting the demands of Congress for fresh troops, so he authorized the organization of a battalion of slaves. He told Rhode Island slaveholders that the state would pay for the freedom of any slave who volunteered for the army. Many people scoffed at the governor's proposal. There were relatively few slaves in Rhode Island, and skeptics doubted that many of them would choose to risk their lives for freedom. These doubters were quickly proven wrong. In an amazingly short time, the battalion was filled. Three fourths of Rhode Island's new regiment were black men who joined Washington at Valley Forge.

With or without their masters' permission, northern slaves made their way into the Continental army. They believed that when the Americans won the war they would also win their freedom. In the South the story was quite different. When the war began the South had 430,000 slaves, who were a primary source of wealth. Planters insisted that without slaves their plantations would be worthless, for who would be left to cultivate them? These slaveholders were determined to free themselves from England while at the same time preserving slavery. Slaves understood instantly the meaning of the revolutionary rhetoric of liberty and freedom that swirled over the South. They waited to see if southern revolutionaries would offer freedom to slaves if they would fight England, but the offer never came. Then on a bleak November day the slave quarters of Virginia were electrified by the news of Lord Dunmore's proclamation.

The Northhampton Committee of Safety reported that during the first days of the proclamation about 200 slaves had rushed to join Dunmore. The state of Virginia responded by organizing hundreds of men to patrol the countryside to prevent more slaves from escaping. Those fugitives who were caught were punished severely. Some were hanged, others were severely beaten, and many were sold out of the area so that they would not contaminate the rest of the slaves with dreams of liberty. Nothing worked; by December, 2,000 slaves had made their way to British headquarters. Soon Virginians were horrified by the sight of Dunmore's new Ethiopian regiment holding high a banner reading LIBERTY TO SLAVES.

The slaves' ability to transmit important information was extraordinary. John Adams was told by one southerner that the slave grapevine could travel several hundred miles in only a week. By

December, Charleston slaves had already heard about Lord Dunmore's proposal, and some of them were ready to take action. On December 6, 1775 the Charleston Council of Safety received a report that hundreds of slaves had fled to Sullivan's Island. They told the captain of the British warships anchored in the harbor that they considered themselves freedmen, and they asked for British protection. Alarmed, the Council took swift action. They ordered a company of rangers under the command of Lieutenant William Withers to attack Sullivan's Island and capture the fugitives. Withers was too late; most of the 500 fugitives had already been rescued by the British. The South Carolina legislature quickly passed an act giving the death penalty to any slave who fled to the British or tried to induce other slaves to flee.

In 1775 in Wilmington, North Carolina hundreds of slaves decided that they also wanted freedom. They seized weapons stored on various plantations and fled into the nearby woods. The revolution was temporarily suspended as both Patriot and Tory slaveholders joined patrols that scoured the forest. It took several days before most of the fugitive slaves were recaptured.

Patriot leaders were now confronted with the danger of trying to suppress the longing of thousands of slaves for freedom while fighting a well organized British army. Southern planters decided they must protect their slave property, no matter how it endangered the revolution. When George Washington issued a desperate plea for more recruits, southern states told the general that they needed to keep their state militia at home to prevent thousands of slaves from deserting to the British. In 1776 the British army abandoned the South to throw all their forces against the northern Continental Army. Lord Dunmore retreated, first to the British fleet in Chesapeake Bay, finally sailing away, leaving soldiers who had enlisted in his Ethiopian regiment to fend for themselves. To the dismay of many slaves, a quick road to freedom had vanished.

In 1778 the Patriots believed that victory was almost within reach. First, there was their stunning victory at Saratoga where General Gates had managed to capture an entire British army led by General John Burgoyne. Next, France finally announced that it was now an ally of the Americans, and would be sending money, troops and their navy to aid the revolution. Patriot leaders believed that

England would now have to send most of their troops to the Caribbean to protect the British West Indies from a French invasion, so they would no longer be able to fight the colonists. The patriots were wrong. England also had a strategy for winning the war. They sent only half of their army to the Caribbean; the other half of their army moved south.

The South was the weakest point in America's struggle against England. Southern colonists did not have a strong regional army because so many of their local militiamen were needed at home to prevent slaves from running away. There was also a sizable minority of southerners who continued to support the British cause. General Clinton, the British Commander, no longer sought total victory over the colonists. What he wanted now was simply a stalemated war. A stalemate would lead to a negotiated settlement, and, if England controlled the colonies from Virginia to Florida they would remain British territories. With Spain, England's ally, in control of Florida plus the vast Louisiana territories, and English Canada pressing down from the north, England believed that the small New England states would find it difficult to survive. Parliament was confident that they would soon have another opportunity to retake their former colonies.

Although England continued to offer freedom to any slave who joined the British army, this offer of freedom was limited only to slaves belonging to the Patriot revolutionaries; slaves belonging to Tory planters were treated as fugitive slaves. England was as conflicted on the issue of slavery as southern Patriots were, because their Tory supporters were some of the largest slaveholders in the South. Britain had to find ways to convince them that they, too, supported their right to have slaves. The message that England used in recruiting slaves for their army was confusing; were the British really offering them freedom, or just slavery under a new master? Yet to many slaves, the British army still represented their best chance for liberty, and thousands fled towards their encampments. Other slaves were more wary; they trusted neither the British nor the Americans to help them win liberty. Instead they escaped into the swamps and woodlands where they organized their own bands, keeping both armies at bay.

In 1780 the British army returned to the South. Their armies forced the surrender of Savannah and Charleston. Thomas Jefferson, then governor of Virginia, was forced to flee Richmond. The governor of South Carolina, John Rutledge, as he fled Charleston, begged

Washington for help, but the General had no troops to spare. The South would have to find another way to save themselves. One leading Patriot, South Carolinian slaveholder, Henry Laurens, thought he had the answer; the South must immediately recruit 3,000 slaves into the Continental army. This would have the immediate advantage of stemming the tide of fugitives fleeing to the British, and give the Revolutionary army desperately needed manpower. Governor Rutledge and Generals Lincoln and Gates, commanders of the southern front, all agreed that black recruitment was the only answer to saving the South from the British. The Continental Congress ordered the enlistment of black regiments to begin immediately. In order to appease southern slaveholders, they also voted to appropriate funds to compensate slaveholders for the loss of their property. Planters were appalled at the vision of an armed battalion of slaves; it would mean the end of slavery. Planters believed that it would be better to lose the battle for independence than face the possibility of destroying the institution of slavery. The legislatures of every southern state refused Congress' demand to enlist slaves.

In 1781 there were only 24,000 men in the Continental Army, 5,000 of them blacks, both slaves and free men. They comprised up to 25% of all of the soldiers in Washington's army. These African American troops were never segregated into black units. They fought and lived side by side with white soldiers, the first and only time black Americans would fight in an integrated American army until the Korean War.

Yorktown was the decisive battle of the American Revolution. Lafayette had just arrived leading 4,500 French troops, while Washington himself rode at the head of 2,000 Continentals. The Americans surrounded the town, but the British were ready for a long siege. General Cornwallis had built a series of well fortified redoubts. These earthen forts were surrounded by deep moats and topped by sharpened wooden stakes. Behind these redoubts the British general placed his most elite troops to guard the road to Yorktown. Informed that a large British fleet was on its way with fresh troops and supplies, Cornwallis knew that his troops only needed to hold out against an American attack for a few weeks. Washington had also heard about the British fleet, and he knew that he must act immediately. If he moved swiftly, Washington believed, he could defeat the British here at Yorktown, and America would finally win its independence. But if he lost this decisive battle, it might well mean the end of America's struggle for freedom from England.

October 14, 1781 Washington decided that the moment for the final attack had come. There were two main redoubts, numbers nine and 10, that must be taken before an assault on Yorktown could succeed. French troops were assigned number nine, and Washington selected his most elite regiments for number 10, among whom were the black soldiers of the Rhode Island regiment. Washington was so determined that the attack be a surprise, that the men were ordered not to load their guns but to fight hand-to-hand with bayonets until after the initial assault. The battles were bloody before both redoubts were finally taken, and Washington was able to march his victorious army into Yorktown.

The American Revolution did threaten the institution of slavery. In the North, Black men, both slave and free, had played such an important part in America's victory that the question of abolition was debated all over the region.

Boston, where the revolution began, became one of the first states to make slavery illegal. There was never any formal legislation to end slavery, but a series of court edicts effectively abolished slavery in the state. The case of the slave Quock Walker was one of the most important of these rulings. In 1781, Walker, imbued with the heady desire for freedom that the revolution had inspired, decided to act like a free man and find a job that would give him a pay check. He went to work for John and Seth Caldwell without getting permission from his master, Nathaniel Jennison. Jennison was furious. He seized Walker and beat him severely then put Walker in prison. Walker decided to sue Jennison for his freedom. His lawyer, Levi Lincoln, argued that under the new Massachusetts Constitution of 1780 and its Declaration of Rights, slavery was illegal and therefore Walker was a free man. The court agreed. Other slaves quickly challenged the right of their masters to keep them in slavery. One man, a black soldier named Felix Cuff, made the fight for his freedom a mass struggle. When Cuff returned home to Waltham, Massachusetts, he was told by his master that he was still a slave regardless of the promise of freedom that had been made during the revolution. Other slaveholders in the area were also refusing to honor the promise of freedom made to

17

black army veterans. Felix Cuff organized these ex-soldiers into a small army. Their headquarters was a deep cave called the Devil's Den. Lieutenant Hastings led a posse towards the cave to reclaim the fugitives for the local slaveholders. They were met with a hail of bullets from the cave and the posse hastily retreated. The fugitives then surprisingly filed a lawsuit against Hastings and his posse for starting a riot, and Lieutenant Hastings instead of Felix Cuff was indicted. No slaveholder in Massachusetts ever again tried to pursue a fugitive slave. By 1800 every state in the North was well on the way to the complete abolition of slavery.

The Paris Peace Treaty, signed on November 30, 1782, stipulated that England would return all property, including fugitive slaves that had been seized from the Americans during the war. Slaveholders demanded the immediate return of the thousands of fugitives still traveling with the British army. General Carleton refused to honor the treaty, because he had given his solemn promise to every slave who had fought under the British flag that they had won their freedom. He told the slaveholders besieging his camp that, since every black man who had enlisted in the British army before November, 1782 under British law was a free man, they could not be considered property as defined under the newly signed treaty. The British troops jammed into New York City, their final stop before boarding the ships that would take them home. Fugitives were deeply worried when they heard that General Washington himself had come to New York to demand that Carleton return runaway slaves to their owners. But to their relief General Carleton refused Washington's demand. At least 3,500 fugitive slaves traveled with British Loyalists to new homes in Canada while thousands more traveled to other British possessions.

The South knew that the war had weakened slavery By the end of the war Virginia planters estimated that their state had lost 30,000 slaves. Georgia reported that over 5,000 slaves had fled, either to fight with the British, or into southern swamps. South Carolina estimated that one quarter of their slave population had escaped. So many slaves had fled that planters were often forced to leave their fields unplanted. When Thomas Pickney, one of South Carolina's delegates to the Continental Congress, returned to his plantation he discovered that all of his slaves had fled. By 1782 the price of an adult slave had escalated from a pre war figure of $200 to the astonishing sum of $1,000.

The swamplands of the South were now filled with fugitive slaves. For years, maroon camps had sheltered escaped slaves, who erected forts and built homes, where they were leading a harsh but free life. After the war southerners moved quickly to destroy these sanctuaries. One of the most important and dangerous of the maroon colonies was the vast swampland that bordered the lower Savannah River between South Carolina and Georgia. Many fugitives had created small communities deep within the swamp and had organized their own guerrilla bands, some of whom had fought alongside the British during the war. Now that the war was over they continued to raid the plantations that bordered the river. They carried off booty and liberated hundreds of slaves. The two states got together and recruited a military force strong enough to invade the swamps and destroy the most dangerous of the fugitive bands. The militia began tracking through the swamp. They suddenly found themselves in front of a well-built fort made of cut logs. It had four foot high walls encircling a site 700 yards long and 120 yards wide. Within its walls were 20 crude log cabins with little gardens. Outside the fort were thriving rice fields. The fugitives had been warned that the militia was coming, and most of them had already fled deeper into the swamp. Leaders of the guerilla band stayed behind to fight the invaders. When the battle was over six of the fugitives were dead while others were wounded or captured. Captain Lewis, one of their leaders, was captured and publically executed. His head was hung on a post in the village as a warning to other slaves who might be planning an escape.

Now that the revolution was over, southerners quickly began to establish tight military control to stop the flow of escaping slaves. Militiamen and local volunteers patrolled the countryside every night; Slaves were not allowed to gather for any reason, even for religious services without a white person present, and they had to carry passes whenever they left the plantation. Patrollers would regularly demand to see the papers of free blacks in case they might be fugitives. When fugitives were captured, they could expect severe beatings or mutilation, such as cutting off an ear, foot, nose or fingers. Sometimes a fugitive might be killed by an angry master. Yet no matter how slaveholders tried to prevent escapes, there were always more fugitives who chose freedom. To make matters worse for slaveholders, once a fugitive crossed the border into a free state, an owner was powerless to recover his property. Slaveholders felt that fugitives were laughing at them from the safety of places like Philadelphia. Something had to be done to prevent southerners from losing property worth thousands of dollars every year to the free North. As long as the states remained independent governments, loosely bound together in a Union under the Articles of Confederation, slaveholders had no legal power to recapture their slave property. Some slaveholders decided to support the proposal to amend the Articles of Confederation, which many of the nation's leaders, like George Washington, were advocating. Maybe as part of a new constitution they could find a better way to prevent fugitive slaves from finding freedom in northern states.

In the summer of 1787, in Philadelphia, delegates from the thirteen colonies wrote a new constitution which established the United States of America as the first modern republic in world history. Never before had a people written the rules and regulations under which they were going to live. For the first time in history there would be no supreme ruler; no king or general would have power over Americans. The creation of this constitution was difficult and complicated and there was no model for the delegates to follow. What was the national government going to look like? Were Americans going to have a parliament like England's, or something different? How would a national leader be chosen? Would a national assembly be elected simply on the basis of population, or would each state send the same number of representatives? Small states wanted each state to have equal representation while the large states wanted the legislature elected only by population. Finally, the delegates agreed on a new kind of legislature that would have two equal bodies – the Senate, which would give each state two senators no matter how large or small the state might be, and the other body, the House of Representatives, that would be based on population

As soon as the delegates had finally worked out this compromise solution to the problem of pleasing both large and small states, a new and bitter struggle broke out between the slaveholding South and the free North. The issue was slavery. The North insisted that since the South considered slaves property, these slaves could not be counted as part of any state's population. The South insisted that slaves be counted as persons, only for the purpose of electing legislators. This lively battle raged for days until finally a compromise was reached; slaves would be counted as three fifths of a person.

The question of the African slave trade was also a contentious issue. The North wanted the hated trade abolished immediately, but

Georgia and the Carolinas, who were still suffering because of the flight of so many slaves to the British or to Florida, insisted they could not end the African slave trade. After another series of bitter debates the convention agreed to allow the detested slave trade to continue until 1808.

Finally, when the delegates were almost ready to go home, weary with repeated arguments and compromises, southern delegates announced that they wanted a Fugitive Slave clause in the new constitution, one that would allow them to go into each state in the new Union and recover their property. Without much debate the delegates passed the Fugitive Slave Clause. Charles Pinckney, one of the delegates, campaigned enthusiastically for the passage of the new constitution. He told fellow slaveholders in South Carolina that, since the new constitution gave slaveholders the right to pursue fugitives anywhere in the new nation, their property was now more secure than ever before. The United States Constitution, by protecting slavery and giving the South greater political power within the new congress (the three fifths rule), helped establish America as the most powerful slave society in the modern world.

It was a terrible blow to those African Americans who had joined the Patriots, believing that, if America won the revolution, slavery would be abolished. Yet black men who had joined the Sons of Liberty and enlisted in George Washington's army had won a partial victory; they had helped destroy slavery in the North. Abolition was a slow process, but by 1830, slavery was illegal in every northern state.

The new constitution was ratified in 1789. Slaveholders hoped that the Fugitive Slave Clause would finally solve the problem of runaway slaves fleeing north by allowing them to recapture their property anywhere in the United States. While slaveholders were celebrating, African Americans, together with a small group of white allies, had just begun to create a small network of escape routes and safe houses, which in time would grow into the formidable organization known as the Underground Railroad.

2

SLAVERY IS HERE TO STAY
THE UNDERGROUND RAILROAD BEGINS

Our Founding Fathers believed that slavery was a dying institution. Then in 1793, Eli Whitney invented the cotton gin. Seed cotton was a crop that grew easily all over the South, but it's seeds were almost impossible to remove. The cotton gin revolutionized southern agriculture because it made the removal of the seeds a simple and easy process. By the 1700's, Europeans had became obsessed with cotton; the rich demanded the most delicate muslin while the poor had to content themselves with rough homespun. By 1800 cotton had become the single most valuable crop in America. Slaves were vital in turning Southeners' plantations into vast fields cottonfields.

In 1796 southerners demanded that Congress pass a Fugitive Slave Law in order for them to enforce the Fugitive Slave clause. Now slaveholders had the legal right to recapture their runaway slaves anywhere in America. The law was devastating to every African American, slave or free. Slave hunters invaded northern states searching for fugitives, sometimes even kidnapping freedmen whom they would sell to unscrupulous slave traders.

Fugitives discovered that they were not always alone when they fled the plantation. There were communities of free blacks and a small group of white Americans eager to help them reach freedom. The Fugitive Slave Law had put this system of support in danger. Antislavery men and women realized that they must create a tighter more organized system of support to help runaway slaves succeed in their escape. Slowly they began building a network which started in the South and stretched all the way to Canada. They needed to find a vast number of secure hiding places and then recruit hundreds of men and women who would be willing to lead fugitives from one hiding place to the next one. Many times fugitives walked from one safe house to another. Other times the runaways might be hidden in a boat, a wagon, or even a carriage. (In 1800 the steam locomotive was used in only a few local areas in England.) For many years this was a secret, illegal, and nameless movement. In 1831, acording to a popular legend, the movement got a name. Tice David was a Kentucky slave who made the decision to escape. As he fled the plantation, David's master realized that his slave had run away and began following his trail. As David reached the Ohio River he looked behind him and saw that his master had almost caught up with him. The fugitive's only choice was to wade into the river and begin swiming towards the Ohio shore and the town of Ripley. Ripley was known as an antislavery stronghold. David hoped that if he could only reach Ripley he might be saved.

David's master never lost sight of his slave bobbing around in the water even when he searched for a skiff. As he launched his vessel he saw that the fugitive was still desperately swimming towards Ripley. He continued to watch as he saw the man wading onto the shore. Then suddenly David disapeared. The slaveholder never saw his slave again. The man would not give up. He knocked on every door and searched every building in the town searching for his escaped slave but the runaway had vanished from Ripley. It seemed impossible that the man could have disapeared in just a few minutes. Frustrated the slaveholder returned to Kentucky. When people asked him what had happened the baffled slaveholder announced that David must have gone on an underground railroad.

In 1830 the first steam locomotives had begun carrying both freight and pasengers. The public was thrilled with this new rapid way of traveling throughout the countryside. Whether or not the story of David's rescue was true or merely a myth antislavery men and women loved it. Proudly they called themselves the Underground Railroad. Rescuers were now conductors, safe houses were now depots and the main network organizers were affectionately known as stationmasters. The railroad tracks of course ran only through imaginary tunnels hidden deep underground invisable to the naked eye.

Tobacco, which had been the most important cash crop in Virginia and Maryland, was destroying the soil. Planters were forced to rotate their crops so more of them were beginning to grow cereal crops such as wheat and barley (which required less labor) along with tobacco. Now planters in the Upper South were faced with the problem of having more slaves than they needed. For a time it seemed that slavery had become a bit shaky in the Upper South. Then came the

Louisiana Purchase. In 1803 President Thomas Jefferson purchased the French colony of Louisiana from Napoleon, opening up a vast new empire for slavery. Now, American slaves faced a new threat to their existence just as devastating as the African slave trade had been to their ancestors. Southern planters swarmed across the mountains and settled on the rich lands of Mississippi, Alabama, and Louisiana. They dreamed of new plantations dotted with miles of white cotton plants. But before these plantations could become a reality, they needed thousands of slaves to cut down the forests, plow up the grassland and drain the swamps. Slaveholders now began a frantic search for a new source of slaves; they found this new source in the plantations of the Upper South.

Slave Auction, Richmond Virgina, 1861.
Source: *Special Collections Dept., University of Virginia Library.*

A whole new world opened up for planters to profit from their slave property; they could now sell what planters called surplus slaves to these western markets. By 1830 over 120,000 slaves had been separated from their families and carried into the frontier states; by the time the Civil War began, over a quarter of a million slaves had been torn from family and friends and transported to plantations in the southwest.

All over the South the threat of being sold to frontier state plantations which were known for their brutality to slaves, made many more slaves decide it was time to leave the plantation. Every slaveholder knew that when slaves discovered that slave traders were on the plantation, runaways increased dramatically.

The internal slave trade affected every slave, those who had been sold away from their families and friends, and those who remained behind. Jesse Torrey remembered how there were always slave traders around the plantation. "The threat always hovered over

24

us that we were about to be sold. Everyone knew that, bad as the plantation was, there were much worse places that we might be sold to. There were the rice-swamps, and the sugar and cotton plantations; we had them held before us as terrors by our masters and mistresses, all our lives. We knew about them all; and when a friend was carried off, why, it was the same as death for we could not write or hear, and never expected to see them again." [1]

Sometimes a whole community decided to run away. In one case, a group of 155 slaves living on a plantation in St. Augustine, Florida heard that they were all going to be sold to a slave trader and taken to Louisiana. When the trader's agent arrived to collect the slaves he discovered that only twenty slaves were left on the plantation. The rest had fled.

The Underground Railroad responded to the desperation of America's slave population by expanding its networks of safe houses throughout the North. Underground Railroad organizers also recruited a group of brave antislavery men and women who volunteered to travel into the South and guide fleeing slaves north. Southerners suddenly discovered that there was a new organization dedicated to stealing their "slave property" and declared war on the Underground Railroad. By the 1830's members of the Underground Railroad were battling a group of powerful political and economic institutions, both in the South and the North.

The new internal slave trade was making members of the white establishment rich, especially planters of the Upper South. The value of a slave was no longer dependent on local markets; it was determined, instead, by the price a slave could bring at the auction block in New Orleans or one of the many other western slave markets. Second only to land itself, slaves were now one of Southerners' most valuable forms of investment. By 1832 slave owners in Virginia alone were selling 6,000 slaves a year. The money they earned was staggering. In 1850 a healthy male adult between 15 and 30 years old sold for a price of $1500. In order to understand what how significant this kind of investment was, in today's economy that same $1500 would be worth around $34,000.

---

[1] Tadman Michael. *Speculators and Slave Masters: Traders and Slaves in the Old South, 2nd expanded edition.* Madison: University of Wisconsin Press, 1996. (Pg. 164).

As early as 1820 slave trading had become a big business. One of the most successful slave trading companies was the firm of Franklin & Armfield in Alexandria, Virginia. They used some of the most innovative capitalist techniques in America to maximize their profits. They purchased their own vessels so that they could transport large numbers of slaves from the coastal communities to many of the most profitable markets in the South. Most merchant ships had an irregular schedule; they sailed only when their cargo hold was filled. The Franklin & Armfield system was different; they announced that their ships would now run on a regular announced schedule no matter if they had a complete cargo or not. If their ships were not filled when a ship was due to sail, they would try to rent out their excess space to other slave traders. After they had unloaded their cargo of slaves they would fill up their vessels with other products like cotton and sugar and sail up the northern coast. By 1835 their company had become one of the most profitable and richest firms in the South.

Now that the frontier states of Georgia, Alabama, Louisiana, Mississippi and Florida were able to purchase all the slaves that they needed, Southerners began creating vast new plantations, devoted to cotton. In Louisiana sugar cane was immensely profitable. Land values in these frontier states had sky rocketed. In 1800 rich bottom land sold for $2 an acre; by 1820 these same lands were selling for $100 an acre. The new slave states had made cotton king. In 1812 the South produced only 300,000 bales of cotton; by 1860 this trade had escalated to four million bales a year. By 1850 cotton had become the largest cash crop in the United States. It was making everyone rich, from southern planters to the mill owners of the North.

Young black men brought the highest prices, but every slave was a valuable commodity. Young women between ages 15 and 20 were also in great demand especially if they had already given birth to a baby, thus proving that they were fertile. Even children were valuable. Twenty percent of this internal slave trade were children 11 to 14 years old. Even babies were considered salable commodities. Two percent of the trade were children under seven years old. By 1860 one out of every three children under fourteen had been sold away from their family. Slavery was not only vital to the South; northern merchants had built their wealth on turning raw cotton into cloth. There were whole towns in New England, like Lowell, Massachusetts whose only industry was the cotton mill. New York merchants filled their ships with raw cotton or woven cloth and traded all over Europe. Cotton had become so vital to the economy of the North that many factory owners, merchants, ship owners and political leaders were now reluctant to question the right of slavery to exist in the South. Some leaders even hesitated to question the right of slavery to expand. Now, however, it became easy for northern industrialists to assuage their consciences by agreeing with their southern partners that slaves were much happier on plantations where they were taken care of by benevolent slaveholders, while they piled up more and more profits.

It was against this formidable combination of southern planters and northern industrialists that members of the Underground Railroad launched their attack against the institution of slavery.

The first great terminal of the Underground Railroad was Philadelphia. By the end of the Revolutionary War the city had become the most important center of free black life in America. There were many reasons for Philadelphia's new role. In 1780 Pennsylvania was the first state to pass a law calling for the gradual abolition of slavery. Even though it would take almost a generation before all slaves would be freed in Pennsylvania, the law's significance was profound. This was the first time an American state had actually condemned slavery as being incompatible with the ideals that the great American republic stood for. The news of this new law traveled swiftly into the South. Many Pennsylvania slaves had already been freed; some ex-slaves had won their freedom because they had fought in the Revolution; other slaves were freed because their owners were devout Quakers and their religion stated that owning slaves was a sin. There were some slave owners who freed their slaves because they had been deeply affected by the ideology of the American Revolution and the Declaration of Independence. Hundreds of these newly freed slaves left the isolated countryside and began streaming into Philadelphia, hoping to make a better life for themselves. They were joined by hundreds of fugitive slaves who had fled the South during the chaos of the Revolution. These fugitives knew that once they crossed the border into Pennsylvania they would be free.

Philadelphia in the 1780's was an exciting place for African Americans. The black community had just established their first two churches independent of white control, Richard Allen's AME Bethel and Absalom Jones' St. Thomas Episcopal. There were decent jobs to be had, and community organizations, like the Free Africa Society, to turn to for help and mutual support. And, at last, there were black schools where their children could learn the forbidden skill of reading.

Then came the Fugitive Slave Law of 1793. Fugitive slaves were now in great danger of re-enslavement. Slave hunters could now legally cross into Pennsylvania, as well as every other state of the Union, to pursue fugitive slaves. Philadelphia was becoming a happy hunting ground for men eager to reap the rewards slaveholders were offering for the return of their slave property. Some unscrupulous slave hunters were even reported to have kidnapped free black men and women and sold them to slave traders who were not overly concerned about where their supply of slaves had come from. Since black men and women were not allowed to testify in court against these kidnapers, there was no way to protect themselves from enslavement.

Philadelphia blacks realized that individual acts of rescue were no longer enough to protect fugitives or even freedmen. It was time to create a real organization, one that might more effectively protect the growing numbers of fugitives turning to them for help.

There had always been a group of antislavery Quakers willing to help a desperate runaway. But now that Congress had passed the Fugitive Slave Law, some of these Quakers worried that helping fugitives would force them to break the law. Most Quakers were a law abiding people and, as long as slavery was illegal in Pennsylvania, they felt justified in lending a hand to the infant Underground Railroad. Now some of these Quakers were confused about what they should do. Must they obey the law and refuse to help these desperate people, or break the law and risk not only a severe fine but a possible jail term as well. There was a core group of Quakers who challenged this conflict; they insisted that Quakers were morally bound to continue their work for the Underground Railroad. After all, these Quakers insisted, there was a higher law than the law passed by a Congress of men. The law of God, insisted these deeply committed men and women, has declared slavery a sin. It was, therefore, their duty to fight this sin by continuing to rescue runaway slaves. Black Philadelphians had no such conflicts. They promptly began organizing one of the most successful terminals in the history of the Underground Railroad. Antislavery Quakers joined the black community in the challenging task of organizing a complex network that would be strong enough to defeat the gangs of slave catchers that had invaded Pennsylvania. Their homes became safe houses and some Quakers also became skillful conductors guiding fugitives from one safe house to another.

By the 1830's something new was added to the operations of Philadelphia's Underground Railroad when the Philadelphia Vigilance Committee opened a public office in the city. The public role of the Committee was that of protecting free blacks from the activities of slave hunters. Its major activity, however, was organizing the most complex far flung terminal of the Underground Railroad. One part of the Road reached all the way down into North Carolina and another led to safe havens in Massachusetts, New York and Canada. The two men primarily responsible for the success of the Vigilance Committee were Robert Purvis and William Still.

Robert Purvis was born in Charleston, South Carolina in 1810. His black grandmother, Dido, was kidnapped from Morocco when she was twelve years old. She was freed when she was still a young woman and she married a German- American settler, Baron Judah. Dido's daughter Harriet met and won the heart of William Purvis a wealthy, white English cotton broker. William Purvis refused to allow his beloved black children to be raised in the slavery-soaked atmosphere of Charleston. He moved his family to Philadelphia when Robert was nine years old. When William discovered that there was no school for black children he established one so that his sons could receive the same kind of education as upper class white Philadelphians. In 1826 Purvis had decided to move his family to England but he died suddenly and Harriet Purvis and the children remained in Philadelphia. Robert Purvis attended Amherst College. With his fair complexion and his wealth, Purvis could easily slip into the white world and live a comfortable upper class life; instead he proudly proclaimed to the world that he was black, shocking some of his Amherst classmates who had assumed he was white.

In 1836 Robert Purvis was hiding a fugitive slave, Basil Dorsey. Suddenly Dorsey's owner, who had discovered where his slave was hiding, appeared on Purvis's doorstep and seized the fugitive. Purvis quickly organized a panel of lawyers to defend Dorsey in court. In case Dorsey lost his court case, Purvis also organized a group of rescuers to grab Dorsey before his owner could return him to slavery. Dorsey was lucky; his lawyers managed to convince the judge that the slaveholder had seized the wrong fugitive, and the man was set free. This experience convinced Purvis that Philadelphia needed an organized method of protecting the hundreds of fugitive slaves who had taken temporary refuge in the city. In its first six months of operation the Vigilance Committee sent fifty-one fugitives to the newly organized New York Vigilance Committee.

In 1839 Purvis became president of the Vigilance Committee, and under his leadership the Committee grew. Purvis moved easily into the world of upper class Philadelphia. He was able to shame some of its members into donating money for the Railroad and even recruit a few aristocrats into full fledged station masters and conductors. Managing a station on the Underground Railroad was a demanding job. Fugitives would arrive at an Underground Railroad station always hungry, their clothes usually in tatters, many of them ill and most of them needing money to survive until they could reach the next station. Some fugitives were able to rest for a while in Philadelphia, and the Committee would help them find places to stay and temporary jobs to support themselves until they were ready to travel north. There were other fugitives who had to be moved immediately because masters or slave hunters were too close. Decisions had to be made instantly. How do you spirit a group of fugitives out of your house when you can see masters and slave hunters riding down your street? Members of the Underground Railroad grew adept at quick costume changes. Men would be put into women's dresses and instantly be transformed into modest Quakers, escorted out of the house and placed tenderly into a waiting carriage by the head of the household right under the noses of the kidnappers. One quick witted Quaker woman, faced with a group of kidnapers knocking at her door, rushed a group of fugitives into a secret hiding place. An infant began crying and could not be quieted. She snatched up a blanket and wrapped it around the baby. When the kidnapers burst into the house they found only a mother rocking and nursing her baby. They looked no further and the tiny fugitive was saved.

Underground Railroad members became expert in recruiting new conductors–farmers who would hide fugitives in hay wagons in order to move them from one safe house to another, draymen who would drive through the heart of Philadelphia with a load of produce and a few fugitives hidden in the bottom of their cart. There were railroad workers who would hide fugitives in freight cars and, at one station, "railroad officials did not feel they were placed there in the interests of Southern masters. They gave tickets to whomever paid for them and asked no questions." [2]

---

[2] Smedley, R. C. *History of the Underground Railroad.* New York: Arno Press and The New York Times, 1969. (Pg. 177)

Although the other great leader of Philadelphia's Underground Railroad, William Still, had never been a slave, he knew from bitter experience the horrors of slavery. His father also had managed to purchase himself and had gone north to make a home for his family. His mother was not so lucky; the first time she ran away with her four children she was recaptured; the second time, she had to make the heartbreaking choice to leave her two sons behind under the care of her mother and just take her two babies with her. All his life William Still watched his mother grieve over the loss of her two oldest sons.

In 1847 when he was 24 years old, Still got a job with the Pennsylvania Abolition Society as a combination janitor and mail clerk. He soon was spending most of his time rescuing fugitive slaves. The old Vigilance Committee had begun to fall apart. By 1852 everyone realized that Philadelphia had to establish a new more tightly organized committee, this time with a full time paid staff member who could devote all of his time to the Committee's work. William Still was the obvious choice. He was a brilliant organizer. He kept the most meticulous records of everyone who passed through the Committee's door. And what a record it was. From Philadelphia the Railroad ran north. Its multiple branches crossed several states. Many of the fugitives decided to settle in communities where they would be protected by the citizens anti-slavery feelings. Fugitives knew they could find jobs in Philadelphia, Boston or New York. The towns of New Bedford, Massachusetts and Troy, New York also had thriving fugitive communities. And because the Canadian government welcomed and protected fugitive slaves, Underground Railroad lines stretched all the way into Ontario.

Still's network also stretched south. His records, which he published after the Civil War under the title The History of the Underground Railroad described an intricate network of conductors, watermen and a few sea captains who regularly aided the escape of hundreds of fugitives from the southern port cities of Richmond, Norfolk and Wilmington. Conductors, like Harriet Tubman, made the office of Philadelphia's Vigilance Committee their final stop, a place where fugitives could be safely delivered into William Still's capable hands.

Because William Still was a brilliant and meticulous organizer, members of his complex network managed to track the activities of masters and slave hunters. When a group of fugitives, eleven men, women, and children arrived at the Lewis family home, their plans were to rest a while and recover from their exhausting flight. Then the Quaker family received an urgent message from Still.

Slave hunters were tracking the fugitives and had discovered where they were hiding. Still's orders were to immediately scatter the group of fugitives into as many different safe houses as possible. Next, each fugitive was to receive an entire change of clothing; every piece of slave clothing must be burned. The Lewis family sent out a call to their Quaker friends to join them in a sewing party. "Dresses were fashioned, bonnets trimmed, veils bestowed, and in a few hours, all was in readiness. It was judged best to send the women and children immediately to Canada by the Reading Railroad." [3] By the time the slave hunters arrived, the fugitives were nowhere to be found.

Wilmington, Delaware was the last stop on the South's Underground Railroad because it was just twenty seven miles from the Pennsylvania border. It was also the home of Thomas Garrett one of the most important members of the Underground Railroad. Most members of the South's Underground Railroad kept their work a deep secret. Even close friends might not know just what they were doing. But Thomas Garrett was different. Even though he lived in the slave state of Delaware, it seemed that the whole world knew that Garrett's home was an important station on the Underground Railroad.

Thomas Garrett was a devout Quaker whose hatred of slavery began early in life. He was just twenty-four years old when a black woman who worked for his family was seized by slave catchers. Garrett leaped on his horse and followed the kidnappers halfway

---

[3] Smedley, R.C. *History of the Underground Railroad.* New York: Arno Press and The New York Times, 1969. (Pg. 176)

across the state of Delaware until he found the right moment to rescue her. It was Garrett's introduction to the Underground Railroad and he instantly volunteered his services. In 1822 Thomas Garrett moved to Wilmington where he opened an iron and coal business and soon became one of the town's most successful entrepreneurs. He was also known throughout the city as one of the most benevolent members of the community.

Garrett began by joining the small network of free blacks who had organized Wilmington's first Underground station, but he soon expanded the Railroad by recruiting other Quakers to become station masters. Garrett was so compelling that he even managed to convince some staunch Democrats to donate money to the Underground Railroad. This principled Quaker refused to hide his activities although he made sure that he was never caught while he was actually aiding fugitives. Because he was such a public figure he was forced to be a bit more cautious about any fugitive who appeared at his door. Garrett knew that slaveholders had tried to trap him many times by sending him their own black agents, pretending to be fugitives begging Garrett for help. Underground Railroad agents who sent fugitives to Garrett's home tried to send a message first so that Garrett would know that the fugitives were indeed genuine rather than spies sent by the various slaveholder organizations. The message might state, "I am sending you two (or whatever the number of fugitives were on their way) bales of black wool," or loads of wood, cotton or other products."

Because he was such a well known antislavery activist he received hundreds of death threats. The state of Maryland even offered $10,000 for his capture. The mischievous Garrett responded by writing an open letter to the Maryland government. He stated that he was insulted by the paltry amount of the reward, insisting that he was worth at least $20,000, and he told the state officials that as soon as they raised the reward to a more appropriate amount he would come to Maryland in person to collect the $20,000. Garrett's friends did not take these threats on his life so lightly. Members of the black community established a regular patrol around his house to make sure that he was protected.

For twenty years slaveholders and their agents tried to find evidence to prove that Garrett was breaking the Fugitive Slave Law, but, even though his house was constantly under surveillance by police and slaveholders' posses, he was never caught. In 1845 Garrett received a letter from John Hunn, a trusted underground agent, stating that the Hawkins family was being held in the Newcastle jail; could Garrett help them? There was a legal question over whether the mother and her two babies were actually slaves but there was no question that her teenage boys were slaves. One of the babies was ill and Garrett somehow convinced the judge to let him temporarily take the whole family out of jail to seek medical care. As soon as the family was released he rushed them into a carriage and soon they were on their way to Pennsylvania and freedom. This was the proof that slaveholders needed so in the spring of 1848, Garrett was arrested and sued by the slaveholder for stealing his property. His trial was swift, his guilt obvious, and the judge ordered Garrett to pay a $5,400 fine. The fine left the sixty- year old Quaker penniless. In order to pay the fine Garrett had to sell everything he owned. When the sale was over the auctioneer spoke, "Thomas I hope you'll never be caught at this again." Garrett responded "Friend, I haven't a dollar in the world, but if thee knows a fugitive who needs a breakfast send him to me."[4]

Slaveholders rejoiced at the verdict. The leading Democratic paper in Wilmington stated that it hoped this severe punishment would remove the rails from the Underground Railroad. Slaveholders did not realize just how beloved a figure Garrett was in Wilmington. Even men who had frowned over his public support of runaway slaves quietly slipped money into the fund his friends had launched to return Garrett's possessions to him. It was not long before Garrett was able to reopen his business. Southerners were furious at this flauting of the Fugitive Slave Law.

One of the most remarkable figures in the history of the Underground Railroad, Thomas Garrett was the southern Railroad's only public member. He lived in the largest city in Delaware among slaveholders and their supporters. His house was under constant surveillance by the police and pro- slavery supporters. Yet of the twenty-nine hundred fugitives that he assisted, not one was ever recaptured.

The first stop for fugitives in the free state of Pennsylvania was often the small Quaker town of Columbia, where some people believe

[4] Buckmaster Henrietta. *Let my People Go: The Story of the Underground Railroad and the Growth of the Abolitionist Movement.* Boston: Harper & Brothers, 1959. (Pg. 151)

the organized Underground Railroad began. In 1787 Samuel Wright, a Quaker, had decided to build a small town on land that he owned, in order to create a Quaker community where he and his friends could live a proper Quaker life. Because the Quaker Church had decreed that slavery was contrary to the Bible, part of this Quaker life meant freeing all of their slaves. Columbia therefore also had a thriving black community of newly freed slaves.

The Susquehanna River was the boundary between the slaveholding states of Maryland and Virginia, and the free state of Pennsylvania. When fugitive slaves reached the banks of the river they had only to cross over the stone bridge and they would be out of the slave South. The black community of Columbia was a place where exhausted fugitives might rest and recuperate before continuing on their trip to Philadelphia.

At the center of Columbia's Underground Railroad were two extraordinary black businessmen, Stephen Smith and William Whipper. In 1805 General Thomas Boude had purchased five-year-old Stephen Smith. Boude was so impressed by Smith's talent that he was made manager of the Boude Lumber Company before he was eighteen years old. In 1816 Smith was a free man but his mother Nancy Smith was a fugitive slave working in the Boude kitchen when her former mistress drove up to the house and demanded that Nancy Smith return to her plantation in Virginia. Stephen and Boude prevented the woman from dragging Smith's mother off. While Boude quickly announced that he would purchase Nancy Smith himself so that he could set her free, Stephen vowed that he would make sure that no other slaveholder would be able to march into Columbia and seize another fugitive. The teenager began organizing a network of safe houses and escape routes that led to Philadelphia's Vigilance Committee.

William Whipper became Smith's partner in both his successful lumber company and the Underground Railroad. In an 1871 letter to William Still, Whipper reminisced about how the early Railroad worked. He reminded Still that he had chosen to build his house on the banks of the Susquehanna River right at the end of the long bridge that connected the Southern states of Maryland and Virginia to Columbia. Fugitives fleeing over the bridge at night could see the welcoming lights of the Whipper home, where they knew that they would find sanctuary. Sometimes this black leader might have as many as seventeen fugitives hiding in his home at one time. Smith and Whipper also hid fugitives in their lumberyard and recruited a number of other black neighbors to provide safe havens for fleeing slaves.

It was not long before the Quakers of Columbia also opened their homes to the runaways. News about the welcoming community in Columbia traveled swiftly into the slave quarters of the upper South and soon hundreds of fugitives were making their way there. Columbia's antislavery community realized that they needed a more permanent organization. Quakers like William Wright and Daniel Gibbons recruited members of their church, not only in the town of Columbia, but Quakers from communities all over Pennsylvania. They soon had a network of safe houses that stretched throughout Chester and Lancaster Counties.

Fugitives Smuggled During Winter.
Source: *Library of Congress, Prints and Photographs Division.*

These station masters quickly developed ingenious strategies to thwart the attempts of slave hunters to capture the runaways. Fugitives were hidden everywhere – under the hay in the barn, or in the eaves of the attic. One inventive woman hid two young women between the mattress and the springs of her bed just as a posse of slave hunters marched into her house to search for the two. When it was time to send fugitives to another station, creativity was always necessary. If possible a message would be sent stating that so many (the exact number of fugitives) bales of black wool would soon be arriving. Sometimes if slave hunters were in hot pursuit a conductor might dress the men in women's clothes, escort them into a carriage then drive them on to their next destination. Other times groups of fugitives would be hidden in farm wagons under bales of hay or other farm produce.

Many times, as slave hunters prowled through a town searching for fugitives and posting guards at every suspected safe house, an experienced conductor would have already gathered up the endangered fugitives and was skillfully guiding them through the thick woods until they reached the safety of another safe house.

In 1834 the first railway line was built linking Columbia with Philadelphia. Now, Smith and Whipper began hiding fugitives among the piles of lumber so that they quickly arrived at Still's office in Philadelphia.

Slaveholders soon learned about Columbia, and some of them decided to hire a group of slave catchers to police the town and identify any place where fugitives might be hidden. They hoped that they would then be able kidnap these runaways before the townsmen could send them north to Philadelphia. While white Quakers believed in non-violence, most African Americans believed passionately in a militant defense. When a slave catcher named Isaac Brooks appeared in Columbia one winter's day, a group of blacks surrounded him, dragged him to a deserted part of town, stripped him, then whipped him. Brooks learned how dangerous it could be to pursue runaways in Columbia; he was never seen in that town again.

Christiana was another Pennsylvania town whose Quaker population joined with the black community to create safe havens for fugitive slaves. William Parker was just seventeen when he escaped from his Maryland master. Although Parker loved and respected the non-violent beliefs of the white Quakers of Christiana, he could never fit into such a passive role. Parker believed, just as did the founders of America, that a revolutionary act was always justified in the cause of freedom. Parker's revolt began on a cold rainy day when his master, David Brogdon, ordered all of the slaves into the fields in spite of the dismal weather. Parker decided not to obey this order and instead tried to hide out in the house, where Brogdon found him. The slaveholder angrily demanded to know why he was not in the field. Parker defiantly told his master that it was raining and he was tired and did not want to work. Such rebelliousness from a slave was unheard of. Brogdon picked up a stick and began beating Parker.

Parker grabbed the stick and began beating Brogdon. As his master called for help Parker ran off to the woods, where he was joined by his brother. That night the two brothers crept back to the slave quarters, whispered their farewells to family and friends and took off for Pennsylvania.

Even in Christiana, Parker was not safe because slave hunters constantly invaded the area searching for fugitive slaves. Slaveholders and their agents felt free to try and enter any house where they suspected fugitives might be hiding. If the homeowner refused to let them in, they did not hesitate to break down the door. Black men working in the fields and black women working in the kitchens of local farmers were frequently snatched by kidnapers and never seen again by their families and friends. Parker was determined to find a way to fight back. The town of Christiana was startled when William Parker led a few black militants into the Lancaster Courthouse to rescue a fugitive who was being claimed by his master. When kidnapers seized a black man and were on their way back to Maryland, Parker led six other armed blacks in a rescue. Even though he was shot in the leg Parker refused to retreat until the kidnapers fled without their prisoner. William Parker decided that it was time to make Christiana safe for fugitive slaves, so he organized a vigilance committee that would regularly patrol the town and farmland around Christiana. These friends of Parker were a militant lot. Their rescue successes became the stuff of legends, and slave hunters became somewhat reluctant to practice kidnapping in the town of Christiana.

By the 1820's New York City had become the center of America's economic life, and cotton was its golden fleece. Fifty percent of all American exports were cotton. In one leg of a great new trade triangle, the South sent its raw cotton directly to New York. Part of that crop was immediately purchased by the mill owners of New York and New England. Southern plantations had changed from self- sustaining little worlds, growing their own food and spinning their own cotton thread, into economic machines dedicated solely to growing raw cotton. Every part of their valuable rich soil was now devoted to that golden crop. It was more profitable for these planters to buy everything else from northern merchants. New York City businessmen controlled this vast new trade. In 1825 the Erie Canal opened linking the port of New York City with the inland seas of the Great Lakes. Now for the first time, New York merchants were able to trade directly with farmers throughout the interior of the country.

Their ships traveled to and from Europe and up and down the coast of America; now merchants were also able to ship their products through the Canal all the way down the Mississippi River to New Orleans.

While upper class New Yorkers piously agreed that slavery was morally questionable they were reluctant to upset their southern cotton producing partners. They saved their most fervent actions to attack the city's small but vocal abolitionist society.

Peter Williams was the respected pastor of St. Philips Episcopal Church, the only black Episcopal Church in the city. He was also a member of the executive committee of the newly organized American Antislavery Society. In 1837 a bloody anti-abolitionist riot rampaged throughout the city lasting almost a week. Black citizens were terrorized and killed. In the midst of the riot, a mob broke into St. Philips Episcopal Church and ransacked the building. Bishop Benjamin Onderdonk, head of the Episcopal Church of New York, never made any comment on the devastation wreaked upon the black community and refused to denounce the rioters. Instead he called Williams into his office and demanded that Williams give up his antislavery work. Reverend Williams was forced to publicly resign from the Society's executive board. It was a public humiliation for one of the black community's most respected leaders and a sign that the Underground Railroad would have a difficult task organizing in the heart of the Cotton Kingdom's northern center.

New York City desperately needed a well-run Underground Railroad terminal. Fugitives living in the city were in constant danger of being kidnapped. Dozens of slave hunters prowled the harbor and the streets of New York ready to seize any suspected fugitive. If the kidnapped victim turned out not to be a fugitive, these gangs could sell their captives to slave traders who were happy to send any kidnapped blacks to Southern slave markets.

In 1834 the white abolitionist, Elizur Wright, began writing a series of articles in two antislavery newspapers, the *Emancipator* and the *Anti-Slavery Standard* to publicize what was happening to both fugitives and freedmen living in the city. He called the series "Chronicles of Kidnapping in New York." New Yorkers read about a seven- year old boy, Henry Scott who was dragged out of his classroom and thrown into jail because he was suspected of being a fugitive. Wright told another story of New York City police raiding the home of Jock Lockley at two o'clock in the morning because a slaveholder insisted that Lockley was his fugitive slave. In spite of Lockley's insistence that he was a free man the police threw the whole family, including a two year old baby into the local jail because he was claimed by a slaveholder as his runaway slave.

George Garnet, the father of Henry Highland Garnet who would become one of the most important African American leaders in the nation, saved himself from a similar fate by jumping out of a second story window when slave hunters knocked on his door. His daughter was not so lucky; she was arrested and brought into court. Abolitionists organized quickly and found a white abolitionist who was willing to lie in court and insist that Eliza Garnet was working for him in New York City at the very time this slaveholder insisted that the entire Garnet family were slaves living on his plantation.

Friends and neighbors were no longer capable of protecting the hundreds of fugitives who were in danger from these slave hunters. New fugitives arrived regularly in the port of New York, most hidden in the ships that traveled from southern ports into the busy harbor. Once their ship had docked, these fugitives typically did not know what to do. Therefore they were in imminent danger of being captured by the groups of slave hunters who prowled the docks, waiting to seize fugitives as soon as they left the safety of their hiding places trying to come ashore.

Black New Yorkers decided that they needed a more organized way to protect these fugitives. In 1836 they organized the New York City Vigilance Committee and persuaded twenty-five year old black leader, David Ruggles to become its director. Ruggles decided that his Vigilance Committee would operate as the most radical organization of the Underground Railroad.

Ruggles was born in Connecticut and had moved to New York City when he was seventeen. He had already spent a great deal of time in the harbor, in fact it was his favorite hunting ground. He was still a teenager when he established a network of contacts who would alert him about fugitives hiding aboard a vessel. Other friends helped him develop clever ways of smuggling fugitives ashore.

Ruggles soon became a specialist in the complex laws of the state of New York covering the subject of slavery. One law, which Ruggles depended on, stated that, if a slave had been brought into New York by his or her master and had been living in the state for more that nine months, that slave could choose to become free. Ruggles delighted in forcing himself into the homes of white

Southerners living in New York City and informing their slaves that they were free under the laws of New York. Those slaves who chose freedom would then march out of their ex-owner's house under the protection of David Ruggles.

Ruggles also decided the Vigilance Committee should mount a campaign against slave hunters. The Committee began publishing a pamphlet called The Slaveholders Directory for New York City and Brooklyn. The pamphlet contained the names and addresses of lawyers, police officers, U.S. Marshals and other individuals, who helped in the kidnapping of suspected fugitives. Ruggles organized a campaign to have Underground Railroad members monitor the activities of these persons. As soon as a slave hunter attempted to seize a fugitive, the monitors would sound the alarm. Ruggles and other members of the Vigilance Committee would follow slave hunters right up to the door of the jail and remind officers that every fugitive must have a hearing before a judge to determine if the prisoner was indeed the fugitive being sought.

If the courts would not free a fugitive, Ruggles might turn to militant methods to rescue the escapee. In 1837, when the court refused to release the fugitive, William Dixon, David Ruggles led a group of African Americans into the courtroom, seized Dixon and spirited him away. Ruggles believed that in the war against slaveholders, if the law was incapable of protecting fugitives, he would happily break the law. More than once Ruggles himself was thrown into jail for his radical methods of defending a fugitive and had to be rescued by other members of the Vigilance Committee. In 1840 black New Yorkers achieved a major victory in the struggle to protect fugitives when the state passed a law requiring a jury trial before any alleged fugitive could be sent back into slavery.

If New York City was the cotton kingdom's financial center, a city where financial leaders quietly supported the South's plantation economy, then Boston prided itself as the city that proudly still upheld American revolutionary tradition. There were many reasons that fugitive slaves flocked to Boston. Slaveholders hated the city passionately. One slave remembered hearing his master bitterly denouncing Boston to his friends, so when the slave made his plans to run away he decided that if his master hated Boston so much it was certainly the city for him.

Boston was celebrated as the most radical city in America, a city where the Boston tea party was still celebrated, and where the statue of Crispus Attacks, the fugitive slave who was the first martyr of the American revolution, had been erected. This was the city where the white radical, William Lloyd Garrison, published the *Liberator,* the most important abolitionist newspaper in America. There were many other white abolitionists in Boston such as Wendell Phillips and Charles Sumner, who were known all over the country.

Some slaves making plans to escape might have heard about Boston's thriving black community with its center in the African Meeting House. The slave grapevine might also have reported on the way black and white abolitionists had reacted to the problems faced by two black women, Eliza Small and Polly Ann Bates. The two women had been passengers on the brig *Chickasaw* when, in August 1836, their ship docked in Boston harbor. A slave hunter boarded the ship and insisted that the women were fugitive slaves and demanded that the captain lock up the women until he could get a warrant for their arrest. The women insisted that they were free persons and that their papers had been illegally taken away from them.

Mrs. Thankful Southwick heard about the plight of Small and Bates and alerted the community. Soon a crowd of black Bostonians gathered on the dock demanding that the captain release the women. Then she marched into the courtroom and demanded that the women be released under a writ of habeas corpus. On Monday, August 9, Eliza Small and Polly Bates were brought into the courtroom of Chief Justice Shaw. The courtroom was filled with sympathetic blacks and a handful of white abolitionists. While a series of legal arguments were being debated in the courtroom the spectators decided not to wait. Someone cried out, "Take them." Men and women rushed over the benches and down the aisles toward the two women. Judge Shaw protested and then rushed to the door to prevent the prisoners from escaping. But the crowd carried the two prisoners down a private stairway and into a carriage. Even though Sheriff Huggerford led a posse in the chase to recapture the prisoners, he failed. Newspapers demanded that the rescuers be arrested. Strangely, law enforcement officials could not find anyone willing to identify members of the crowd and the investigation ended in failure. One of the reasons for the collapse of the investigation might have been the fact that the chief investigator, C. P. Sumner, the High Sheriff of Boston, was the father of Charles Sumner, who, in 1852 would be elected to the United States

Senate as Massachusetts' first abolitionist senator.

The slave grapevine might also have spread the word about some of the remarkable men who were part of Boston's black community—men like Robert Morris who had become the first black lawyer in America, or William Nell who, in 1844, had just organized the first boycott in the nation against Boston's segregated school system. These men were soon joined by Leonard Grimes. Grimes had been a successful businessman in Washington D C, owner of a fleet of horses and carriages. His taxi services were popular with Washington's upper classes. He was also one of the most daring members of the city's Underground Railroad, using his carriages to transport fugitives out of the city. He was finally caught and sent to prison for the crime of aiding in the escape of fugitive slaves. While in prison, Grimes became a minister. When he was released, Grimes realized that Washington had become too dangerous for him, so he decided to move to Boston. This did not mean that Grimes had abandoned his commitment to the Underground Railroad. In 1848 Grimes was invited to become the minister of the tiny (it only had 25 members) 12th Street Baptist church. Grimes was a mesmerizing minister. Under his dynamic leadership the church quickly grew to a membership of 250. Its congregation was so filled with fugitive slaves that Bostonians began calling it the Church of the Fugitives.

One member of Rev. Grimes' congregation was Lewis Hayden, a fugitive slave from Kentucky. Hayden's story was a powerful indictment of slavery. His mother was a beautiful woman. When Hayden was just a boy his owner sold his mother to a man who wanted her for his mistress. Hayden's mother fought gallantly against this man's sexual advances. Her owner was furious and he began beating her with such brutality that she became insane. Hayden was later sold away from his brothers and sisters for a pair of carriage horses. He never saw his family again. There were more tragedies. He fell in love with Esther, a slave woman from another plantation; they married and had a baby. Esther was owned by Henry Clay, the senator from Kentucky and one of the most powerful political leaders in America. One day Hayden discovered that his wife and son were about to be sold. He pleaded with Henry Clay not to sell his family but Clay was completely indifferent to Hayden's grief in fact he seemed surprised that Hayden would care so much about losing his family. He never saw Esther or his son again. It was a long time before Hayden allowed himself to build a new life. However, when he met Harriet, a slave woman with a baby son, he started over again; her son became his son and eased some of the pain of losing his own baby.

In 1844 Hayden met Delia Webster, a white abolitionist from Vermont. She was so impressed by Hayden that she asked him if he wanted to escape. Not without my family he replied. Touched by his love for his family she introduced him to Calvin Fairbank, a white conductor of the Underground Railroad. Fairbank was equally impressed by Hayden and the two abolitionists agreed to rescue the whole family. Fairbank's plan was to rent a carriage, hide the family inside and drive the coach to a dock on the Ohio River. A member of the Underground Railroad would help Hayden, Harriet and the baby board the waiting ferry. As soon as the boat docked on the Ohio side of the river they would be able to slip ashore and move quickly to an Underground Railroad station. The plan worked, and soon the Hayden family was on their way north to freedom.

Webster and Fairbank were not so lucky. When they returned to Lexington, Kentucky they were promptly arrested for slave stealing. The arrest of Delia Webster horrified northerners. It was the first time that a middle class white woman had ever been put into prison. Her jailors were not quite sure what to do with her. Webster had served only two months of her sentence when Calvin Fairbank made a deal with the Kentucky government. Fairbank promised to plead guilty to the crime of slave stealing if the authorities would free Delia Webster. Fairbank was sentenced to fifteen years in prison.

Hayden could never enjoy his freedom while Fairbanks' languished in jail. He wrote a letter to his old master offering to raise the money to buy his freedom if, in exchange, the slaveholder would petition the state to free Fairbanks. The slaveholder agreed, Hayden sent 650 dollars to his old master and, in 1849, Calvin Fairbank was released from prison.

Hayden had become one of the most important leaders of Boston's black community and began organizing one of the most militant Vigilance Committees in America. By1850, Theodore Parker, one of Boston's most famous theologians, claimed that between four- to six- thousand fugitives were living in the city.

Northern states had passed various laws which they hoped would protect their free black citizens from being kidnapped and sold into slavery. In 1842 the United States Supreme Court issued a ruling which made all of these laws unconstitutional. Edward Prigg was a slave hunter who had been hired to find and return Margaret Morgan and her children to Maryland. Morgan had been living in Pennsylvania for over five years and was now married to a free man. Prigg had traveled into Pennsylvania, seized Margaret Morgan and her children and taken them back to Maryland without first appearing in any Pennsylvania courtroom. Prigg was arrested under the laws of Pennsylvania, which required that a slaveholder or his representative prove that his prisoner was indeed a fugitive slave. Maryland appealed the Prigg conviction to the Supreme Court. In 1842 Justice Story, speaking for the majority, announced that the Pennsylvania law was unconstitutional because the Fugitive Slave Law was a federal law, therefore Prigg did not have to get permission to kidnap Morgan and take her back into slavery. This Supreme Court decision terrified not only every fugitive slave living in the North but most free African Americans as well. With the highest court in the land taking away the power of a state to protect its black citizens, the South had just won a major political victory

Before Boston's antislavery leaders even began analyzing the impact of the Prigg decision, news reached them that another fugitive slave had just been seized. George Latimer and his wife Rebecca had recently fled Norfolk, Virginia. Rebecca was expecting their first baby and she was determined that her baby would not be born a slave. The couple made a daring escape. First the two slipped aboard a vessel bound for Baltimore. They were hidden under the fore-peak lying flat against the stone ballast for nine hours until the ship docked in Baltimore's harbor. Later they were able to sneak off the ship

Now that they were in Baltimore, the harsh part of the escape was over. George Latimer, whose father was white, had purchased a first class ticket on a ship bound for Philadelphia. He walked boldly up the gangplank his face somewhat disguised by a distinctive Quaker hat. Rebecca walked behind him dressed as his male servant. The couple made their way quickly to their first class stateroom and traveled in comfort all the way to Philadelphia. They settled in Boston, but, eleven days later, George Latimer was recognized by an acquaintance of his owner, James Grey. On October 20,1842 George Latimer was arrested and thrown into the Leverett Street Jail. There had been no legal warrant for his arrest, the constable had not been given proof that Latimer was a fugitive slave, and the city constable had jailed Latimer only because of a request made by James A Grey delivered by his Boston lawyer, Elbridge Austin.

Boston abolitionists were outraged. It was the first time a man suspected of being a fugitive slave had been kidnapped on the streets of Boston. One group of abolitionists quickly organized a series of protest meetings. The streets were soon filled with placards and handbills demanding Latimer's release and denouncing the Boston police for acting like slave hunters. Another group of abolitionists began searching for the best lawyer to defend Latimer in court. They hired Samuel Sewall, one of the city's most eminent attorneys. Sewall immediately petitioned Boston's Chief Justice Lemuel Shaw to release Latimer under the 1837 Massachusetts law, which guaranteed every suspected fugitive the right to a trial by jury before he could be returned to a slaveholder or his agent. The Chief Justice of the Supreme Court ruled that, under the new Prigg ruling, the Massachusetts law was now unconstitutional.

Angry abolitionists began to rally Massachusetts citizens to demand Latimer's freedom. Latimer committees sprang up all over the state. It was the first time most of them had heard about the Prigg decision. Interest in Latimer's case was so high that Boston's Latimer Committee began publishing a daily newspaper called the *Latimer and North Star Journal*. Amazingly, the Journal soon had 20,000 subscribers. These Latimer Committees understood that they could not legally win Latimer's freedom, so they began raising money to purchase the fugitive. While negotiations over the sale price were going on between abolitionists and Grey, three hundred blacks patrolled the jailhouse to make sure that Grey did not try to spirit Latimer out of his cell onto a ship bound for Virginia. Grey was so worried that these African Americans might break into the jail and rescue Latimer that he finally agreed to give up his claim to Latimer for $400. The money poured in and within a month they had raised the $400 needed to free Latimer. Rebecca had been whisked away and hidden the moment Latimer was arrested; now she and Latimer were reunited and their baby was born in freedom.

This was just the beginning of the struggle. A few abolitionist lawyers had discovered an unusual provision in the Prigg ruling, a legal loophole, which was big enough to change the Prigg decision from a victory for Southern slaveholders into an antislavery weapon. Judge Shaw had ruled that the Fugitive Slave Law of 1796 was a federal law so states could not pass any laws that might annul its provisions; however he also ruled that because it was a federal law no state or local officials were required to enforce the law. The Latimer Clubs now began organizing a massive campaign to demand that the Massachusetts Legislature pass a series of laws that would prohibit any state or local official from cooperating in any way with slaveholders or their agents. By May 1843 they had collected 65,000 signatures on petitions, which they presented to the legislature.

The legislature acted quickly. They passed a law known as the Latimer Law which prohibited state judges from hearing fugitive slave cases; barred the use of any state facility, such as a jail, to incarcerate a suspected fugitive; and prohibited state officials from participating in any way in the capture of a suspected fugitive slave.

CHAPTER

3

WE MUST ESCAPE THIS HELLISH PLACE
THE UNDERGROUND RAILROAD IN THE SOUTH

Slaveholders were always obsessed with the problem of fugitive slaves. Local newspapers were filled with reports of chronic runaways. There was Jack, a North Carolina slave who began running away when he was fifteen and, in spite of frequent whippings, was considered a notorious absconder by the time he was thirty. Peter was another chronic runaway, a man who spent more time between the years 1824 and 1830 in jail as a runaway than working for any of the men who thought they might be able to control him. Finally, in December 1830, Peter succeeded in escaping for good. Sarah, a Charleston slave, was labeled a notorious runaway by one of her numerous owners.[1]

Slaveholders were baffled by these chronic runaways. The "learned" Dr. Samuel A. Cartwright of the University of Louisiana offered this explanation. These slaves were suffering from a peculiar form of mental disease which manifests itself by a propensity to run away. He named this disease Drapetomania. His suggested cure for this disease: whipping the devil out of them.

The Louisiana planter Isham P. Fox believed that severe beatings might actually cure his slave, Little Charles. Fox was baffled and completely frustrated by his slave's annoying habit of running away at every opportunity. In 1836 Fox felt that he had enough, so when Charles had been caught again his owner decided to follow Cartwright's advice. Cartwright ordered that Charles be whipped all night long without pause. Fox was still not sure that the devil had been whipped out of his recalcitrant slave, so even after a physician who had examined the runaway and reported that most of his skin was literally "cut off him," Fox decided Charles had not been punished enough. The next day Fox ordered that a heavy iron chain be placed around Charles' neck and then forced the runaway to drag his bruised body all the way from the plantation to Baton Rouge. Charles survived

---

[1] Franklin, John Hope and Loren Schweinger. *Runaway Slaves: Rebels on the Plantation.* New York: Oxford University Press, 1999. (Pg. 38-39)

his punishment for a few days before dying of his wounds.[2]

Slaveholders had seen their slave property vanish during the chaos of the American Revolution. They were absolutely determined that the problem of runaway slaves be handled on a federal level so that the North would not become a safe haven for fugitives. The Fugitive Slave Law of 1796 was only the first step in the building of a fortress around the South to keep their slaves from fleeing. Southern states also created an elaborate system of laws to control every aspect of a slave's life. There were laws which required that every slave who left the plantation carry a pass. Other laws forbade slaves gathering together in groups, not even for a religious meeting, without white supervision. Slaves were never supposed to leave the plantation after dark except with their master's permission. These laws were brutally enforced by armed local slave patrols who rode through the southern countryside every night searching for any slaves not on their owners' plantation. One slave recalled how the patrollers, when they discovered slaves who were away from the plantation without passes, would beat them black and blue. John Capeheart, a Norfolk Virginia constable, described how, as a patroller he was allowed by law to arrest any slave or even a free black man holding a meeting after dark without white supervision. Capeheart reported that the punishment for this crime was thirty nine lashes.

Slaves captured by hunters. Source: *Library of Congress, Prints and Photgraphs Division*

After the Revolution a new kind of business began to thrive in the South–slave hunting. A slave hunter made his living by collecting the reward money for recapturing a runaway. These slave catchers were usually poor white farmers who had been pushed by more affluent plantation owners onto the poorest land with the thinnest soil. Most slave hunters watched as their families struggled to escape bitter poverty. They hated both the slaveholder and the slave.

---

[2] Ibid (Pg. 93)

Slave hunters had packs of bloodhounds used to track fugitives through forests and swamps. These dogs were trained to viciously attack any fugitive that they were able to trap. Most fugitives regarded these bloodhounds as one of the most terrifying dangers they could face if they decided to run away. Frederick Law Olmstead, the famous landscape designer of New York City's Central Park, as a young man was so curious about slavery that he decided to take a trip south. There he spent his time visiting all kinds of southerners, rich planters, merchants, poor farmers and even a few slave catchers. Olmstead returned home and wrote his first book, "The Cotton Kingdom." In that book he reported his surprise that so many slaveholders told slave catchers to let their hounds tear up chronic runaway slaves. These slave catchers frequently returned fugitives to the plantation with an arm or leg torn off, a face ripped or an eye missing. It was a sight meant to terrify every slave on the plantation, especially any other slave who was thinking of running away. Olmstead was shocked. He had been told by so many planters that, unlike northern factory owners, they always took such very good care of their slaves because slaves were so valuable. Slave catchers had a different story. They explained to Olmstead that chronic runaways had already lost most of their value because everyone knew that these runaways were a risky investment.

The question that puzzled slaveholders was, how did their slaves learn so much about the outside world when their masters believed that they had worked so hard to keep them isolated and ignorant? The answer was simple: slaves learned about the outside world from their masters.

Slaves used white conversation as a kind of television newscast. House slaves listened avidly to whatever white folks discussed around the dining table, in the parlor, or in the carriage. Whatever house slaves heard was transmitted to the entire slave community Information was swiftly carried by coachmen, draymen, boatmen, and every other slave sent on an errand outside the plantation.

John Adams was told about this remarkable communications system in 1775 from two Georgia delegates to the Continental Congress. "The negroes have a wonderful art of communicating intelligence among themselves: it will run several hundreds of miles in a week or fortnight." [3] It was called the slave grapevine.

During the War of 1812, for example, household slaves heard their masters fuming to one another about the astonishing fact that some British regiments had armed black soldiers from Canada. Slaveholders told their slaves how fugitives were freezing to death in that icy land. Slaves smiled at each other and decided that if slaveholders hated Canada so much it must be a good place for them.

When slaveholders bitterly denounced the city of Boston, at least one slave planning his escape decided that Boston was the city for him. Many slaves had heard the news through the grapevine that northern states were beginning to abolish slavery. The question was, for many slaves who were planning to run away, how to find these northern states. A few slaves got their answer when they heard slaveholders murmur that they would like to rip the north star right out of the heavens. Soon slaves were talking about how if you followed the north star it would lead you to the land of freedom.

Some slaves who were fleeing from Maryland plantations were helped by black teamsters who regularly traveled into Baltimore, their wagons filled with produce. Sometimes they hid fugitives among the crops. Other times they might simply give a fugitive directions on how to find the first station on the Underground Railroad The historian, R.C. Smedley, writing one of the first histories of the Underground Railroad in Pennsylvania, was told about one elderly black man who lived outside Baltimore near the Susquehanna River, which separated Maryland from Pennsylvania "This man would go in the night, see them across the river and direct them to the house of Isaac Waters... then return before morning." [4]

It did not matter how often patrollers rode through the countryside; it did not matter how cruelly fugitives were punished when they were caught; slaves continued to escape.Lucretia Alexander was 89 years old when she was interviewed for the Federal Writer's Project in 1941, but she had never forgotten what happened to slaves who tried to run away. She told the interviewer "But lord I've seen such brutish doins' runnin' niggers with hounds and whippin' them till they were bloody. They used to put them in stocks, used to be two

---

[3] Diouf, Sylviane. *Slavery's Exiles: The Story of the American Maroons*. New York: New York University Press, 2014. (Pg. 117)

[4] Smedley, R.J. *History of the Underground Railroad*. New York: Arno Press, 1969. (Pg. 229)

people would whip em the overseer and the driver." [5]

Most runaways were quickly recaptured; it was a miracle that a small number of fugitives who attempted to escape actually succeeded. Slaveholders were obsessed by the fact that so many slaves made the attempt. Their answer to the constant battle to control runaways was to punish any person, black or white, whom they suspected might be helping a fugitive. These punishments were extreme, especially for whites. Slaveholders, because they refused to believe that slaves had the ability to plan escapes on their own, decided that it was white abolitionists who were enticing their slaves to run away. After all, they had been promoting the idea that slaves were helpless, sub-human creatures who could not function on their own. Therefore it must be evil whites who were dazzling slaves with fairy tales about how wonderful life was in the North and in Canada.

Slaves who were planning on running away tried to get as much information as possible about what to expect when they escaped and how to avoid the many hazards along the way. Many fleeing slaves had never heard about the Underground Railroad. They counted only on their family and friends, the people that could always be counted on to lend a hand to the runaway. Sometimes that helping hand was a hiding place deep in the woods or in a nearby cave where the fugitive might stay for a time, supplied with food and information about just when and where the patrollers would be riding that night. Other times it might be a forged pass, written by a slave friend who had secretly learned to read and write. Fugitives might then be passed on to other family members or friends. Most of the time, however, once these fugitives left their homes, they were on their own.

When fugitives needed help, whom could they trust? Sometimes desperate fugitives turned to strangers, usually other black folks, who might lend a hand. William Singleton tells the story of how, as a young and frightened boy, he made the decision to trust a stranger. He stood on the banks of the Lower Neuse River. He knew that he must cross the river before dark or else the slave patrols would certainly find him. In the distance he saw a solitary fisherman. Singleton could not tell if the man were black or white. He hesitated for a moment, then decided to approach the fisherman because he knew that white men rarely fished, instead relying on freedmen or slaves to supply their table with fresh fish. The frightened boy drew close to the man

---

[5] Yetman Norman R. *Life Under the "Peculiar Institute" Selections from the Slave Narrative Collections.* Huntington, New York:Krieger Publishing Co., 1976. (Pg. 12)

who was a black boatman. The man not only rowed Singleton across the river, but gave him instructions on how to find the slave quarters of Piney Point plantation where Singleton's mother now lived.

Slowly the Southern Railroad began to grow. The slave grapevine was very adept at collecting and sharing information about how an escaping slave might succeed. Fugitives were told that they must travel only by night and hide by day; their guide was always the north star. In order to make sure that they were actually traveling north they should always check the trees every day because moss grows thickest on the north side of a tree trunk. Fugitives were instructed on how to build rafts so that they could cross the many rivers and streams on the road north. Runaways were told that as soon as they heard the sounds of braying dogs, find a body of water immediately, a lake, river, stream or even a boggy piece of land and quickly plunge into the water. They were instructed to try to stay submerged until the dogs had left. Because dogs cannot follow a man's scent through water, this was the only way to prevent slave catchers from following their trail.

Fugitives were also told how to find signs and symbols that indicated where a secret station of the Underground Railroad might be found. Rev. Robinson learned about these symbols of the Underground Railroad from his father. When Robinson decided to escape, he was able to find friends by reading these secret signs. Robinson found a friendly black woman who told him about a secret cave overlooking a stagnant pond, where he found 19 runaways hiding from a posse of slave hunters. Thanks to the help given by another black man who brought them food and information, they were able to stay in the cave until the danger had passed.

Even slaves who knew nothing about the world outside the plantation sometimes decided to run away anyhow. John Brown was just such a man. He was a slave who had never even heard about the free states in the north when he slipped away from his cabin one night. All he knew was that there was a country called England where everyone was free. Brown had no idea that England lay across the Atlantic Ocean. Brown simply began walking. During the day he hid in the woods and swamps, living off of the berries and other plants that he found growing. Since Brown was traveling blindly¬and had never heard of the North, he suddenly found himself at the foot of the Smokey Mountains. While Brown was frantically trying to find a route around the mountain range, he was caught and returned to his master, Decatur Stevens. Brown received a terrible beating. Beatings could not stop Brown from trying to escape. When he was captured again, this time by a local posse led by a pack of dogs, Brown was beaten until he nearly died. Stevens then put a twelve pound helmet, which had large horns and bells attached to it, around Brown's head. He had to wear this torturous device both day and night. It would be many years before Brown found the Underground Railroad and rode its rails to freedom.

Many fugitives heard about one group of white southerners who might help them in their escape the Quakers, because their church opposed slavery. One of these Quakers was Levi Coffin. He came from a large family of North Carolina Quakers, all of whom hated slavery. Coffin began his Underground Railroad activities when he was just a child. He loved to wander in the woods surrounding his home in New Garden and, in his rambles, he sometimes discovered bands of fugitives who were hiding there, many of whom were on their way north. He promised them that he would not betray them and explained that his family were Quakers who hated slavery. He also promised to return with food. As the fugitives ate, they told the youngster about their lives as slaves and why they were so determined to be free. Soon the word got out that the woods around New Garden were a good place to hide when you were working your way north. Sometimes, when someone was very ill or the weather was too harsh to stay outdoors, the Coffins would hear a tentative knock on the door. Levi Coffin was soon hiding fugitives in his bedroom. By 1820 the various Coffin family homes had become stations on the Underground Railroad.

Many slaves chose to run away in groups. William Still tells of one incredible escape of twenty eight fugitives from Maryland. The band included several families with their children, including babies. Knowing that the slave catchers would soon be on their trail, the young men of the party carried with them three revolvers, three double barreled pistols, swords, knives and other weapons, for they were resolved to be free or die. They had provisions for only one day. They left during a blinding rainstorm. The rain continued for three days when they ran out of food, living only on parched corn and a few crackers. Some of the children became sick, but the band kept on until they at last reached the promised land of Philadelphia and the tender care of its Underground Railroad director William Still.

On Dec. 20,1845 the *Baltimore American* reported that over 100 Maryland slaves had made a mad dash for freedom. Most of them had been recaptured, but an unknown number had succeeded in their escape.Henry Predo, a twenty- seven- year old Maryland slave, found out that his master intended to sell him. He quickly contacted a member of the Underground Railroad for help in escaping. Seven other slaves were also planning to escape and, for three days, the eight fugitives managed to evade the traps that slave catchers had set for them. On the third day they discovered that a reward of $3,000 had been posted for their capture. The reward proved too much for the conductor who was leading them to the next station, and he betrayed them. The fugitives were dragged off to the Dover, Delaware jail. The six men and two women fought back bravely. While the sheriff waved a gun at the band and ordered them into the jail, they pushed him aside, fled into the Sheriff's private apartment, smashed a window, jumped twelve feet to the ground, then fled into the darkness. William Brinkley, a black member of the Underground Railroad of Dover, told a friend what happened next. He took his carriage to the spot where the fugitives were hiding, hid them in his carriage, and drove them nineteen miles to a safe house. Brinkley then had to drive back home so that, when the patrollers wanted to search his home for the escapees, he would be able to say honestly that he certainly was not hiding any fugitives.

On hearing of the disaster,Thomas Garrett sent a message to the Underground Railroad members who were now hiding the band. Garrett had heard that the owners had stationed a number of people along the only road going north, knowing that sooner or later the fugitives had to pass along that road. Garrett suggested that the fugitives remain hidden for at least two weeks until the slave catchers got tired and went home. The band was quickly rescued by members of the Underground Railroad, who hid the group until the hunt for the fugitives was over and they could safely travel on to Philadelphia and freedom.

There was one place in the South where fugitives knew that they could always find permanent sanctuary, the Great Dismal Swamp. This was an immense boggy wilderness of about one thousand square miles which began just a few miles inland from the Atlantic Ocean. This swamp stretched from Norfolk, Virginia

through Elizabeth City, North Carolina. The Great Dismal Swamp had been home to fugitive slaves since before the Revolutionary War. By 1830 one estimate stated that there were two thousand fugitives living within its protected spaces. Some of these settlers were the grandchildren of fugitives who had fled into the swamp before the Revolution. Government officials, as well as slave hunters, regularly launched raids into the swamp to try to destroy these black maroon settlements, but the fugitives had their own military bands, and were able to fight off these invaders. The battle skills of these black maroons would become an important asset to the Federal government during the Civil War.

There was more contact between the fugitives and the outside world than the white world realized; a well established trade with other blacks living close to the swamp. Maroons would supply game and fish to plantation slaves in exchange for necessities such as salt (for preserving meat), guns and cloth, as well as such luxuries as sugar and coffee. The same trade went on with the poor whites in the area. Enterprising maroons also found ways to earn money, because the Great Dismal was an important source of shingles which were used for roofing in construction products. The best shingles were made from the pine and cedar trees growing in the swamp. The Dismal Swamp Shingle Company hired hundreds of workers to cut these shingles. Many laborers, instead of working in the yard, would take the raw shingle material and vanish. Workers would return with many more shingles than they could possibly create on their own. Everyone knew that workers had taken unprocessed shingles into the Great Dismal where fugitive families would finish them. The fact that the money was shared with runaway slaves never bothered the company because they were making a substantial profit from this secret working arrangement.

In the 1800's, before railroads crisscrossed the nation, the only way for people to travel long distances, and for goods to be shipped to market, was on the vast system of rivers, lakes, streams, and creeks that covered America. These waterways began in the Appalachian Mountains and flowed down through Southern towns and plantations before emptying into the Atlantic Ocean. Hundreds of slaves became expert in navigating the South's river system. Products like cotton, tobacco, timber, tar, and corn were piled high on boats, barges and rafts. Some of these vessels traveled only a few miles to a local town market, but there were other boats that might travel over 100 miles from the rich interior farmlands to the major port cities of the South. Some of these slave watermen traveled alone for weeks at a time, unsupervised by any white man.

There were black watermen everywhere. Slave river men traveled on rivers that flowed deep into the heart of the South, rivers that separated the South from the North, rivers that began in the South's interior and flowed down to the sea. These watermen, as they traveled up and down the rivers, were the most vital link in the slave grapevine. They delivered messages between family members and friends separated by the slave trade. Watermen also passed on information about national and world events. Many slaves first learned about the Haitian Revolution, the abolition of slavery in the North, and John Brown's raid on Harper's Ferry from them. It was watermen who frequently spread the word throughout the South about the existence of the Underground Railroad.

As mentioned earlier, many watermen were themselves conductors on the Underground Railroad. They were skilled at hiding a fugitive, or even a band of fugitives, under the bales of cotton or sacks of tobacco stacked up on their rafts and boats. The fugitives would remain hidden sometimes for over a week until the riverman reached his final destination. Sometimes that destination was a port city or town. Other times the waterman's destination might be another town or village along the way. There were usually temporary hiding places, sometimes with friendly slaves or freedmen; other times fugitives were forced to hide within the vast network of swamps, dense forests, and tidal marshes that covered many parts of coastal Virginia and North Carolina. If they were lucky, some fugitives would be hidden within a port city where they waited for a ship to carry them north. Fugitives might have to wait for weeks or sometimes months until a member of the Underground Railroad could find a seaman or a ship's captain who would smuggle them aboard an ocean vessel.

While most members of the South's Underground Railroad were dedicated individuals, there were other people who who used the Underground Railroad as a way to make money. These people demanded money from every fugitive that they helped along the way. Fugitives found many ways to raise the funds to pay for their freedom. Many of the fugitives hiding in the Great Dismal Swamp were working with white woodcutters in order to pay for a ship's hiding place. Other fugitives found jobs in the port cities even while they hid from slave hunters.

Slaveholders knew that some of the watermen might be conductors on the Underground Railroad, but, because the entire maritime economy was dependent on slave labor, especially slave pilots, southerners felt powerless to control the activities of black watermen. Without boats to carry the cotton, tobacco, rice and sugar cane from the plantation to the sea there would be no way for southern crops to reach their markets in the North and Europe. Slave pilots were the only people who had the training to navigate the complicated river systems, filled with shoals, murky currents, lurking sandbars, and unexpected turns.

Wilmington was the largest town with the best harbor in North Carolina. So many fugitives headed for that port city hoping to find a ship that might take them north, that one frustrated North Carolina planter called Wilmington "an asylum for Runaways." [6]

The *Wilmington Journal* complained that "It is almost an every day occurrence for our negro slaves to take passage [aboard a ship] and go North." [7] The *Norfolk American Beacon* of Norfolk insisted that slaves were escaping "almost daily" from their Virginia city. In 1854 the newspaper claimed that more than $30,000 worth of slaves had been lost "by the aid of abolitionists." [8]

The slaveholders were right; the Underground Railroad had

---

[6] Cecelski, David. *"The Shores of Freedom: The Maritime Underground Railroad in North Carolina, 1800-1861.* The North Carolina Historical Review, April 1994. (Pg 177)

[7] Ibid (Pg. 174)

[8] Grover, Kathryn. *The Fugitive's Gibraltar: Escaping Slaves and Abolitionism in New Bedford, Massachusetts.* Amherst: University of Massachusetts Press, 2001. (Pg. 242)

organized a complex network of escape routes based on the cooperation of at least four sea captains and scores of seamen, and other maritime workers. According to records kept by William Still, four men, Alfred Fountain, captain of the sailing ship *City of Richmond,* William D. Bayliss, captain of the *Kesiah,* and Captains William Lambdin and Robert Lee were all involved in this network. Some of them would just hide a single or a few fugitives. Captain Fountain, who boasted that he was never caught hiding a fugitive, once smuggled twenty one fugitives aboard his ship.

Southerners living in port cities demanded that the government enforce stricter control over the hundreds of black-operated boats that sailed in and out of Chesapeake Bay. They believed that most of the fugitives were able to slip aboard these ships given the help of black seamen. They were right: many black and a few white seamen were important members of the South's Underground Railroad.

When fugitives arrived in a port city, they needed some way to contact the Underground Railroad. If a runaway was lucky enough to have traveled to a port city hidden in a black pilot's vessel, the fugitive was most probably already under the protection of the well-organized escape network that honeycombed most of the South's coastal communities. But there were other fugitives who reached the city alone and in desperate need of help to find the Underground Railroad.

Many times the fugitive would approach members of a black church, always the heart of any black community. Church members frequently knew the names of someone who was a member of the Underground Railroad. Other times the fugitive might slip into a barber shop and ask for help. Barbershops were one of the few black businesses approved of by the white establishment, and so barber shops operated as a kind of social and political club for the entire community, one of the few places blacks could gather together without whites becoming suspicious.

If a fugitive escaped to Wilmington, North Carolina, he or she might be guided to a slave pilot whose name was Peter. Peter had been running a thriving station of the Underground Railroad for years. His master was a rich merchant and ship owner, and Peter skillfully towed large vessels in and out of Wilmington Bay. He had many friends among the crews of these ships, so he knew which of these seamen would be willing to hide a fugitive. Peter regularly stowed fugitives aboard his barge and slipped them aboard northbound ships. Peter was not alone; he had allies. Two white Quakers, Fuller and Elliot were oyster men who fished in the waters of the bay and also hid fugitives in their sloops. Whites finally got suspicious of the three men. They warned the two Quakers to stay away from blacks. Elliot fled north. Fuller was not so lucky; he disappeared suddenly from Wilmington and his family never heard from him again. Although his body was never found, his family believed that he was murdered by white vigilantes. Peter was sold and his family never heard from him again.

Even after the Underground Railroad had made arrangements for a shipboard hiding place, the fugitive still had to be smuggled aboard the vessel. Slaveholders and their agents haunted southern harbors constantly searching for runaways. Many fugitives were seized just as they were trying to slip aboard. Fugitives turned to a group of dedicated rescuers, such as Eliza Baines. Baines was a Norfolk, Virginia slave whose owner hired out her services to a number of sea captains while their ships were in port. This gave Baines unlimited access to every vessel in Norfolk. Baines had an amazing knowledge of the sailing times, friendly crew members, even antislavery sea captains, that made her remarkably successful in finding secure hiding places for her fugitive clients. Sometimes Baines had to wait weeks before she found a safe ship. Many times she hid fugitives in her own house. One time Baines heard that a posse was on the way to her home to search for runaways. She ran home and sent her group of fugitives out into the garden to hide among the tall rows of corn. One of them remembered how, when the fugitives were finally safely aboard the ship, Baines lifted up her voice and sang "It's all right hallelujah, glory to God." Baines was so skillful that she was never caught and remained an Underground Railroad operator until the end of the Civil War.

Henry Lewey, a slave, was one of the key Railroad operators between Norfolk, Virginia and the Philadelphia Vigilance Committee. Lewey was skilled in finding safe houses for newly arrived fugitives waiting for a ship to take them to Philadelphia. He recruited crew members and sometimes captains to hide fugitives on their vessels. He regularly sent letters to William Still using his code name of Blue Beard. These letters alerted the Vigilance Committee that a new group of fugitives were on their way to Philadelphia. Lewey sometimes got letters from fugitives who had successfully escaped with messages for their family and friends. Then one day it was Lewey's turn to escape. In the summer of 1856, the authorities began to suspect that he was aiding fugitives. A quick witted thinker, Lewey managed to convince the authorities that he was innocent. He went home and immediately arranged for his young wife, Rebecca, who was also a slave, to escape. As soon as he heard from Still that she was safe, Lewey slipped aboard one of the friendly ships in the harbor and sailed away to freedom.

There were many other Underground Railroad agents who worked on wharfs all over the South. Some were market women who delivered fresh food. Other agents were stevadores who carried cargo up the ships' gangplanks. Laundry women brought newly washed clothes aboard and wandered unnoticed throughout the ship, depositing clean piles of laundry in various cabins. Amid all this hustle and bustle these agents managed to slip hundreds of fugitives aboard ships bound for the North.

Robert Purvis remembered that "The most efficient helpers or agents that we had were two market women, who lived in Baltimore, one of whom was white, the other "colored." Another most effective worker was a son of a slaveholder, who lived at Newberne, N. C. Through his agency, the slaves were forwarded by placing them on vessels engaged in the lumber trade, which plied between Newberne and Philadelphia and the captains of which had hearts." [9]

When groups of fugitives needed to board ships, special arrangements had to be made. Sometimes a ship would take off for a northern port, then secretly sail into a deserted cove where a small boat holding the fugitives would quickly row out to meet the ship. The fugitives would climb aboard, and the ship would set sail for the North. Even after a fugitive was safely hidden the danger was still acute. Slaveholders frequently insisted on searching a ship just before it sailed. Sometimes they even fumigated the ship which forced any runaway to abandon his hiding place before he choked to death.

Even when the fugitives reached a northern port they were still not safe as we know since slave hunters haunted the harbors searching for fugitives. One member of Boston's Vigilance Committee routinely sailed his boat after dark to rescue fugitives from the docks so that the ever-present slave hunters could not see them.

Robert Lee, a white sea captain living in Portsmouth Virginia, was part of William Still's network. In 1857 four slaves came to him for help in planning their escape. Lee told them he would find a boat and sail them to Philadelphia. The four fugitives met Lee at a deserted cove near Portsmouth where the captain had a skiff

---

[9] Smedley, R.C. *History of the Underground Railroad.* New York: Arno Press and The New York Times, 1969. (Pg. 355)

waiting. Lee sailed his boat to a deserted beach outside Philadelphia and the four fugitives quickly made their way to William Still's Vigilance Committee. Captain Lee returned to Portsmouth where he was promptly arrested for slave stealing. He was tried convicted and sentenced to 25 years in the state penitentiary. His sentence also included five lashes daily for ten days. Lee died in prison. His wife and two young children were brought to Philadelphia where they were cared for by the grateful members of the Underground Railroad.[10]

A white Philadelphian member of the Underground Railroad, Seth Concklin, was deeply moved by his friend Peter Still's grief because, while Still was free, most of his family were still slaves. Concklin told Still that he would travel to Alabama and rescue his family. Concklin succeeded in helping the Still family flee the plantation. He led them to the skiff that he had hidden in the bushes, and soon they were sailing north on the Tennessee River. Whenever they stopped, Concklin pretended that he was their master and this deception worked until the runaways reached Vincennes, Indiana. There a group of slavehunters who had been given a description of the entire family recognized the fugitives. They arrested the entire Still family and had them jailed. When Concklin tried to run away he was caught. The slave hunters then began beating Concklin on this head. A few days later his body was found in the river, his skull fractured.

Captain Fountain was one of the most daring and heroic conductors on the Underground Railroad. His ship collected cargo from every port in the Upper South. The slaves knew his name and everywhere his vessel dropped anchor he was immediately besieged by desperate fugitives trying to escape. Slaveholders also knew his name and reputation, so whenever Captain Fountain was in port, his ship was under close surveillance. Yet, although he had many close calls, Fountain was never caught. The captain gleefully told William Still about one such encounter with the mayor of Norfolk. His schooner was anchored at the wharf while stevedores loaded a cargo of wheat. A rumor quickly spread all over town that Fountain was hiding a group of fugitives somewhere aboard his ship. The rumor was true; twenty one fugitives were hiding below the deck. The mayor, led a posse of men up the gangplank and demanded to search the ship. A smiling Fountain graciously agreed and even offered to help in the search. Members of the posse believed they knew just where the fugitives

[10] Still, William. *The Underground Railroad.* Chicago: Johnson Publishing Company Inc., 1970. (Pg. 101)

were hiding and they began spearing the bales of wheat stacked in the hold but reluctantly decided that there were no fugitives hiding in the wheat. Next they swung their axes chopping sections of the deck

to find a secret compartment. Fountain took his own ax and began swinging as he asked the mayor where he wanted to search next. The baffled mayor, somewhat nervous at the sight of the wild Captain Fountain swinging an ax, decided to leave. Captain Fountain sailed off and in a few days delivered twenty-one fugitives into the waiting arms of William Still.

Mayor & Police of Norfolk Searching Captain Foutain's, Schooner. Source: *Project Gutenberg* TM *License.*

These sea escapes haunted southern slaveholders. The sea was like a sieve where fugitives slipped through every net that southern society had erected to prevent the escape of their slave property. There were many men and women ready to help these fugitives. Slaveholders organized posses that constantly patrolled the docks for fugitives. Even when northbound ships were smoked, to force fugitives out of their hiding places it did not always work. Frederick Douglass tells of one determined fugitive woman who was hidden in a ship's hold bound for Boston. The fumes almost suffocated her, but she decided that she would rather die than return to slavery. Luckily she survived the ordeal. It was obvious to southerners that the only way to keep fugitives from escaping would be to quarantine their entire coast. Obviously that solution was impossible.

Southerners talked about banning blacks from the docks, but they realized that such a ban was impossible because most of the working people loading and unloading the ships, repairing the vessels, servicing the crew and even operating the tiny shops that crowded the shore, were black. Southerners reluctantly faced the fact that their entire maritime culture was run by African Americans, both slave and free.

Sailors were another problem. Most seamen were still white, but a growing minority of ships' crews were black. Southerners hated these free and independent mariners, and soon most coastal states had passed a series of draconian laws to prevent black seamen from having any contact with their slaves. The South Carolina Negro Seamen's Act was typical. Any black crewman from a ship docking in a South Carolina harbor must be taken from the ship and placed in the local jail until that ship was ready to sail. The cost of this jail stay had to be paid by the ship's owner. Any captain who did not place his black crew in jail would be subject to a fine of one thousand dollars. Even though the U.S. Supreme Court declared this law unconstitutional, Charleston continued to enforce it until the Civil War. Georgia, North Carolina, Louisiana, Florida, and Alabama also passed their own black seamen's law.

The North was outraged by these laws, not just for humanitarian reasons but for practical reasons as well. Many black sailors refused to sign up on ships that were traveling South. It became harder to recruit crews. Merchants were infuriated that they had to pay jail costs for members of their crews. Yet in spite of everything southerners did to control the escape of their slaves, the sea remained the most successful escape routes on the Underground Railroad.

The Underground Railroad also recruited some extraordinary people to travel into the slave South and gather up groups of slaves and guide them North. The most famous of these conductors was, of course, Harriet Tubman. She had escaped from her Maryland owner in 1849 after the death of her old master. The slave quarters had buzzed with the rumor that she was about to be sold. For two years nobody in her family had gotten any message from Tubman. Her family wondered if her escape had been successful or perhaps she was lying dead in some unmarked grave. Then one night they heard a knock on the cabin door. They opened the door and saw their beloved Harriet. Why, they cried out, had she returned from freedom back into danger? Why, to bring you all out from slavery into freedom, she answered. Tubman became a legend within Maryland plantations. From 1850 until the Civil War, Tubman made nineteen trips from Maryland to Philadelphia. One of her resting places was usually the Wilmington home of Thomas Garrett. Her final destination was always William Still and the Philadelphia Vigilance Committee.

She asked no funds from any of the abolitionist societies; instead she would work as a domestic until she had saved enough money to finance another rescue. She was so strong that she could lift a man in her arms and run with him if she felt that he was moving too slowly to suit her. When Tubman was young she had been hit on the head with an iron bar and sometimes lapsed into a temporary coma. Maryland slaveholders put a price on her head of five thousand dollars but she was never betrayed. There is a legend that she once fell into a coma right under one of these wanted posters.

Nobody really knows just how many fugitives Tubman rescued; the numbers grew each time somebody repeated the legend of Harriet Tubman. She was known affectionately throughout Maryland as Moses. The signal that she was about to lead a new rescue was sometimes a person singing the song "Go Down Moses." She even managed to rescue her aged parents, a trip that had to be meticulously planned since they were too feeble to walk the hundreds of miles that her other rescues required. The legend of Harriet Tubman became an inspiration to every slave in Maryland and created a virulent form of paranoia in the minds of slaveholders.

Harriet Tubman was only the most famous of an intrepid group of conductors who regularly made their way south for rescue missions. There was the famous Canadian Dr. Alexander Ross, who was also one of the world's leading ornithologists. Ross visited most of the coastal south from Virginia to Georgia studying the habits of American birds. Plantation owners welcomed this celebrated man into their homes. What they never knew was that he had met with leaders of the Underground Railroad. These leaders had given Ross detailed information about hundreds of routes and stations that began deep in the South and led to safe havens in the North. Ross was committed to sharing that information with interested slaves. On his first trip into Virginia, he met with 42 slaves in Richmond. They all promised to pass on the information that he gave them. Nine slaves were ready to escape immediately. Ross gave them each a few dollars, a pocket compass, a knife, and as much cold meat and bread as they could carry. Other times Ross became a conductor himself, leading bands of runaways out of the South.

John Fairfield was certainly a surprising conductor. He was born into a family of Virginian slaveholders, but he hated slavery. He decided he had to live somewhere free of slavery's contamination so, as soon as he reached adulthood, he left Virginia and moved to Ohio. Fairfield didn't leave the South by himself; he took with him his boyhood friend, a young slave of his uncle. For this crime Fairfield discovered, when he returned to Virginia for a visit, there was a warrant out for his arrest. He fled Virginia but not without some excess baggage a group of fugitive slaves. Fairfield brought them all safely to Canada. The word of his success spread throughout the black Canadian settlements, and Fairfield was besieged by fugitives bringing him their small savings and begging him to rescue their relatives. Fairfield had a new career as a conductor on the Underground Railroad. For each mission he began by questioning his new clients to learn everything possible to guarantee the success of the rescue. Who were the slaveholders; what were their personalities and habits? What was the geography surrounding the plantations? He wanted full descriptions of the neighborhoods. When he had gathered all this information he was ready to begin his dangerous trip south. He always presented himself as a southern businessman, sometimes even pretending to be a slave trader. He loudly proclaimed his pro-slavery feelings. Rarely did anyone associate him with the strange disappearance of a group of slaves around the same time he was leaving.

For 12 years Fairfield traveled into almost every southern state, rescuing slaves. His work was so secret that we might never have heard of him were it not for Levi Coffin, living in Cincinnati, who regularly took charge of Fairfield's bands of fugitives. Even William Still had never heard his name until Fairfield knocked on the door of the Vigilance Committee claiming that he was hiding a band of desperate fugitives, and he had run out of money. Still telegraphed Coffin asking who was this charming but unknown Virginian. Coffin wired back immediately to give John Fairfield anything he needs.

Fairfield was tough, and only fugitives ready to fight for their freedom were welcomed into his company. Coffin tells of one such rescue. Fairfield was visiting one neighborhood disguised as a merchant buying chickens and eggs. He managed to interview 10 or 12 slaves who had already resolved to win their freedom or die in the attempt. One of these rescued fugitives described to Coffin his experience of Fairfield" I never saw such a man as Fairfield. He told us he would take us out of slavery or he would die in the attempt, if we would do our part, which we promised to do. We all agreed to fight until we died rather than be recaptured." They were attacked several times by patrollers, but managed to drive them off. One night patrollers ambushed both sides of a bridge that they needed to cross. These slave hunters believed that such a heavy attack would certainly cause the fugitives, who were surrounded, to surrender. Fairfield ordered his band to charge to the front and attack. The patrollers scattered and ran like scared sheep to Fairfield's glee. Levi Coffin, a devoted Quaker, was appalled by Fairfield's use of violence, and tried to convince the rescuer that "We should love our enemies." Fairfield's response was that, "When I undertake to conduct slaves out of bondage, I feel that it is my duty to defend them, even to the last drop of my blood." Fairfield made a final trip to Cincinnati, and then seemed to disappear. Nobody ever heard from him again.[11]

Slaveholders were especially upset at the terminal in Washington D C. The city was the capital of the most democratic nation in the world, yet it was also a slave city and the center of the South's power base. Washington was surrounded on all sides by slave states and, in the streets, one could frequently see groups of chained slaves marching towards one of the largest slave auction houses in the nation.

The city was also the home of a large community of free African Americans. One of these African Americans was Thomas Smallwood, a Maryland slave who bought his own freedom in 1831 for $500. In 1840 Smallwood and his wife Elizabeth organized Washington's first Underground Railroad terminal with a network that led from the city to Baltimore, where the black leader, Jacob Gibbs, had established his own active terminal.

Charles Torrey was a young Boston aristocrat who had begun his antislavery activities by helping organize Boston's Vigilance Committee and through his writing for several antislavery newspapers. The young man decided to travel to Maryland to write about a state slaveholders convention that would be held on January 12, 1842 in Annapolis. The delegates were in the midst of debating

---

[11] Coffin, Levi. *Reminiscences of Levi Coffin. Abridged and edited by Ben Richmond.* Richmond Indiana: Friends United Press, 1991. (Pg. 293-294)

a proposal to force every freedman to leave the state. Torrey leaped
to his feet and told the 150 slaveholders that blacks would die rather
than be forced to leave their slave families and friends. The delegates
responded by seizing Torrey and sending him to jail on charges of
mutiny, and distributing incendiary material. A judge soon freed
the reporter from these illegal charges, but his arrest changed
Torrey forever. He was ready for some direct action and, in 1842,
he met Thomas Smallwood, who recruited him into Washington's
Underground Railroad

They were an interesting team. Smallwood ran the Washington
terminal while Torrey, who lived in Albany, New York, was the line's
chief conductor, making frequent trips into the Washington area to
rescue slaves. The two men had recruited a group of carriage owners
who would hide fugitives in their vehicles, drive them out of the city
and deliver the fugitives to the next station.

Leonard Grimes was one of the most successful of these drivers.
Grimes was a free born Virginia black man living a seemingly
respectable life in Washington DC, as the owner of a profitable hack
rental company. Grimes used his carriages to slip down into Virginia
and fill his vehicles with runaway slaves. It was on one of these
trips that Grimes was arrested while rescuing a slave family with
seven children. He was sentenced to two years in the state prison in
Richmond.

Torrey was able to raise money from the small group of
antislavery congressmen, as well as other political figures around
Washington, such as Gamalied Bailey, editor of the New Era, even
though Bailey publicly rejected Torrey's radical antislavery activities.
Some of these political leaders were also suspected of hiding fugitive
slaves.

Torrey and Smallwood had a philosophy that differed from the
secretive ways of most of the Underground Railroad operators. While
they kept their identity secret, they delighted in baiting slaveholders
in the Chesapeake area. Torrey had become the editor of the *Tocsin
and Patriot* newspaper. Smallwood wrote for the newspaper, a series
of letters under the name Samivel Weller Jr., named at Torrey's
suggestion after one of the characters in Charles Dickens' Pickwick
Papers. In November 1842 Samivel Weller boasted in one of his letters
that Washington's Underground Railroad had helped 150 escapees,
thereby relieving slaveholders of property worth around $75,000.
There was a reason for this defiant letter. The two men wanted to
shake the slaveholders confidence in their ability to retain their hold

on their slaves. Using the persona of Weller, the two men taunted and belittled Chesapeake slaveholders by sending them copies of Torrey's newspaper. In each paper the superior skills of conductors of the Underground Railroad were glorified.

The strategy of creating paranoia among Chesapeake slaveholders backfired. Instead of making slaveholders think about giving up their property, it only made them decide that they must get rid of Torrey and his cohorts any way they could. In the summer of 1843, Smallwood got word that he was about to be arrested. He quickly packed and, with his family, fled to Toronto in Canada. Torrey was not so lucky. He was arrested and sentenced to six years in a Maryland jail. Torrey died in prison in 1846.

If slaveholders thought that by getting rid of Torrey and Smallwood they had crippled Washington's Underground Railroad, they were mistaken. William Chaplin, another member of Boston's elite, and the newest Washington correspondent for a group of abolitionist newspapers, had just moved to the city. Chaplin had idolized Torrey and he vowed that the Underground Railroad terminal that Torrey had helped to create would continue to thrive. William Chaplin was about to become part of one of the most spectacular rescue attempts in American history.

The rescue began innocently one evening when Captain Daniel Drayton sat smoking his pipe on the deck of his ship, which was tied to one of Washington's many wharfs. An elderly black man boarded the boat and began a seemingly idle conversation. Within this random conversation a few key questions had been asked. The man confirmed that Drayton was from the North. He had heard that most Northerners were abolitionists. Drayton paused for a moment then nodded. The black man took a deep breath and revealed that he knew of a black woman and her five children who desperately needed to escape. "Will yah talk t' her? Kin ah bring her on the bo't?" Drayton hesitated for a moment then nodded.[12] This was the dangerous way that blacks recruited new conductors for the Underground Railroad. Either they got a new member or they might find themselves in jail. It was remarkable that so many of these anonymous members of the Underground Railroad were willing to take that risk over and over again. Chaplin learned about this new recruit almost as soon as

---

[12] Buckmaster, Henrietta. *Let My People Go: The Story of the Underground Railroad and the Growth of the Abolitionist Movement.* New York: Harper & Brothers, 1941. (Pg. 152-153)

Drayton had delivered his first band of fugitives. He wrote a letter
to Drayton telling him that there were a number of slaves who were
longing to run away but who needed some way to travel north. Did he
want to help them?

On April 13, 1848, Daniel Drayton slipped the schooner *Pearl*
into its moorings on the Potomac River. On board were three white
men, Drayton, the ship's owner Edward Sayres, and the seaman
Chester English. They were waiting for night to fall. Drayton had
promised members of Washington's Underground Railroad that the
three men would transport as many fugitives as the ship was able to
hold. The schooner was scheduled to sail in three days. Chaplin, who
had recruited Drayton and Sayres for this mission, was now busy
spreading the word that the *Pearl* was going to sail on Thursday,
April 13 and that anyone who wanted to be free must be aboard before
Thursday.

When Drayton boarded the boat on Saturday ready to set sail he
was astonished to find seventy eight men, women, and children hiding
below deck, eager to begin their journey north. It was a wonder that
the small ship did not sink under the weight of this cargo.

Their plan was to sail down the Potomac River to the sea
during the night and reach the open waters of the Chesapeake before
daybreak but the weather was against them. There was no wind and
the ship barely moved. On Sunday the wind was too strong for the
small ship to venture out into the ocean. This delay was fatal. Sunday,
when slaveholders discovered that so many of their slaves were
missing, they believed that only a ship would be capable of carrying
so many fugitives at one time. When they heard that Drayton's ship
was also missing, thirty armed volunteers, under the command of
Washington, D.C. magistrate W.C. Williams, set sail on the steamer
Salem in swift pursuit. The pursuers found the *Pearl* still at anchor at
two o'clock Monday morning. The fugitives, caught by surprise, had no
way to resist; they were quickly chained below deck on the *Pearl*. The
three white men, Drayton, Sayres and English were arrested and
taken aboard the *Salem*. At seven-thirty Tuesday morning, the two
ships docked. The fugitives, with the three white prisoners leading
the way, were marched along Pennsylvania Avenue towards the city
jail. Among the fugitives were thirty-eight men, twenty six women,
and thirteen children, some of them infants in their mothers arms.
A furious mob lined the streets shouting angry threats at the three
white leaders of the escape. Magistrate Williams was so worried that
the three men might be harmed by someone in the crowd that he

decided to put them in a hack and send them as fast as possible on to the jail.

By evening the fugitives and their rescuers were safely in jail, but the crowd was still angry. Tuesday night several hundred people gathered at the building that housed the abolitionist newspaper, *The National Era;* they smashed some windows and rammed open one of its doors. Only police intervention saved the building from destruction. The next night an even larger crowd assembled in front of the building, demanding that *The National Era* building be torn down. Walter Lenox, a member of the Board of Aldermen, along with other members of Washington's elite, temporarily calmed the mob by promising to get Gamaliel Bailey, publisher of *The National Era*, to immediately close down the newspaper.

A delegation of fifty quickly walked to Bailey's home. They told him about the mob and begged him to remove his press from the city to prevent any more violence. Bailey, who had dealt with mob threats before in Cincinnati calmly replied, "that he would rather die than surrender his rights as a 'representative of a free press'." [13] When the delegation returned with Bailey's answer, the infuriated rabble again tried to burn the building down. Only the police, joined by a large group of volunteer citizens, managed to save *The National Era* building. Gamaliel Bailey's friends were so worried by these threats that they rushed to his house, lifted his six children from their beds and took them to a safe house. Bailey and his wife Margaret stayed behind to confront the mob. The mob also searched Washington to find William Chaplin, the man they believed had organized the entire escape. They blamed him for recruiting Drayton and spreading the word that the *Pearl* was ready to carry fugitives north. Chaplin was never found. As soon as his friends had told him about the capture of the *Pearl*, he fled the city because he knew that his life was in danger.

On Tuesday, April 18 Joshua Giddings, an antislavery Congressman from Ohio, presented a resolution to the House demanding to know on what authority "men, women and children" were being held "without being charged with crime...other than an attempt to enjoy that liberty for which our fathers encountered toil, suffering, and death itself." [14] This resolution, of course was instantly voted down, but southern representatives were furious because such

---

[13] Harrold, Stanley. *Subversives: Antislavery Community in Washington D.C.* Baton Rouge: Louisiana State University Press, 2003. (Pg. 122)

[14] Ibid (pg. 130-131)

a resolution would certainly encourage slaves to escape and, even more infuriating, the resolution assumed that African Americans had rights. The next day Giddings again defied the mob by appearing at the jail along with two attorneys. They demanded to meet with the prisoners. The jailor took the three men upstairs; Giddings was just permitted to peek at the fugitives, but was not allowed to meet with Drayton, Sayres and English. On the way down the stairs the three men were attacked by a mob led by the notorious slave trader, Hope Slatter, who owned the largest slave market in Washington. Giddings and the two lawyers managed to escape without harm.

Even President Polk began to worry. Polk was already trying to decide if slavery was going to expand into every one of the new territories won by the United States after its victory in the war with Mexico. The possibility that slavery might extend into territories where slavery, under Mexican law, had always been illegal, was already beginning to tear the country apart. Now the President was faced with the fact that a Southern mob was threatening one of the most popular abolitionist newspapers in America, which might further inflame the North. Because he believed that the preservation of the Union was at risk, Polk decided that he had to control the riot. He appealed to government clerks asking them to act as "conservators of law and order." These clerks volunteered to join a hundred law enforcement officials in a show of force to quell the riot. On the fourth day peace was finally restored to the nation's capital.

It was an uneasy peace. Common folks stood on the sidewalks or looked out of their windows and watched as most of the *Pearl* fugitives were marched to the railroad station. The cries of anguish of husbands and wives, mothers and children, as they were separated from each other, probably forever, was a sound that most observers had never heard before. For the first time Washington's citizens were forced to face the reality that slave families loved each other as devotedly as white families. This was the first time that so many whites were forced to confront the horror of the slave trade.

The battle over the *Pearl* fugitives had just begun. It now moved into the halls of Congress. Representative Giddings demanded an investigation to determine how the nation's capital had been taken over by a Southern mob for three days. Southern congressmen responded angrily that the mobs had the right to attack those people who publicly were inciting their slaves to run away. Inciting slaves to run away was "slave stealing" which was a crime in every southern state. Furthermore these congressmen insisted that every

72

man had the right to protect his property. Giddings responded by announcing that blacks had the same right to freedom as whites. Southern congressmen angrily went on the attack. John Calhoun, the most important southern leader in the senate, stated that the *Pearl's* attempted rescue was a Northern attack on a Southern port. He insisted that unless something more was done to protect slave property in the capital and to counteract northern resistance to the Fugitive Slave Law there would be a worse slave revolt than the one that resulted in the independent black republic of Haiti. Meanwhile Senator Jefferson Davis, the future president of the Confederacy, threatened immediate secession unless the slave stealing abolitionists of the *Pearl* were prosecuted.

Forty-one indictments were drawn up against Drayton and his two associates. When Drayton was convicted he was singled out for the most extreme punishment. The government had fined him $ 10,000, a sum impossible for him to raise, therefore Drayton was facing a lifetime in jail. Abolitionists immediately began trying to raise money to pay the fine, but the amount was formidable. In those days a person ordered to pay a fine would be kept in jail until the fine was paid. As he faced this horrible fate, Drayton had one piece of comfort. His abolitionist friends assured him that they would always take care of his family.

The memory of the *Pearl* would not die. Northern newspapers were filled with heart-wrenching stories about the *Pearl* fugitives who had been sold to slave traders. There were stories about how families had been ripped apart. Other stories speculated about why some of the beautiful young women were bringing such high prices. Was it because these women were being sold as concubines? Drayton and Sayres were celebrated all over the North as heroes. Meanwhile Chaplin was raising money all over the North to purchase the freedom of several of the *Pearl* fugitives. Finally in August 1852 President Millard Fillmore, yielding to northern pressure, granted pardons for both Drayton and Sayres.

In August 1850 William Chaplin returned to Washington. He probably had been back in Washington already, since he had never given up his role as a conductor of the Underground Railroad. This time, working with Warner Harris, a Washington freeman, the two men were planning to rescue Allen and Garland, slaves and body servants of two prominent Georgia Congressmen, Alexander H. Stephens and Robert Toombs. The two fugitives had already escaped and were hiding in the home of the free black man, Noah Hanson,

73

waiting for transportation north.

On the evening of August 8th Chaplin was hiding the two men inside the carriage he had just rented when he saw Captain Goddard riding towards him, leading a detachment of the Washington Guard. The rescue had been betrayed. Chaplin and the two fugitives began firing but were outnumbered and taken prisoner. The Washington court charged Chaplin only with stealing slaves; but as soon as that trial ended, Maryland courts were ready to charge him with the serious crime of assault with intent to kill. Northen abolitionists worried that Chaplin would receive a long jail sentence just like Torrey. They vowed that they would not let this happen again. Their plan was simple. They would raise enough money to bail him out of jail with the understanding that he would flee Washington into the antislavery communities of the North where he would never be extradited. The committee did not forget the other two prisoners. They began a national campaign to raise the fines for Harris and Hanson. It took eight months to collect Harris' fine and, in 1854, Hanson received a presidential pardon.

On August 21, 1850 a unique convention was held in Cazenovia New York. It was called the Fugitive Slave Convention. There were over fifteen hundred delegates including at least thirty-five fugitive slaves. There were several guests of honor, but the acknowledged hero of the convention was William Chaplin. The delegates enthusiastically nominated Chaplin for president of the United States.

CHAPTER
4

WE ARE ALREADY FREE
FLORIDA AND THE SEMINOLES

Florida had been the favorite destination for Georgia's fugitive slaves since colonial days. It was a Spanish colony, but Spanish control was very loose. Florida's interior was a vast swampland ruled by the Seminole Indians, a hospitable people who seemed delighted to welcome runaway slaves to settle among them. The slaveholders of Georgia were outraged that Spain seemed indifferent to this stream of fugitive slaves moving into Florida. Southern leaders insisted that the United States government demand that the Spanish government use their army to return these fugitives to their rightful owners. But since the Spanish colonial government was too weak to prevent fugitives from settling in Florida, by 1812 it was apparent to the South that protests to Spain were useless.

President James Madison next approached the Seminole chiefs with offers of bounties and other gifts if they would round up the fugitives living in their midst and return them to the Georgia slaveholders. The Seminoles listened politely and did nothing. Americans could not understand why these Seminole chiefs were so indifferent to their generous bribes.

Just what was the relationship between the Indians and fugitive slaves? Southerners believed that all fugitives were Seminole slaves, but if this were their actual status, then no American slave ever lived the way these Seminole "slaves" did. Blacks, whether free or slave, were treated as equal members of the Seminole nation. Black Seminoles had their own independent tribes and elected their own chiefs. They lived in their own villages under the protection of a Seminole Chief; their only duty to their tribe's Protector was to provide troops in case of tribal war and to pay him a yearly tribute, which was usually about ten bushels of corn and a slaughtered pig or two. By 1812 Black and Indian Seminoles had already become more like one people. Abraham, the great chief of the Black Seminoles married the widow of one of the Seminole chiefs. Chief Osceola's wife was the daughter of a fugitive slave. The father of John Horse, one of the chiefs of a Seminole tribe, married a black woman and John Horse himself became the Principle Chief of one of the Black Seminole tribes.

Slaveholders in Georgia and the Carolinas told President Madison that the entire institution of slavery was threatened by Florida's lax border, and they insisted that he order the invasion of Florida and make it part of the United States. Southerners had another powerful argument to convince the president that the United States must annex Florida: England and France were in a long, bitter battle for control of Europe. America had struggled for years to remain neutral. In the shifting world of European political alliance, Spain was first an ally of France then of England. If America were to get dragged into this war, then Florida, with its growing population of fugitive slaves, would certainly create a dangerous situation for the security of the United States. Southerners pointed out to the president how England had recruited an army of fugitive slaves during the revolution.

President Madison, a slaveholder himself, was compelled to find some solution to the problem of Florida. In 1811 the president met with Congressional leaders and agreed on a secret plan to annex Florida. Southerners must begin recruiting men to settle in Florida's St. John River area, which was a sparsely settled valley ideally suited for a plantation economy. Madison believed that a flood of new settlers would soon overwhelm the local Spanish population. This plan was very successful; by 1812 land hungry Americans filled the St. John River valley with hundreds of thriving plantations. Now that the American settlers were strong enough, part two of the president's secret plan would begin. The settlers would revolt against Spanish rule and Madison would immediately send gun boats and armed American volunteers to support the insurrection. Everyone knew that Spain was so weak it could not prevent the settlers from setting up an independent government. Congress, as part of the secret agreement, would quickly recognize the new settler government; the settlers would petition the United States to be admitted as a new territory and Florida would become part of the United States.

On March 14, 1812 a group of volunteer militiamen, who called themselves the Patriots, marched into East Florida, supported by a fleet of American gunboats. A few weeks later the Patriots planted their new territorial flag firmly on Florida soil and began a siege of St. Augustine. They believed that St. Augustine would quickly surrender and then all of East Florida would be theirs. The Patriots forgot that East Florida was not only a Spanish colony, but the home of the Seminole Indians, who were not about to let their homeland be taken from them.

On July 25 the Seminoles launched a series of raids on the plantations of the St. John River. Hundreds of newly liberated slaves rushed to join the Seminole war parties. Now the Seminoles, in a series of brilliant raids, attacked the Patriot forces until the siege of St. Augustine was lifted.

Southerners had been surprised by the sight of black and native bands of Seminoles fighting side by side. Their surprise turned to astonishment on the day that a band 40 Seminoles, led by the Black Seminole chief, Prince Witen, attacked a wagon train escorted by a body of Patriots and United States Marines. The Patriot leader Colonel Smith reported to Georgia Governor Mitchell that he could not attack St. Augustine without at least 300 more men. The Governor of Georgia could not send fresh troops, so Smith was forced to lift the siege of St Augustine and temporarily returned to his base in Georgia.

On June 18, 1812 the United States declared war against England. President Madison needed the army to fight on every American frontier where the British, or its Spanish ally, might invade the United States. He adopted a new strategy towards East Florida. Instead of attempting to conquer all of East Florida, President Madison sent out a small military force whose objective was just to destroy all of the Seminole villages close to the Georgia border. With the villages destroyed the Seminoles would be forced to flee south. This would create a vast barren space between Spanish Florida and the Georgia border. The Seminoles were outnumbered on the battlefield but they were masters of guerrilla warfare. During one battle United States troops were marching towards a Seminole village when they were attacked by a band of Black Seminoles. This war band fought so fiercely that the entire Seminole village had time to find a safe haven in the swamp. When the news reached the Black Seminole band that the villagers were safe, the band also slipped away allowing the American army to find their way back to their base camp. The United States army succeeded in their mission to destroy the major Seminole villages bordering Georgia, but the Seminole people were still close enough to the Georgia border to entice any slave wanting to escape to join their war bands. These fugitives delighted in harassing slaveholders as they tried to recapture their runaway slaves.

In the spring of 1814 the British army ordered Lieutenant Colonel Edward Nicolls to gather up the remnants of his West Florida army and establish a new fort at Prospect Bluff on the east bank of the Apalachicola River, the new boundary between Spanish and American Florida. It was called the British Fort. Traveling with Nicolls were around 100 fugitive slaves, veterans of the West Florida battlefields. Nicolls wanted these fugitives to be the primary defenders of the fort, and they happily agreed. On December 24, 1814 the United States and England signed a peace treaty that ended the War of 1812, and the British went home. Most of their Florida forts were abandoned and stood empty. All but one – the British Fort.

The fugitive defenders of the fort refused to leave. Florida was their home and they were determined to defend it against the Americans whom they knew would soon be coming. The British had left behind thousands of pieces of small arms, crates of ammunition, several pieces of light artillery and six small cannons. The fort, newly named the Negro Fort, was now ready for battle. The fugitives also had a new leader whose name was Garcon. Garcon issued an invitation to every slave living in Georgia and the Carolinas to join him. Soon a stream of runaways traveled the Underground Railroad south to Florida. One thousand fugitives settled on the banks of the Apalachicola River. Fifty miles of flourishing farms and rich pastureland thrived under the protection of Garcon and the Negro Fort.

Southerners were appalled by the Negro Fort. There it stood, only sixty miles from the Georgia border, an inspiration to every slave in Georgia. The fort defied every justification that slaveholders had to keep black men in chains. These fugitives had begun creating a flourishing community and had assembled a band of black fighters able to defend their territory. The most dangerous problem of all for slaveholders was that the Negro Fort had become a Mecca for every restless slave in the lower south. How could a southerner prevent his most valuable property (in 1814 a prime field hand might sell for as high as $600) from fleeing the plantation when there was such an alluring alternative only sixty miles from America's border.

Posses of Georgia planters rode down into Florida trying to find their runaway slaves, but Garcon's army successfully fought them off. Frustrated Southerners then insisted that the Spanish colonial government dismantle the fort but the governor of Florida simply

78

shrugged and insisted that he was powerless to disarm Garcon. Now desperate Southerners turned to the United States government and demanded that they do something to prevent their continuing great loss of property.

In 1816 General Andrew Jackson built a new fort at the mouth of the Apalachicola River on the boundary between Georgia and Florida. Jackson gave the command of the fort to General Gaines. On July 10 Gaines ordered Lieutenant Colonel Duncan Clinch to sail down the river with a battalion of regular soldiers. Gaines gave Clinch secret orders that if Garcon fired on his ship, Clinch could then attack the fort and destroy it. It was obvious that Garcon could not allow an army of American soldiers to sail past his fort, so, on July 11, he attacked a party of sailors in a small rowboat who were trying to land on the banks of the river. That was all Clinch needed. The American forces surrounded the fort and demanded that Garcon surrender. His answer was swift. The fugitives shouted and jeered at Clinch, then hoisted the Union Jack as well as a red flag of death. Shots from Clinch's cannon rang out, and the American gunboats moved up the river and began firing. The battle had begun. American soldiers and fugitive slaves fought fiercely; then suddenly a shot from one of the gunboats hit the fort's magazine; there was a terrific explosion and the fort blew up killing most of its defenders. The fugitives, who were living on the banks of the river, had slipped into the forest when the American ships began firing. There they watched in horror at the sight of the fort bursting into flame, and knew that immediate flight was the only way to protect themselves from re-enslavement. By the time slave hunters arrived at the ruined fort most of the fugitives had vanished into south Florida's vast swampland and the sanctuary of the Seminole tribes who lived there.

The skirmish over the Negro Fort was just the beginning of the undeclared war that the United States was waging against the Seminole Indians. The War of 1812 frightened Americans because they saw that England and Spain could easily raise an army against them simply by promising fugitive slaves freedom and citizenship, promises America could never make.

General Andrew Jackson decided to invade East Florida; his goal was the complete surrender of the Seminole people who lived on the fertile land coveted by American planters. Jackson began the first Seminole War by attacking Seminole villages and demanding that their chiefs surrender. Many of the chiefs, overwhelmed by the fighting power of the American army, yielded. Other Seminoles fought back.

In retaliation Jackson ordered their villages burned to the ground. These Seminole chiefs, both Indian and Black were forced to abandon their blackened villages and flee into south Florida. There they joined other Seminoles whose villages were built deep in the swamps where, they hoped, the white man would have no further interest in pursuing them.

In 1821 Spain gave up the struggle to keep its colony and ceded Florida to the United States. The South was jubilant. Florida was now part of the United States. They believed that the southern frontier was now a stronger fortress to prevent slaves from fleeing now that that fugitives no longer had a sanctuary in Florida.

Southerners were wrong. Slaves from the Carolinas, Georgia and the thriving plantations of Florida's panhandle regularly took off for the Black Seminole villages of South Florida. Slaveholders complained to the government that, as long as South Florida remained a refuge for runaways. they had no real security.

In 1830 Andrew Jackson, now President of the United States, was working on a plan that would please every slaveholder in America. It was called the Indian Removal Act. Jackson sent to Congress a bill that would allow the American government to seize the rich tribal lands of all the Indian nations living in the Southern states in exchange for other land located in the barren undeveloped territory of Oklahoma. This would give Southerners large tracts of land to develop into new plantations. Supposedly this was to be a voluntary removal, but, since most Indian tribes did not want to leave their ancestral homeland, the Indian Removal Act became a struggle between the United States government and most of the Indian nations of the South. It was an unequal fight that the Indian tribes quickly lost. Soon most of the South's Indian people were rounded up by American troops, forced to leave most of their possessions behind, herded into caravans, then marched at least 2,000 miles to the Oklahoma territory. It was one of the most shameful acts in American history.

In 1832 the United States government invited the leading Seminole chiefs to send a delegation to inspect the Indian Territories of Oklahoma. Everyone knew that this invitation was the first step in the well orchestrated Indian Removal Act. As soon as the delegation had completed their survey the chiefs were presented with a treaty stating that they approved of this new land and were ready to support the United States government's plans to remove the entire Seminole Nation to Oklahoma.

The Seminole Indian chiefs indignantly refused to sign the document, but the American army officers announced that the delegation would not be permitted to return to Florida until they had signed the new treaty. Under this threat of permanent exile, the chiefs signed the document: but as soon as they returned home, most of the chiefs disowned this forced treaty.

One of the leaders of the delegation to Oklahoma was the Black Seminole chief, Abraham. Abraham was born in 1787, a slave to an American living in Pensacola, Florida. During the War of 1812 Abraham heard that the British were offering freedom to slaves who joined their army. Abraham quickly escaped and joined one of the Seminole war bands fighting alongside the British army. Abraham rose rapidly within the tribe because of his exploits as a warrior, and became the Chief Interpreter to Mikanopi who was the leading chief of the Seminole nation. Abraham's position as Interpreter was similar to the position of Prime Minister in a European country. When Florida became an American territory, Abraham, as Chief Interpreter, traveled to Washington several times as Makanopi's representative. One can well imagine the shock that American government officials, many of them slaveholders, must have felt at having to negotiate with a black man. Abraham was a wily diplomat. He never allowed the Americans to know what he was really thinking. Most American officials believed that Abraham was a shallow, easily led lackey. Only after the Second Seminole War began did they learn their mistake.

While most of the chiefs bitterly denounced the forced treaty, Abraham remained silent. He wanted the Americans to believe that, with sufficient flattery, they might win his support for their Indian Removal Policy. Abraham knew that only Indian Seminoles were going to be sent west. Black Seminoles were going to be rounded up and returned to slavery. Even those who had been born free would be enslaved since most of them had mothers or grandmothers who had been fugitive slaves. Abraham's plan was simply to string the Americans along while he convinced the Seminole chiefs to unite in a war against the Americans.

Abraham first had to present a plan to the members of the Seminole council, one that would prevent the Seminole people from the humiliation of being shipped west like cattle. Even though some chiefs believed that the Seminoles would be better off if they did leave a place where white men were terrorizing the Seminole people to satisfy their insatiable hunger for land, most of the chiefs wanted to remain in Florida. How would it be possible, they asked Abraham, to defeat the American army in open combat? The first Seminole War had taught the chiefs a bitter lesson about the power of the United States army. Abraham had an answer. He suggested that the Seminoles must make the war so costly to the United States that they might grant the Seminoles a few important concessions. One of those concessions, Abraham suggested, might be to allow Seminoles who did not want to leave Florida to remain in the southern tip of the territory where swamps covered the land so completely that even land hungry whites had no interest in developing it.

The most important concession that Abraham wanted the tribal council to agree to was the right of Black Seminoles to be included in those Seminoles who decided to move to the Indian Territories. On the other hand, one of the chief demands made by government negotiators was that Seminoles return all the fugitive slaves living among them to their slaveholder masters. These negotiators never seemed to realize that Abraham himself was a fugitive slave. There was a heated debate within the tribal council. When one of the older tribal chiefs suggested that some of the fugitives who were recent escapees be turned over to the Americans most of the chiefs refused. The young Chief, Osceola, whose wife was the daughter of a fugitive slave and would be included in such a return, was enraged at such a suggestion. The tribal council agreed that Black Seminoles must remain an integral part of the Seminole nation.

Many of the Black Seminoles had married Seminole Indians; but according to American law their children were still considered fugitive slaves and their children would not be included in the trip west. When a band of white slave hunters raided the village of old Chief Oconchattemicco, one of the few Seminole chiefs who had supported the American Removal Policy, and carried off a large group of Black Seminoles, they also took the chief's half- black granddaughter. When the Seminoles heard that she had been sold to a slaveholder in Georgia, it sent shockwaves throughout the Seminole nation. The Seminole council secretly voted to declare war, and they made Abraham the war leader of the Seminole nation.

A new group of young Seminole chiefs was ready to join Abraham in planning for the war. Osceola had already become a major war leader, and he would soon be joined by Wild Cat, the son of Chief King Philip, and John Horse, one of the chiefs of the Black

Left: John Horse
Below: Abraham
Right: Wild Cat

Left: John Horse, Credit: *Engraving by N. Orr, 1848,* Source: *Rebellion, www.johnhorse.com*
Middle: Abraham, Credit: *Engraving by N. Orr, 1848,* Source: *The Origin Progress.*
Right: Wild Cat, Credit: *Engraving by N. Orr, 1848,* Source: *Smithsonian American Art Archives.*

Seminoles. These three friends would lead a guerrilla Seminole army that the United States army, with all of its military might, was never able to totally defeat.

For three years Abraham continued to negotiate with the American army, even as he was organizing the Seminoles into a powerful fighting force. He also was able to secretly recruit hundreds of slaves from the plantations of the St. John River area who would be ready to join the Seminole war as soon as he gave the signal. Then Abraham turned to a group of free blacks living in St. Augustine who were angry because most of the rights that they had possessed under the Spanish were rapidly disappearing under American rule. Abraham asked them to begin collecting weapons and supplies so that the Seminoles would be well prepared when the war began.

Finally the United States government grew tired of these convoluted negotiations. After all, most of the other Indian tribes had already begun to move west; now it was time for the Seminoles to leave as well. In December the government told Abraham that, by the end of January 1836, all of the Seminoles must assemble at Tampa Bay where ships would be waiting to take them west. If this order was not obeyed, there would be swift retaliation. The U.S. retaliation would begin by the army's immediately rounding-up the Seminole people, and forcing them into unpleasant military compounds. Such a roundup, Abraham was told, frequently became violent. Certainly, the government insisted to Abraham, no one wanted that to happen. Abraham listened and said nothing. The United States government sat back and waited confidently for the Seminoles to gather in Tampa.

Abraham was ready. On December 28, 1835 a Seminole war party attacked and destroyed a troop of 100 soldiers led by Major Dade. At the same time Osceola led another band of warriors in an attack against General Thompson. The next day, John Caesar led a band of 250 slaves in a series of attacks on the plantations lining the St. John River banks. The second Seminole War had begun.

Abraham's Seminole forces, augmented by 400 slave recruits, had become masters of guerilla warfare. The South Florida swamps were the perfect battleground. Only the Seminoles knew how to travel on the dry paths that lay hidden amid the tangled jungle growth and murky waters of every swamp in their homeland. The Seminoles would swiftly attack an American patrol, then just as quickly take refuge in the nearest swamp. It was impossible for the army to pursue them. The United States government was completely frustrated because, after a whole year of war, Seminole resistance had still not been crushed.

Then in early January John Caesar led his band of slaves in a raid on a plantation just two miles west of St Augustine. Even though John Caesar was killed in the attack, the people of St. Augustine were panicked over Black Seminoles attacking at the very gates of their city. They demanded that Washington end the war as soon as possible.

In December 1836 a new General was named commander of the United States forces in Florida. General Jesup's orders were to end the war quickly by convincing the Seminoles to leave Florida. It did not take Jesup very long to realize that he could not end the war unless he convinced Black Seminoles to support the move to the Indian Territories.

Jesup sent a letter to Washington explaining that this was a Negro war not an Indian war. The only way he could get a majority of the Seminoles to agree to leave Florida was to find a way to include Black Seminoles as part of the Seminole nation. Washington instructed Jesup to do whatever he had to in order to end the war.

On March 6, 1837 General Jesup and the principal Chiefs of the Seminoles signed a truce agreement which stated that the Seminoles and their allies, who would come in and emigrate to the west, shall be secure in their lives and property and that their "bona fide" property would accompany them to the west. The phrase bona fide property was a thinly disguised code word for Black Seminoles who were legally considered the property of the Seminole chiefs. The agreement signed by Jesup and Abraham had stated that this resettlement was a voluntary move. To show the Seminoles that the treaty was a voluntary one that only applied to those who wished to travel west, Chiefs Mikanopi, Jumper and Cloud agreed to become American hostages until the removal was complete. Soon hundreds of Seminoles, both Black and Indian, had moved into the Tampa Bay encampment. General Jesup warned Washington that his agreement with Abraham must be honored because, "the Negroes rule the Indians and it is important that they should feel themselves secure; if they should become alarmed and hold out, the war will be renewed." [1]

There were still, of course, many Seminoles who decided to remain in the Florida swamps, but General Jesup was not anxious to pursue them. If the majority of the Seminoles left Florida, his mission would be a success.

It did not take long for pressure from southern planters to cause Washington to break the truce agreement. American planters were allowed to enter the Seminole camps searching for fugitive slaves; the peace treaty had been broken. On the night of June second, three young Seminole chiefs, Osceola, Wild Cat and the Black Seminole chief, John Horse, led a band of Seminoles up to the compound and forced the gate open. Hundreds of Seminoles fled, vanishing into the protective swamp. The warriors searched the compound until they found the three hostage chiefs and carried them off to safety. The Seminole War grew even bloodier under its new war leaders, Wild Cat, Osceola, and John Horse.

In September 1837 General Jesup captured King Philip, Wild Cat's father. As soon as he heard the news, Wild Cat reacted. He put on his finest clothes, placed a white crane's feather in his silver headband and as a sign of peace, carried a flag of truce. He traveled to the American camp in St. Augustine, leading a delegation of chiefs including John Horse and Osceola, hoping to negotiate the release of his father. Jesup's response was to arrest the delegation. The general threw his prisoners into the jail at Fort Marion. The prisoners were locked in a room which already held 20 other prisoners including the

[1] Porter, Kenneth W. *The Black Seminoles: History of a Freedom-Seeking People.* Gainsville: University Press of Florida, 1996. (Pg. 78)

elderly King Philip. The cell measured 18 by 33 feet. It was lighted only by a narrow window 15 feet above the floor. Outside of a sleeping platform three feet above the floor, the room was completely bare. Although escape seemed impossible as soon as the jail door closed, the young chiefs began planning their escape.

They had help. Someone, probably one of the slaves working in the jail, slipped them a file. It took 6 weeks for the captives to file through one of the window bars. Next they tore the canvas bags upon which they slept into strips and braided these strips into a strong rope. On the night of November 29, the escape began. First one of the tallest and strongest of the warriors leaped onto the platform, then lifted another prisoner onto his shoulders. That man, using a series of toeholds which the Seminoles had carved into the prison walls climbed up to the window ledge, the rope gripped between his teeth. Then he tied the rope to the remaining window bar. Next, he tied a rock to the other end of the rope and tossed it out of the window. It was a grueling escape. Each Seminole had to wiggle out of the window exit which was only 8 inches wide, then slide down the rope; then they had to jump into a moat which was 20 feet below them, hoping that the thick mud which filled the moat would cushion their fall. The Seminoles then took off to find the remnants of King Philip's band.

Osceola alone remained in the cell, for he was dying of malaria. As he lay dying, the famous painter George Caitlin visited him in his jail cell and was so impressed with the nobility of the young chief that he painted Osceola's portrait. This portrait was reproduced in newspapers all over the country. Osceola was now the most famous Seminole in America, and his death created a wave of sympathy for the Seminole cause throughout the nation. Even in Congress, questions were being raised about this undeclared war.

The war continued. The youthful Colonel Zachary Taylor, the future president of the United States, had been ordered to find and defeat the militant Seminole chiefs. For months he had been doggedly tracking Wild Cat, John Horse and Alligator. Finally, in late December, he learned that the three Seminole Chiefs with their band of 400 warriors were slowly retreating towards Lake Okeechobee.

On Christmas day Taylor, leading 1,000 troops, reached the Seminole camp, which had been hastily evacuated. Taylor eagerly pushed on; he crossed a peaceful prairie where he could see cattle peacefully grazing in the distance, then suddenly he found himself facing a wet murky swamp. It was so dense, the soldiers had to abandon their horses and proceed on foot. Colonel Taylor suddenly realized that the Seminoles had led him into an ambush. The battle raged for several hours but, in the end, the Americans were forced to retreat.

General Jesup understood that, to end the war, he had to negotiate in good faith with John Horse and the other Seminole chiefs. Before he met with the chiefs, he informed Washington that Black Seminoles must be protected from slave hunters, or Florida would never be a safe place for Americans. The war had cost America over 30 million dollars, one of the most costly wars in American history. This time, when the Seminoles gathered in Tampa Bay to travel west, Black Seminoles were protected by the United States Army against slave hunters, and all Seminoles made the trip together to Oklahoma.

John Horse and Wild Cat remained in Florida. They were still skeptical, and John Horse especially wondered if he could ever trust the word of an American officer. Abraham traveled back from the Indian Lands to meet with John Horse. He told him that the group of Black Seminoles who had traveled west with him were living free. He explained to John Horse that the white man would never allow Black Seminoles to remain in Florida. White Americans would try to kill every Black Seminole because they dared not allow black men to live free in a world of southern slavery. He told John Horse that they must move their people west while they still had the chance. John Horse agreed and, in 1838, Black Seminoles traveled west along with most of the remaining Seminole Indians.

But there were other bands of Seminoles who refused to leave. The Seminole War dragged on until August 14, 1842, when Colonel Worth was told to end the fighting, even though several hundred Seminoles still remained in Florida. When Seminoles today talk about their history, they proudly proclaim that they are the only Indian nation never defeated by the United States army. The United States government was happy to end the conflict. There were still a few Black Seminole bands among the remaining tribes. Florida remained a major stop on the Underground Railroad for those fugitives who chose to join the swamp Seminoles. The Seminole War had been the most costly Indian war in American history.

87

5

THE RAILROAD MOVES WEST

By the 1830's Americans were moving west into the frontier states of Ohio, Illinois, Missouri, and Michigan, and so did the Underground Railroad. The Mississippi River, like the Atlantic Ocean, became an important line on the Railroad. Over the years hundreds of fugitive slaves would be hidden aboard the ships that regularly sailed from New Orleans to Cincinnati, Ohio.

The Ohio River was the dividing line between slavery and freedom, and one of the most vital lines of the Underground Railroad. On the south bank of the river was the slave state of Kentucky and on the northern bank were the free states of Ohio and Indiana. The Ohio River ran for 160 miles dividing North and South, and slaves whispered among themselves that the Ohio River was the new River Jordan. If only you could cross the river you might have a real chance at being free. By 1840 some people living in towns perched on the northern bank of the river had opened new terminals of the Underground Railroad. The South quickly declared war on this new frontier of freedom. The war was a violent one with gangs of southerners invading northern river towns and attacking both black and white citizens suspected of being part of the Underground Railroad.

Cincinnati, Ohio was the sixth largest city in America, a thriving port on the Ohio River. Southerners sent their cotton, rice and sugar to Cincinnati merchants and bought the countless manufactured products produced in the North. The city's businessmen thrived on this lucrative southern trade. Most of its white citizens supported slavery, and many of its settlers came from the South; yet Cincinnati was also home to the largest black community in Ohio.

In 1839 to placate Kentucky slaveholders, the Ohio legislature had passed a law permitting Ohio officials to aid slaveholders in the capture of fugitive slaves. Whenever slave owners or their representatives suspected that fugitives might be hiding in the city, government officials would join slave hunters in searching homes and businesses of Cincinnati blacks to find the suspected runaways.

In spite of these obstacles, Cincinnati was a key terminal in the Underground Railroad. Fugitives who had been hidden on steamships sailing up the Mississippi or who managed to cross the Ohio River were told to look for two landmarks, the Bethel AME Church where Augusta Green was both the pastor of the church and an agent of the Underground Railroad, and the Zion Baptist Church, known throughout Cincinnati's black community as the Railroad's headquarters. Fugitives were also told to look for the Iron Chest Company. Most fugitives knew that black churches provided sanctuaries for runaways, but what, they wondered, was the Iron Chest Company? The Iron Chest Company was a unique institution. The buildings, three large warehouses sitting on the banks of the Mississippi River, were owned by a group of black businessmen, but were rented out to white tradesmen. These black businessmen were also dedicated members of the Underground Railroad, so when they built their warehouses they made sure that there were plenty of hiding places inside each building. They painted the name Iron Chest in large letters so that fugitives would be able to clearly identify the buildings.

There were also groups of black dockworkers and boatmen who regularly patrolled the waterfront in search of fugitives. These men were skilled at preventing the re-capture of fugitives, in spite of the teams of slave hunters who regularly patrolled the docks. Cincinnati had many safe houses for fugitives, but the Iron Chest Company was one of their favorites, because so many white businessmen used the warehouse that slave hunters rarely searched what were essentially white business establishments.

The Dumas Boarding House was another key elememt in the complex working of Cincinnati's Underground Railroad. Slaveholders traveling up and down the Mississippi River would usually stop in Cincinnati along with their personal servants. These slaves would be housed at the Dumas along with river men and other free black travelers. It was easy for fugitive slaves to mingle among the other African American guests.

William Casey was one of the most daring members of Cincinnati's Underground Railroad. He was born in Virginia in 1804, probably free, but, by the 1830's, had moved to Cincinnati. He worked as a boatman, one of the key jobs on the Railroad. Not only was he able to spirit fugitives into the city, but he frequently made secret trips into Kentucky, meeting with slaves planning to escape, and agreeing to row them across the river. As someone who volunteered to become a conductor for Kentucky slaves, Casey had chosen one of the most hazardous roles within the Underground Railroad. The Kentucky side of the river was constantly patrolled by slave hunters. Any black man caught helping a fugitive could be sold into slavery, sent to prison, or even killed.

The black Underground Railroad in Cincinnati soon had some important white allies, the most important of whom was Levi Coffin. Coffin had left North Carolina along with most of the other antislavery Quakers, who had been forced to leave the state because of the hostility of slaveholders towards any religion that opposed slavery. He first settled in the small town of Madison, Indiana where he quickly discovered that the town had no organized Underground Railroad station. The small black community was the only place where fugitives might find refuge. These black homes were not really safe because they were always the first place slave catchers would search for runaway slaves. Since they were black homes, the local government had no real interest in providing any protection against these illegal invasions.

Coffin took immediate action. His first step was to offer his home as the major Underground Railroad depot in Madison. Next, Coffin confronted local Quakers with a searing question. What are you personally doing to protect the fugitives who are appealing to us for protection? Most of them replied with various excuses. The first reason was that they would be breaking the Fugitive Slave Law and that they were a law abiding people. They also stated that it was too dangerous to hide fugitives because there were so many slave hunters in the area. Coffin was indignant. What was more important, obeying an evil law or obedience to God's decree which condemned slavery as a major sin? Coffin soon had a thriving Underground Railroad station in Madison with links to depots throughout Indiana and Ohio. When Coffin moved to Cincinnati his reputation as a Railroad organizer was firmly established. Cincinnati gave Coffin the opportunity to organize the Underground Railroad on a much larger scale because of his ties with Quakers communities all over the North. He helped create hundreds of new lines. Abolitionists called Levi Coffin, with deep affection, the President of the Underground Railroad.

For many years Ohio had some of the most restrictive Black Codes in the nation; but northern Ohio was beginning to fill up with settlers from New England who brought their antislavery beliefs to the region. The state government began to reflect this changing political reality. One case in particular had outraged many Ohio citizens. This was the case of Matilda, a young woman slave from Missouri, who had been brought to Ohio by her master, who was also her father. The young woman had never been in a city without slavery and she longed to be free. She begged her father to free her but he refused. She fled and hid within Cincinnati's black community until her father left for home. Then she emerged from hiding believing she was now safe, and went to work in the home of James Birney, one of the city's most distinguished abolitionists. In 1837 Matilda was discovered by a slave catcher who brought her before a judge asking that she be returned to her father/owner in Missouri.

Salmon Chase a young lawyer, who in 1861 would become Abraham Lincoln's Secretary of the Treasury, eloquently defended her right to remain in Ohio. Matilda's plea for freedom touched the hearts of many Ohioans. The judge ruled that he had no choice under the Fugitive Slave Law of 1793 but to return Matilda to Missouri. Many Ohioans demanded that the state do something to prevent slaveholders from bringing their slaves into Ohio where slavery was supposed to be illegal.

In May, 1841 Ohio's Supreme Court issued a ruling declaring that when any slaveholder voluntarily brings a slave into the State of Ohio or permits a slave to travel into the state, that slave becomes a free man. This ruling upset many whites in Cincinnati. They felt that their livelihood depended on trade with the South, and they knew that southern merchants would be very upset if they were no longer able to bring their personal slaves into the state. The whole city was on edge.

In the summer of 1841 tensions in the city were high. Gangs of young white boys roamed the streets attacking any blacks that they might find. Black leaders were deeply disturbed because they knew that it was very possible that a full scale riot could break out at any time. Riots against blacks had taken place in 1829 and in 1836 with disastrous results for the African American community. This time they were determined to fight back. City blacks began arming themselves and they elected a leader to organize a campaign of armed resistance if a white mob should invade their community. The man they selected was 28-year-old J. Wilkerson, a black man whose white grandfather had been an officer in George Washington's Revolutionary army. Wilkerson resolved that if another riot broke out, this time blacks would drive the invaders out.

On Friday September 3, flocks of Kentuckians had entered the city to swell the angry crowds that had gathered in the Fifth Street Market, ready to attack the black homes and businesses that lined the nearby streets. City officials looked on but did nothing to disperse the crowd. At eight o'clock the mob began to move with their guns in hand. They first wrecked a black confectionary shop and attacked a few blacks who were unfortunate enough to still be on the street. When they arrived at New Street, the mob was met with a counterattack. Wilkerson ordered his black defenders to open fire from the strategic positions where he had stationed them. The white mobs were fired upon from inside homes, from rooftops, and in alleys. The battle raged all night long until finally the mayor sent in some troops to force the mob to leave the black community. The riot went on for days with hundreds of whites invading the black community and its defenders forcing them to retreat. Finally the mayor declared martial law and sent in armed troops. This riot remains one of the most violent attacks against a black community before the Civil War, but it was also the first riot where blacks had been able to drive invading white mobs out of their community. Even though three hundred black men were arrested for rioting and marched off to jail, it was an experience that African Americans remembered with pride.

John Rankin, Abolitionist. Source: *retro.cincnnati.com*

To many slaves the Ohio River was their own River Jordan; on one side was Kentucky and slavery, on the other side was Ohio and freedom. Ripley with its narrow crossing from shore to shore was an ideal place to cross. When desperate fugitives crossed the river to Ripley they might find John Rankin or one of his sons reaching down to help them climb ashore just as they had done for Tice Davids. John Rankin was not the only station master in Ripley; he was just its most well known member.

It was on New Years Eve,1821, that John Rankin, a white Scottish Presbyterian minister, crossed the Ohio River into Ripley. Rankin had chosen Ripley as the new home for his family in part because it was a favorite crossing for fleeing Kentucky slaves. It was not long before Rankin began meeting with black members of the Underground Railroad, most of whom lived in the tiny town of Sardinia just next door to Ripley. He promised these black leaders that he would recruit the members of the Scotch Presbyterian Church to organize another branch of the town's Railroad network. By the time the legendary Tice Davids crossed the Ohio River, Ripley had a multitude of safe houses crisscrossing the black and white community. These hideaways succeeded in baffling the flocks of slave hunters who regularly invaded Ripley trying to capture fugitive slaves. By the late 1830's, hundreds of slaves had passed through the town, the first step of their journey to reach the promised land of Canada.

One of the most important members of Ripley's Underground Railroad was John Hudson. He came to Ripley as a boy of nine and, by 1820, was already guiding runaways from Ripley to one of several safe houses. He quickly understood the importance of finding white sanctuaries for these fugitives. Slave hunters, when they were searching for runaways, would immediately head for Sardinia because they knew it was the most likely place for fugitives to hide. Now that Rankin had recruited a number of whites to become new station masters, Hudson would be able to guide the fugitives into the homes and barns of white Ripley. Hudson became renowned as a man who brilliantly evaded slave catchers, but who, if he had to, was tough enough to fight them off. He was the conductor who escorted more runaways to the next Underground Station than anyone else in town.

Ripley had become such a well known station that Kentucky slaves had begun to sing a song to each other. It was the secret

musical roadmap to Ripley and John Rankin for anyone who was
planning to run away:

Follow the drinking gourd
(*the big dipper which points to the north star*)

Follow the drinking gourd
For the old man is a-waiting for to carry you to freedom
(*JohnRankin*)

If you follow the drinking gourd
The river bank will make a very good road
The dead trees show you the way
Left foot peg foot traveling on
Follow the drinking gourd
The river ends between two hills
Follow the drinking gourd
There's another river on the other side
Follow the drinking gourd
Where the great big river meets the little river
Follow the drinking gourd
The old man is a- waiting for to carry you to freedom
If you follow the drinking gourd [1]

Slaveholders were dismayed when they realized how many of
their slaves had succeeded in escaping because of the help they were
given by Ohio's Underground Railroad. Ripley was a particularly sore
spot. How dare the leaders of the Underground Railroad operate so
freely in the town? Kentucky slaveholders declared war on Ripley. In
April, 1838 they began by placing posters offering rewards of up to
$2,500 for the abduction or assassination of the suspected leaders of
the Underground Railroad. Among those named were the ministers
John Rankin and John Mahan, These wanted posters were nailed to
trees, affixed on the doors of local saloons, even hung on the pillars
of courthouses, in every town and village in northern Kentucky.

---

[1] Hagedorn, Ann. *Beyond the River: The Untold Story of the Heroes of the Underground Railroad*. New York: Simon & Schuster, 2002. (Pg. 39)

Kentucky government officials turned a blind eye to this public call for murder.

There were greater shocks to come. In June the Rankin family had temporarily hidden a fugitive named John before moving him to a safer hiding place. His owner, William Greathouse, came riding into town claiming that some one had stolen his slave valued at $1,500 and that he was going to find his slave and have that slave stealer arrested. He insisted on searching every home in Ripley suspected of being a station on the Underground Railroad. Leaders of the Railroad kept moving John from one hiding place to another until they reached the home of John Mahan, who lived in Sardinia. He decided to keep the fugitive hidden in his own home until Greathouse and his party finally left the area and John could be moved to a safer depot away from the river. When it was finally safe to travel, Mahan asked Jackson Meyers to take John to William Mahan's farm. Meyers decided that he would also guide John all the way to Canada. The Ripley/Sardinia Underground Railroad leaders breathed a sigh of relief when they heard that John had arrived safely.

William Greathouse was angry and, because he had heard that John Mahan had helped more than one of his slaves to escape, he decided on a scheme to entrap the minister. That August a white man named Rock, and a black woman knocked on Mahan's door. The white man asked for the minister's help. He claimed that the black woman was searching for her husband, John, who had been a slave of William Greathouse. Mahan told the visitors that John was now in Canada. Rock then asked if Mahan could help the slave woman reach Canada. Mahan of course agreed and gave Rock a note to another station master. On August 14 a grand jury in Mason County Kentucky indicted John Bennington Mahan for stealing William Greathouse's slaves.

On Monday, September 17, 1838 Greathouse led a posse of Kentuckians into Sardinia. He had with him a writ signed by Robert Vance, governor of Ohio, allowing Mahan to be taken into Kentucky to be tried in that state's court for the crime of stealing slaves. The posse dragged Mahan from his home under the horrified eyes of his wife and children. By nightfall he was locked in Kentucky's Washington County jail.

Mahan's arrest worried many white Americans, even those who opposed the abolitionists. If slaveholders were permitted to attack the legitimate although misguided actions of abolitionists, who would be next? Did slaveholders feel that they had the right to put any

American in jail who vigorously opposed slavery? Many citizens of Ohio were especially outraged by Mahan's arrest, and they blamed Governor Vance for signing the extradition papers. Vance knew he was in trouble and he desperately tried to get the Kentucky governor to release Mahan. But the Kentucky governor ignored his requests. In slaveholders war against Ohio's Underground Railroad this trial was going to be their first victory. In 1836 Vance had been a very popular leader who had been elected as the first Whig Governor by a majority of six thousand votes; but now, in 1838, angry at the governor's complicity in Mahan's arrest, the voters turned on Vance and voted him out of office.

On a dark rainy morning of Nov 14, 1838, in the small town of Washington, Kentucky Mahan's historic trial began. Since Mahan's lawyers easily proved that their client had not stepped onto Kentucky soil for over ten years, he could not be tried for breaking any laws of that sovereign state. So why was he being tried in a Kentucky courtroom? The prosecutors responded that they had proof that Mahan was enticing their slaves, their most valuable property, to run away simply because they knew that once they reached Ripley they would find a network of people who would help them reach the North and Canada. The state had proof of Mahan's enticement of slaves in the letter he gave Rock. Mahan therefore was breaking the Kentucky law against stealing slaves. Mahan had to be tried in Kentucky because he had broken no Ohio law, since slavery was illegal in that state.

The jury debated for two hours then surprisingly returned with a verdict of not guilty. Mahan, they stated, had not committed a crime on Kentucky soil, therefore could not be tried in a Kentucky courtroom. There were victory celebrations all over Ripley; people believed that their troubles were over, but the slaveholders were just biding their time. If the law had failed them then they would try a different tactic.

In early March of 1838 a group of Kenucky slaveholders decided on a new way to attack black members of Ripley's Underground Railroad.They began to conduct a series of raids on Sardinia's African American community. The aim of these raids was to arrest suspected Railroad members and carry them back to Kentucky. Most of the raids failed because the black community successfully fought back. On April 30 tragedy struck when Sally Hudson was shot in the back trying to protect her brother Jacob. Sally Hudson's murder profoundly affected the citizens of Ripley. That spring three hundred men and women joined the newly organized Ohio Antislavery Society.

John Parker was a Virginia slave who had been sold away from his mother when he was just eight years old. The pain of that separation never left him. His hatred of slavery grew stronger every year. Even though Parker was able to purchase his freedom and become a successful businessman something was missing from his life. He wanted to become part of the fight against slavery. Parker believed "Ripley was the real terminus of the Underground Railroad." In 1850 Parker moved his business to Ripley and began his new career as a Railroad conductor.[2]

Parker's forays into Kentucky became legendary. On one trip he was able to find ten fugitives who were lost in the woods still twenty miles from the river. Another time Parker was in Kentucky ready to rescue a slave family. The mother said she would not go because her master had taken her baby. The slaveholder believed the family was getting ready to run away and was holding the infant in his bedroom to prevent the escape. Parker slipped quietly into the bedroom, lifted up the baby and silently fled.

John Parker became so notorious in Kentucky that slaveholders offered a reward of one thousand dollars for his capture dead or alive. Parker boasted in his autobiography that, in spite of the posted reward, he had rescued 440 slaves and never lost a fugitive.

After the dangerous passage through the border towns of Ohio or Indiana, fugitives would find themselves in towns that were more hospitable. Oberlin, Ohio was so welcoming that it publicly welcomed any fugitive to make their home in the community. The town was also the home of one of the most remarkable colleges in America. Oberlin began as a small manual institute, but in1834, a series of events at Lane Theological Seminary in Cincinnati, one of the most prominent colleges in the nation, would change the school and the town of Oberlin forever.

Theodore Weld, son of a prominent Congregational minister, was one of the most brilliant students at Lane. He was also a dedicated abolitionist anxious to spread the ideology of antislavery to a wider audience. He decided that the best way to reach Lane

[2] Sprague, Stuart Seely editor. *His Promised Land: The Autobiography of John P. Parker*. New York: W.W. Norton & Company, 1996. (Pg. 87)

students was to hold a series of evening meetings to discuss the subject. At the end of the series the seminary students voted to organize an antislavery society whose mission was simply to approach slaveholders and convince them that slavery was an evil institution. These students planned to use the Bible as their main argument. Theodore Weld was still a young and naive idealist who believed that the South could be converted to antislavery. He would become one of the most sophisticated leaders of the abolitionist movement. The new Lane Abolitionist Society members began their crusade by moving into the city of Cincinnati. Some of them began lecturing on the evils of slavery. Others, since Cincinnati barred black children from the public schools, created small schools and libraries so that blacks could receive an education. These student activists were pursuing a very conservative course. They were totally opposed to slave revolts, and did not even oppose the Fugitive Slave Law. They never suggested that their members help any of the many fugitive slaves who were hiding out in the city. They believed that their main mission as seminary students was to appeal to the conscience of the slaveholders.

Even this minor attack on slavery was enough to alarm Lane's Board of Trustees, most of whom were merchants involved with the lucrative southern trade. They quickly passed a resolution banning any organization that was not directly associated with school activities. The Board went even further in appeasing the merchants of Cincinnati; they passed another resolution forbidding the discussion of any subject that would distract from studying, particularly issues that were "a matter of public interest and public excitement."

Lane students were outraged by the attack on their freedom. Many of these abolitionists, who had already created small groups throughout Cincinnati, decided on a new and radical program. They dedicated themselves to the rescue of fugitive slaves. These Lane students became some of the most active members of the Underground Railroad. Thirty-nine of them immediately resigned and began looking for a new school. Members of the Oberlin Institute's Board of Trustees were looking for a way to expand their tiny school into a full scale college. They needed an infusion of money and students. They happily agreed to invite the Lane rebels into their school. To demonstrate Oberlin's antislavery commitment, they made Asa Mahan, a prominent abolitionist, their new president. In return, abolitionist businessmen agreed to fund the expansion of their school. Soon Oberlin was flourishing. Its unique student body included blacks and women, two groups that were still excluded from most colleges in America. Fugitives happily settled in this welcoming community which boasted that no fugitive would ever be taken from their town.

Fugitive Slave Group in Lean-to on River Bank.
Source: *Schomburg Center for Research in Black Culture, New York Public Library.*

By the 1840's settlers were streaming west by the thousands. These settlers, mostly from New England, had been deeply affected by the religious revival movement that was sweeping the North. The New England settlers agreed with the Lane students that slavery was immoral. While most of the settlers felt that they could not demand that the South abolish slavery, since protection of slavery was part of the Constitution, they felt that they had no duty to return runaway slaves to their masters.

William Cratty lived in central Ohio and, because slavery was illegal in his state, believed that slavery had nothing to do with him. Then one day he saw a fugitive with an iron band around his neck with prongs curved up and over his head. It was a sight that he could never forget. In 1836 his home became an important station on the Underground Railroad. Cratty claimed that he had helped three thousand fugitives on their road to freedom. Slaveholders must have believed him because they posted a reward of $3,000 if Cratty were delivered to them, dead or alive.

Pittsburgh, because it was situated on the banks of the Ohio, Allegheny and Monongahela rivers, was a major terminal for many of the Underground Railroad lines. There were many fugitives who regularly arrived by boats or on foot, and these weary travelers needed help. Black Pittsburgh responded by organizing one of the most efficient associations of the Underground Railroad, the Philanthropic Club. One of the committee's youngest officers was Martin Delany who began studying medicine in 1833 and became one of America's first black physicians.

In 1839 the Philanthropic Club achieved a remarkable victory in ending white mobs' periodic attacks on Pittsburgh's black community. That year Dr. McClintock, a good friend of Martin Delany, was elected mayor of the town. On April 27, 1839 Martin Delany was told that an angry group of whites were getting ready for an attack on the black community. Delany announced that the community must defend itself and the Philanthropic Club began passing out guns. Delany told his friend the mayor that Pittsburgh blacks were prepared to fight any attacks against their community. A few hours later Delany got a message from Mayor McClintock. The mayor told Delany that he should pick a group of the most responsible young black men and McClintock would choose a group of equally responsible young white men who would all be appointed as special police officers. A white and a black officer would then be paired to patrol the area closest to the black community, so as to prevent any riot from beginning. Hundreds of white men were beginning to march when they were startled to discover these black and white armed policemen. Ringleaders were promptly arrested and later tried as rioters. This was the first time a city government had ever intervened to prevent the invasions of a white mob into a black community.

The Underground Railroad thrived in the northern cities and towns that bordered Canada. Sailors who worked on the steamship lines that traveled up and down Lake Erie regularly hid fugitives aboard their ships and carried them to the Canadian shore. William Wells Brown, a fugitive slave himself, claimed to have carried sixty-nine fugitives to Canada in 1842 alone. In 1836 a slave trader, Bacon Tate, came to Buffalo, New York to capture the Stanfords, a couple and their six year old child. Tate found out that the three fugitive slaves were now living in St. Catharines, Canada, just across the border. They believed that because they lived in Canada they were safe from the bands of slave hunters that patrolled black communities all over the North. Tate refused to be thwarted by the international law, which protected every black fugitive living in Canada. He hired four men to kidnap the family and bring them back to the United States. The kidnappers slipped quietly into St. Catharines on a Saturday night, seized the Sanfords, tied them up and forced them into a carriage and drove them into Buffalo. The news of the kidnapping reached members of Buffalo's Underground Railroad on Sunday and they immediately swung into action. Fifty armed men including William Wells Brown managed to rescue the Stanfords. As they were putting the family onto a ferry bound for Canada, the sheriff of Erie County, New York, along with a posse of seventy men reached the banks of the river. The sheriff announced that the rescuers were breaking the Fugitive Slave Law and he was determined to prevent the rescue. A pitched battle began. One rescuer was killed but the Stanfords escaped and sailed back to Canada. Twenty-five of the rescuers were arrested but they were only given fines. Slaveholders were upset that enforcement of the Fugitive Slave Law was treated so cavalierly in that northern town.

Detroit River Front, 1800's. Source: *Detroit News Archives.*

Michigan was a hotbed of Underground Railroad activity. Detroit, a major border city between the United States and Canada was a vital terminal on the Underground Railroad. Each year hundreds of fugitives were hidden aboard the ferries that regularly sailed across the narrow Detroit River to Canada. Even before Detroit had organized a formal branch of the Underground Railroad, black

Detroiters had developed their own way of dealing with slave catchers. In June, 1833 Ruth and Thorton Blackburn, who had fled Kentucky in 1831 and believed that they were safe in this northern city, heard that a slave hunter from Kentucky was at that very moment in court demanding that the couple be arrested under the Fugitive Slave Law. They had no time to flee before they were arrested. Detroiters were angry; the *Detroit Courier* told readers that Thorton Blackburn was "a respectable, honest and industrious man." On June 15, 1833 a judge ordered that the couple be turned over to the slave hunter immediately.

Blacks who had filled the courtroom angrily denounced the verdict and vowed that the sentence would never be carried out. The next day was Sunday and, down by the Detroit River, a group of black men armed with clubs had begun patrolling the wharf where the steamboat *Ohio* was docked. The ship's captain was so worried that he refused to set sail until the next day. The patrollers were pleased. They needed a day for their rescue plans to succeed.

Meanwhile back at the jail, the first steps in the rescue had already begun. Visitors crowded the jail, tearfully begging the jailors to let them say a last goodbye to their dear friends. The sympathetic jailors allowed the visitors to pack the cells. One of these visitors was Mrs. George French who somehow managed to remain in Ruth Blackburn's cell until after dark. During this time she and Ruth exchanged clothes, and shortly after dark Ruth Blackburn walked quietly out of jail along with the other visitors. She was then quickly whisked across the Detroit River to safety in Windsor.

Thorton Blackburn's rescue took place on Monday. That morning armed blacks were patrolling both the dock and the jail waiting for Blackburn to make his appearance. When Sheriff John Wilson, his deputy, and the slave hunter came down the steps, expecting to put the fugitive into the prison carriage, they found themselves surrounded by this organized group of rescuers. Blackburn asked the sheriff if he could say a few words to the crowd. When the sheriff happily agreed Blackburn leaped into the carriage, whipped out the gun that one of the rescuers had slipped to him, aimed it directly at his captors and shouted "Get back damn you!" Both the deputy and the slave hunter fled back into the jail, but Sheriff Wilson was not so lucky; a shot rang out and Wilson was hit and almost killed. While the fray was at its height, an elderly black woman, Sleepy Polly and an old black drayman Daddy Walker hustled Blackburn into Walker's dray and sped away while a group of black women dismantled the prison carriage, making pursuit impossible. The rescuers carried Blackburn to the Rouge River where a boatman was waiting to carry both the fugitive and several of his liberators to safety in Canada.

Blackburn's rescue threw Detroit into a panic. Whites began talking about the riot as the first "Negro Insurrection." Troops were called from Fort Gratiot to restore order. Blacks, whether or not they had been part of the rescue, were arrested; many of them were held in jail without a trial. Black Detroiters demonstrated in the streets demanding the release of the protesters. In July the mayor of Detroit decided to punish black residents by demanding that they post a bond of $500. Most black Detroiters decided to leave the city and headed for Canada. It took four years before the black population of Detroit regained its former strength.

William Lambert had fallen in love with Detroit the first time he saw it as a young seaman working on the Great Lakes. By the time he settled in Detroit in 1838, Lambert was an experienced member of the Underground Railroad who had spent many years hiding fugitives aboard his vessels and smuggling them into Canada.

Detroit had already become the busiest gateway from the United States to Canada for fugitives traveling on the Underground Railroad. Black Detroiters needed to organize a Vigilance Committee to protect the flood of fugitives as they waited to be transportered to Canada. In 1842 William Lambert and George DeBaptise organized one of the Railroad's most efficient Vigilance Committees. The Committee's most spectacular action was the rescue of Robert Cromwell. Cromwell was a fugitive slave who had successfully escaped from his Mississippi master and, in 1846, settled in Detroit. Cromwell so longed for his daughter, whom he had left behind in slavery, that he finally wrote a letter to his old master, David Dunn, offering to purchase his child. Dunn pretended to agree to the purchase and suggested a meeting at the Detroit courthouse to discuss the exchange. As Cromwell approached the courtroom where the meeting with Dunn was to take place, a friendly clerk warned him that the meeting was a trap.

Cromwell had not been completely naive. Before leaving for the courthouse he had alerted William Lambert and George De Baptiste about his meeting, and they were waiting just outside the building. In spite of the warning, Cromwell was dragged into the courtroom and Dunn locked the door. The friendly clerk dropped his key out of the window and Lambert and De Baptiste rushed into the courtroom. They attacked Dunn, and Cromwell managed to escape. He was soon on his way to Canada. White Detroiters joined the black community in demanding that Dunn be arrested for the attempted kidnapping of a Detroit citizen without a legal court hearing. Dunn was jailed for six months and barely escaped a long jail sentence on the charge of kidnapping.

For several years black Detroiters had been looking for ways to bring their families and friends out of slavery. At first they signed a series of contracts with a notorious gang of criminals known as the McKinseyites, a band of sixty men who had been terrorizing the southwest for years. The committee would pay this gang to rescue a slave or group of slaves. The McKinseyites had a completely mercenary approach to any rescue. First they would collect money from family members in Detroit, then they would rescue the slave from the plantation and sell him to another plantation owner. Later they would steal the slave from this owner also. Sometimes they might sell a slave three or four times until the fugitive finally reached Detroit. It did not take long before Lambert and the others decided to take charge of rescuing fugitives themselves. They met with a group of Underground Railroad members and created a radical team of rescuers known only as the African American Mysteries. William Lambert remembered that one of the few whites admitted into the Mysteries was John Brown. Brown became one of Lambert's closest friends. Lambert remembered that John Brown escorted more than two hudred fugitives into Detroit.

The western part of Michigan was even more dangerous for slave hunters than Detroit was. Most of these towns were settled by groups of Quakers and other men and women who had been deeply influenced by the religious movement known as the Great Awakening. These settlers agreed with their religious leaders that slavery was a national sin, therefore they were duty-bound to do everything in their power to fight slavery. Their communities welcomed black settlers of all kinds, and they soon became safe havens for hundreds of fugitive slaves, most of whom came from Kentucky. News about these fugitive slave settlements infuriated Kentucky slaveholders, and a group of Bourbon County planters organized into an association to find ways of retrieving their human property. Their first step was to send a secret agent to travel to Michigan to make a series of maps that would give slave hunters information about just where their fugitive slaves were living. Members of the Underground Railroad had also heard rumors that slave owners were about to send teams of slave hunters into western Michigan, and an agent was sent to the Michigan

Underground to warn them about the coming invasion.

One morning in the summer of 1847 Francis Trautman led three slave hunters into the village of Marshall armed with one map which showed just where Adam Crosswhite, a fugitive slave, his wife, and family were living. Crosswhite and his friends were ready. The moment Crosswhite felt he was in danger he would signal his friends by firing his gun. Trautman's band opened the door of the Crosswhite cabin and immediately seized the mother and four babies. Crosswhite quickly fired his gun. The slave hunters were suddenly surrounded by one hundred black and white citizens. The startled kidnapers released the Crosswhites. The rescuers swiftly rode to the train station and put the fugitives on a train to Detroit. Members of Detroit's Vigilance Committee had been alerted; they met the train and quickly arranged for the Crosswhites to cross the Detroit River to Canada.

Slaveholders in Kentucky were deeply concerned over Michigan's violation of the Fugitive Slave Law. They decided to file a lawsuit against many of the leading citizens of Marshall to recover the value of their chattels, as well as damages that they had incurred because of what they called the abolitionist riot. It took over a year before a jury finally awarded them a verdict of $1,900. This was a very large amount of money, for middle class Americans to raise, in 1848, and people in Marshall were very worried that some of their citizens might end up in jail. So many Michiganders were outraged at the verdict that a massive fund drive was launched and the fine was soon paid.

Kentucky's Bourbon County planters were not satisfied by a simple fine, and they soon planned their second raid into western Michigan. This time they would send a larger force to make sure that their slaves were returned to them. On a hot summer day in August, 1837 a party of thirteen slave hunters driving covered wagons arrived in the town of Battle Creek, pretending to be selling farm equipment. This gave them the excuse to prowl the countryside searching for fugitives. Before they could organize their kidnapping operations, Erastus Hussey invited them into the village tavern and told them that the villagers knew that they were slave hunters and that they had better leave immediately. If they tried to kidnap any of the fugitives living in the area, they said, the slave hunters would certainly be in danger of action on the part of the citizens of Battle Creek. The Kentuckians wasted no time in packing up and leaving Battle Creek.

Frustrated, these Kentucky slave catchers decided that they could not return home without capturing a single fugitive, so they slipped into Cass County where their maps identified at least fifty fugitives living in various communities throughout the county. These runaways would make a rich haul. Their plan was to raid as many fugitive homes as possible at the same time, then flee Michigan with their captives into the more slavery-friendly state of Indiana. These slave hunters invaded farms, smashed down doors and were able to seize nine fugitives who had not heard the warning about the kidnapers. They began to move towards the Indiana border pursued by hundreds of rescuers. Angry threats were shouted out by both kidnapers and rescuers, and it looked as if violence might break out at any moment.

Some of the Quaker leaders of the rescuers calmed the crowd by suggesting that the Kentuckians follow Michigan law and take their victims into the courtroom to prove that they had captured actual fugitive slaves rather than innocent freedmen. Three hundred of the rescuers then escorted the Kentuckians into the nearest village of Cassopolis where a hastily organized courtroom was convened in the local tavern. The abolitionists were masters of manipulating the law to protect fugitives. First their lawyers asked for a delay in the hearings. Next they secured a writ of *habeas corpus* to release the so called fugitives on bail. The temporarily freed fugitives were quickly sent on to freedom in Canada, leaving a frustrated group of Kentuckians in Michigan who had lost every fugitive that they had set out to capture. The Bourbon County slaveholders had lost all chance of regaining their human property. The Kentucky slaveholders' frustration turned to rage when the court indicted the slave hunters for trespass and kidnapping. These charges were dropped when news reached Cass County that the fugitives were safe in Canada. It was obvious to southerners that the Fugitive Slave Law could not be enforced in the state of Michigan.

6

MUST WE GIVE UP OUR LIBERTY TO SAVE THE UNION?

In 1793 the governor of Pennsylvania, Thomas Mifflin, sent a letter to Virginia's governor, Beverly Randolph, demanding that he extradite three Virginians who were accused of kidnapping a black Pennsylvanian citizen, John Davis. Randolph refused the extradition request on the basis that John Davis was a fugitive slave. Mifflin stated that Davis was a free man and, as governor of the sovereign state of Pennsylvania, he had the right and duty to protect Davis and prosecute his kidnappers. A mini war between the two states over these two conflicting issues seemed inevitable.

In the North the question of who was a free man and who was a slave was very different. Every black man or woman in a free state was presumed to be a citizen of that state. A slaveholder or his agent had to prove not only that a particular black man or woman was a fugitive slave, but also prove that this particular fugitive was their own property. As soon as the law was passed there was a small group of northerners who had raised the difficult question of how to enforce the Fugitive Slave Clause, while at the same time protecting their own black citizens from being kidnapped and sent into slavery.

Southern slaveholders turned to the new president for help. George Washington, a slaveholder himself, was sympathetic to southern concerns over protecting their and their agents' right to cross into free states to recapture runaways. The President sent a message to congress asking that they pass a Fugitive Slave Law that would give slaveholders the legal right to recapture their runaway slaves anywhere in the North.

Many northern congressmen tried to include a provision in the new bill that would protect the rights of free black citizens from the real danger of being kidnapped. These congressmen proposed making the kidnapping of a free citizen a crime punishable by jail or at least a heavy fine. Southern congressmen rejected every one of these proposals because they insisted that the right to recapture runaways was a basic right guaranteed to them in the Constitution. Southerners insisted that this right of recapture was a more important right than the rights of any black man, even if he were a freedman. It took over a year before a compromise Fugitive Slave Law finally passed in 1796.

The first Fugitive Slave Law gave a slaveholder or his representative the right to seize a fugitive anywhere in the United States. The law allowed a claimant or his agent to appear before any court or magistrate with a simple affidavit stating that this particular black man, or woman was a fugitive. The affidavit was usually granted in the state court where the claimant lived. As soon as the affidavit was approved by the magistrate, the claimant was free to whisk the alleged fugitive out of the state where the black man or woman was residing. The fugitive had no way to prove that he or she was actually a free person since a black man or woman was not permitted to take the stand in his or her own defense .Children of a fugitive mother, no matter where they were born, were considered the property of the mother's owner. The law also made it a Federal crime to help an escaping slave.

For African Americans, both fugitives and freedmen, this new law was a threat to their liberties, as every black citizen was in danger of being kidnapped and dragged into the slave South. Even Richard Allan, the most respected African American minister in the United States, was seized on the streets of Philadelphia by a slave hunter and charged with being a fugitive. Allen was saved only because a group of prominent white Philadelphians heard about his arrest and rushed into the courtroom to establish their friend's identity and testify as to his status as a freedman.

In 1796 four freed slaves from North Carolina traveled to Philadelphia in order to meet with Absalom Jones, the president of the Free Africa Society, and beg him for help. The Free Africa Society was created to help members of Philadelphia's black community, many of whom had been freed during the American Revolution, to navigate through the complex world of urban living. The Society set up schools for both children and adults, advised laborers and small businessmen how to operate in a capitalist society. The Society was also the primary welfare organization for Philadelphia's African Americans helping such vulnerable people as widows, orphans, the sick, the newly arrived, and other members of the black community who were in need of help. It was also the first black organization to celebrate the African heritage of black Americans. By 1796 the Free Africa Society had become the most important black secular organization in Philadelphia.

Jupiter Gibson began by telling Jones a disturbing story. When the war ended, some North Carolina slaveholders, who believed in the ideals of the Revolution, had decided to free their slaves. The state legislature, alarmed at the growing free black population, passed a series of laws that permitted the re-enslavement of recently freed slaves unless that freedom was granted because of "meritorious services." Hundreds of freedmen living in North Carolina had been seized and sold back into slavery. This had turned into an extremely profitable business for slave hunters. Gibson told Jones how he and his family had been pursued by armed men and dogs. His father, mother and brothers had all been captured by kidnapers, even though they had been freed by their owner. Gibson alone managed to escape the kidnapers, fleeing to Philadelphia as a safe haven. Now he realized that, even in this free Quaker city, he was not safe because slave catchers, encouraged by the newly enacted Fugitive Slave Law, were now prowling the city searching for any black man or woman that they could claim was a fugitive. Gibson begged Jones to lead Philadelphia's black community in a struggle against this dangerous legislation.

Absalom Jones knew just how dangerous this law was to every black American, fugitive or free, yet he was reluctant to lead another struggle against the leaders of Philadelphia's white society. Jones had established the first black Episcopal church in the nation, St. Thomas Episcopal Church, and Jones was completely dependent on white support for its survival.

Absalom Jones and Richard Allan had just led the first great civil rights struggle in American history. This struggle began in 1787 when the St. George Methodist Church made the shocking decision to segregate its black members. The Methodist Church had been founded as a democratic, antislavery, evangelical church. Its members had been recruited from among the poor whites and blacks of the community. Any member of the church could become a preacher if he felt the call. Both Allen and Jones had received the call and were now Methodist ministers..

Over the years many members of St. George had become more prosperous and also more conservative. These conservative members were now the leaders of the church, and they wanted to force out the black members. They abruptly announced a new ruling; black members of the congregation could only be seated in the balcony.

Absalom Jones and Richard Allen refused to accept this segregationist ruling. One Sunday morning as Jones and Allen led their black members to their seats in the church, then knelt and began praying white church leaders led a suprise attack. They began pulling the black Methodists from their old pews, blacks refused to leave and continued to pray. Jones fought off his attackers until he had finished his prayer. Then he and Richard Allen led the entire black congregation out of the church.

Absalom Jones, Richard Allen and the angry black congregation decided that the time had come to create their own church, independent of white control. Richard Allen still believed deeply in the basic tenets of the Methodist church. He led a group of the congregation in creating the first African Methodist Episcopal Church in America, which became the mother church of one of the most powerful national black church movements in the nation. Absalom Jones had become completely disillusioned with the Methodists, and decided to find a new home for those black members of St. George who shared his feelings. Jones met with a group of leaders of St John's Episcopal Church and suggested to them that he build a black sister church. With consummate diplomacy Jones convinced the church leadership that this new black church must be an independent church with the power to choose its own minister. It was the first time a black church had been given such power by any Protestant denomination. In 1794 St. Thomas Episcopal Church opened its doors with Absalom Jones as its first ordained deacon.

Although Jones knew that, if he decided to lead a campaign against the Fugitive Slave Law, he would be risking his greatest accomplishment, the creation of St. Thomas, he did not hesitate. In 1796, with the support of Richard Allen, he launched a petition campaign to amend the Fugitive Slave Law. The conservative white benefactors of St. Thomas were appalled by the sight of its minister publicly leading a political struggle of any sort. They told Jones that they would withdraw their support from St. Thomas if he did not abandon the petition drive. Jones, who had anticipated just how upset these conservative Episcopal church leaders were going to be, had lined up his own group of supporters, the leaders of Pennsylvania's Antislavery Society. This organization had been founded by Benjamin Franklin. Its leaders, who advocated a very gradual abolition of slavery, were members of Philadelphia's elite society. These respected citizens, together with Absalom Jones' own formidable powers of persuasion, managed to convince the church leaders to drop their opposition to the petition campaign.

In 1797 Congress was astonished to receive a stack of petitions addressed to the "President, Senate, and House of Representatives of the Most Free and Enlightened Nation in the World!!!" The petitions stated "The law (Fugitive Slave Law) allows men of cruel disposition to kidnap and re-enslave blacks who have been freed in Southern states." They asked the legislators to amend the law to protect the rights of free citizens. The petitions were signed by hundreds of Philadelphia's black citizens.

Southern congressmen were dismayed not only because these petitions challenged parts of the Fugitive Slave Law, but also because this demand was raised by black people, some of them ex slaves. How did these "inferior" people learn to grasp our political system so well that they were able to craft an amendment that would weaken a law written to protect slavery? Southern congressmen insisted that the petitions be tabled immediately without discussion. A small group of Northern congressmen were intrigued by the boldness of these black citizens, and insisted on holding a discussion on the merits of the issue before they called for a vote. Fifty congressmen voted to table the petitions but a surprising thirty-three congressmen voted for further discussion. This vote gave black Philadelphians hope. Maybe with a more vigorous campaign they might succeed in amending the Fugitive Slave Law.

This hope was dashed forever when Eli Whitney invented the cotton gin which made cotton the most important cash crop in America. In 1800, when Representative Robert Waln of Pennsylvania presented a new group of petitions to amend the Fugitive Slave Law, he was greeted with angry demands that the petitions be immediately tabled. This time the House of Representatives tabled the petitions without further discussion, with only one dissenting vote.

Some Americans were upset that free black citizens could be kidnapped off the streets of their towns and cities, and that state laws seemed powerless to protect them. Southern leaders had a disturbing answer for these Americans. The Federal government and every one of the thirteen individual states who had signed the Constitution had agreed to protect slavery. It made no difference that many of the states had already abolished slavery. Southern political leaders now advanced the theory that the commitment to protect slavery overrode every other issue of states rights, including the right that every state had to protect its own citizens. Recapture, slaveholders insisted, was an essential part of this protection of slavery. Any attempt to thwart their right to pursue fugitive slaves anywhere in the country would mean that the basic contract of the Constitution had been violated and, therefore, slave states would have the right to secede from the Union.

Northerners were so intimidated by Southern threats to secede that, for a time, the North agreed to every demand the South made. When the abolitionist movement launched a campaign to send antislavery pamphlets, tracts, and newspapers into the South in the hope that they might convince slaveholders to abandon slavery, Southerners took immediate action. At midnight on July 29, 1835, a mob broke into the Charleston post office and burned sacks of the abolitionist literature. The United States Government refused to take any action. The Postmaster General of the United States claimed that this mob action was legal because abolitionist literature was a threat to slavery. Only a handful of Americans questioned the undeniable fact that the Federal government was refusing to enforce one of the nation's fundamental laws: It was a Federal crime to interfere with the delivery of the United States mail.

One piece of abolitionist literature spread terror among slaveholders because it was written by a black man, David Walker, whose father had been a slave, although his mother was free. He had been born in Wilmington, North Carolina, but he hated the southern world of slavery, and soon left Wilmington for the freer world of Boston. Walker's Boston home was a station on the Underground Railroad, but he was determined to do more to fight against slavery. In September, 1829, Walker wrote a pamphlet called "Walker's Appeal." This document was a radical departure from every other piece of abolitionist literature. Walker rejected appeals to the moral or religious beliefs of the nation. Instead Walker predicted bloody slave revolts if slaveholders refused to end slavery. "Remember, Americans, that we must and shall be free and enlightened. Will you until we shall, under God, obtain our liberty by crushing the arm of power? [1]

Southerners quickly passed laws that made distributing, or even reading this dangerous piece of literature illegal. The Virginia

---

[1] Walker, David. *Walker's Appeal in Four Articles.* New York: Arno Press and The New York Times, 1969. (Pg. 80)

legislature held a secret session to discuss how to deal with the Appeal. The Mayor of Savannah asked the Mayor of Boston to arrest Walker. A group of Southerners offered a reward of $1,000 if Walker's dead body was sent South, and $10,000 if the author was delivered alive to Southern authorities.

Most Northern abolitionist leaders were equally upset by the Appeal. These leaders believed that non-violent appeals to the conscience of Americans was the only way to end slavery, however Boston blacks loved and supported the Appeal. As soon as it appeared, they gave a dinner party in Walker's honor to toast its publication. The Appeal enjoyed brisk sales, and had to be reprinted three times.

William Lloyd Garrison, a white antislavery editor, read Walker's Appeal and was deeply disturbed by its content. Garrison was still committed to the cause of gradual emancipation along with many of the ideas of the American Colonization Society. This organization was dedicated to solving the problem of slavery by sending black people back to Africa. Their first step had been to purchase land in Africa. (That land is now the nation of Liberia.)

Garrison and his partner, Benjamin Lundy, were the editors of an antislavery newspaper called *The Genius* published in Baltimore. In November, 1829 Garrison wrote an article chiding Francis Todd, a Massachusetts ship owner, for his business connection to Austin Woolfolk, one of the most prominent and successful slave traders in America. Garrison was certainly not unique in his condemnation of slave traders. Most Americans, no matter how they felt about slavery, disapproved of the business of slave trading. To everyone's great surprise, in February, a Maryland grand jury indicted Garrison on a rarely used law against having published "a gross and malicious libel against Francis Todd." [2] Maryland's government had now taken the unusual stand that any attack on the institution of slavery, no matter how insignificant, violated a slaveholders rights under the Constitution. Even freedom of the press was no longer a sacred right, if it conflicted with the South's demands that slavery must be protected no matter what the cost. Garrison was sentenced to either pay a fine of seventy dollars (at this time Garrison's salary was six dollars a week) or serve six months in jail. Garrison refused to pay the fine and, on April 17, 1830, he defiantly entered the Baltimore jail.

---

[2] Mayer, Henry. All On Fire: *William Lloyd Garrison and the Abolition of Slavery.* New York: St Martin's Press, 1998. (Pg. 84)

Garrison left jail a changed man. He decided to move to Boston and consider his future. "Walker's Appeal" had begun his education. Living in the city of Boston completed his conversion to radical abolitionism. Boston's black community had some of the most sophisticated political leaders in the nation. These leaders convinced Garrison to abandon his old beliefs that gradual emancipation and persuading blacks to move to Africa was the way to end slavery. Garrison now believed that only immediate abolition would wipe the sin of slavery from America, and he dedicated his life to that mission. Garrison began his dedication to the cause of immediate abolition by publishing his own newspaper. Financial support came first from Boston's black community, and soon spread to black communities all over the North.

On New Years Day, 1831, the first issue of Garrison's *Liberator* came off the press. In the first editorial, Garrison proclaimed that he would make slaveholders and their apologists tremble: "On this subject (slavery) I do not wish to think or speak or write with moderation. No! No! Tell a man whose house is fire to give a moderate alarm ... I will not retreat a single inch ... AND I WILL BE HEARD" [3]

This first issue of the *Liberator* electrified the country. The nation's traditional antislavery societies had always called for a program of gradual emancipation, modeled after the abolitionist laws passed in the North after the Revolution. Garrison's ringing demand for immediate emancipation radicalized the entire white antislavery movement. Two years later fifty-six men and four women gathered in New York City to create the National Antislavery Society, an organization which called for the immediate abolition of slavery. Americans worried how the South would react to this revolutionary new organization and its radical attack on slavery. People had hoped that the Missouri Compromise had settled that disturbing issue. Now these radicals were determined to upset the hard-won compromise by demanding slavery's immediate abolition. Some Americans reacted violently. Anti-abolitionist riots broke out all over the North. Surprisingly, many of these riots were led by respectable members of the community. Even Boston, cradle of the American Revolution, was not immune to these anti-abolitionist riots.

In 1834 the Boston Female Antislavery Society invited both William Lloyd Garrison and the British abolitionist, George

---

[3] Mayer, Henry. *All On Fire: William Lloyd Garrison and the Abolition of Slavery.* New York: st. Martin's Press, 1968. (Pg. 112)

Thompson, to address one of their meetings. Thompson was an extremely controversial speaker because many people thought that he was an agent of Great Britain. The women were unable to rent a hall for their meeting, as there had been some threats of violence. The ladies decided not to advertise the meeting and hold their gathering in an upstairs room of the *Liberator*. Even though they had not publicized the meeting, the news still got out. The women opened the meeting with a prayer but were soon drowned out by the shouts of a mob of over two hundred men who crowded the street outside the *Liberator* building. The worried mayor of Boston begged the women to leave immediately before someone was hurt. Beautiful and aristocratic Mrs. Maria Weston Chapman astonished the mayor by quietly stating that "if this is the last bulwark of freedom we may as well die here as anywhere" [4]

Then the ladies heard the sound of a door being smashed and soon a mob was streaming up the stairs. Garrison quickly made his escape through a back window, as some of these mob leaders had vowed to kill him. The thirty women followed the mayor down the stairs. The ladies defied the mob as they walked two by two, a white and black woman, side by side out of the building into the angry mob. The mob parted and let them through, unnerved by the courage of these abolitionist women.

Now the mob spread out searching for Garrison. When they found him they put a rope around his neck and marched him through the streets of Boston. The mayor and his constables finally forced the mob to release Garrison into their custody. They decided that the only safe place for Garrison was the city jail until the city returned to normal.

In November, 1838, something happened that profoundly shocked Northerners. Elijah Lovejoy a white abolitionist, had recently moved to Alton, a town in southern Illinois. When Lovejoy announced that he was going to publish the Observer, an antislavery newspaper, in their town, the pro-southern citizens were indignant. Missouri slaveholders, who lived just across the Mississippi River, warned the townsmen that if Lovejoy and his newspaper were not immediately silenced they would refuse to trade with the citizens of Alton. Town meetings were held to demand that Lovejoy suspend publication, but the editor was adamant. This country is a democracy, Lovejoy reminded the protestors, and he had the right to publish any kind of

[1] Buckmster, Henrietta. *Let My People Go.* (Pg. 88-89)

Mob attacking the Warehouse of Godfrey Gilman & Co., 1887.
Source: *Library of Congress, Prints and Photographs Division.*

newspaper that he chose to. Lovejoy proclaimed that the pro-slavery beliefs of the people of Alton must be challenged. A mob secretly slipped into Lovejoy's warehouse, seized his printing press and threw it into the Mississippi River. The mob's violence did not stop Lovejoy; he immediately purchased another printing press. That press also was seized by a mob and tossed into the river; a third press was also destroyed. Lovejoy's fourth press arrived at his warehouse at three o'clock in the morning. Lovejoy's friends vowed that this press was going to be saved. Fifty men met in front of the warehouse doors and remained there all day guarding the precious press. That night a mob of thirty men rode up to the warehouse and demanded that the guards open the doors and give them the press. Lovejoy's friends cried out," Never!" Their leader then drew out his pistol and announced that they would protect the press with their lives if necessary. He was answered with a round of bullets and the gunfire continued as some members of the mob climbed onto the roof of the warehouse carrying a blazing torch. The building was set on fire and everyone, both defenders and mob members, began fleeing the burning building. Lovejoy, who was still in the warehouse, came to the door to see what was happening. More shots were fired and Lovejoy fell to the ground, dead. His body had been pierced with five bullets.

Elijah Lovejoy had become the abolitionist movement's first great martyr. Americans were deeply upset by the fact that a man was murdered, not because he had been helping fugitive slaves, which was, after all, against the law, but simply because he wanted to publish an unpopular newspaper. Freedom of the press was considered one of the most sacred American rights under the Constitution. Some Americans began to wonder just how many of their rights they would have to give up in order to satisfy the paranoia of slaveholders.

In 1839 William Seward, Governor of New York, reacted to the anger so many Northerners felt over the murder of Elijah Lovejoy. That summer Seward received a letter from the Governor of Virginia asking that three black sailors be extradited to his state because they had broken Virginia law. It was not an unusual request except for one fact- the law that these three men had broken was the law that made aiding a fugitive slave a crime, the crime of stealing a slaveholder's property. Governor Seward refused. The three seamen were citizens of New York and, under New York law, they had committed no crime, since in his state slavery had been abolished. Furthermore, the New York governor reminded the Virginia governor, under the doctrine of "States Rights" the South's most precious dogma, the only time a citizen of a state or country should be extradited is when some universal law had been broken such as murder. Seward told the governor of Virginia that, since slavery had been made illegal in almost every civilized nation in the world, the crime of helping a slave to escape was only a crime in the American South. Many people in the North were happy that at last there was one Northern leader who dared challenge the South's demand that the Fugitive Slave Law supercede every other civil right of American citizens.

In 1836 the American Antislavery Society launched a new crusade, this time directed at the United States Congress. It began with a mass petition drive which asked Congress to ban slavery in Washington DC. The Constitution allowed the people of each state to decide how to regulate slavery. They could choose to live under slavery or abolish it, but Washington D.C. was a different matter; this city was governed by the United States Congress, therefore Congress did have the power to abolish slavery. The petitions asked Congress to use its power to abolish slavery in the capital of the United States.

In a time when the telegraph or the telephone had not yet been invented and travel took so long, Congressmen rarely saw their constituents during the legislative year. Hence, a petition campaign was a very popular and effective form of political expression.The House of Representatives considered petitions such an important

117

expression of popular will that the first few weeks at the begenning of each new Congressional session were devoted exclusively to them. The petitions were all introduced, then discussed, and then either tabled, which meant that no further action would be taken, or they would be sent to the appropriate committee for legislative action.

On December 16, 1835, Congressman John Fairfield of Maine stood up and introduced a petition signed by 172 ladies in his district prayerfully asking that Congress end slavery in the District of Columbia. He moved that this petition be referred to the Committee on the District of Columbia. The Congressman, as well as the rest of the members of the House of Representatives, expected that this petition would suffer the fate of every other petition asking for the abolition of slavery; it would be tabled, meaning no action would be taken.

A group of South Carolina Congressmen had a different idea. For years they had been very concerned because abolitionists were regularly presenting petitions to Congress. Now they decided it was time to put an end to these antislavery petitions. These representatives insisted that the Constitution had expressly banned congress from discussing the question of slavery, and that, therefore, any antislavery petition must automatically be rejected without even the courtesy of the House of Representatives allowing the petitions to be formally received.

There were a number of reasons that these congressmen gave for wanting to completely ban abolitionist petitions. The first reason southerners gave for demanding a total ban was because antislavery petitions were an insult to the way of life in every southern state. A more compelling reason to pass the ban was the possibility that these petitions might incite civil insurrections like the Virginia slave revolt in 1831 led by Nat Turner that resulted in the deaths of 55 whites. (The fact that over 250 African Americans subsequently also lost their lives was never part of the debate.)

Southerners did not talk about another reason they needed to ban abolitionist petitions. Somehow their slaves had learned that the House of Representatves had received hundreds of antislavery petitions. This kind of information encouraged slaves to feel that if only they could reach the North a fugitive might find people willing and able to help him.

Democrats and Whig politicians did not ever want to discuss slavery so they were happy to support the ban. On May 16, 1836, the House of Representatives voted that henceforth "all petitions, memorials, resolutions, propositions or papers relating in any way or to any extent whatever to the subject of slavery or the abolition of slavery shall, without being printed or referred, be laid upon the table and that no further action whatever should be taken." This new rule was known as the Gag Rule. The few Congressmen who questioned the legality of the Gag Rule were easily silenced by the leaders of both political parties.

Only one Congressman was brave enough to challenge the right of congress to revoke the right of Americans to petition their elected officials on any issue that concerned them. John Quincy Adams was the 68 year old former President. To the amazement of the country, instead of retiring from politics, Adams had chosen to return to Congress in a new and more humble role, that of the representative of his home town of Quincy, Massachusetts. He had become one of the most distinguished members of the House. Adams was not an abolitionist, although he hated slavery, but he cared deeply for the Constitution. When the vote on the Gag Rule was taken, Adams rose from his chair and denounced the rule as a violation of the Constitution. The Speaker of the House banged his gravel and announced "Mr. Adams you are out of order!" The battle against the Gag Rule had begun.

Northerners took a look at this new southern demand and they did not like it. They had been ready to let southerners keep their "peculiar institution" as long as they left the North alone. Now slaveholders were challenging the right of Americans to petition their government.

The American Antislavery Society understood that the Gag Rule gave them a great opportunity to convince northerners that slavery was not just a southern institution, but a system that infringed on the rights of every American. In order to publicize the twin evils of slavery and the Gag Rule, they sent out a call to begin collecting thousands of petitions in order to give Congressman Adams plenty of ammunition to challenge it.

The leaders of the American Antislavery Society soon realized that they did not have enough men to collect these signatures. In desperation they turned to antislavery women for help. Women had always played a private role in the abolitionist movement, holding bazaars and fairs to raise money for the antislavery cause. A few women wrote unsigned antislavery tracts. Many of their homes were stations on the Underground Railroad, and some women even helped transport fugitives from one safe haven to another. These activities were all very private acts that were part of the proper feminine role in a world where women were never allowed a public voice. In 1835 women were still legally under the control of their husbands. The American Antislavery Society itself did not permit women to become members of their organization. Antislavery women had to create their own auxiliary organization. There had been a terrible uproar when, at the founding convention of the American Antislavery Society, Lucrecia Mott stood up in her balcony seat and asked to speak.

Abolitionist women had been very successful in collecting signatures at gatherings of women. Leaders of the petition drive asked these women if they would begin collecting signatures of men as well. It was very hard for these abolitionist women to venture out in public to collect signatures. At first they circulated signatures in safe places like local antislavery fairs and bazaars. Sometimes they would leave petitions with friendly shopkeepers. Then as more and more women joined the campaign, the ladies grew braver and they ventured out into the community. At a time when women were not allowed to even speak up at a mixed gathering of men and women, these ladies bravely walked down unfamiliar streets to knock on strangers' doors. Many of these women had to fight against public criticism, the jeers of men, and even the outright commands of husbands or fathers. By the end of the year, women had become the mainstay of the petition campaign. Soon wagonloads of petitions were arriving on Adams' doorstep.

The petition campaign taught women that they had the power to influence the American political system. In 1848 two abolitionist women, Elizabeth Cady Stanton and Lucretia Mott, organized the first women's rights convention in world history. The convention, held in Seneca Falls, New York, passed a most revolutionary demand that American women be given the right to vote.

For five years Adams led the fight against the Gag Rule. It was one of the wildest fights in congressional history. Adams' goal was to disrupt the proceedings of the House of Representatives until the Gag Rule was repealed. He would innocently present a petition to carry out the principles of the Declaration of Independence in Washington D C. Then in a softer voice he would whisper, "including Africans." There were shouts that he was violating the Gag Rule, and Adams would question in a shocked tone whether Americans were no longer allowed to discuss the Declaration of Independence in congress. The leaders of the House of Representatives tried every way they knew to silence Adams, but they never succeeded. One of most masterful strategists in congress, Adams would use every parliamentary trick he knew to present his antislavery petitions.

Whenever he could, Adams would rise up to participate in some ongoing House debate, then suddenly slip in a demand to introduce a new batch of petitions which he would insist must be read before the Speaker could rule whether or not they violated the Gag Rule.

Southerners were angry; they demanded that the House of Representatives do something about that obstinate Congressman, John Quincy Adams. In 1841 the House voted to formally censure Adams. Year by year the struggle against the Gag Rule had been gaining support all over the North. By 1841 Adams had been joined by a handful of northern congressmen. The censure vote, by which southern members of the House of Representatives had hoped to end Adams attack on the Gag Rule, backfired. Northerners who had been indifferent to the issue of abolition were surprised to realize that an ex-president was on trial for defending the Constitution. Adams quickly became the hero of the nation. Day after day this 75 year old man stood on the floor of the House for hours on end defending his right to fight against the illegality of the Gag Rule. He challenged his adversaries to explain to the nation why congress was so afraid to even question anything which touched on the subject of slavery.

The country began to listen. Newspapers regularly reported on the censure trial and described the courage of an elderly man fighting for the right of every American to petition his government. The editorials of newspapers throughout the North proclaimed their support for Adams. Petitions against the censure motion began flooding congress. The issue of slavery, which the South had tried to ban from Congress, became one of the main topics of discussion throughout the nation. In the process, John Quincy Adams had become one of the most popular men in the North. After weeks of turmoil, the House of Representatives voted to table the Censure Resolution. A triumphant Adams now took the floor to present 200 new antislavery petitions. The abolitionists had won their first major victory.

Slaveholders were furious at this defeat, and they looked around for another way to punish those radical congressmen who had dared lead the fight against the Gag Rule. In 1842 their moment came when Joshua Giddings, an Ohio Congressman, introduced a resolution to deal with the fate of a group of African Americans on the American slave ship *Creole*. It was a resolution guaranteed to anger every southern congressman.

The American brig, *Creole*, had set sail from Hampton Roads, Virginia; her only cargo was 135 slaves who were to be sold in the slave market of New Orleans. Madison Washington was one of those slaves. Washington was a fugitive who had been living a free life in Canada while his wife, Susan, was still a slave on a Virginia plantation. He missed her so much that he decided to return to Virginia and rescue her. His friends begged him not to go. They told him that it was too dangerous, that he would be risking his own freedom. Washington replied that, "Liberty is worth nothing to me while my wife is a slave." [5]

Revolt Aboard The *Amistad*. Source: *The Norton Anthology of English Literature*.

Washington was captured as he crept into the room where Susan was sleeping. He tried to beat off his attackers, but he was clubbed to the ground. The wounded fugitive was immediately sold to a slave trader, to be sold on the New Orleans auction block. The 135 slaves were put aboard the *Creole*, the men in one cabin the women in another. Washington, because he was a fugitive slave, was put in irons and chained to the floor.

Even though Washington was brokenhearted over losing Susan, he was still determined never to be a slave again. Before leaving Canada, he had hidden some tiny files, miniature saws, and other tools inside his clothing just in case he was captured. He had already created a new plan, and now he began recruiting a group of the most militant men aboard the ship to join him in a revolt. They used his tools to break apart their chains, then they waited until the time was right. On the ninth day at sea the weather turned nasty. While the crew were absorbed in dealing with the weather, Washington led his 18 recruits out of the cabin. First they quickly searched the ship for weapons. Next they crept onto the quarter deck and, brandishing their weapons, they overpowered the crew. Most of the crew surrendered

[5] Brown, William Wells Brown. *The Negro in the American Rebellion: His Heroism and His Fidelity*. New York: The Citadel Press, 1971. (Pg. 29)

immediately. Only one crew member fought back and he was killed in the fighting. The captain and first mate were wounded. As soon as the fugitives were in control of the *Creole*, Madison ordered the fighting stopped, then commanded the crew to turn the ship towards Nassau, the port city of the British Colony of the Bahamas. Washington even dressed the wounds of the white officers and crew who had been hurt in the fighting.

Now Washington led his men down into the female cabin to free the women. Opening the cabin door Washington was overwhelmed with joy to see his wife Susan. Cheers and hurrahs followed the happy couple as they climbed up to the deck to watch the sun rise over the water. The next morning the *Creole* landed at Nassau. Since slavery was illegal in every British territory, the moment the Creole rebels stepped ashore they were declared free men.

In 1842 Congress demanded that England compensate slaveholders for the liberated slaves. Some southern extremists even threatened war with England if the debt was not paid. On March 21, in the midst of this debate, Josiah Giddings stood up in the House of Representatives and wondered whether congress even had jurisdiction over the Creole issue. After all, Giddings innocently inquired, haven't Southern legislators claimed for years that slavery was an issue that could only be decided by individual states? They had proclaimed over and over again that the Federal government had no power to legislate on any issue concerning slavery. If the Constitution forbad any Federal interference with the institution of slavery then congress had no authority to demand compensation from England for the slaves aboard the *Creole*, since the Creole revolt took place at sea outside the territorial limit of any American state. Giddings then introduced a resolution asking the House of Representatives to end the debate on the Creole. This resolution created instant turmoil on the floor of the House because it raised a dangerous issue. According to Giddings' argument, while the delegates to the Constitutional Convention had passed a series of pro-slavery clauses, they had also required the Federal government to be neutral with respect to slavery. This meant that it was the slaveholders rather than abolitionists who were violating the Constitution. Southerners did not dare allow any discussion of the limitation of Federal power in support of slavery. Instead, southern representatives demanded that Giddings be censured. The very next day, on March 22, a majority of House members voted to censure Giddings without even granting him the courtesy of a trial.

Josiah Giddings immediately resigned from Congress and returned to Ohio. The governor of Ohio ordered new elections held in late April to fill Giddings' vacant seat. Giddings announced that he would run again for his old congressional seat. The Whig Party regulars knew that they would have to defeat Giddings in order to placate southern Whigs. The party organization lavished money on his opponent, circulated thousands of leaflets, hung hundreds of posters trying to stop his election. Nothing worked; Giddings was re-elected by an overwhelming majority of the voters. It was a stinging defeat for the South.

CHAPTER

7

THE UNDERGROUND RAILROAD GOES PUBLIC
FUGITIVES TELL THEIR STORIES

By the late 1830's, southerners needed a new approach to combat the growing antislavery mood of the North. Slaveholders began to advance the novel idea that slavery was a great blessing to American slaves. In newspapers, magazines, churches, and lecture halls, southerners insisted that slaves were child-like creatures who were unable to take care of themselves. Slaveholders were benevolent masters who protected "their people" and provided them with all their needs. They even made Christians out of these once- savage Africans.

Southerners painted an idyllic picture of happy slaves, singing in the cotton fields, living in cozy cabins with plenty of food and warm clothing. They compared the fate of elderly slaves to that of older workers in the North. Slaveholders boasted that when their slaves got too old to work they were tenderly taken care of by kindly masters. Southerners compared this happy secure existence to the life of northern factory workers who had nobody to take care of them when they were sick, out of a job or simply too old to work.

So many northerners loved this charming picture of plantation life that abolitionists became worried. They needed something powerful to combat this rosy picture of slavery. They did not have long to wait. This idyllic picture of slavery began to crumble the day Frederick Douglass escaped from slavery.

In the summer of 1841, the 21 year old fugitive was attending his first abolitionist meeting. Douglass suddenly felt compelled to stand up and say a few words about his own experience as a slave. The audience was spellbound. William Lloyd Garrison, editor of the *Liberator*, leaped onto the stage and thundered out the question " Is this a man or a thing?" The audience shouted "a man! a man!" One of the greatest abolitionist leaders was born that evening.

The six foot Douglass was a commanding presence on the abolitionist stage. Word spread about the story that this fugitive was telling about the realities of slavery. The public was eager to hear for themselves what this late "graduate" from the south's "peculiar

125

institution" with his diploma written on his scarred back, had to say about the idyllic life of a slave. Douglass described to his audiences the rage of his church-going master, Captain Auld, when he discovered that Douglass was teaching a Sunday school for slave children. The punishment Douglass received for this "crime" was to be sent to a notorious slave breaker, Edward Covey.

The job of a slave breaker was to crush the independence of a slave and turn him into a docile submissive creature. Douglass said that all during that terrible summer Covey tried to break his spirit by overwork, daily beatings, and almost starving him to death. Douglass confessed that by August he was so desperate that he thought about suicide. Douglass then electrified the crowds that gathered to hear him when he told them how he suddenly made the decision that if he were going to die he would die fighting. He described how, on that hot August day as Covey began whipping him, Douglass turned on him and beat him to the ground. The audience cheered as Douglass proclaimed that, "this battle with Mr. Covey was the turning point in my career. I was a changed being after that fight. I was nothing before; I was a man now." [1] Then audiences would burst into laughter as he described the look on Covey's face when Douglass knocked him into the filth of the cowpen. He concluded his story by proudly remarking that Covey never hit him again. Douglass had begun his career as an antislavery lecturer by simply talking about his own experience as a slave, but he soon began linking his own experiences to a deeper evaluation of slavery. He pointed out that it was not that his old master, Captain Ault, was born a wicked man; it was the institution of slavery that turned decent men into cruel taskmasters, because the only way to keep a man in slavery is by the threat of brute force. Douglass told his audience that every man hungers to be free. No matter how kind and Christian a slaveholder might want to be, in the end he can only keep a man in chains by the threat of violence.

Before movies, radio or television, Americans flocked to religious revivals, political rallies and the lecture circuit, which were the major events that broke up the monotony of everyday life. Abolitionist lecturers were becoming an important part of this entertainment circuit. People flocked to these lectures, some to cheer, many others to heckle the speaker. It was part of the fun to see how

---

[1] Douglass, Frederick. *Life and Times of Frederick Douglass.* New York: Bonanza Books, 1962. (Pg. 143)

these speakers would handle themselves. Frederick Douglass was a master at handling audiences. He could silence hecklers by using humor, as well as his powerful oratory. Douglass' very presence on the lecture circuit challenged the notion that slaves were sub human people. Slaveholders began spreading the rumor that Frederick Douglass had never been a slave because he was too literate and much too sophisticated a lecturer. Douglass felt that he must answer these critics at once, before his value as an abolitionist lecturer was destroyed.

Douglass decided that he must write his autobiography, and, this time, the book would not be ghost written by a white abolitionist; Douglass would be the only author of his autobiography. In order to prove to the world that he was indeed a fugitive slave, he decided not to hide his real slave identity. In his book he gave his slave name, Fred Bailey, and the name of his owner. Wendell Phillips, when he first read the manuscript, advised Douglass to burn the book before it went to press because he would no longer be safe in America. Douglass understood the danger that he would now face; he would now become the target of every slave hunter in America. Douglass insisted that the book must be printed anyhow. His friends were so impressed by his courage that they decided to send him to England for a grand lecture tour where he would be safe from kidnapping.

His autobiography, *The Narrative of the Life of Frederick Douglass,* was published in May, 1845, and became an instant best seller. The autobiography became an instant best seller in America, and it was translated into French and German. In England, where Douglass was lecturing to standing room only- crowds, his autobiography went into nine editions.

The role that fugitive slaves played in advancing the cause of antislavery was a vital one. People in the 1840's loved a great adventure story just as much as they do today. Antislavery lecturers, when they introduced a fugitive speaker, promised the audience that they were about to hear a true tale more thrilling, more filled with danger and pathos than any story they might read.

The speakers usually began with their own tales of life under slavery, which contradicted the southern myths of a loving plantation society between slaves and owners. Fugitives described the life of brutal labor, savage beatings they received, and the tearing apart of families. Every fugitive had stories about the anguish they felt when family and friends were sold to slave traders, knowing that they would never see their loved ones again. Josiah Henson described his profound struggle in trying to remain a good Christian in spite of all the pain and suffering he had endured. His story, many believe, was the inspiration for the fictional Uncle Tom in Harriet Beecher Stowe's *Uncle Tom's Cabin*, one of the most influential novels in American history.

Henry Bibb, one of the most effective speakers on the abolitionist circuit, brought audiences to tears when he talked about how much he had loved his wife and the anguish he felt when she was sold away. They applauded his courage when he described how many trips he made down South to try and rescue her, and his despair when each rescue attempt failed.

Northerners were startled to realize that, in the South, slave marriages were never considered legal or even recognized as a holy institution by any southern white church. Slaveholders tried to convince their critics by insisting that black men and women easily forget their mates and children just as the cows in the pasture immediately forgot their calves. Ex-slaves refuted this callous explanation the moment they described the reality of slave life.

Northern audiences wept as fugitives told them about their pain at parting from beloved husbands or wives; mothers described the anguish of having children torn from their arms, or fathers spoke of the agony of watching as slave traders carried off their little sons and daughters. The horror of slavery suddenly became a reality to northerners who had been blinded by southern myths about plantation life.

Audiences especially loved hearing the story of the actual escape. Their excitement mounted as fugitives told about what it felt like to be pursued by bloodhounds; how they sometimes had to submerge themselves in a river, stream, or even a murky swamp to prevent these murderous dogs from following them. Audiences roared with laughter as speakers described the many clever ways that they were able to outwit slave catchers trying to re-capture them. Abolitionists decided that these stories must reach a larger audience than could be reached by the lecture podium, so they urged the most articulate of these fugitive slaves to write their own autobiographies.

Best selling books were a new phenomenon in American life, along with cheap popular newspapers and mass produced pamphlets.

Ever since the invention of the printing press in 1440 the paper used in these presses had always been made laboriously by hand, using rags. The cost of a book or even a newspaper had always been much too expensive for most Americans. In the1820's a revolution took place in the printing industry with the invention of machine made paper. Now newspapers, pamphlets, and books could be produced so cheaply that everyone could afford to buy them. Suddenly there were newspapers everywhere. Every small town in America had its own newspaper. Political parties, religious organizations, and mass movements, were able to publish their own newspapers. Magazines and pamphlets could be found everywhere. Even books were being mass produced. Americans were enchanted with this avalanche of printed material. By the 1830's they were the most literate people in the world. Many of the slave narratives became best sellers. Audiences all over the North wanted to hear from these ex-slaves, so the American Antislavery Society recruited even more ex-slaves to become lecturers on the antislavery circuit.

The life of an antislavery agent was a hard one. The lecture circuit was a major form of entertainment. The audiences were made up of antislavery supporters as well as others who hated abolitionists. In many communities organized crowds would regularly physically attack the speakers, hurling rotten eggs, tomatoes and even stones, as he or she stood at the podium. They would shout out epithets as the agent tried to speak. Black agents were an especial target of these mobs. Douglass describes some meetings where he was forced to flee the meeting hall in the middle of a speech, followed by howling mobs screaming "kill the dammed n-----r" as he fled through the streets searching for a safe hideout.

Years later the Quaker abolitionist Rebecca Lewis told the historian R. C Smedley about one time when Frederick Douglass came to Lancaster as one of the featured speakers at an abolitionist meeting, " The meeting was broken up by a mob which threatened the life of the distinguished orator." The meeting broke up and the speakers fled. Later Douglass somehow got separated from the other speakers. Lewis recalled how, "Mr. Douglass was overtaken and mercilessly cut and bruised by the mob who thought that they had

Frederick Douglass resisting an Indiana mob.
Source: *Library of Congress, Prints and Photographs Division.*

killed him." [2] It took weeks of nursing before Douglass was well enough to leave his sick bed, but as soon as he was able to travel he was back on the abolitionist circuit.

Discrimination followed the black agent wherever he or she went. They were not allowed a seat on trains; instead they had to travel in filthy boxcars. Many times when they arrived in a town, while white speakers were invited into antislavery homes or at least found housing in cheap hotels, black speakers discovered that there was no home or hotel willing to let them in and they were forced to sleep on hard church floors or even in open fields.

Even fugitives who had no special ability to make speeches or write books could become powerful weapons in the war against slavery. Levi Coffin understood how to use that power. In 1847 Coffin moved from Indiana where he had already built up a successful network of Underground Railroad stations to Cincinnati where he immediately began recruiting new members for the Railroad. Coffin understood what the sight of a desperate runaway had on the conscience of decent people. On one occasion Coffin invited several prominent Cincinnati citizens to his home to show them a "curiosity" that he had just received from the South. Coffin's guests were shocked when they discovered that the "curiosity" was a refined black woman and her son, both fugitive slaves. When Coffin asked whether they would help these fugitives find freedom, his guests quickly raised enough money to send the family to Canada. Many of these guests became regular contributors to the cause.

While the escapes of most fugitives were very quiet affairs, the escape of Henry Brown was so sensational that it became a legendary event. Henry Brown had been content to remain a slave because he

---

[2] Smedley, R. C. *History of the Underground Railroad.* New York: Arno Press and the New York Times, 1969. (Pg. 187)

was working hard to purchase freedom for his slave wife and baby. Brown earned this extra pittance because, after he finished every task demanded by his master, he would find small jobs on his own. Every week he paid his wife's master his meager outside earnings as a down payment on his family's freedom. Then, on the most disastrous day of his life, Brown discovered that his wife's master had just sold his wife and baby to a North Carolina slaveholder. Brown learned which street the slaveholder's wagon would be driving down. Brown watched in agony as the wagon carrying his child went by. Then he saw a group of chained slaves. His wife among them. Brown ran up to her, seized her hand and whispered "We shall meet in heaven." Brown managed to run beside her for four miles. Then, Brown remembered, "We were obliged to part, the look of mutual love which we exchanged was all the token which we could give each other." Brown never saw his family again.[3]

Brown could no longer tolerate being a slave and he decided on a daring escape plan that would bring him either freedom or death. He turned for help to a white businessman who was a member of the Underground Railroad. Brown built a wooden box just large enough to hold himself. He drilled a few air holes, just barely enough for him to breath but not enough to attract the attention of any railroad workers. Then Brown went to Mr. Smith's shop and slipped into the box. Smith

Henry "Box" Brown. Source: *Library of Congress, Prints and Photographs Division.*

handed Brown a bladder of water and a few small biscuits. Then Smith nailed the box shut and addressed this human package to William H. Johnson, a member of Philadelphia's Vigilance Committee.

The trip was a nightmare. At one stop the box was transferred from the railroad car to a steamer and the box was stored standing on end. Brown felt his eyes swelling as if they would burst from their sockets When he tried to lift his hand to his face he found that the hand seemed paralyzed. Brown believed that he was about to die. Luckily after an hour and a

---

[3] Brown, Henry Box. *Narrative of the Life of Henry Box Brown written by Himself.* New York: Oxford University Press, 2002. (Pg. 52-54)

half someone wanted to sit down and moved the box to a horizontal position and Brown was saved.

Meanwhile the Philadelphia Vigilance Committee had received a mysterious message stating that an important box was arriving on the three o'clock train from Virginia for Mr. Johnson. Committee members rushed to Johnson's house. The hours dragged by until finally there was a knock on the door. Johnson carried the box gently into the parlor, the door was locked, then James McKim rapped quickly on the lid and called out "all right?" praying that the fugitive was still alive. To the great relief of everyone there was a muffled answer, "All right sir." The men quickly broke open the box and found Brown curled up inside. He reached out his hand and said simply "How do you do gentlemen." [4]

Brown's thrilling escape from slavery became a national sensation. People all over the North overflowed meeting halls to hear more about his miraculous escape. They re-named him Henry Box Brown. Sheet music was even written to celebrate his exploit. There was no way that supporters of slavery could explain why a man like Brown would choose to risk the possibility of a horrible death rather than remain a Virginia slave.

In the midst of a growing antislavery ferment, Theodore Weld, now that his battalion of abolitionists were blanketing southern Ohio with their antislavery message, launched a new project. He decided to write a book about slavery called "American Slavery As It Is." When it was published in 1839, it shattered forever the South's claim that slavery was a benevolent institution. Weld had used only southern sources to describe the harshness of slavery. Americans found the real facts on southern slavery hard to deny as soon as they began the book. Weld's introduction promised readers that: "A Majority of the facts and testimony contained in this work rests upon the authority of slaveholders, whose names and residences are given to the public, as vouchers for the truth of their statements" [5]

The book was filled with advertisements for the capture of fugitive slaves. These advertisements talked about fugitives having

---

[4] Ibid.

[5] Theodore Dwight. *American Slavery as it is: Testimony of a Thousand Witnesses.* New York: Arno Press, 1968. (introduction).

the scars of beatings and mutilations. Some mentioned the fact that the fugitive might be found searching for a child, husband or wife who had been sold away. Other articles might talk about punishment meted out to runaways, or the absolute power that a slaveholder had over his slave, a power no court in the South would oppose even if it resulted in the torture or murder of a slave. This book destroyed the professed Christianity of slavery and its uplifting effect on the slave

Ellen and William Craft's escape also escalated the debate over slavery. Their escape attracted national attention, not only because it was amazing, but because Ellen Craft was a beautiful woman who appeared as white as any woman in America. She was a Georgia slave whose father was a white *Planter* and whose mother was one of his slaves. Ellen was a lovely child who was frequently mistaken for a member of her father's white family. Her father's wife hated Ellen passionately, and she delighted in abusing the child. When Ellen was eleven years old her father gave her to one of his legitimate daughters as a wedding present.

The anguish of being sold away from her mother never left Ellen. She made a vow that she would never have children unless she was a free woman. This vow was shaken when a handsome young man named William moved to Macon with his master. Ellen and William fell deeply in love and they began talking about marriage. William was wise enough to realize that Ellen would be miserable in a slave marriage. He knew that he must find a way for them to escape. But how? Their situation seemed hopeless. The nearest free state, Pennsylvania, was one thousand miles away, an impossible barrier to freedom.

Then one day William came to Ellen with a plan. It was a dangerous scheme, and it depended on Ellen's white skin and her ability to act. Ellen would disguise herself as an invalid white *Planter* who was seeking medical treatment in the North. William would act as her slave man-servant. The only flaw in William's plan was that neither of them could read or write, and Ellen would have to sign papers and register at hotels along the way. Ellen came up with a brilliant solution. She would bind up her right hand in a sling so that she would be unable to write. Ellen also suggested that she cover part of her face with a poultice so that she would have a good reason not to talk to anyone.

The poultice turned out to be a brilliant idea because as the train pulled out of the station Ellen discovered that the passenger sitting next to her was a friend of her master. Feigning illness, she remained silent throughout the trip while William, acting as the most devoted of slaves, was always on hand to help his very ill master and explain her unsociability. The two played their parts so convincingly during the hazardous four day trip that no one suspected the truth. They pulled into the Philadelphia train station on Christmas day, 1848. They were free at last.

William Wells Brown, a fugitive slave himself, and now a well known abolitionist lecturer, heard about the Crafts' remarkable escape. He rushed over to meet with William Still, the brilliant black head of Philadelphia's Vigilance Committee. The Crafts, Brown told Still, will be a sensation as abolitionist speakers. Their story had everything, young love, great courage, pathos and finally a triumphant arrival in Philadelphia. Brown was right. Audiences loved the story of their thousand mile escape and the many dangerous situations that they overcame by using their quick wits. Most of all, northerners loved Ellen Craft. Audiences were disturbed because this beautiful woman looked so much like their own wives and daughters, yet she was a slave. Northerners wondered what kind of father would heartlessly separate a gentle, beautiful child from her mother at such a tender age. The Crafts and William Wells Brown traveled all over New England attracting huge audiences at every stop.

By the 1840's the Underground Railroad was moving into high gear. Most of the Railroad conductors who made the dangerous trip South were anonomous heroes but one of these liberators became a national folk heroine. Harriet Tubman began her forays into the South in the 1850's. Tubman boasted that although she made 19 trips she never lost a fugitive.

In 1839 Jo Norton, a Maryland slave, met one of these nameless rescuers on a dark Sunday evening. This white man offered Norton his help if he wanted to flee slavery. Three weeks later Jo Norton and four other slaves of Colonel Hardy began their escape on the Underground Railroad. A few days later a copy of the newspaper *The Liberty Press,* published in Albany, New York, was sent to Colonel Hardy with an article marked for his attention. A Washington, D.C., newspaper reported on what happened next.

"Now we learn that Colonel Hardy, a tobacco *Planter*, residing in the district about five miles from the city lost five slaves last Sunday evening. They were pursued by an excellent slave catcher, but no trace of them was discovered. The search was abandoned this morning." The article went on, "Arrived this morning by our fast line three men and two women. They were claimed as slaves by Colonel Hardy of the District of Columbia, but became dissatisfied with the Colonel's ways and left the old fellow's premises last Sunday evening arriving at our station by the quickest passage on record." The article ended with the statement, "Now Colonel Hardy, please give yourself no trouble about these friends of yours, for they will be safe under the protection of the British Lion before this meets your eye." [6]

While a completely baffled Colonel Hardy was wondering how the Underground Railroad could smuggle fugitives north faster than a first class train, Jo Norton's actual escape indicates the sophisticated methods that Underground Railroad operators were beginning to use. Norton and the other four fugitives were nowhere near Albany. They were actually hiding in Baltimore, not too far from Colonel Hardy's plantation, waiting for the search to be over before they headed north. Southerners were so amazed over these Underground Railroad reports of miraculous escapes that a few of them actually began to believe that there really was a mysterious underground road that carried their runaways north.

Jonathan Walker was a decent man who felt that he must follow his Christian conscience, no matter what the cost. He was a New England businessman who had been hired to help build a Florida railroad. In Florida, railroad construction was done by slaves. Slaveholders would rent out their slaves to the railroad company until the job was complete. Walker was a unique boss. He refused to treat his slave workers inhumanly; He sat at the same table and shared the same food with his workers. He led the slaves in prayer. This was a man who might be recruited into the Underground Railroad. In 1844 one of the slaves cautiously approached him and tried to find out what he thought about slavery. Walker told the man that he did not like slavery. The next day seven men begged Walker to help them flee their masters.

Walker found an open boat and the seven men crowded aboard. They pushed off from a bay in Pensacola and set sail for the Bahamas. Neither Walker nor the fugitives knew much about navigation. By the time they rounded the southern tip of the Florida coast they were lost. They were found by a sloop and taken aboard as prisoners. Walker

---

[6] Buckmaster, Henrietta. *Let My People Go: The Story of the Underground Railroad and the Growth of the Abolitionist Movement.* Boston: Beacon Press, 1941.(Pg 109)

was jailed in Pensacola, where he was chained to the floor for fifteen days. After his trial he was stood in a pillory for an hour while he was pelted with rotten eggs. Next, by order of the Federal Court, a branding iron was heated and the letters SS (slave stealer) were burned upon his hand. Then he was taken back to his prison cell and again chained to the floor. The State of Florida decreed that Walker would remain in jail until he had paid both for the cost of the trial, and the fines that the court had imposed for stealing seven slaves. The court also added a jail term for Negro stealing. Slaveholders expected Walker to remain in jail for years, but, within the year, abolitionists had raised the money to pay all of the fines. The embarrassed Florida government decided to waive the jail sentence. Jonathan Walker became an abolitionist hero and a popular speaker on the abolitionist circuit. He had but to hold up his branded hand to convince audiences of the brutality of slavery.

The country had barely recovered from the savage treatment Florida had given Jonathan Walker when the news about Calvin Fairbank and Delia Webster made headlines throughout the North. Calvin Fairbank was a student at Oberlin College in 1837 when he began his career as an Underground Railroad conductor. His father had sent him down the Ohio River to sell a raft of lumber. At Wheeling, Virginia he fell into conversation with a young slave. His antislavery feelings must have been apparent because the young man mentioned his desire to be free. Fairbank loaned the man his raft and that night the fugitive slipped across the river. A few days later Fairbank arrived in Kentucky. There must have been something about the man that made slaves trust him because a slave woman begged him to rescue her and her seven children. That very night Fairbank rafted the entire family across the river.

By 1844 Fairbank had helped forty-one slaves to escape. He had become an expert on conveying fugitives out of the south, using simple but effective devices for their escapes. He put men into women's clothing and women into men's clothing to confuse slave hunters. Whenever possible Fairbank tried to put fugitives on horseback, into buggies, wagons, or carriages, anything to make the trip faster. He hid them under loads of hay, fresh produce, old furniture, even boxes and barrels. He hired boats to take them across the Ohio River. Once, when that proved impossible, he found a large log and a long piece of board and paddled a young fugitive woman across the river to Ohio. He had become a legend among members of the Underground Railroad. No fugitive rescued by Calvin Fairbank was ever captured.

In 1844 Fairbank was approached by Lewis Hayden, a Kentucky slave, to help rescue his family. Hayden was owned by one master; his wife and son belonged to another family. When Fairbank asked Hayden to tell him something about his life, Hayden told him this heart wrenching story.

When he was just a child, his mother, a lovely young black women, was sold to a slaveholder who wanted her for his mistress. She consistently refused his advances. For her bravery she was beaten and tortured until she was finally driven insane. Her pitiful pleas for her children gave her master some hope that, if she actually saw them, her sanity might be restored. Hayden remembered the day when he was seven years old and found his mother in their cabin. "She sprung and caught my arms and seemed going to break them and then said, 'I'll fix you so they'll never get you!' I screamed...They came in and took me away. They tied her and carried her off." [7]

Hayden fell in love with Esther Harvey and they were married. Soon after the wedding, Esther was sold to Henry Clay, one of the most prominent leaders of the United States Senate. Esther and Lewis had a baby son. One day Esther came to him in tears. Henry Clay had just sold her and the baby to a slave trader. They were leaving tomorrow. Helplessly Hayden watched as his wife and baby were dragged off. Hayden had now lost his entire family. His mother, sisters, and brothers, had all been sold away from him. He told Fairbanks that the loss of his son caused him such unbearable pain that he could never talk about it. Yet life went on. Hayden had recently re-married. Harriet, his new wife, had a young son, Joseph, a child that Hayden loved as deeply as if he had been his own. Harriet was owned by another master and there was talk that after the busy Lexington summer season was over one of them might be sold. Hayden told Fairbank that he could not bear the agony of losing another family. Fairbank was deeply moved by Hayden's story and agreed to help his family to escape.

Fairbank recruited a young New England school teacher, Miss Delia Webster, to help in the escape. Webster had graduated from Oberlin College, a hotbed of abolitionist activity, and had

---

[7] Strangis, Joel. *Lewis Hayden and the War Against Slavery*. North Haven, Connecticut; Shoe String Press, 1999. (Pg. 2)

recently moved to Kentucky to become the principal of the Lexington Female Academy. Fairbank rented a carriage and a driver for the last weekend of September. He had been in the habit of taking Miss Webster for carriage drives on pleasant weekends, so renting a carriage was not unusual .

On the Saturday night of September 27, Hayden slipped away from the restaurant where he worked and walked to the Bain house where Harriet and Joseph waited. Hayden rapped on the window. Harriet opened it up and lifted the seven year old Joseph into Hayden's arms, then Harriet climbed out of the window. The carriage with Fairbank and Webster inside was waiting for them. It was a sixty-five mile trip with toll houses all along the way. The toll collectors were always on the lookout for fugitive slaves, so Fairbank used a variety of strategies to hide the Haydens. Sometimes he would disguise them as white travelers by covering Harriet's face with a veil, and using enveloping cloaks for Lewis and Joseph. Other times he would hide Joseph under the seat while Harriet and Lewis would pretend to be Delia's servants. Finally they crossed the Ohio River and landed in the town of Ripley. Soon the Hayden family was on their way to Canada and freedom.

When Fairbank and Webster returned to Lexington, disaster struck. A letter had been found that linked Fairbank with the escape of the Haydens. Fairbank and Webster were arrested and immediately locked up in the local jail for the crime of "Negro stealing." Fairbank's arrest was not unexpected; Kentucky officials had long suspected that Fairbank was a member of the Underground Railroad. Slaveholders were pleased that at last they had caught him.

The arrest of Delia Webster, a middle-class white woman, created a sensation in Lexington. It was unheard of for such a woman to be jailed no matter what the crime; never in Lexington history had a woman been jailed before her trial had even begun. The evidence against her was very weak, but, to the surprise of most people outside Kentucky, the jury found her guilty.

Why was Delia Webster treated so harshly when other women, arrested for much more serious crimes were treated with that chivalry for which Kentucky was famous? It was, of course, the issue of slavery. In 1844 the price of a slave had reached an all time high. The city of Lexington had become an unofficial center of the slave trade. Kentucky slaveholders were selling their slaves to the highest bidders and collecting big profits. At the same time, Ohio and freedom was just a river away. Slaves like Lewis Hayden, faced with the imminent danger of being sold, were finding ways to escape, and conductors on the Underground Railroad were only too happy to help them. Something had to be done to teach these "Negro stealers" a lesson. Sending Delia Webster to prison would send a message to other misguided abolitionists about the high cost of aiding fugitive slaves. Delia Webster was sentenced to two years in the Kentucky State Penitentiary. This harsh sentence horrified people all over the country. Even the jury who found her guilty sent a message to the governor asking him to commute her sentence. But Lexington slaveholders insisted that the governor hold firm.

Calvin Fairbank's trial began in February 1845. At first Fairbank pleaded not guilty insisting on arguing the immorality of slavery but he decided to make a deal with the governor of Kentucky. If the governor would pardon Webster, he would change his plea to guilty. In February Webster was released from prison and Fairbank was sentenced to fifteen years in the state penitentiary, five years for each of the slaves he helped free.

Lewis Hayden was safe in the North, but he was haunted by the price that Fairbank had paid for his freedom. Hayden decided he must raise the money to pay his old master. He began talking to abolitionist audiences about the heroism of Webster and Fairbank. He soon had raised enough money to pay for his own freedom, hoping that this would win freedom for Fairbank. The Kentucky governor pardoned Fairbank in 1849.

Calvin Fairbank never stopped working for the Underground Railroad. In 1851 he helped another fugitive, Tamar, to escape from Kentucky to Indiana. This time Fairbank was dragged back from Indiana to Kentucky, tried again for slave stealing, and was, again, sentenced to fifteen years in the state penitentiary. Only in 1864, in the midst of the Civil War, long after Lincoln had issued the Emancipation Proclamation, was Fairbank given a pardon.

It was a bitterly cold February day in 1838 when a Kentucky slave mother heard that her master was about to sell her two year old baby to a slave trader. There was no time to waste. Snatching up her baby, the woman headed for the Ohio River. It took her all night to reach the river. When she reached its banks the sun was beginning to rise. She saw that the river was no longer frozen solid but had broken up, and was filled with floating ice floes. It was too dangerous to cross.

139

She had heard there was an old white man who had a cabin on the banks of the river who was known to help fugitive slaves. The woman knocked on his door. The man brought the two fugitives inside, set them before his fire and fed them. They hid in his cabin all day. When she went down to the river that night she saw that the river was still filled with blocks of floating ice. Then she heard the sound of braying dogs and she knew the slave catchers were right behind her. Quickly she wrapped her baby in her shawl, then tied the shawl around her neck and waded into the river. She stepped onto the first block of ice, then jumped onto another block. Sometimes she slipped off the ice into the frigid water. Other times the cake of ice would sink under her weight and in desperation she would lay her baby on another block of ice and drag herself up by her hands. Finally she reached the Ohio shore. A man who had been watching her escape with incredulous eyes reached down to help her climb up the bank. It was Chancey Shaw, a notorious slave catcher. Any other time Shaw would have seized the fugitive and claimed his reward, but this time was different. He spoke to her softly, "Any woman who crossed that river carrying her baby has won her freedom." Then he guided her to a steep cliff; on its peak was the house of John Rankin. For the moment Harris was safe.[8]

The Rankin sons were concerned that there were slave hunters searching homes in Ripley, so they quickly moved her to an inland safe house. The slave mother and her baby was ferried from station to station until at last she reached Sandusky, her final stop. Now dressed as a boy with her hair cut short, she boarded a boat and sailed across Lake Erie to Canada.

Harriet Beecher Stowe had heard the story of this unnamed slave mother's dangerous flight over the ice floes and it haunted her. In 1850 Stowe decided to write a novel that would expose the reality of slavery. She called it *Uncle Tom's Cabin*. In her novel Stowe's depiction of the slave mother (that she gave the name Eliza) leaping from one chunk of ice to another, her baby clutched in her arms, became one of the most compelling indictments of slavery ever written.

"Eliza" real life story was even more remarkable than the tale depicted in Stowe's novel. On the day she left Ripley, she told John Rankin that she would be back to rescue her daughter and four grandchildren. Rankin was skeptical. "Eliza" had faced so

---

[8] Hagedorn, Ann. *Beyond the River: The Untold Story of the Underground Railroad.* New York: Simon & Schuster, 2002. (Pg. 137)

George Pecks grand revival of Stetson's *Uncle Tom's Cabin.* Source: *Library of Congress, Prints and Photographs Division.*

many dangers in her first escape that he wondered if, once free, she would risk her freedom to return to Kentucky to liberate the rest of her family.

Yet on a bright June day in 1841, Rankin, working in his garden, saw what appeared to be a man climbing the steep cliff to his house. When the man entered his garden, Rankin was astonished to see that it was "Eliza". That night she crossed the river into Kentucky and hid in her daughter's cabin. The next night she gathered her grandchildren together and began walking back towards the river. It took longer than they expected, and dawn was breaking before they reached the banks of the Ohio. Rankin, who had been waiting all night for "Eliza" to appear, saw with dismay a group of men on horseback with their dogs and guns searching for the family. Rankin noticed that for some reason the dogs were unable to pick up the scent. All day long the slave hunters searched but they never found the fugitives. John Rankin had an idea about where they might be. He found them hiding in the river itself completely submerged, using river reeds to breath. Rankin sent a friend with a message of instructions for "Eliza". Just at twilight one of the Rankin sons slipped across the river, put on a woman's dress, and then led the slave catchers on a lively chase while another agent slipped the fugitive family aboard a boat and rowed across the river.

In 1837 Edward Prigg, a slaveholder of Maryland, received a warrant from a Pennsylvania justice of the peace to recapture a suspected fugitive slave, Margaret Morgan, and her children. Prigg appeared before another justice demanding the right to remove the fugitives immediately; this second justice refused to hear the case, ordering that before Prigg could take the suspected fugitives back to Maryland, the fugitives must first be given a jury trial to determine if they were indeed the fugitives described in Prigg's warrant. A jury

141

trial was mandated by Pennsylvania's Personal Liberty Law. Prigg ignored this judicial order and immediately returned home, carrying Margaret Morgan and her children with him.

Six months later a Pennsylvania grand jury returned an indictment against Prigg for kidnapping. The Pennsylvania governor asked the state of Maryland to extradite Edward Prigg so that he could stand trial for flauting the Pennsylvania law. The governor of Maryland angrily refused. He insisted that the right of re-capture under the Fugitive Slave Law gave any slaveholder in the United States the right to reclaim a fugitive without first getting the permission of any state court.

The issue had become so divisive that the two states decided to appeal to the Federal courts for an answer. The case worked its way through the Federal courts up to the Supreme Court. On March 1, 1842, the Supreme Court announced its decision. They announced that the right of recapturing fugitives was part of the agreement that the states had made when they approved the Constitution. Therefore, Prigg was within his rights when he seized the fugitives Margaret Morgan and her children. In this ruling the court refused to consider the rights of free black citizens. The South breathed a sigh of relief, happy that their right of recapture was now re-affirmed as the law of the land.

The South celebrated too soon; the Federal court had created one important loophole in the Prig decision. The case of George Latimere, a fugitive slave, would dramatically illustrate that loophole. Latimer had been living quietly in Boston for many years. In 1842 his owner James Grey suddenly appeared before a Boston judge and demanded that Latimer be returned to him. The fugitive was immediately arrested and thrown into jail. Antislavery leaders demanded that Latimer be released on a Writ of Habeas Corpus. When the Massachusetts Court announced that it did not believe that fugitive slaves had any legal rights under the Fugitive Slave Law, based on the new Prig decision, Boston abolitionists called a public protest meeting. On October 30, 4,000 people crowded into Faneuil Hall to protest Latimer's arrest. This meeting became more than a demonstration when they heard what a group of lawyers had to tell them. The lawyers had carefully read the complete ruling and discovered that, even though the court had given slaveholders the right to pursue their runaway slaves, they also ruled that, since the Fugitive Slave Law was a Federal law, state officials did not have to aid in the recapture of any fugitives. A statewide Lattimore

Committee was quickly organized which began circulating petitions directed to the state legislature.

These petitions asked for a state law forbidding any state official from participating in the enforcement of the Fugitive Slave Law.

On February 17, 1843, petitions bearing 64,526 signatures were delivered to the Massachuset State Legislature. Five weeks later the legislature passed a measure dubbed by delighted abolitionists, the Latimer Statute, which prohibited the use of any state officials, including police, sheriffs and their deputies, judges, or any judicial officers including state marshals in the enforcement of the Fugitive Slave Law. The new law also forbade the use of any state property, such as jails, and courthouses in the arrest or detention of any alleged fugitive slave. The anger against Latimere's arrest increased every day. There were so many protests and demonstrations that the committee began publishing a newspaper, *"The Latimer Weekly* and *North Star Journal."* James Grey, Latimer's owner, was so upset and shocked at all this agitation that he offered to sell the fugitive for only $400. The money was quickly raised and George Latimer became a free man.

Other states quickly followed the example of Massachusetts and passed their own Personal Liberty Laws. Slaveholders found themselves on their own when they tried to enforce the Fugitive Slave Law. If slaveholders or their agents made a mistake in identifying a fugitive and captured a free citizen of a northern state, they might find themselves in court facing a kidnapping charge. Dismayed southern lawmakers turned to Congress for help. They demanded a tough new Fugitive Slave Law that would plug the loophole in the Prigg decision, but northern Congressmen of both parties refused to amend the Fugitive Slave Law. The split between slave and free states was growing deeper.

8

CANADA THE PROMISED LAND

On November 25, 1783 the American war of independence was finally over. On that day the last group of British soldiers set sail for England.

Boston King was a fugitive slave who had chosen to enlist in the British army in exchange for freedom. For weeks King, along with 3,000 other black Loyalists, had been waiting to find out whether England was going to honor that commitment. The peace treaty signed in April 1783 promised that England would return all property seized during the war. The Loyalists worried that this agreement included slave property as well. George Washington, speaking for the American government, insisted that slaves were the most important property taken by the British and he demanded that they be return to American slaveholders. General Carleton, who had taken over command of the remaining British forces in America, said no. His government, he told Washington, had made a solemn promise of freedom to their black soldiers and he intended to honor that commitment.

The political struggle lasted all summer but Carleton remained firm. Boston King remembered how "Each of us received a certificate which dispelled all our fears, and filled us with joy and gratitude." [1] On May 4, 1783 a fleet of 300 ships carrying both white and black settlers set sail for the Canadian province of Nova Scotia. Their destination was the sparsely populated harbor town of Birchtown. These black loyalists looked forward to their first experience as free citizens of Great Britain.

The first surprise came when they discovered that their new town, Birchtown, was a satellite community of Shelburne. Shelburne was filled with slaveholding southern loyalists along with their slaves because, in 1783, slavery was still legal in the British Empire. These slaveholders were not eager to welcome a group of black ex- soldiers into any part of Canada. Slaveholders made up a significant proportion

---

[1] Wilson, Ellen Gibson. *The Loyal Blacks*. New York: Capricorn Books, 1976. (Pg. 100)

of Canada's white elite, and they wanted to make sure that black loyalists were isolated and kept far away from their own slaves. Freedom was a "dangerous" ideology which spread quickly through any slave community.

Slaveholders' fears were justified. In the 1790's, before the United States Constitution had been ratified, the Articles of Confederation Government had passed a law banning slavery in the Northwest Territory. That news inspired a trickle of Canadian slaves from Montreal and the Maritime provinces to flee south to this American territory which included the future states of Ohio, Michigan, Illinois, Indiana, and Wisconsin.

The promise of free land had enticed both black and white men to enlist in the British army, and black Loyalists expected the British government to live up to that promise. Thomas Peters, a former slave in North Carolina, had joined the British regiment, Guides and Pioneers. When the war ended Sergeant Peters had become one of the most important leaders of the black Loyalists. Peters reminded Governor Parr in a petition he sent to him in 1784 of the promise made to black Loyalists that they would receive "land & provitions the same as the rest of the Disbanded Soldiers." [2]

A few of the black Nova Scotia settlers received small land grants of fifty acres or less. "The majority received no land. This guaranteed that most newly freed blacks would become a rootless servant class.....their hopes to become independent yeomen were dashed." [3]

Nova Scotia blacks struggled to survive any way they could. Some of the luckier black Loyalists who had received a parcel of land might still have to work part time on someone else's land in order to support their families. Landless blacks were frequently forced to indenturing themselves to a white farmer or businessman for a full year. For some of the more desperate families the contract was simply an exchange of labor for food and other provisions. Other blacks negotiated an indenture contract that called for a small cash payment at the end of the year.

Thomas Clarkston, the British abolitionist, believed that the major problem faced by black Loyalists was the influence of southern white loyalists and some British officers on the Canadian

---

[2] Ibid (pg. 100), [3] Ibid (pg. 101).

government..."made frequent and successful attempts to reduce again to slavery those negroes who had so honourably obtained their freedom." [4]

On July 26, 1784 a race riot broke out in Birchtown. Benjamin Marston , the deputy surveyor of Shelburne, wrote in his diary "Great Riot today. The disbanded soldiers have risen against the Free negroes to drive them out of Town because they labour cheaper than they-the soldiers." Simon Perkins, a Nova Scotia businessman, sent this report to London: "Some thousands of People Assembled with Clubs & drove the Negroes out of the town & threatened Some People." [5] It is no wonder that so many black Loyalists leaped at the chance to leave Canada and help establish the new British African Colony of Sierra Leone.

By 1790 many Englishmen had become troubled at the cruelties of the African slave trade. A powerful movement, led by the great British abolitionists Thomas Clarkson and William Wilberforce, worked to pass a law that would make the African slave trade illegal throughout the British Empire. To make such a law effective they needed a land where rescued Africans might find a new home. The place they selected was Sierra Leone located on the west coast of Africa. This tiny colony had recently been so ravaged by disease that only 64 settlers had survived. The British government had just begun a mass recruiting drive among blacks in order to turn Sierra Leone into a thriving colony.

Thomas Peters had heard about this recruiting drive. The black population of Nova Scotia were so upset over their treatment by white Canadians that many of them talked longingly of a return to Africa. Peters decided to seize the moment. The black leader somehow raised enough money to travel to London. There he met several times with Thomas Clarkson, describing the living conditions of the black Loyalists. Peters told Clarkson that there were hundreds of black Loyalists in Nova Scotia who were eager to help build a new colony in Sierra Leone. On January 21, 1792 a fleet of ships set sail for Africa. Aboard these ships were 1,190 blacks who had chosen freedom in Sierra Leone over semi slavery in Canada.

[4] Wilson, Ellen Gibson. *The Loyal Blacks*. New York: Capricorn Books, 1976. (Pg. 181)
[5] Ibid (Pg. 92-93)

Slavery was becoming a very unpopular institution in Canada. Most Canadians wanted to live in a society where they did not have to compete with slave labor. Soon after the mass exodus of black Loyalists from Nova Scotia provincial governments began passing laws to abolish slavery in their regions. In 1793 the governor of Upper Canada (now Ontario) decided to end slavery in his province, the first of England's colonies to rule against slavery, forty years before England itself abolished the institution.

A few years later a group of African Americans living in Cincinnati, Ohio were facing a crisis. In 1829 the city had just gone through a summer of racial violence with white mobs continually rampaging through the streets of black communities. The city decided it must take action. Rather than controlling the actions of the white gangs, city officials told its black citizens that they were no longer welcome in their city. They were going to enforce an old law that required any black person who settled in their city to post a bond of $500. This was an impossible requirement since the average yearly salary in 1830 was only seventy dollars.

Blacks realized that they were being forced to leave a city that some of them had lived in for years. Hastily they sent a delegation to Canada to ask the question if they would be welcome? The answer they received from the Canadian government was heartwarming. "Tell the Republicans that we royalists do not know men by their color. Should you come to us you will be entitled to all the privileges of the rest of Her Majesty's subjects." [6] The blacks of Cincinnati began packing up in such great numbers that the city fathers began to worry that they were losing a vital part of their work force. They quietly abandoned any attempt to collect the $500 from blacks still living in the city.

Many Cincinnati blacks had already left the city and refused to return. For most of them the trip to Canada was too difficult and expensive so they settled in those northern communities where they felt more welcome. A few families decided that they wanted genuine freedom and they accepted the Canadian government's offer of a new home.

[6] Buckmaster, Henrietta. *Let My People Go: The Story of the Underground Railroad and the Growth of the Abolitionist Movement.* New York: Harper & Brothers, 1941. (Pg. 45)

After Canada abolished slavery a few of the most resolute fugitives decided that they wanted to live in a land that offered them real freedom. The journey to Canada in the early 1800's was a very long and difficult much of it through an uncharted wilderness. By the 1820's there was a small population of black settlers scattered throughout what is now southern Ontario.

When the War of 1812 began Canadian blacks enlisted in overwhelming numbers to fight for their new country, the nation that had given them freedom. The news that black men were fighting side by side with white soldiers spread into slave cabins all over the South. For some slaves planning their escape, Canada seemed like the new Promised Land.

When Cincinnati blacks decided to settle in Canada they did not want to make the same mistakes that had overwhelmed black Loyalists. Land ownership, they believed, was the key to freedom and happiness in their new home. They turned to a few antislavery religious institutions and a handful of wealthy abolitionists to help finance a new colony. Somehow they needed to raise enough money to make a down payment on 4,000 acres just north of modern London, Ontario which would guarantee that the new settlers would not be landless.

Families moved onto their property and began clearing the land, building cabins and a schoolhouse. They invited blacks from America to come and join them. By 1835 the colony, now named Wilberforce, had 166 inhabitants. The new colony faced many problems. Many settlers did not understand that they were supposed to purchase the land that they had been temporarily allowed to farm. They believed that the land had been donated to each new settler as a gift. Some settlers arrived at Wilberforce so destitute that the colonists had to provide long-term food and shelter. The leaders of Wilberforce understood that if the colony was going to thrive it needed to become self- sustaining, but they never understood just how to turn a colony, designed to rescue poverty stricken fugitives, into a thriving farming community. Wilberforce leaders continued to depend on raising money from sympathetic antislavery organizations and philanthropists to keep their colony afloat. Within six years the Wilberforce settlement had disintegrated and its settlers had scattered.

Dawn was a different kind of settlement. It was founded in 1842 by the charismatic black minister, Josiah Henson. Henson was a fugitive slave who may have been the inspiration for Harriet Beecher Stowe's hero, Uncle Tom, in her novel *Uncle Tom's Cabin*. In Henson's autobiography, published in 1849, he tells the story of how he was promised his freedom over and over again by his master. When he realized that his owner was making plans to sell him South, Henson took immediate action. In 1830 the 44-year-old slave along with his wife and four children took off for Canada. In his book Henson describes how he carried his two youngest children on his back, how he was helped by friendly Native Americans as they traveled through the Ohio wilderness, and how on the last lap of the journey friendly sailors hid the family aboard their boat until they reached the safety of Canada.

In the 1830's the province of Ontario was always short of laborers, and Henson quickly found work. He soon became a prosperous farmer. Many of the other fugitives who had found their way to Canada were not as lucky as Henson; they were having trouble surviving. Visitors to the many small black communities scattered around southern Ontario found some of these refugees living in utter destitution. In 1840 Henson decided to create a new colony that would not only rescue these emigrants but teach them the life skills that would help them prosper. He had met two men, Hiram Wilson, a missionary from the American Antislavery Society, and James Canning Fuller, a Quaker from New York who agreed that too many of the refuges needed more help than charitable individuals were able to provide. These two men decided to help Henson finance his new colony. Henson used their money to purchase 200 acres in Dawn Township near the town of Dresden and invited fugitives to join him in the new colony. Soon one could see men clearing the land, planting wheat, corn, and tobacco. At its peak just before the Civil War Dawn had around 500 settlers.

The center of Dawn's community life was the British American Institute, a manual education school that held classes for both children and adults. The Institute had an outstanding reputation and attracted both black and white students from the town of Dresden. Dawn became a center of the Underground Railroad where rescuers were recruited to make the dangerous trip South to rescue family members and friends. Dawn settlers knew that volunteering as a rescuer was not only an extremely dangerous enterprise but an expensive undertaking as well. So many of the refugees had family members still in slavery whom they longed to rescue. Henson's church became a fundraising center for those wanting to hire a rescuer.

Henson was always troubled by the fact that while he was enjoying a life of freedom he had done nothing to alleviate the suffering of his fellow slaves. He decided that he must become a rescuer. Henson's first trip South was to Kentucky to rescue the family of James Lightfoot, a Dawn neighbor and friend. After the Civil War Henson claimed that he personally had rescued dozens of slaves.

Canadians were so impressed by the loyalty and fighting abilities of their black citizens during the War of 1812 that they welcomed every fugitive who managed to flee across the border. Even though prejudice still existed in Canada, there was a world of difference in the way its black citizens were treated. The law itself was color-blind. Canadian blacks could purchase property, sue other Canadians, testify in court, and sit on juries. But to black Canadians their most precious right of all was the right to vote. In 1819 the new Lieutenant Governor of Canada, Sir Peregrine Maitland, established an African American military colony in the wilderness area of Oro Township. The new settlers were veterans of the war, and Maitland was happy that these intensely loyal ex-soldiers would now be part of his first line of defense should hostilities break out again between his government and the Americans.

By the 1820's the Canadian government had developed a policy of refusing to return fugitive slaves to American slaveholders. Even England was feeling the pressure of a growing antislavery movement. In 1826 Albert Gallatin, the American minister to England, after several years of negotiations over the return of runaway slaves, was told that the British government stood by the principle "...that every man is free who reaches British ground." [7]

In the 1820's the Canadian towns that bordered the Detroit and Niagara Rivers were not completely safe for fugitive slaves since slave hunters had no hesitation in crossing over into Canada and kidnapping runaways and returning them to slavery. Toronto became one of the most popular destinations for new emigrants. The city was located on the north shore of Lake Ontario and most slave hunters disliked making such a long and expensive trip through hostile territory. The people of Toronto seemed especially welcoming to the

[7] Bordewich, Fergus M. *Bound for Canaan*. New York: Harper Collins, 2005. (Pg. 247)

fifty black families that had settled in that northern city. There was never any segregation in its churches, schools, or places of public entertainment.

In 1837 a serious rebellion broke out against the Conservative government of Canada. The rebels were demanding major reforms, and some were even talking about an independent Canada. Black settlers were passionately loyal to the Conservative Party which had resolutely protected them against every demand of the United States government. When the government asked for volunteers to put down the rebellion, blacks were quick to respond. Nearly one thousand blacks enlisted in a single month. Josiah Henson was one of the most enthusiastic of these recruits. He led a black militia company that helped defend Fort Malden. Black militia companies had the lowest rate of desertion in the entire colonial forces.

By the 1840's there were around 12,000 black men and women living in Canada among whom were the fugitive slaves Ruth and Thornton Blackburn. They were about to make international history. On the night of June 17,1833 Thornton Blackburn[8] along with his seven rescuers had crossed the Detroit River and landed in Sandwich, Ontario. The men believed that they were finally free, but their ordeal was just beginning.

The sheriff of Ontario's Western District, William Hands had just received a message from the mayor of Detroit, Marshall Chapin, to hold the entire Blackburn party including Ruth Blackburn, because he was about to begin formal extradition proceedings against them under the Fugitive Offenders Act. This was a new agreement just signed by Canada and the United States which delineated under what circumstances suspected criminals who had fled from one nation to the other would be returned for criminal prosecution.

Canadian officials promptly arrested the Blackburns and their party and placed them in the Sandwich jail. The Executive Council of Canada was very cautious about how they ruled on the first case under the Fugitive Offenders Act. The Blackburn case would set the standard for the way all future cases involving fugitive slaves from America would be handled. The agreement required first of all that

---

[8] See Chapter 5; *The Railroad Moves West*. (Pg. 102-103)

there be reasonable proof that a crime had been committed, and that that crime must be of a capital nature. A capital crime was one under which punishment would be death, flogging, or incarceration at hard labor. A final loophole allowed the Lieutenant Governor of Upper Canada (now Ontario) to decide not to extradite a criminal.

The crime that the Blackburns had committed, according to the extradition request, was inciting civil unrest which resulted in an attack against the sheriff. For three days the Canadian government debated the issue. Then on July 19, 1833 they issued this ruling which stated that every man has the right to fight for his freedom, and Thornton Blackburn was simply acting in self defense when he attacked Sheriff Wilson. The Blackburns were freed and welcomed as new citizens. Canada had just amended the Fugitive Offenders Act to exclude fugitive slaves even when they committed an act of violence protecting their liberty.

The Blackburns moved to Toronto where Thornton became a leader of the black community and also one of the important business leaders of the town by establishing the city's first taxi cab system. In 1843 Thornton risked both his new prosperous life and his very freedom when he decided to return to Kentucky and rescue his elderly mother. With help from the Underground Railroad, Thornton made the thousand mile journey to Kentucky to locate his mother. After their tearful reunion, mother and son together made the hazardous trip back to Toronto.

In 1842 Nelson Hackett, a fugitive slave, turned to William Lambert, a member of Detroit's Vigilance Committee for help in crossing the Detroit River. Lambert found a boat and rowed the fugitive across the river. Hackett's former master soon discovered that his runaway was living in Canada and demanded that his slave be returned to him, not because he was a fugitive, but because he was a thief. When Hackett escaped he had also stolen several items belonging to his master.

The Governor General of Canada ordered Hackett's arrest. On the night of February 8, 1842 Hackett was secretly rowed back across the river to Detroit. There was a tremendous uproar all over Canada. The Colonial Office in Britain demanded to know how a runaway who had sought asylum on British soil had somehow been sent back to slavery in America. The British Government decided to issue new orders to make sure that no fugitive would ever again be sent back to America. The new rules demanded that all extradition cases involving a runaway would have to be sent to England for a final decision. Nelson Hackett was the last fugitive slave ever extradited from Canada.

In 1850 the United States Congress passed a tough new Fugitive Slave Law which put runaway slaves and even free African Americans living in the North in danger of being forced back into slavery.[9] The Fugitive Slave Act set off an exodus of blacks from almost every northern city. "One newspaper account estimates that 3,000 fugitive slaves arrived in Canada within weeks of the passage of the... Act." [10]

White Canadians were alarmed by the numbers of black Americans who were seeking safety in their country. The Toronto Colonist on April 27, 1855 stated, "We fear that they are coming rather too fast for the good of the Province...fugitive slaves are by no means a desirable class of immigrants for Canada, especially when they come in large numbers." [11]

Black leaders both in America and Canada knew that they had to deal with the concerns of white Canadians. William Troy, a black minister living in Windsor remembers that, during the 1850's, fugitives were fleeing to Canada at a rate of around 2,000 every year. "Some have come fifteen hundred miles, traveling at night and hiding by day. Coming stripped of nearly everything, many need in the beginning, a helping hand." [12] In order to extend this helping hand, two new settlements were established.

Henry Bibb was born in 1815 in Kentucky. His father was a white slaveholder, but his mother was a slave. As a child Bibb experienced some of the worst features of slavery; his six brothers were sold away; he himself was sold to an abusive master.

Bibb made several attempts to escape but he was always caught. Then, when he was eighteen, he fell in love and married a fellow slave, Malinda, and the couple had a daughter. Now Bibb's escape plans included his wife and baby. In 1837 Bibb escaped to Cincinnati where

---

[9] The Fugitive Slave Law is described in detail in Chapter 9.

[10] Rhodes, Jane. *Mary Ann Shadd Cary*. Bloomington: Indiana University Press, 1998. (Pg. 29)

[11] Frost, Karolyn Smardz. *I've got a Home In Glory Land*. New York: Farrar, Straus and Giroux, 2007. (Pg. 299)

[12] Ibid (Pg. 299)

he made contact with the Underground Railroad. Bibb traveled all the way to Canada, worked hard and saved enough money to return to Kentucky to rescue his family. The first rescue was a failure. Bibb himself was recaptured, but he managed to escape. Bibb tried several more times to rescue his family without success.

In 1842 a heartbroken Bibb finally gave up any further rescue attempts. He settled in Detroit and became an abolitionist lecturer. In 1849 he published his autobiography *Narrative of the Life and Adventures of Henry Bibb an American Slave.* In 1850 after the new Fugitive Slave Law was passed, Bibb and his new wife Mary took off for Canada.

The Bibbs settled in Windsor, Ontario. The couple quickly realized the desperate situation of the new fugitives who regularly arrived in their town. The city of Detroit had grown from a small village to a major city. Its population had grown from a mere three thousand in 1830 to twenty-one thousand in 1850. It was now the busiest terminal on the Underground Railroad. Windsor, the first stop for so many of these refugees, was still a small western village incapable of handling such an unexpected overflow of population. Frederick Douglass in an article written for his newspaper describes what he found when he visited this frontier town. "The vast barracks erected during the last war (1812) may be seen here rapidly falling to decay. They are now occupied by fugitive slaves, and among them both poverty and suffering are visible." [13] Henry and Mary Bibb appealed to friends in the abolitionist and religious communities to help fund a small colony for Windsor's growing fugitive population.

In 1851 the Refuge Home Society invited American blacks to settled on the 2,000 acres the society had just purchased. Each family would get 25 acres. They had to farm the land for three years then they would own five acres. They had nine years to pay for the remaining 20 acres.

Mary, a school teacher, was especially anxious to build a community schoolhouse; education was always a vital part of every black Canadian colony. Henry Bibb also became famous for publishing the first black Canadian newspaper, *Voice of the Fugitive.*

The Bibbs hated the practice of "begging" which meant depending on the antislavery community for funds to support the colony. The couple always hoped for a time when most of the settlers

---

[13] Rhodes, Jane. *Mary Ann Shadd Cary.* Bloomington: Indiana University Press, 1998. (Pg. 35-36)

would become independent farmers able to completely support themselves, but that time never came. Throughout the 1850's Windsor remained a small frontier town with very few businesses, therefore most of the emigrants had no place where they might earn even a small wage. Most new settlers arrived penniless, needing help with food, clothing and seed just to survive. Bibb continued to depend on donations to support the colony. By 1860 the Refugee Home Society was home to one hundred and fifty settlers. Bibb died suddenly in 1854; he was just 39 years old. The colony struggled on under the leadership of Mary Bibb until the end of the Civil War.

For those emigrants, both fugitives and freedmen, who wanted to live among a community of blacks and who had some access to funds, there was another pleasanter option, the Elgin Settlement. William King was a white Presbyterian minister whose wife was the daughter of a wealthy Louisiana *Planter*. When his wife died in 1846 King discovered that he had inherited fifteen slaves from his late father-in-law. King hated slavery and he vowed that he would free these slaves as soon as possible. He realized that simply freeing these slaves was not enough; he felt he had to make sure that they could survive in a hostile world. In 1848 King told the Toronto Presbyterian Synod that he wanted to establish a different kind of colony for fleeing African American blacks, one that would demonstrate what blacks could accomplish once they had their freedom. The Synod became part of a group of shareholders who purchased the nine thousand acres that became the colony of Elgin (also known as Buxton).

When the people of Chatham heard that King was planning to bring hundreds of blacks into the adjacent community, many of them were upset. Local newspapers wrote angry editorials against the proposed colony. Protest meetings were held all over Chatham. Hundreds of people signed petitions hoping that King would organize his new colony someplace else. King ignored the anger of the community and, in 1850, the first settlers, King's fifteen ex-slaves, arrived in Elgin.

King established some very rigid rules for any individual who wanted to join the settlement. First and most important, every member of the settlement must own their own land, and the land could only be owned by blacks. Even King himself could not own land in Elgin. Every individual who purchased land in Elgin signed an agreement that the family must own and farm the land for ten years before they had the right to sell their property. The use of alcohol was frowned upon.

The appearance of the colony was important to King as well. He designed the kind of houses that settlers should build and he gave out prizes each year for the homes with the most curb appeal. A visiting reporter from the *New York Tribune* described to his readers "tidy whitewashed cabins, and gardens blooming with phlox, poppies, and cornflowers." [14]

King and the shareholders understood that the settlement needed more than a community of successful farmers if the colony was going to thrive. They also had to create an assortment of small businesses. Very quickly the Elgin stockholders invested in a sawmill, grist mill, potash and pearl-ash factory. Elgin townsmen also opened a dry goods store, a brickyard and a blacksmith shop. The Elgin settlement even opened its own hotel to accommodate the many guests who flocked into town to see for themselves the most successful black community in Canada.

Class photo in front of the Elgin Settlement School. The only school in Canada built by slaves.
Source: *Buxton National Historic Site*

In 1860 Elgin had 1,200 settlers. The cornerstone of Elgin, and its pride and joy was its school, the Buxton Institute. Most schools in Ontario offered its students a basic education in reading, writing and arithmetic taught by men or women who had just graduated from similar schools themselves. The Buxton Institute offered its students a classical education including Latin and Greek. Its fame

---

[14] Bordewich, Fergus M. *Bound for Canaan; The Underground Railroad and the War for the Soul of America.* New York: HarperCollins Publishers, 2005. (Pg. 392)

spread throughout the Chatham area and white students clamored to be admitted. Buxton became the first, and for many years, the only integrated school in Canada.

Other black Canadians rejected the notion that black emigrants needed protected settlements in order to live a normal happy life in Canada. These groups of emigrants believed that it was important that fugitives show white Canadians that they were as independent a group as any other Canadian pioneer settling in Canada West.

Like the Blackburns many of these new arrivals were attracted to Toronto which soon had a small black community with it's own business and professional leaders. The town of Chatham also became a popular destination. In 1852 Abraham Shadd decided that he had had enough of the Fugitive Slave Law, and he convinced most of his family and several friends to leave Pennsylvania for Canada. Abraham Shadd had been one of the most important leaders of the black community in West Chester, Pennsylvania. He had also operated as one of the most successful stationmasters of the Underground Railroad.

Shadd was one of the organizers of Chatham's Vigilance Committee. Why did he believe that Chatham needed a vigilance committee in a nation where every black person was a citizen? No Canadian black could ever forget the ties that bound them with their black brothers still in slavery. A constant stream of money was needed to finance ex-slaves who longed to rescue family or friends had the funds to make the dangerous trip south themselves or hire a rescuer to do the job for them.

Canadian rescuers were surprisingly successful considering all of the hazards they had to surmount. A great part of their success lay in the fact that they were returning to a community and friends that they knew intimately. They also were familiar with most of the safe houses scattered along the escape route.

There was a second reason that Chatham needed a vigilance committee. Some of the more determined slave owners and slave hunters managed to slip across the border in order to seize runaway slaves. In 1858 Sylvanus Demarest was seized by a white man claiming to be his master. When the train stopped in the Chatham station more than 100 blacks stormed the train and rescued Demarest.

By the middle of the 1850's Chatham had become the center of black Canadian life. It had 800 black settlers, which was 25% of the town's total population. Since Canadian blacks had the right to vote, they became an important political constituency. In 1862 Abraham Shadd was elected alderman for Kent County, the first black man to be elected to public office in Canada.

The most well known of all the Shadds was Abraham's daughter Mary Ann. She had come to Canada in 1850 completely disillusioned with America. She had taken a job as a teacher in the Refugee Home Society. Shadd tried to make the school one that would welcome white as well as black students, but the white community of Windsor refused to attend. She decided to open her own school in the more friendly atmosphere of Chatham. It was hard for Shadd to attract paying students even with the financial support of the American Missionary Association and, after several years of struggle, she was forced to close the school. Teaching alone could never satisfy this enormously gifted woman. At the same time Shadd was struggling to make her school a success, she was also writing an encyclopedia of Canada which became the definitive guide to this northern nation. Her book *Notes of Canada West* was the first detailed study of Canada that informed African Americans what to expect should they decide to move to this northern country. The book told readers that the climate was temperate not frigid as slaveholders had been telling their slaves forever. *Notes of Canada West* described a nation where so much of the land was still unclaimed and was selling for $1.62 an acre. On these unclaimed acres, she told her readers, was valuable timber which could be easily harvested. After the timber was cut they would find that the cleared land was exceptionally good for farming.

While she admitted that prejudice was still a part of Canadian life, it still differed from the racism that every African American experienced living in the United States. Mary Ann Shadd quickly became the most well known advocate for Canadian emigration in North America.

Mary Ann Shadd. *American-Canadian anti-slavery activist*. Source: *Library of Archives, Canada.*

In 1852 Mary Ann Shadd reached out to conquer another new arena. She decided to publish her own newspaper. At a time when women could not even hold property in their own name and, if they worked, their wages belonged to their husbands, it was unheard of for a women to publish a newspaper. But Shadd always ignored barriers. In the beginning there was so much opposition to the idea of a woman publisher, that she asked Samuel Ward, a well known African American abolitionist, and her brother Isaac, to place their names on the masthead of the *Provincial Freeman*. However it was not long before everyone knew who the real publisher of the newspaper was, and, within a few years, her name appeared as the publisher. Shadd was the first black woman to publish a newspaper in North America. After the death of Henry Bibb in 1854, the *Provincial Freeman* became the only black periodical in Canada.

In the spring of 1858 a famous white abolitionist rode into Chatham. John Brown had decided that the only way to end slavery in America was by a revolutionary act. Before he decided on a final plan, he decided to consult with many of the most important black leaders who had chosen to emigrate to Canada. He first met with Martin Delany and the Shadd family. They agreed to hold a secret convention in Chatham.[15] Thirty-four delegates discussed Brown's plans to create Underground Railroad stations throughout the South hidden deep in the Allegheny Mountains. These camps could be defended from attacks by small armed groups of blacks. For some reason, Brown changed his plan. In October 1859 John Brown led a group of black and white guerrillas in an attack on the federal arsenal at Harper's Ferry. One of the members of the raiding party was Osborn Anderson, the Provincial Freedman's young printer. After John Brown and most of the raiders were either captured or killed, Anderson managed to escape. He returned home to Chatham and, together with Mary Ann Shadd, wrote his autobiography, A Voice From Harpers Ferry. This book is the only document we have which tells the inside story of that historic raid.

In 1863 after Lincoln signed the Emancipation Proclamation, many black men who had settled in Canada rushed to enlist in the

[15] See chapter 11, *John Brown at Harpers Ferry.*

Union Army. Among these men was Isaac Shadd. After the war he settled in Vicksburg, Mississippi. He was elected to the Mississippi legislature and became speaker of the House from 1774-1776. Mary Ann Shadd, whose husband Thomas Cary died in 1860, was asked by Martin Delany to become a recruiting agent for the Union army. For two years she traveled throughout the North then after the war she settled down in Washington D.C.

Mary Ann Shadd became one of the few black women to lead the National American Woman's Suffrage Association. She continued her career as a reporter and had many of her articles published in various magazines and newspapers. In 1883 this remarkable women decided, when she was sixty years old, to enter Howard University Law School. Shadd became only the second black woman to practice law in the United States.

Scholars estimate that from the beginning of the Republic to the Civil War over 100,000 slaves found freedom by fleeing slavery. Forty thousand of these fugitives found their way to Canada. Even though this is a relatively small number compared to the total slave population in the South, the very existence of the free nation of Canada made slaveholders seethe. First of all there was the loss of property. In 1860 an adult slave was worth $500. This meant that over the years the South had lost over $20,000,000 in human property.

To American slaves Canada was something even more important than a final destination, a place which most of them would never be able to reach. For years they listened as slaveholders ranted about this northern country where black people, even former slaves, were treated as citizens. Stories of black Canadians in the army, owning land, even voting, spread throughout the slave quarters. Canada became the symbol of The Promised Land.

9

THE COMPROMISE OF 1850 – HAS THE NATION BEEN SAVED?

In 1848 Americans were delighted that the two-year war with Mexico was over. People were celebrating all of the new territories the country had acquired because of the nation's victory. The United States owned not only California, but the New Mexico territory which included the futute states of Arizona,New Mexico, Utah, Nevada and parts of Colorado and Wyoming. Congress settled down to the task of organizing these new lands. Then a disturbing issue cancelled the festivities. What was Congress going to do about slavery in these newly conquered regions?

In 1819 America had experienced its first crisis over slavery when the territory of Missouri petitioned Congress to be admitted to the Union as a slave state. Antislavery feelings in the North flared. Angry meetings were held in Massachusetts, New Jersey, and Pennsylvania demanding that Congress refuse to admit Missouri. In the South equally indignant citizens declared that Congress had no right to bar slaveholders from taking slaves, their legal property, into any territory in the Union. For a time it looked like the Union might split apart. Then in 1820 Kentucky Senator Henry Clay brokered a compromise. Missouri would be admitted to the Union as a slave state while at the same time Maine would be admitted to the Union as a free state, thus maintaining the balance between slave and free states in Congress. However the most significant part of the compromise, any other territory that the United States acquired would have a line drawn known as the Mason-Dixon line. North of this line slavery would banned. Congress believed that it had permanently solved the issue of the expansion of slavery.

Because most of these new lands were south of the Mason-Dixon line southerners expected to bring their slaves into California and most of the New Mexico territories. Northerners disagreed; they felt it was morally wrong to introduce slavery into a region where slavery had been illegal for years (Mexico had outlawed slavery in 1829). Most northerners, whether or not they approved of slavery still wanted the West to remain a land of modest farmsteads not a place that was carved up into large plantations that had to be worked by slave labor. The debate grew so heated that some southern states threatened to secede if their right to bring slavery into these new lands were blocked by Congress.

For nine months the debate over whether or not to allow slavery in the new territories paralyzed Congress. The clashes between those legislators who wanted to expand slavery and those who insisted on a ban became so acrimonious that every issue became a power struggle. Even the most basic task of government became impossible. The House of Representatives was unable to organize a single congressional committee and so in 1849 the House did not pass a single piece of legislation. Everyone agreed that something had to be done to end the crisis but nobody seemed to have an answer.

Senator Henry Clay, the leader of the Whig party, was known to legislators as their greatest negotiator. Clay was the author of the Missouri Compromise and he had a plan that might save the nation from collapse. The senator began by crafting a series of five bills which had to be passed as one package. The bills were designed to give each region a part of what they had been demanding while at the same time both the North and South would relinquish other demands. Clay told northerners that if they gave up their demand that Congress ban slavery from all of the new territories, California would be admitted to the Union as a free state. The senator also told northerners that his Compromise included another important demand the slave trade in Washington D.C. would be banned, although slavery itself would still be legal in the nation's capital.

Southerners did not want to give up California, the richest of the new territories, the land where gold had just been discovered. Southerners dreamed of becoming rich by having their gold mines operated by slave labor. Clay promised southerners that if they gave up California, Congress would pass the toughest fugitive slave law that could be written. Southern legislatures reluctantly agreed to give up California in exchange for a new Fugitive Slave Law. In 1850 southern representatives voted for Henry Clay's compromise.

Northern congressmen were unhappy at the provisions of the new Fugitive Slave Law. This law took the power to decide on the fate of suspected fugitive slaves away from the state courts; instead the new law created special Federal commissioners to decide on the status of suspected runaways. The accused fugitives, under the new law, did not have the right of a trial by jury; they could not even take the stand in their own defense. The owner did not have to appear to identify his slave; his agent had only to swear that the prisoner was the fugitive in question, and the agent was free to carry the fugitive slave back into slavery. There was no appeal from a commissioner's decision. Even more objectionable was the fact that a commissioner would get ten dollars if he returned a fugitive to slavery, and only five dollars if he freed the fugitive. The proposed law would make it a criminal offense to hide a fugitive, hinder slave kidnappers in any way, or try to free a fugitive in custody. Anyone convicted of these acts would have to pay both a large fine as well as serve time in jail. The worst feature of this new law required that any person could be drafted by slave kidnappers into a posse to re- capture a fugitive and, if that person refused to be part of the posse, he would be subject to a sizeable fine. Clay convinced reluctant northern congressmen that, if they did not support the new Fugitive Slave Bill, the South would secede and the Union would be destroyed. On September 4, 1850, after months of angry debates, Clay's compromise was finally passed.

Most Americans, both in the North and the South, rejoiced when the Compromise of 1850 was finally passed. They believed that the issue of slavery, which had been tearing the country apart since 1846, had finally been resolved. Northerners expected that, with the passage of the new Fugitive Slave Law, the threat of southern secession was over. The nation had been saved yet again. One North Carolina Whig wrote that "the firm course of the Administration in the execution of the Fugitive Slave Law has given a new lease to slavery...Property of that kind has not been so secure for the last twenty five years." [1]

Poster created after passing of the Compormise of 1850.
Source: *pixgood.com, political poster collection.*

Other Northerners believed that the Fugitive Slave Law should never have been passed, even to save the Union. Mass resistance to this harsh new law began almost immediately. In Boston, Underground Railroad leaders reacted quickly. On October 14, Boston's Vigilance Committee

---

[1] McPherson, James. *Battle Cry of Freedom: The Civil War Era.* New York: Oxford University Press, 1988. (Pg. 77)

held a protest meeting of 3,500 people in historic Faneuil Hall. The audience took a pledge that they would fight the Fugitive Slave Law by legal means if they could, and illegal means if they must.

The Vigilance Committee was especially worried about Boston's most prominent fugitives, Ellen and William Craft. This couple were among the most popular speakers on the lecture circuit, and they were always the target of slave catchers. Early in October 1850, when a visitor entered William Craft's cabinetmaking shop, Craft was immediately suspicious. The man, Knight, a white person who had worked with Craft in Macon Georgia, pretended to be delighted to see him so successful, and asked William to take him on a tour of Boston. Craft refused and instead asked his friends on the Vigilance Committee to learn more about Knight. They quickly discovered that Knight and his partner Hughes were slave hunters, and that their only reason for being in Boston was to kidnap Ellen and William Craft. When Knight's first attempt at kidnapping William failed, the two men immediately went to court and obtained warrants for the arrest of the Crafts under the Fugitive Slave Law.[2]

The Vigilance Committee sprang into action. Ellen was immediately taken out of the city and hidden at the country home of Dr. Henry Bowdich, a white committee member. William refused to leave; instead he gathered a number of guns, then barricaded himself inside his small cabinetmaking shop. Outside the shop members of Boston's Vigilance Committee mounted guard. "No man could approach within 100 yards of Craft's shop" one reporter observed "without being seen by a hundred eyes, and a signal would call a powerful body at a moment's warning"

Meanwhile, other members of the Committee promptly began a series of legal harassments to force the slave catchers out of Boston. First, they had Hughes and Knight arrested for slander. Bail was set at $10,000. The next day, after the two slave catchers had posted bail, the two men were back in jail charged with the attempted kidnapping of William and Ellen Craft. Bail was set again at $10,000.

The Vigilance Committee also appealed to Bostonians to show their support for the Crafts. The Committee posted handbills all over

---

[2] Blackett, R. J. M. *Beating Against the Barriers: The Lives of Six Nineteenth Century Afro Americans.* Ithaca: Cornell University Press, 1986. (Pg. 92)

the city that described the two slave hunters' physical appearance. Now, in many parts of the city, the two men could not walk on the streets without being accosted by angry crowds shouting "Slave-hunters! Slave hunters!"

As the situation grew more tense, William slipped out of his shop and moved into the home of Lewis Hayden, chairman of the newly organized League of Freedom, a group dedicated to armed resistance in the fight against the Fugitive Slave Law. Hayden had placed kegs of gunpowder in the basement of his house. His black neighbors had armed themselves with guns, swords, and knives in case the kidnapers decided to attack. When Hayden announced that he would blow up his house rather than let William Craft be taken, Hughes and Knight could not find a single marshal willing to arrest William Craft.

Finally, as the two slave hunters left the courtroom after answering another legal charge initiated by the Vigilance Committee, and tried to enter their carriage, they found themselves surrounded by a large, angry mob of blacks. Their coachman whipped the horses into a gallop, but the mob followed. Hundreds joined the chase and the coachman finally stopped, opened the carriage door, and fled the mob. Hughes and Knight were left alone to face the crowd. The two slave hunters were told that if they left town immediately they would not be hurt. They quickly left Boston. When southerners heard about the treatment that the two slave hunters had received in Boston, they were very upset. They wondered if this was a sample of how the North was going to enforce the Fugitive Slave Law.

There was more bad news for southerners. The citizens of Chicago were so outraged when they understood the terms of the new Fugitive Slave Law that they demanded their city government send a resolution to the Federal government protesting the new law. On October 21, 1850, the Chicago City Council adopted a series of resolutions which nullified the law and released city officials from obeying any of its provisions, in direct defiance of the Federal law. In a surprising move, the city council also enrolled a special branch of Chicago's police force, a small cadre of black policemen whose only task was to patrol the streets monitoring every slave catcher prowling the city in search of fugitive slaves.[3]

Resistance to the new law was spreading. Mass meetings were held all over the North protesting the Fugitive Slave Law. Audiences at these meetings vowed that they would never become man hunters no matter what the law required.

On October 8, 1850 a black man was arrested in Detroit as a fugitive. The word spread quickly and, before the fugitive could be brought from the jail to the courthouse, hundreds of armed blacks rushed into the street. The authorities did nothing; in fact, they advised the slaveholder to agree to sell the fugitive in order to avoid bloodshed. Members of the Underground Railroad quickly raised 500 dollars to purchase the fugitive. His owner, who had spent 200 dollars to re-capture his slave, ended up with a paltry 300 dollars for a slave who was worth at least 800 dollars in the slave markets of the South.[4]

The supporters of the 1850 Compromise had not expected such an angry response to the Fugitive Slave Law. Southerners proclaimed that, if the Fugitive Slave Law were not properly enforced, they would secede from the Union. Northern businessmen quickly assured their southern friends that the opposition to the law was the work of only a lunatic fringe, that most responsible Northerners were anxious to support the new law.[5]

In New York City, at a meeting called by prominent merchants, ten thousand people signed a resolution supporting the Fugitive Slave Law as the best way to preserve the Union. When Henry Long, a fugitive slave, was arrested in January, 1851, these same merchants quickly hired one of the most prominent city attorneys to support the right of Long's owner to recover his fugitive. Long was promptly returned to Virginia, and Southerners acknowledged their pleasure over the co-operation they had received from the respectable citizens of New York. Yet even this support left southerners questioning the effectiveness of the Fugitive Slave Law, since the cost of retrieving Long had been one thousand four hundred dollars.

[3] Campbell, Stanley W. *The Slave Catchers*. Chapel Hill: University of North Carolina Press, 1970. (Pg. 54)
[4] Ibid (Pg. 115), [5] Ibid (Pg. 117).

Almost unnoticed in all the furor over the northern response to the Fugitive Slave Law was an event that was occurring on the border between Texas and Mexico. In the summer of 1850 officials in the Mexican village of Piedras Negras were startled to see 200 Seminole Indians led by John Horse and Wild Cat wading across the Rio Grande River into their town. The two chiefs rode up to the town hall and formally asked permission for their band to enter Mexico.

By 1850 John Horse, Principal Chief of the Black Seminoles and his close friend Wild Cat, Principal Chief of his own band of Indian Seminoles, decided that the Indian territories were no longer safe for their people. The demand for slaves had increased dramatically. In 1849 the price of almost any healthy slave, including children, was rising. Slave hunters had moved close to Seminole territory. Now slave hunters were regularly swooping down into the Black Seminole settlements, kidnapping tribesmen, women and children, and selling them to slave traders. John Horse and Wild Cat had been negotiating for many months with Mexican officials for a safe haven. They knew that the northern Mexican border communities were being devastated by raiding Apache and Comanche Indians. Wild Cat and John Horse had offered to use Seminole warriors to protect the settlers on Mexico's northern borders in exchange for a grant of territory so that the Seminole people could establish their own community. The Mexican government agreed. They offered the two chiefs a temporary home in the town of Nacimiento, and a grant of farm land which surrounded the town, in exchange for Seminole protection.

In 1851 John Horse and Wild Cat were leading Seminole warriors in a series of battles, not only against hostile Comanches and Apaches, but also against Jose Carvajal, a man who was leading a rebellion against the government of Mexico. Carvajal wanted to create his own nation in northern Mexico, which he called the Independent and Slaveholding state of the Rio Grande. If Carvajal were successful, not only the freedom of Black Seminoles but that of thousands of other fugitive slaves who had fled to Mexico would be in jeopardy. The Seminoles defeated Carvajal and his rebellious followers, and a grateful government granted the Seminoles Nacimiento as a permanent home in Mexico. The Underground Railroad had a thriving new station in Mexico where slavery was illegal, a safe haven that fugitives could reach simply by crossing the Rio Grande.

Texas slaveholders angrily demanded that the Federal government do something to stop the Mexican government from encouraging American slaves to run away.

In November, 1852, John Horse was visiting Piedras Negras when he was shot during a gun fight. A Texas man, Captain Adams, heard that John Horse was wounded and unconscious and he swiftly crossed the border and captured the Principal Chief of the Black Seminoles. Adams carried his unconscious prisoner across the border to Fort Duncan, Texas. Adams then sent word to Wild Cat that he was demanding a ransom of 500 dollars and a dozen Black Seminole men whom he could sell in American slave markets as payment for John Horse's safe return. Wild Cat agreed to pay the ransom and a few days later a pouch filled with gold was delivered to Adams. The Seminole people were known throughout the West for the scrupulousness with which they regarded a promise. Adams was so confident that he would soon be sent the dozen Black Seminoles that he immediately released John Horse. Then Adams sat down to count his money. He was horrified to discover that each coin had been carefully dipped in blood. Adams got the message and quickly left town.

John Horse was the most revered leader of the Black Seminoles. Legends grew up around his ability to protect his people against the frequent changes in the Mexican government. He kept the Seminoles neutral during all of the bloody struggles for power among Mexico's national leaders. Even his death seemed part of John Horse's legend. In 1882 a crisis developed for the Seminoles in Nacimiento. The original owners of the Seminole territory, the Sanchez family, ignoring the 1852 grant which gave the town of Nacimiento and the surrounding land to the Seminoles in exchange for their services to the government of Mexico, sold the town and the land to an Englishman, John Willett. Willett ordered the Seminoles to leave Nacimiento immediately. The Seminoles turned to the seventy year old John Horse for help. John Horse announced that he would leave for Mexico City immediately to meet with the president of Mexico, Porifiro Diaz.

The next morning John Horse, dressed in his finest clothes, mounted his favorite white horse and rode off. He was never seen again. There is no record that he ever met with Porifiro Diaz and it was assumed that John Horse died sometime during that last trip. Yet, mysteriously, John Willett abandoned his demand to expel the Seminoles from Nacimiento. Black Seminoles are still living in Nacimiento today.

Another challenge to the Fugitive Slave Law came in the city of Boston on the morning of February 15, 1851. Shadrack Minkins, a Virginia fugitive, was seized by a slave-hunting constable from Norfolk, Virginia and rushed into the Boston Court House. Federal officials hoped that the secrecy of the arrest would prevent any of the demonstrations that had so upset southerners when Federal officials tried to capture Ellen and William Craft four months earlier. Legally everything was in place. The constable, John Capehart, had already secured a warrant for Minkins' arrest with papers identifying the prisoner as a fugitive slave belonging to John DeBree.

Daniel Webster was the senior senator from Massachusetts and one of the most respected political leaders in the North. In 1850 he had thrown his support behind the Compromise and, because of his popularity, he had convinced most of the people of Massachusetts to give the Compromise a chance, in spite of their hatred of the new Fugitive Slave Law. Webster, who had just been appointed Secretary of State by President Fillmore, believed that if Shadrack Minkins could be returned without incident to Norfolk it would go a long way toward convincing southerners that the Fugitive Slave Law would be enforced all over the North.

Daniel Webster's hopes were about to be dashed. The news that Shadrack had been arrested had already spread throughout black Boston. When the hearing began, black and white members of the League for Freedom were seated in the courtroom. Other members were massed outside the courtroom waiting to see what would happen. The judge asked Shadrack if he wanted a lawyer because the government was determined to follow the letter of the law. It was unclear just what a lawyer could do for Minkins since he could not testify or call any black man in his defense, but Minkins firmly announced that he wanted one. A half hour later, two lawyers representing Boston's Vigilance Committee marched into the courtroom. They insisted that they needed more time to prepare their case, so the hearing was adjourned for three days. As the deputy marshal attempted to clear the courtroom one tall black man called out to Shadrack, "Don't be afraid; We'll stand by you." That black man was Lewis Hayden. When he heard these encouraging words Shadrack Milkins straightened up to his full height, stripped off his coat and with a determined look spoke to his supporters. "If I die I die like a man!" [6]

Marshal Patrick Riley immediately cleared the courtroom. By 12:30 only Riley, five deputies and one of Shadrack's lawyers, Robert Morris, the first black lawyer to be admitted to the Massachusetts bar, and a white reporter, Elizur Wright, remained in the courtroom. Outside the courtroom the crowd refused to leave and, in fact, had grown larger.

Meanwhile Marshal Riley was struggling with his own problem. He could not put Minkins in the city jail because using the jail was illegal under the Massachusetts Personal Liberty Law. No one had yet figured out if the new Fugitive Slave Law superceded the Personal Liberty Law. Nervous about breaking the Personal Liberty Law, Boston's policemen were reluctant to aid the Federal marshals. Finally, Marshal Riley decided to detain Minkins in the courtroom until he could find a safe place to hold his prisoner overnight. Meanwhile Wright began taunting Riley about his role as a slave hunter. Angrily Riley ordered Wright to leave and opened the door a crack to push the reporter out of the courtroom.

This was the break that Hayden had been waiting for. The rescuers shoved aside the marshals guarding the door and forced open the courtroom door. As the crowd streamed in, Shadrack pulled away from the marshals guarding him, even though Riley called out to him that, if he tried to escape, he would be shot. In the melee that followed, an officer named Byrnes called out, "Kill the big nigger." Elizur Wright, who had been forced back into the courtroom by the surging rescuers, hollered back, "Not in this courtroom you don't." [7] Twenty rescuers seized Minkins and rushed him down the stairs. The marshals tried to follow but, by the time they reached the steps of the courthouse, Shadrack had disappeared somewhere inside the black community. Marshals forced their way into over one hundred homes of black Bostonians and searched them from top to bottom. They were especially diligent in searching Hayden's house, but Minkins seemed to have completely vanished. While all the searching was going on, Minkins was hiding in the attic of an elderly black woman, Mrs. Elizabeth Riley, a woman of such complete respectability that her home was never entered.

---

[6] Collison, Gary. *Shadrack Minkins: From Fugitive Slave to Citizen.* Cambridge, Massachusetts: Harvard University Press, 1997. (Pg 121)

[7] Ibid (Pg. 126)

When it was dark and the marshals had left the area, Hayden appeared at Mrs. Riley's doorstep in a rented cab. Shadrack quickly stepped inside and Hayden drove him to Cambridge. The next day Hayden drove Shadrack 15 miles to Concord. From Concord Shadrack traveled north on the Underground Railroad until he reached Montreal, Canada. He was finally free. Boston abolitionists were jubilant. They were proud that they had carried on Boston's most cherished tradition, that no fugitive slave had ever been turned over to slave hunters in the city of Boston.

Conservative Bostonians, on the other hand were outraged. "Mob law triumphs" complained the *Boston Daily Courier*.[8] On February 18, the Mayor and Board of Aldermen ordered the City Marshal to make the whole police force available to any Federal marshal who requested their help if there was ever another attempted rescue of a fugitive slave from a Federal courtroom.

In Washington the Federal government was even more upset. Secretary of State, Daniel Webster, fumed that Shadrack's rescue was treason. President Fillmore called an emergency cabinet meeting and then issued a proclamation demanding that Boston officials put those rescuers on trial. Senator Henry Clay defended his Compromise by reminding southerners that it had been only black men who were responsible for Shadrack's rescue, sabotaging the Fugitive Slave Law and subverting his hard won Compromise. Clay asked his Senate colleagues whether a "government of white men was to be yielded to a government of black men." [9]

The government immediately arrested Elizur Wright, Robert Morris, Lewis Hayden, Shadrack's other attorney Charles Davis, and four more suspected rescuers for the crime of disobeying the Fugitive Slave Law. Hayden's trial was held first. Although Hayden's defense team produced witnesses who claimed that at the time of the rescue Hayden was at home eating lunch, there were other witnesses, including U.S. marshals, who claimed that Hayden was the leader of the rescuers. The jury debated for hours, then announced that they could not agree on a verdict. Eleven jurors had consistently voted guilty but one juror refused to agree with the majority and continued to vote not guilty. The judge was forced to declare a mistrial. Abolitionists often wondered about why this one juror had

---

[8] Ibid (pg 136)

[9] Levy, Leonard W. "*The Sims Case: The Fugitive Slave Law in Boston*". Journal of Negro History, January 1950. (Pg. 41)

been so strongly in favor of Hayden's innocence. Richard Henry Dana learned the real reason for Hayden's mistrial a year later when he was chatting with a new acquaintance. The man asked if Dana had been one of Shadrack's attorneys. Dana nodded and they both began to talk about the case. When Dana commented on his gratitude towards the one juror who voted for Hayden's acquittal, his new acquaintance just smiled and then announced, "I was the twelfth juror in that case, and I was also the man who drove Shadrack over the state line." [10]

President Millard Fillmore and his Secretary of State, Daniel Webster, knew that it was crucial to prove to Southerners that the Federal government would enforce the Fugitive Slave Law even in that hotbed of abolitionism, Boston. The two men made plans to mobilize Federal troops the moment another fugitive was arrested in that defiant city. That moment came just two months later on April 3 when Thomas Sims was arrested on a warrant claiming that he was the fugitive slave of James Potter. It was nine o'clock in the evening when two police officers spotted Sims outside his home and tried to arrest him. Sims fought back; he whipped out a knife and tried to stab one of the officers, but was quickly overpowered by other members of the posse. As the police forced him into a waiting carriage Sims cried out in anguish, "I'm in the hands of kidnappers." [11] Sims' frantic cry was heard by neighbors who quickly informed members of Boston's Vigilance Committee.

The next morning, citizens of Boston woke up to the most astonishing sight. The City Marshal, Francis Tukey, had ordered iron chains to be wrapped around the entire courthouse. The sidewalks leading to the courthouse door were also barricaded with a series of ropes and chains. The door was so covered by chains that anyone doing business in the courthouse had to bend down almost to the floor and crawl under the chains to enter the building. Even judges attempting to enter their own courtroom had to endure this humiliating procedure. Five hundred policemen patrolled the area, and no one but authorized persons were permitted by the police to enter the courthouse. The Federal government and Boston officials were determined that this time there would be no humiliating rescue.

---

[10] Strangis, Joel. *Lewis Hayden and the War Against Slavery.* North Haven, Connecticut: Shoe String Press, 1999. (pg 79)
[11] Levy, Leonard W. "Sims Case: The Fugitive Slave Law in Boston in 1851" *Journal of Negro History* January 1950 (pg 44)

While the lawyers of Boston's Vigilance Committee wrote a series of brilliant appeals addressed to state and federal judges, challenging Sims' arrest, other committee members were already planning another spectacular rescue. They sent an urgent message to the white Unitarian minister, Thomas Wentworth Higginson, to travel to Boston immediately. The twenty-eight-year-old minister, a member of Boston's Vigilance Committee, had been explaining to his Newburyport congregation that, because the Fugitive Slave Law was a law against God's law, they had a right to use violence to protect fugitive slaves. Higginson arrived in Boston that evening, ready to plan the rescue of Thomas Sims. The key player in the rescue of Sims was going to be the Reverend Leonard Grimes.

After his release from the Richmond jail, Grimes decided to leave Washington, moving to Boston to become a Baptist minister. In 1848 Grimes was invited to asume the pastorship of the 12th Street Baptist Church. Grimes' new church was struggling; it had only twenty-three members, but, by the time Thomas Sims became a member of the congregation, its membership had grown to two hundred and fifty. The church was known throughout Boston as the Church of the Fugitives because so many of its members were fugitive slaves.

Reverend Grimes was essential to the rescue of Sims because he was the only person who would be able to discuss the Vigilance Committee's escape plans with Sims. Jail had not tamed Grimes' spirit, so when Vigilance Committee members asked him to deliver their message to Sims, Grimes immediately agreed. The marshals tried to keep Grimes from meeting with Sims, but he insisted that Sims had the right to religious counsel by his minister. On Wednesday Grimes entered the courtroom and told Sims about the rescue plan organized by the Vigilance Committee This dangerous plan would require immense courage and trust from Sims. The room where the trial was being held was on the third floor of the courthouse, and Higginson had noticed that one window in that room had no grating. Grimes told Sims that the only way that he could escape was through this window. Grimes told Sims that, at a set hour that evening, he was to casually stroll over to the window as if for a breath of fresh air and then jump out of the window onto the street below. Timing was everything in this desperate escape. The Committee promised that, minutes before Sims made his leap for freedom, they would lay mattresses on the street to break his fall and a fast carriage would be waiting to whisk him to freedom. Sims told Grimes that he would rather die than remain a slave, so he enthusiastically agreed to the plan. Dusk was falling when Higginson and a friend strolled down the street and turned into Court Street. Looking up at the window where they expected to see Sims getting ready for his heroic leap, they saw instead workmen busily fitting iron bars into the windows. Behind them Higginson saw the mournful face of Thomas Sims. There would be no escape that evening.

On Friday Sims' last appeal was rejected by the court. An unhappy group of Vigilance members met that night in William Lloyd Garrison's newspaper office, desperately seeking some other way to rescue Sims. At about three o'clock in the morning they looked out of the window and saw an unbelievable sight. Hundreds of armed policemen and volunteers were beginning to gather in front of the courthouse. At four- fifteen in the darkness, the main doors of the Courthouse swung open and Sims, surrounded by armed guards was escorted down the steps. Tears were streaming down his face as he viewed the armed force assembled to send him back to slavery. Rescue was out of the question. The mayor and City Marshal Tukey ordered the troops to begin marching. Only a small group of abolitionists watched as Sims was escorted down the street toward the docks. They cried out "Shame! Infamy! Where is Liberty!" Some abolitionists tried to break through the lines but they were pushed back by police holding swords. Finally the troops reached Long Wharf where the brig Acorn, owned by a Boston merchant who had donated it to the government, waited to return Sims to slavery. Sims was quickly moved aboard and the ship sailed away. Sims was delivered to Savannah,where he was publicly lashed thirty nine times.

The newspaper, *Commonwealth,* spoke for all the "respectable" citizens of Boston when they happily stated that "Boston is redeemed... the Fugitive Slave Law has been enforced." [12] Southern politicians, who had fought for the passage of the Fugitive Slave Law, boasted that 15,000 of Boston's most wealthy and respected citizens had thrown their support behind the law. Perhaps the South would now be reassured that the Fugitive Slave Law would be enforced even in Boston. Yet what none of these respected leaders talked about was the fact that It had cost twenty thousand dollars to return Sims to slavery. Two weeks later antislavery Bostonians had their revenge against Daniel Webster. Webster's Senate seat had remained vacant ever since the senator had become the new Secretary of State. Now the

---

[12] Ibid (Pg. 74)

Massachusetts Legislature elected Charles Sumner, one of the most radical abolitionists in Massachusetts, to take Webster's old seat.

(During the Civil War a fugitive slave crossed over into the Union lines and volunteered to enlist in the army. It was Thomas Sims. After the war he returned to Boston, a free man at last.)

Syracuse, New York was very different from Boston. The city did not have any rich cotton merchants or ship owners who wanted the North to placate the slaveholding South. Syracuse citizens were free to express their indignation at the new Fugitive Slave Law. On October 4,1850, hundreds of people crowded into City Hall to protest the law. The mayor chaired the meeting, and speaker after speaker stood up and proclaimed their opposition. Then J. W. Loguen, one of the most popular black ministers in Syracuse, mounted the podium. He looked over the crowd and announced to the surprise of all that he was a fugitive slave. He told the assembly that, under the terms of the Fugitive Slave Law, he could be kidnapped at any time and sent back into slavery. The crowd gasped in surprise. He told the assemblage that many of his friends had begged him to take his family and flee to Canada, but Loguen declared that he was determined to stay in Syracuse and fight for his right to live in his own home among his own people. He asked the audience if they would support him, "whether you will permit the government to return me and other fugitives who have sought asylum among you to the Hell of slavery. Whatever may be your decision, my ground is taken...I don't respect this law..I won't obey it! ..I will not live a slave, and if force is employed to re-enslave me I shall make preparations to meet the crisis as becomes a man... If you will stand with us in resistance to this measure, you will be the saviors of your nation." [13] The audience cheered loudly as Mayor Hovey announced: "The colored man must be protected---he must be secure among us." [14] The meeting went on to denounce Daniel Webster, who until now had been one of the most beloved senators in the North, and President Fillmore for approving the law. Finally the crowd called for the city to organize an official Vigilance Committee whose job would be to protect every fugitive in Syracuse.

One week later on October 12, City Hall was again jammed with people waiting to hear how the Vigilance Committee was going to keep the Fugitive Slave Law out of Syracuse. The mayor and city

[13] Loguen, J.W. *The Rev. J. W. Loguen as a Slave and as a Freeman: A Narrative of Real Life.* New York: Negro University Press, 1968. (Pg. 398)
[14] Ibid (Pg. 395)

leaders, along with the rest of the assembly, stood and cheered when the Committee chairman read their resolution announcing that: "No man shall be taken from Syracuse a slave, and no power shall force the fugitive slave law upon it." [15] The president of the Syracuse and Utica Railroad added to the roars of approval when he announced that he had given orders to his men that if they saw any fugitive slave in irons being put into any of his railroad cars they should stop the train, take off his irons, and set him at liberty.

When Daniel Webster visited Syracuse later that year and heard about the anti-Fugitive Slave Law protests he told the people that their proposed resistance to the law was treason. He declared that the Fugitive Slave Law would be executed everywhere, including Syracuse. Yet in spite of Webster's fiery attack, Loguen, the most public fugitive slave in America, remained free.

Monument to Jerry Rescue, Syracuse, New York.
Credit: Debra Millet, Source: *Dreamstime.com*

There were other fugitives living in Syracuse who agreed with Loguen's choice. Jo Norton who, since his escape from slavery had become a popular lecturer on the local abolitionist circuit, told his friends that Syracuse was his home, his business was thriving, his children were happy in school and besides, he declared, there were not men enough in Virginia to carry him out of this city.

On August 1, 1851, the United States government decided it must enforce the Fugitive Slave Law in Syracuse. The city was

---

[15] Ibid (Pg. 397)

hosting the State Convention of the radical anti-slavery Liberty Party. The delegates included many of the most important white abolitionist leaders of the area, including the pacifist minister Samuel May, the wealthy radical Gerrit Smith, along with black militants J. W. Loguen, Samuel Ward, and Jo Norton. The session had just begun when a man rushed into the hall and shouted that a government marshal had just arrested one of our fugitives and that he was being held in the office of U.S. Commissioner Sabine. Instantly the convention voted to adjourn and they all began marching to the commissioner's office. Meanwhile one of the delegates, William Crandall, rushed to the Presbyterian church and began ringing the bell. Instantly all the churches in the town began ringing their bells as well.

As the Commissioner began a preliminary hearing, Gerrit Smith pushed his way into the hearing room and sat down beside the fugitive, Jerry McHenry, and announced that he would be representing the fugitive slave. "Will the crowd support me"? McHenry asked Smith. Smith told the fugitive that the courtroom was filled with his friends. McHenry immediately jumped across the defense table and fled the courtroom. The crowd opened a path for him then formed a tight line to prevent the deputies from pursuing the fugitive. McHenry only got a few blocks before he was recaptured. The Vigilance Committee, deeply impressed by the courage of McHenry, vowed that they would not let the slave catchers take him out of Syracuse. They immediately began planning McHenry's rescue.

The government, worried about the crowd gathering in the street outside the courthouse, decided to hold an immediate trial. The marshal hoped that the proceedings would be over quickly and he could leave with his prisoner before nightfall. But so many citizens pushed their way into the courtroom that the judge decided to adjourn the trial for supper while the marshal and his deputies stood guard over McHenry. The nervous marshal watched as the crowd in the street increased hourly. The marshal shouted out of the window that he was armed and would shoot anyone who attempted to rescue the prisoner.

This threat did not bother the leaders of Syracuse's Vigilance Committee, who were ready to begin McHenry's rescue. Jo Norton gave a signal and suddenly a group of stout black men appeared carrying a twenty foot long log on their shoulders. At Norton's command this battering ram was hurled at the outside door and, as soon as the door was smashed, Norton led the rescuers up the stairs waving a crowbar in his hands. They reached the door to the room where McHenry was being held. Norton battered down the door and the marshal fired at the rescuers. Norton attacked the marshal, who then fled by jumping out of the window. The rescuers tied up the remaining deputies and began searching for McHenry. They heard his call coming from an inner room and quickly broke down the door. The rescuers found McHenry bound and chained, lying almost naked on the floor. He was covered with blood, and they could see that he had a broken rib from the beating he had received. The rescuers had to carry the fugitive down the stairs because he was too weak to walk. When the crowd saw McHenry emerge from the courthouse they began cheering. He was quickly put into a carriage drawn by a white horse and driven off. As part of the rescue plan, dozens of other carriages also drawn by white horses immediately began driving out of the city. The pursuers were completely baffled. McHenry was taken to a safe house until his wounds healed and he could regain his strength. Then he was taken in stages to Oswego where a friendly sea captain took him across the lake to Kingston, Ontario.

The United States Government, frustrated by these defiant New Yorkers, promptly arrested twenty-four of the most respected citizens of Syracuse for the crime of "constructive treason." Samuel May, Charles Wheaton, and Gerrit Smith were some of the New Yorkers now facing prison. There was an arrest warrant issued for Jermain Loguen, but he was finally convinced by his family that he was in extreme danger and took off for Canada. Jo Norton also fled when he discovered that slave hunters were already on his trail.

The United States attorney ordered the arrested men to be brought to Auburn for questioning. To his astonishment, one hundred citizens of Syracuse accompanied the prisoners. The U.S. attorney demanded that the court set a bond for each of these so called criminals and, to the attorney's great discomfort, William Seward, governor of the State of New York, was the first man to sign the note for the bond. The twenty-four men were never tried; the government found it almost impossible to mount a case. The town of Syracuse celebrated the "Jerry Rescue" every year as a civic holiday until after the Civil War.

The Vigilance Committee of Philadelphia was at the center of that city's resistance to the Fugitive Slave Law. William Still organized a special committee to watch the activities of slaveholders and their agents. When Edward Gorsuch appeared before the

The Christiana Tragedy.
Source: *Library of Congress, Prints and Photographs Division.*

Philadelphia commissioner asking for a warrant for the arrest of four of his fugitives living in Christiana, Still sent an urgent message to William Parker telling him that Deputy Marshall Henry Kline, Edward Gorsuch and his son had organized a posse and were already on their way to Christiana. Parker immediately called for a meeting of his vigilance team. Seven men, including two of Gorsuch's fugitive slaves, immediately moved into Parker's house and waited.

At dawn Henry Kline led his posse of fifty men up to Parker's door and demanded that, under the terms of the Fugitive Slave Law, he open the door and let his men in to search for the fugitives. Parker appeared at his window shouting to Kline to get away from his house. Kline then ordered his men to pile straw around the house, then set the piles on fire to force the fugitives out. While Parker and Kline shouted at each other, Eliza Parker (William's wife) crept up to the attic and began blowing on a horn: this was the signal to the neighbors that the slave hunters were attacking their house. Kline demanded to know why she was blowing the horn and he ordered his men to shoot her. Eliza crouched down below the window and continued to blow the horn while bullets pelted around her.

Kline, worried that the horn might be some kind of signal, gave the order to attack. He believed that the battle would be over quickly because there were just a few desperate men in the house. Then he looked up and saw an army of black men marching towards him. The battle of Christiana had begun. By noon Edward Gorsuch lay dead upon the ground; his wounded son lay close beside him. Marshal

Kline, who had also been wounded, had fled into the fields to hide. William Parker and the fugitives hiding in the house disappeared from Christiana.

The United States government was horrified by the battle of Christiana. Politicians had never expected this kind of defiance of the Fugitive Slave Law. Federal troops were sent into Christiana to restore order and arrest the black vigilantes. The government arrested thirty African Americans, most of whom were not even remotely connected with the fighting. They combed the area searching for Parker and the other members of his vigilance committee but they never found them. Government officials arrested Eliza Parker and her sister, but they soon released the two women because they realized how foolish they would look charging two women with leading a major rebellion against the Fugitive Slave Law.

Instead,the government arrested two white Quakers. These men had stood in front of the Parker house begging both sides to stop fighting. Kline had turned to them and demanded that the Quakers join the posse. The men indignantly refused Kline's order reminding the deputy that the Quaker religion forbade its followers to participate in violence of any kind. Now Kline insisted on their arrest under the clause in the Fugitive Slave Law that made it illegal to refuse to join a posse pursuing a fugitive slave.

The trial became national news when the government announced the indictment that they were leveling against the two Quakers, along with thirty-eight black men. It was treason! This was the first time in American history that men and women, whose only crime was helping fugitive slaves escape, would be tried for such a crime. Congressman Thaddeus Stevens, one of the defense lawyers, laughed out loud over this ridiculous charge. He asked the jury to carefully consider this indictment "That two non-resisting Quakers and thirty-eight Negroes armed with corn cutters, clubs and a few rusty muskets, headed by a miller in a felt hat, without coat or arms, levied war against the United States? Blessed be God our Union survived such a shock." [16]

People around the country rushed to the defense of the prisoners with both money and powerful political pressure. The prisoners began to be treated as heroes rather than criminals. Some of the black

[16] Buckmaster, Henrietta. *Let My People Go: The Story of the Underground Railroad and the Growth of the Abolitionist Movement.* Boston: Beacon Press, 1941. (Pg. 210)

prisoners mysteriously disappeared from jail and were never found.

In spite of all this pressure, the Federal government was determined to make the Christiana trial the test of the Fugitive Slave Law, especially that portion of the statute that made resistance to the law a treasonous crime. The government's determination to punish the forty defendants for treason was rather difficult since the real leaders of the Christiana riot, William Parker and the members of his Vigilance Committee had all escaped arrest.

The government could not prove that the thirty-eight blacks and two Quakers had ever been involved in the rebellion. It took the jury only twenty minutes to declare the defendants not guilty. Southerners were very angry that the people of Pennsylvania had refused to convict any of the defendants who had defied the Fugitive Slave Law and were responsible for the death of a southerner.

The Underground Railroad had sent William Parker north. All during the trial he had been hidden in the home of his old friend, Frederick Douglass. When it was finally safe to leave this sanctuary, he made his way to Canada where he was greeted with the news that the Governor of Pennsylvania was demanding his extradition on the charge of murder. Parker asked for a meeting with Canada's Governor General, Lord Elgin. Canadian government officials met to discuss the extradition request. When the meeting was over Lord Elgin emerged from his office and announced to Parker "You are as free a man as I am." [17]

When *Uncle Tom's Cabin* was published in 1851 it immediately became a literary phenomenon. It first appeared as a serial in the magazine, *National Era*. It was so popular that, in 1852, it was published as a book. Ten thousand copies were sold in only a few days. By year's end, three hundred thousand copies had been sold in the United States alone. The book became an international best seller translated into thirty-seven different languages including Arabic and Armenian. Seventy-five editions were published in Germany alone. No one has ever been able to put a figure on how many books were sold worldwide.

Uncle Tom's Cabin was made into a play which packed the New York City theater for months, and toured every northern city to overflow audiences. The play was also produced in Europe where it was so popular that in both London and Paris the play ran in two

---

[17] Bacon, Margaret Hope. *Rebellion at Christiana*. New York: Crown Publishers, Inc. 1975. (Pg. 190)

theaters at the same time.

Uncle Tom's Cabin had a political impact that had never been seen before and has never been equaled since. The story of *Uncle Tom's Cabin* seems to have reached almost every citizen in the North. It became the Bible of America's anti-slavery movement.

Southern politicians began to question whether they should have voted for the Compromise of 1850. They had given up California in exchange for the new tough Fugitive Slave Law, but that law had not stopped the flow of fugitives fleeing North. In fact, it seemed to worried slaveholders that the Underground Railroad was growing even stronger. Daniel Webster tried to calm the fears of southerners by pointing out to them that the most influential citizens in the North were doing everything in their power to enforce the law. Webster insisted that it was only a small minority of radicals who were resisting the law. Have patience, he pleaded with them, and the Fugitive Slave Law will soon be enforced all over the North.

Southerners were becoming skeptical. Even when a fugitive was returned to an owner, it was not necessarily a complete victory. For example when the fugitive Henry Long was arrested in New York City, the actual cost of returning Long to Virginia was $2,250. Most of this money had been raised by New York City businessmen, anxious to convince southerners that they wholeheartedly supported the Fugitive Slave Law. Long was quickly sold for $750, but many slaveholders wondered how effective the new law really was if the cost of recovering a fugitive exceeded his actual value as slave property.

The Compromise of 1850 was supposed to bring peace to the nation, but an uneasy South watched as the Fugitive Slave Law created an anti-slavery mood that swept through the North. This mood became a tidal wave when the Kansas territory was ready for statehood.

10
KANSAS BLEEDING KANSAS

In 1854 Kansas settlers petitioned Congress to allow their region to organize as a legal territory of the United States, the first step in becoming a state. This routine request would launch one of the greatest political crises in American history.

Stephen A. Douglas, Democratic senator from Illinois, hungered to be the next president of the United States. In 1854 he saw his chance to win southern support for his candidacy. In the midst of a routine debate on the organization of the Kansas territory, Douglas stood up and proposed that the Kansas territory be divided into two states, Kansas and Nebraska, and that each state decide for itself whether or not they wanted to be slave or free. He called his proposal "Popular Sovereignty." Since both Kansas and Nebraska were north of the Mason Dixon line, Douglas was proposing that slaveholders be allowed the right to bring slaves into territory where slavery had always been barred. Popular Sovereignty would overturn the Missouri Compromise which so many Americans believed had saved the nation in 1820.

To many southerners, the Compromise of 1850 had been a bitter failure. They had reluctantly given up one of their most important demands, that California enter the Union as a slave state, in order that Congress would pass a powerful new Fugitive Slave Law. Slaveholders had believed that this tough new law would weaken the Underground Railroad and stop the flow of runaway slaves. Unfortunately for them the law was not working. Slaves, especially in the upper South, were running away in ever increasing numbers. Slaveholders were also appalled at the way in which northerners were flouting the Law. Southern newspapers were filled with stories about mass protests against the Fugitive Slave Law, as well as reports about the spectacular rescues of a few fugitive slaves. Southerners were convinced that the new Fugitive Slave Law was a failure. They may have been right about the failure of the new law. From 1850 to 1860 only about two hundred escaped slaves were returned by order of Federal commissioners to their former owners.

Sophisticated southern leaders were facing a new, more complex problem. So many people from northern states were moving westward that Southerners worried that, in time, there might be more free states than slave ones. If that happened the balance of power in Congress would tip toward the North. A key group of southern leaders were beginning to discuss secession as the only way to preserve their slave society. When Douglas introduced the idea of Popular Sovereignty, southerners hoped that the Kansas Nebraska Act would restore the balance between slave and free states, and allow the South to maintain its control of Congress.

Missouri slaveholders had a more urgent reason to support passage of the Kansas Nebraska Bill. Their state was already surrounded by the free state of Illinois to the east and Iowa to the north. If Kansas became a free state Missouri would be bordered by free states on three sides, and the danger of losing even more slave property would be increased. Slaveholders in Missouri insisted that Congress support Popular Sovereignty because "there was great danger that too many of their slave property which might take legs and run." As one newspaper, the *Westport Frontier News* warned its readers: "We every day see handbills offering rewards for runaway negroes from Jackson and neighboring counties. Where do they go? There is an underground railroad leading out of western Missouri.[1]

On May 22, 1854, after three months of bitter Congressional arguments, capped with seventeen hours of continuous debate, the Kansas Nebraska Act was passed. Conservative northerners, who had supported the Compromise of 1850 for the sake of national harmony, felt betrayed. Many northerners announced that if the South chose to repeal the Missouri Compromise then they were released from enforcing the Fugitive Slave Law.

In New York City members of the Union Safety Committee, who had been the most active supporters of the Fugitive Slave Law during the struggle over the capture of the fugitive slave Sims, after the passage of the Kansas Nebraska Act suddenly changed their minds. The committee held a huge meeting in New York City protesting both the Kansas Act and the Fugitive Slave Law. New England clergymen, who in the past had been very critical of the abolitionist protesters,

---

[1] Goodrich, Thomas. *War to the Knife: Bleeding Kansas 1854-1861. Mechanicsburg, Pennsylvania:* Stackpole Books, 1998. (Pg. 48)

decided to become protesters themselves. These religious leaders collected 3,000 clergy signatures on a petition to Congress protesting the repeal of the Missouri Compromise.[2]

Senator Stephen Douglas soon found out that, instead of becoming the leading Democratic presidential candidate, the Kansas Nebraska Act had made him unpopular all over the North. When he traveled home in August he stopped to give a series of lectures on the new act. He got cold receptions wherever he held public meetings and, in one New Jersey town, Douglas was actually booed. The popular senator discovered that he was now in deep trouble even in his own state of Illinois. On September 1, 1854 Douglas arrived in Chicago and announced that he would hold a mass meeting in the public square that evening to defend his Kansas Nebraska Act. It did not take long before he discovered just how formidable a task it was going to be. That afternoon all the flags in the harbor were lowered to half mast, and an hour before Douglas was to address the public, church bells began to toll as if announcing the death of a prominent person. Ten thousand people had gathered in the square. As Douglas mounted the podium he was greeted only with an ominous silence. Then as he began to defend his law the boos and hisses began. The senator continued with his impassioned speech but the angry crowd grew louder and soon drowned out the speaker. Douglas tried to get the crowd to listen but at midnight he gave up and stalked angrily out of the square.

Two days after the passage of the Kansas Nebraska Act, Anthony Burns, a fugitive slave, was arrested in Boston. It was a quiet spring afternoon, Burns had just locked the door of the clothing store where he worked as a clerk and had started to walk up the street when he was stopped by Deputy Marshal Butman. A small curious crowd gathered and asked what was going on. Butman replied that Burns was

Rendition of Anthony Burns. Source: *ClipArt Etc.*

[2] Campbell, Stanley W. *The Slave Catchers: Enforcement of the Fugitive Slave Law 1850-1860*. New York: W. W. Norton Company, 1968. (Pg. 84)

being arrested for breaking into a jewelry shop. Suddenly a group of men rushed out of the shadows, seized Burns and dragged him across the street to the courthouse where he was confronted by his master Colonel Charles Suttle of Virginia.

At nine o'clock the next morning, attorney Richard Henry Dana was walking past the courthouse on the way to his office when he was stopped by a man who told him that a fugitive slave was being held in the courthouse. Dana rushed to the courthouse and demanded to see Burns. The lawyer walked into the room where Burns was being held and offered his services. Burns was extremely depressed and he also was not sure he could trust this white lawyer. He told Dana that he did not want to fight the charges because "They will get me back and if they do I shall fare worse if I resist." [3]

The next morning Burns had another visitor, his minister, Leonard Grimes. Grimes told Burns that he was not alone because he had friends and one of these friends was Richard Dana. That afternoon when Dana met with Burns he found a changed man; Burns was now eager to fight for his freedom.

The Boston Vigilance Committee had decided on a quick rescue of Burns. The day after his arrest, Lewis Hayden and Thomas Higginson led a small group of black and white rescuers up the stone steps of the courthouse and began battering down the door. There was a brief struggle between the rescuers and the armed guards, but the rescuers were outnumbered and they were forced to retreat.

Sentries were quickly stationed at every entrance to the courthouse. The corridors were so filled with troops that it was almost impossible for Burns supporters to even enter the courtroom. Two small pieces of field artillery were placed in the square to discourage any further rescues. United States Marshal Freeman also ordered Marines from the surrounding army forts to march into Boston to help preserve order. Reluctantly, Vigilance Committee members decided that it would be impossible to mount a new rescue attempt.

Boston began to look like an occupied city. Even conservative cotton Whigs began to regret their support of the Compromise of 1850 since it now seemed there was no way of satisfying the demands of slaveholders. The traditional Whig newspaper, *Atlas,* seemed to speak for the entire city when it declared itself disgusted with the exorbitant demands of the "slave power." Members of the conservative Merchant's

---

[3] Von Frank, Albert J. *The Trials of Anthony Burns: Freedom and Slavery in Emerson's Boston.* Cambridge: Harvard University Press, 1998. (Pg. 2)

Exchange, who had publicly volunteered to help return Sims to Virginia in 1851, announced that they now opposed the Fugitive Slave Law. Members of the organization then began to circulate petitions to repeal the Law. Black and white waiters were refusing to serve food to the troops who were guarding Burns. Colonel Suttle, Burns' owner, was so terrified that he begged southern students at Harvard to volunteer to guard him against angry Bostonians.

Members of the Vigilance Committee asked Suttle if he would be willing to sell Burns. The slaveholder was overjoyed at such an easy solution to his problem. Leonard Grimes quickly raised Suttle's asking price of $1,200. The United States District Attorney, Anthony Hallett, rejected the offer over the vehement protests of Colonel Suttle. There was a reason that the government insisted on rejecting this offer. For years when fugitive slaves had been captured in the North abolitionists would contact the owner and offer to purchase the runaway. Antislavery activists found it easy to raise the money to free a slave while the owners of these slaves were eager to accept the purchase price. Slaveholders realized that once a slave was known to have run away his market value was dramatically reduced. The slave grapevine was spreading the news that simpathetic northerners had purchased and freed a number of well known fugitives.

President Pierce understood the danger of even a handful of fugitives winning their freedom after being captured. The President believed that, if Burns was purchased by abolitionists and set free, it would certainly encourage other slaves to run away in the hopes that they, too, would be rescued by sympathetic northerners. The President was anxious to send a strong message to the South that the Fugitive Slave Law would be enforced even in the abolitionist city of Boston. Allowing Burns to be set free, no matter what his owner wanted, would destroy that message.

The trial was short. Commissioner Loring ruled that Burns was not entitled to the protection of *habeas corpus* since fugitives had no legal right to a trial by jury. Under the rules of the new Fugitive Slave Law, Burns did not even have the right to testify in his own defense. The only evidence that the commissioner needed was the sworn statement of Colonel Suttle that Anthony Burns was his slave. Commissioner Loring quickly ruled that Burns must be returned to Colonel Suttle immediately. For a moment there was dead silence in the courtroom. Then people one by one walked quietly up to Burns and whispered words of sympathy until the courtroom finally emptied.

United States Attorney Hallett was prepared to carry out

the decree as soon as it was announced. He had a telegram from President Pierce authorizing him to "incur any expense in executing the law." [4] Hallett began by commandeering a revenue cutter to sail Burns back to Virginia. Hallett's most difficult task was how to get Burns out of the courtroom and through the streets of Boston where a large and increasingly hostile crowd was gathering. He planned the move through Boston's streets to the wharf as if he were organizing a battlefield campaign. To lead this military operation, the Adjutant General of the Army was ordered to Boston along with troops from Rhode Island, New Hampshire, and New York. Boston's mayor was ordered to call out the entire militia corps of the city, 1,500 men, to assist the police in keeping order; they were issued orders to fire upon the crowd if necessary

Bostonians felt that their town had become an occupied city and, on this day they were united in their determination to show the nation their anger. All the businesses in the city had closed; their windows were draped in black. A coffin covered with black cloth hung suspended across State Street. The popular newspaper, Commonwealth, lowered three flags edged in black from its windows. With loaded rifles and fixed bayonets the soldiers began clearing the courtyard square and the streets leading to the Long Wharf where the ship was docked. The crowd was so dense that it took the troops three hours to clear a path for Burns to leave the courthouse. People climbed onto rooftops and filled the side streets. They were held back from freeing Burns only by the overwhelming number of armed troops. As Burns was moved slowly down State Street, cries of "shame" echoed throughout Boston. The people pressed forward. Troops attacked the crowd knocking down and beating some of the spectators. In the midst of the uproar the twenty year old Burns walked alone, somberly, his head held high. As the army continued to march down State Street people began moving in behind them. By the time Burns reached the harbor, he was followed by a crowd of 50,000. Burns was hurriedly taken aboard the cutter and thrust into a cabin.

It cost the federal government $40,000 to return Burns to slavery. Although the president and most Southerners claimed that this was a victory for the enforcement of the Fugitive Slave Law, many other Southerners were dismayed. The *Richmond Examiner* stated that "A few more such victories and the South is undone." [5]

---

[4] Ibid (Pg. 206)

[5] Buckmaster, *Henrietta. Let My People Go: The Story of the Underground Railroad and the Growth of the Abolitionist Movement.* Boston: Beacon Press, 1941. (Pg. 235)

The fallout from the Burns affair changed many Bostonians forever. A conservative Whig reported that after he saw Burns being marched to the ship: "I put my face in my hands and wept." The textile magnate Amos A. Lawrence reported that, "We went to bed one night old fashioned conservative compromise union Whigs and waked up stark mad abolitionists." [6]

Colonel Suttle was still anxious to sell Burns, but he was afraid of Virginia public opinion, so he relied on subterfuge. He sold Burns to a North Carolina slave trader who in turn sold Burns to an unknown purchaser. The unknown buyer was actually a group of Bostonians, and Anthony Burns returned to Boston a free man. Burns was the last fugitive slave in New England to be arrested under the Fugitive Slave Act.

On March 10, 1854, Joshua Glover, a fugitive living quietly in Racine, Wisconsin, was seized by a United States deputy marshal and the man claiming to be his owner, B. W. Garland of St. Louis. Glover fought furiously for his freedom. The marshal beat him until he was unconscious, carried him to a waiting wagon, and the two men were driven off to Milwaukee where Glover was put into a jail cell.

As soon as the news of Glover's arrest reached Racine, the people sprang into action. The courthouse bell began ringing and a huge crowd gathered in the square. It was the largest meeting that Racine had ever held. The people passed a resolution declaring that, because Congress had passed the Kansas Nebraska Act, all the legislation that had been part of the Compromise of 1850 was now repealed. "We as citizens of Wisconsin are justified in declaring and do declare the slave catching law of 1850 disgraceful and repealed." To emphasize this resolution, 100 citizens of Racine traveled to Milwaukee and joined the 5,000 people who were holding their own protest meeting. Sherman Booth, one of the leaders of the abolitionist movement in Wisconsin, told the crowd that if the people let their feelings about the Fugitive Slave Act be known the law could never be enforced, because no lawyer would aid the slave catchers, and Federal officers would resign their posts before assisting in enforcing this odious law.[7] The crowd roared their approval.

---

[6] Von Frank, Albert J. *The Trials of Anthony Burns: Freedom and Slavery in Emerson's Boston.* Cambridge: Harvard University Press, 1998. (Pg. 207)

[7] Baker, Robert H. *The Rescue of Joshua Glover a Fugitive Slave, the Constitution, and the Coming of the Civil War.* Athens, Ohio: Ohio University Press, 2006. (Pg. 22-23)

The protesters marched to the Milwaukee courthouse and demanded that the jailer give them the keys to the jail so that they could free Glover. The jailer refused. James Angove, a husky blacksmith, picked up a six by six wooden beam and declared that this was a good enough key and began ramming the beam against the jail door until it broke open. Glover was carried through the broken door and out into the street, to the applause of the crowd. John Messinger, a local businessman, offered his carriage to the escaping fugitive. Sherman Booth rode horseback next to the buggy as the crowd cheered and Glover doffed his cap to them crying "Glory Hallelujah." [8]

Messinger drove his carriage to the nearest Underground Railroad station, which was in the town of Waukesha. There, Glover was hidden until abolitionists felt it was safe to move him to Racine. Glover only had to make a quick trip across Lake Michigan to Canada and freedom.

The Glover rescue promptly became a national symbol of defiance against the Fugitive Slave Law. There were mass meetings all over Wisconsin where the rescuers were publicly thanked. Congratulations poured in from people all over the North, and many northern cities used Racine's defiant words in their own resolutions against the Fugitive Slave Law.

The Federal government again was forced to prove to southerners that the Fugitive Slave Law would be enforced. The government indicted two of the rescuers, Sherman Booth and John Rycraft. The local courts refused to try them. The United States government then moved the case into Federal court, which found Booth guilty. The Wisconsin State Supreme Court, in spite of the fact that it was a Federal, not a state case, reversed the guilty decision on the grounds that the Fugitive Slave Law was unconstitutional. The case finally went to the United States Supreme Court in 1859 where Justice Taney, speaking for the majority of the court, ruled that the Fugitive Slave Law was constitutional, and Booth was arrested.

Local citizens were outraged by this decision. They showed their indignation by marching into the jail and freeing Booth while the jailer looked on. On August 6, the courageous Booth spoke before an antislavery rally in Ripon and announced that there was a U.S. marshal in the room and dared the officer to arrest him. Marshal McCarty stepped forward and attempted to make the arrest. The crowd attacked him and he was forced to flee. Finally in 1860 the

---

[8] Ibid. (Pg. 23)

federal government was able to send Booth to jail but, just a few months later, President Buchanan decided to grant Booth a pardon.

In Chicago a throng of people protected a dozen fugitives from capture by a marshal who was leading a cadre of federal militia. The militiamen realized that they were powerless against this determined crowd, so they left Chicago without their prisoners. *The Warsaw Illinois Press* supported the action of the crowd. The newspaper stated that "Before the repeal of the Missouri Compromise, in all contests between the slaveholders and abolitionists our sympathies were decided in favor of the former but since that act of treachery we have not one word to say...One year ago there were thousands of men who would have aided you slaveholders in the capture of your slaves, who now say hands off." [9]

The Compromise of 1850 was beginning to unravel. It was not only the fact that some northerners were defying the Fugitive Slave Law; it was also that so many northern states had passed new Personal Liberty Laws. Rhode Island's new law, for example, made it illegal for any official to participate in helping return a fugitive to slavery. Any judge or state officer who violated this new Personal Liberty Law would be subject to a five-hundred-dollar fine or six months in prison.[10]

Other Personal Liberty Laws imposed severe penalties, including imprisonment, for the crime of kidnapping suspected fugitives. Some state laws made it illegal to house any fugitive in a state or local jail, which made it almost impossible for a slaveholder to find a secure place where a fugitive might be confined overnight. These Personal Liberty Laws were the most important evidence to southern extremists that the North was no longer willing to support the rights of slaveholders.[11]

In 1855 the issue of Kansas exploded throughout the nation. When the territorial governor called for elections to choose members of the first territorial assembly, slavery supporters sent out word to every Missourian to do whatever necessary to assure that Kansas

[9] Nevins Allan. *Ordeal of the Union: A House Dividing 1852-1857.* New York: Charles Scribner's Sons, 1947. (Pg. 153)

[10] Campbell, Stanley W. *The Slave Catchers: Enforcement of the Fugitive Slave Law 1850-1860.* New York: W. W. Norton Company, 1968. (Pg 171-172)

would become a slave state. Thousands of armed Missourians crossed the state line into the Kansas territory. They rode into free soil towns and tried to intimidate the population by attacking campaign rallies and smashing antislavery presses. When the polls opened, these armed bands terrorized citizens so they were unable to go to the voting booths, then stuffed the ballot box with pro-slavery votes. Not surprisingly the newly elected legislature was pro-slavery. The Kansas legislature, known as the Leavenworth Assembly, quickly passed one of the most draconian slave codes in all of America, including a provision that called for the death penalty for anyone convicted of aiding a fugitive slave. The Kansas legislature also declared that a citizen could be sent to jail for two years simply for possessing abolitionist books, newspapers, or pamphlets.

Northerners were not going to allow slaveholders to capture Kansas. The call went out for free soilers all over the North to buy land in Kansas. Emigrant Aid Companies were quickly organized to raise money to finance the enterprise. Soon thousands of free soil families were on their way to Kansas. On September 5,1855, the northern settlers met in Big Springs to organize their own party, the Free State Party, and hold a new convention. They insisted that the Leavenworth Assembly was an illegal legislative body which had been fraudulently elected. On December 15, these Kansas voters adopted the Topeka (Free State Party) Constitution by a vote of 1,731 to 46 and sent this new constitution to Congress.

President Pierce added to the increasing violence in Kansas when he announced on January 24, 1856, that the Free Party legislature of Topeka was an illegal government and its existence was a revolutionary act against the legal Leavenworth government of Kansas. In April the U.S. House of Representatives sent a Congressional Commission to Kansas to investigate the two elections. When they returned, the commission reported that only one sixth of the votes cast for the Leavenworth constitution were legal, but Pierce ignored the report. Kansas now had two competing governments.

On May 21 a band of slavery men rode into the center of free soil settlers, Lawrence, Kansas. They ransacked the town, destroying homes and businesses. The band searched for and found the town's two printing presses which published the local newspaper, as well as election material and pamphlets of all kinds, hauled them into the

---

[11] Ibid (Pg. 169)

street and. smashed them. Then they moved on to the Free State Hotel and burned it to the ground. One man was killed during the raid.

A few days later Massachusetts Senator Charles Sumner delivered a passionate speech in the United States Senate denouncing the "Crime Against Kansas" and finished his speech by condemning South Carolina's senator, Pierce Butler.

The very next day Congressman Preston Brooks of South Carolina, a cousin of Butler, decided to punish Sumner for his attack on southern slavery. Brooks entered the Senate chambers where Sumner was seated at his desk and, brandishing his cane, proceeded to beat Sumner over the head until he was unconscious. The deeply divided Senate refused to sanction Brooks for the attack on Sumner.

The attack on Sumner horrified northerners. Protest meetings were held in towns and cities. The government of Massachusetts vowed to keep Sumner's Senate seat vacant until the senator recovered from the paralyzing effects of the beating. The beating was so severe that it would take three years before Sumner recovered and was able to return to the Senate. The South's response to the attack on Sumner was quite different. Brooks received hundreds of canes, some inscribed with the motto "Use knock- down arguments."

John Brown had been a deeply committed abolitionist all his life. Wherever he lived his home had immediately become a station on the Underground Railroad. Brown believed that Kansas had become the center of the antislavery struggle, so, in 1856, he and four of his sons left their farm in upper New York and moved to Kansas. Brown believed that abolitionists must challenge the pro-slavery bands that had invaded the territory and threatened to turn Kansas into a slave state. He believed that God was calling upon him to organize bands of free soilers to defeat these invaders. Because Brown's free soil militia won a few skirmishes against the pro-slavery invaders, he soon became one of the most famous free soilers in Kansas.

Northerners began to examine the political landscape to decide which party would be the most effective vehicle to challenge the Slave Power that seemed to dominate the federal government. They looked at the Whig Party, the traditional home of most antislavery northerners, but the Whig party was in shambles after their crushing defeat in 1852, and its leaders were afraid to confront the issue of Kansas.

Many northerners decided that they needed a new party, one that would not be dominated by the South. On June 17, 1856, 1,000 delegates met in Philadelphia to create the Republican Party. It was a wonderfully diverse gathering. For the first time dedicated antislavery men like Joshua Giddings and Samuel Chase joined such staunch Whigs as Thurlow Weed, William Steward, Charles Francis Adams and Abraham Lincoln, as well as antislavery Democrats such as David Wilmot. Excitement filled the air. The delegates looked for someone who would have lots of popular appeal and they found him in John C. Fremont, the famous explorer who had crossed the Rocky Mountains and helped win California for America. When his name was announced as the unanimous choice of the delegates, the convention rang out with enthusiastic shouts of "Free Speech, Free Soil and Fremont." The Republican platform opposed the repeal of the Missouri Compromise and the policy of Popular Sovereignty. They demanded that Kansas come into the Union as a free state.

The Democrats rejected President Franklin Pierce as their candidate; delegates felt that his role in the Kansas disaster was a recipe for defeat. Instead the delegates nominated James Buchanan, a man who had been out of the country because he was minister to Great Britain during the heat of the Kansas debacle. The Democrats' main platform was very simple – a vote for Republicans would most certainly force the South to leave the Union.

In spite of the fact that the Republican Party was not on the ballot in any southern state, Fremont received 1,342,345 votes while Buchanan, the winner, received 1,836,072 votes. Even though the Republican Party had lost the election, southerners were disturbed. Southern politicians realized that, for the first time, they were facing a real challenge to the southern domination of the country. Radical southern politicians were now proclaiming that the only way to preserve slavery was by seceding from the Union.

The new president, James Buchanan, was determined to pacify the South, no matter what the cost. Since Congress could no longer be counted on to protect the interests of slaveholders, the President turned to the Supreme Court to help end the national crisis over slavery. There was one case Buchanan believed might be used to end the slavery controversy. This was the case of Dred Scott. Scott was a slave who had been purchased in 1833 by Dr. John Emerson, a surgeon in the United States Army. During the years that Emerson owned him, Scott had served in military forts in both the free state of Illinois and the free territory of Wisconsin. In both of these lands, slavery was illegal since the Missouri Compromise, the Wisconsin enabling act, and the Northwest Ordinance, which outlawed slavery.

Scott never challenged his slave status until after the death of his owner, John Emerson. When he approached Emerson's widow with a request to purchase his own and his family's freedom, she refused. Finally in 1846, Dred Scott, with the support of a friendly antislavery lawyer, sued Mrs. Emerson for his freedom based on the legal argument that, since he had been brought into both a free state and a free territory by his master, John Emerson, he had become legally free under all three Federal laws.

For years the Dred Scott case moved through the Missouri court system. Sometimes a jury declared Scott a free man, then Mrs. Emerson appealed the decision. Finally it reached the Missouri Supreme Court, which ruled in Mrs. Emerson's favor. Scott then appealed to the United States Supreme Court and, in 1856, the court agreed to hear his case.

Then something extraordinary happened. President-elect James Buchanan, knowing that the court had a majority of southerners, wrote a letter to one of the justices, John Catron, a personal friend. In this letter Buchanan suggested that the case needed to be heard as quickly as possible and that the court reach a verdict that would be broad enough to end the slavery controversy forever.

President Buchanan's action in trying to influence a decision of the Supreme Court in the Dred Scott case clearly violated one of the foundations of the United States Constitution, the separation of power between the presidency, the legislature, and the courts. On March 6, 1857, one of the most infamous Supreme Court decisions in American history was handed down. Chief Justice Taney delivered the opinion of the court. It was as broad an opinion as President Buchanan could have wished for. Taney declared that no black man, either slave or free, could ever be a citizen of the United States. The Chief Justice claimed that the drafters of the Constitution had viewed all African Americans as "beings of an inferior order and altogether unfit to associate with the white race, either in social or political relations, and so far inferior that they had no rights which the white man was bound to respect"

Also in the Dred Scott decision, Chief Justice Taney, in an effort to end the slavery controversy forever, declared that territorial legislatures had no legal right to ban slavery. A slaveholder, Taney insisted, had as much right to bring a slave into any U.S. territory as a farmer had to convey a herd of cattle. President Buchanan and Chief Justice Taney were convinced that the American people would accept this sweeping decision as law. They were certain that, since the issue of whether the territories would be slave or free was finally solved, the danger of southern secession was over.

Northerners were shocked at the Dred Scot decision. They believed that this Supreme Court ruling meant that slavery was now legal in every territory in the United States. Citizens in the North also wondered what would stop slaveholders from bringing their slaves, not only into the territories, but into the free states as well. A wave of protest and denunciation of the Taney decision swept across the North and West.

The New York legislature announced that "New York would never permit slavery within its borders. Any slave brought into New York would instantly become free and any person trying to hold a slave even in transit was liable to imprisonment for two to ten years," [12] Other Northern states soon followed suit. Thomas Hart Benton, the venerable senator from Missouri, announced that the Dred Scott ruling was a political decision which could not be enforced. Instead of ending the slavery controversy, the Dred Scott decision split the Democratic Party into northern and southern wings, while the Republican Party grew even stronger.

The response of Ohio's citizens to the Dred Scott decision was not long in coming.

It began on a spring day in the small town of Mechanicsburg. Everyone in town knew that Addison White was a fugitive slave who had a job working on the farm of the white abolitionist Udney Hyde. On May 21, 1857, White was plowing the field when he saw a group of men headed towards him. To his dismay the first man he saw was his former owner, Daniel White, leading a posse of two United State marshals, Elliot and Churchill, along with five other slave hunters. Addison White wasted no time. He ran as fast as he could to the safety of Hyde's farmhouse and hid in the loft. Hyde told his daughter to get help as quickly as possible.

Marshal Elliot began climbing the ladder to the loft to arrest White but White, armed with a pistol, began firing. Eliot quickly climbed down the ladder. He soon found that his posse was

---

[12] Nevins, Allan. *The Emergence of Lincoln: 1857-1859.* New York: Charles Scribner's Sons, 1950. (Pg. 114)

surrounded by thirty armed men, and the slave catchers were forced to beat a hasty retreat. Addison White was hidden by members of the Underground Railroad until it was safe to send him on to Canada.

Federal government officials tried again to show southerners that they would not allow the Fugitive Slave Law to be flaunted. They sent officers to arrest Udney Hyde and his family for obstructing the federal law. Hyde had gone into hiding, but the officers arrested his son and three friends. The local court immediately issued a writ of *habeas corpus* for the release of the prisoners. When Sheriff Layton attempted to serve marshal Churchill, the marshal responded by first knocking down the sheriff with his revolver, and then viciously beating him. A local judge quickly issued a warrant for the arrest of the two marshals and the other posse members for assault and battery with intent to kill. The judge then ordered the release of the Hydes and their friends.

The next act of this drama took place in Cincinnati where a Federal judge ruled that, even though the State of Ohio had issued a writ of *habeas corpus,* the two United States marshals did not have to obey the court order. The judge explained that, since the officers were attempting to do their duty under the Fugitive Slave Act, they were allowed to use any degree of force necessary to retain custody of their prisoners.

Next the United States Attorney ordered the arrest of all those persons who had tried to prevent the enforcement of the Fugitive Slave Act. This new list not only included the four original prisoners but Sheriff Layton and the judge who had issued the writs of *habeas corpus.* The new charge was resisting federal officers in the discharge of their duties.

Samuel Chase, the outspoken abolitionist governor of Ohio, informed the Federal government that his state was on the verge of an explosion if some compromise could not be worked out over the Hyde case. President James Buchanan reluctantly agreed. A compromise was worked out between Chase and the President. Funds would be raised privately to pay Daniel White for the loss of his slave and Buchanan agreed to quash all prosecutions of Ohio citizens under the Fugitive Slave Law.

The people of Ohio's battle against the Fugitive Slave Law was just beginning. Oberlin often boasted that it was the most abolitionist town in America. It was the home of Oberlin College which had been re-created in 1835 by the antislavery rebels of Lane College. The college remained true to the vision of those Lane rebels. In a time when neither blacks nor women were welcome in most American colleges, Oberlin gloried in its diverse student population. Oberlin graduates went off to teach or to establish churches and wherever they settled they quickly established new mini stations of the Underground Railroad.

The town of Oberlin was a major terminal on the Underground Railroad. In 1858 attorney John Langston, was elected township clerk, the first elected black official in America. Langston was able to use his new position to help any needy fugitive who arrived in Oberlin. With the unspoken support of the townsmen, Langston simply listed the fugitive in the town records as a pauper, transient, or poor stranger, so that the fugitive would be eligible to receive help from the town's charity funds. John Price was one of the fugitives who had been given temporary help when he first arrived in Oberlin too ill to work. When Price recovered, black community leaders assured the

Oberlin Rescuers, 1859.
Source: *Library of Congress, Prints and Photographs Division.*

fugitive that he was as safe in Oberlin as he would be in Canada. No slave hunter would ever dare seize a fugitive in their town.

It was just after noon on September 13, 1858, when Oberlin citizens heard the alarming news that John Price had been seized by slave hunters. Members of the Underground Railroad sprang into action. They learned that the kidnappers were holding Price in the attic of a small hotel in the nearby town of Wellington. Forty armed black and white townsmen immediately set off on the nine mile trip to Wellington. Some traveled on horseback, others piled into wagons. Their leader was Charles Langston, John Langston's older brother. It was not long before an angry crowd of rescuers surrounded the hotel demanding that the kidnappers release Price.

Violence seemed imminent. Charles Langston temporarily convinced the crowd to hold off charging into the hotel until he had tried every legal means to free Price. Langston met with the village constable and suggested that he arrest Price's captors on a charge of kidnapping, but the constable rejected the proposal. Next Langston proposed that the constable issue a writ of habeas corpus so that Price could be taken before a judge, but again the constable refused. United States Marshal, Jacob Lowe, who was becoming increasingly nervous about the angry rescuers, begged Langston to try and disperse the crowd. Langston replied that his rescuers were determined to rescue Price at any cost. He suggested that if Lowe wanted to avoid a riot he should urge the kidnappers to give Price up. When Lowe refused Langston got up from the bed where the two men were sitting and told the marshal, "We will have him anyhow." A small armed group of black and white rescuers met Langston at the back door of the hotel. He told them that the negotiations had failed. Instantly the rescuers sprang into action. They overpowered the guards, rushed up the stairs to the attic, burst open the door and led Price down the stairs and into a waiting buggy. He was whisked away, to the cheers of the crowd.

In dispatches to newspapers ranging from *Western Reserve* weeklies to the *New York Tribune*, Oberlin citizens crowed: "The Fugitive slave Law can't be did in this part of Ohio at least." [13]

Again the Federal government insisted that everyone involved in the rescue must be punished, so, in early November, a federal grand jury was impaneled in Cleveland. To guarantee that indictments would be issued, prosecutors insisted that only members of the Democratic Party could serve as members of the jury. Thirty-seven Oberlin and Wellington residents were indicted.

The first trial began on April 5, 1859. The trial judge was the same man, Judge Willson, who had presided over the grand jury; the jurors had all been selected based on their support for the Fugitive Slave Law. The trial lasted only a few days; the government was sure they would get a guilty verdict. John Bushnell, the man who had driven John Price out of Wellington, was quickly declared guilty.

The prosecution confidently moved on to its next case, that of Charles Langston. United States Attorney George Belden was

---

[13] Cheek. William and Aimee Lee Cheek. *John Mercer Langston and the Fight for Black Freedom 1829-65*. Urbana: University of Illinois Press, 1989. (Pg. 328)

accustomed to routine convictions of black defendants on only the flimsiest evidence. Langston was the most prominent of the defendants, and Belden expected to win another quick victory. The prosecutor believed that, with Langston's conviction, the other defendants would quickly plead guilty and the supremacy of the Fugitive Slave Act would be firmly established.

The defense team was led by John Mercer Langston. Langston fought the prosecution brilliantly on every issue, forcing Belden to put on a string of witnesses to prove his case. The trial dragged on for weeks, but, as expected, the jury brought in a verdict of guilty. On May 12, Judge Willson delivered his routine invitation to Charles Langston to address the jury before he passed the sentence.

Charles Langston rose and delivered one of the most famous speeches in American courtroom history. He began by stating:

"I was tried by a jury who were prejudiced; before a Court that was prejudiced; prosecuted by an officer who was prejudiced."

Then in an impassioned climax Langston pledged himself to do again what he had done for John Price:

> *"Unprotected by law I must take upon myself the responsibility of self protection; when I come to be claimed by some perjured wench as his slave, I shall never be taken into slavery. And in that trying hour I would have others do to me as I would call upon my friends to help me. As I would call upon you, your honor to help me, as I would call upon you (the prosecution attorney) to help me, and you and you so help me God! I stand here to say that I will do all I can for any man thus seized and held ...We all have a common humanity, and you would all would do that; your manhood should require it, and no matter what the laws might be you would honor yourself for doing it, while your friends and children to all generations would honor you for doing it, and every good and honest man would say you had done right."* [14]

Judge Willson, struggling to control his emotions, told Langston that he was mistaken in believing that nothing he could say would influence the court in its sentencing. The Judge then pronounced a sentence of a scant twenty days in jail along with a small fine of one hundred dollars.

---

[14] Ibid (Pg. 331-332)

Charles Langston now led the Oberlin rescuers in a unique protest strategy. He refused to pay his fine and instead elected to go to jail. Thirteen other black and white defendants also refused to pay their fines. The rescuers gleefully took up residence in the Cleveland jail. Under the control of an indulgent antislavery sheriff, the prisoners became popular martyrs. Newspapers were eager to interview them; the most prestigious of the national magazines, *Leslie's Weekly,* featured the jailed rescuers on its cover. There was a steady stream of visitors to the jail. The prisoners were asked to supply sermons to visiting pastors. They wrote their own pamphlets, which circulated throughout the North. Finally, because there was so much interest in the prisoners and their activities, the rescuers began publishing a newspaper called the *Stone Castle* (the popular name of the Cleveland jail).

Meanwhile their attorneys were attacking the legality of the Fugitive Slave Law before the Ohio State Supreme Court. Joining this appeal in behalf of the defendants was the Ohio Attorney General. President Buchanan was furious. He told Ohio's Attorney General that he would never compromise and, to emphasize his determination to win this case, he ordered the United States warship, *Michigan,* to sail into the port of Cleveland in case of violence. The day before the Supreme Court was to hear the case, a crowd gathered at the jail and called upon Charles Langston to give a speech. When he finished his address the crowd was so wrought up that the other speakers felt forced to caution the crowd against violence.

Buchanan was forced to retreat from his determination to jail the rescuers of John Price. The situation in Ohio was so volatile that there was a danger that there might be a pitched battle between state and Federal law enforcement forces. The Federal and Ohio government reached a complex compromise. Since an Ohio grand jury had just indicted Andrew Jennings and his three companions on a charge of kidnapping John Price, the Ohio Supreme Court agreed to drop this charge in exchange for the United States Government's promise that it would drop all charges against the Oberlin/Wellington rescuers. Even more important to the Federal government, the Ohio Supreme Court decided not to rule on the legality of the Fugitive Slave Law.

Meanwhile in Kansas tensions continued to rise. In 1857 the newly appointed territorial governor wanted the issue of two separate Kansas governments to be settled by vote of the settlers, so he asked the Federally recognized Lecompton government to submit their constitution to the settlers for their vote. This southern- supported legislature refused. Instead, under pressure, it offered to submit only Article 7, the section that would allow new slaves to be imported into the territory, with the caveat that, even if no new slaves would be permitted into Kansas, those slaves already in the territory would be allowed to remain as slave property. Free soiler settlers were outraged and announced that they would refuse to participate in such an illegal referendum. Even Stephen Douglas was upset over the flouting of the rules and regulations of the law of Popular Sovereignty which stated that the people of the territory would decide for themselves the issue of slavery.

Even though free soilers boycotted the election of December 21, and Article 7 received only 6,428 votes, the governor declared that over half of these votes were fraudulent. On January 4, 1858, the free-soil legislature at Topeka launched their own referendum; this time the voters adopted the free- soil constitution with a vote of 10,226.

The Lecompton constitution was narrowly accepted by the U.S. Senate, but soundly defeated in the House of Representatives. Northerners were troubled by the situation in Kansas and, in the elections of 1858, defeated most of the Democratic legislators who had supported Popular Sovereignty. Republicans now filled these seats.

On April 27, 1860, Charles Nalle, a fugitive slave living in Troy, New York, was seized by federal marshals. Harriet Tubman had been visiting friends in the city when she heard the news and took immediate steps to plan a rescue. On the day of Nalle's trial, Tubman walked slowly towards the open door of the courtroom disguised as a weak and crippled old woman, a shawl partially covering her face and carrying a basket of food on her head. She was clutching the arms of two black women for support and she whined pitifully to be admitted into the courtroom. The guards decided that she must be a relative of Nalle so they let her in. When the verdict that Nalle must be returned to Virginia was announced by the Commissioner, his lawyers responded that they had already obtained an order that the decision would be reviewed by a judge of the New York Supreme Court. Deputies began moving the manacled Nalle towards the state courthouse.

This was the moment Tubman had been waiting for. She straightened up her body and leaped to the window. She shouted out to the thousands of people milling about in the streets, "Here he comes! Take him!" Then she bounded down the stairs, quickly overtaking the guards, locked her arms around Nalle and cried out to the crowd, "This man shall not go back to slavery. Take him, friends! Drag him to the river! Drown him! But don't let them take him back." People in the crowd hurled themselves at the marshals trying to force them to release Nalle. The marshals fought back, attacking anyone who approached them. Tubman, although she was repeatedly beaten on the head, continued to hold tightly to Nalle's arm. The mob continued to assault the marshals until they were finally forced to release their hold on Nalle to protect themselves. Tubman quickly led him to the river where a skiff waited.

This was just the beginning of the battle for Nalle's freedom. There were marshals waiting across the river for Nalle's boat to land, They seized the fugitive and rushed him to Justice Stewart's office where barricades were quickly erected to prevent a new rescue. Tubman saw what had happened to Nalle and commanded her troops to rush to the local ferry. Four hundred rescuers boarded the ferry (all the boat could hold). The ferry sailed across the river and, when it landed, the rescuers began marching down the street ready for another battle. Tubman led the way. First they demolished the barricade, then they battered down the door and moved up the stairwell. They were met by a hail of bullets. There was a momentary retreat until someone shouted "They can only kill a dozen of us-come on." The door was pulled open by a powerful black man who was killed by Deputy Sheriff Morrison. Other rescuers were also hit by bullets but nothing could stop them. Tubman led a band of women into the room, seized Nalle and disappeared into the crowd.[15] He was soon on his way to Canada, safe at last from government kidnappers. Tubman was now a wanted woman. Southerners demanded her arrest, and some slaveholders insisted that she be executed for her role in the rescue of Nalle. What slaveholders did not know was that Harriet Tubman had been seriously wounded during the rescue. It would take months before she was fully recovered.

---

[15] Larson, Kate Clifford. *Bound For the Promised Land: Harriet Tubman Portrait of an American Hero*. New York: Balantine Books, 2004. (Pg. 80-82)

John Brown believed that there was nothing more he could do in Kansas. However, before Brown left Kansas, he led the most spectacular fugitive escape in American history.

When Jim Daniels, a Missouri slave, met John Brown he was a desperate man. He and his family were a part of a Missouri slaveholder's estate, which had been divided and given to several heirs. Slaves, who were part of the estate, had already been sold to a number of different slaveholders. In just two days he and his wife and babies were going to be separated forever. Daniels told Brown that he was their last hope of keeping the family together, and he knew of other slaves who were also eager to escape. Brown realized that he had to move quickly, so, the very next evening, he led a small group of antislavery men into Missouri.

While this rescue began in secrecy as did every other rescue, something happened at one plantation that would change everything. One of Brown's men, Aaron Stevens, had slipped into slaveholder David Cruise's house to bring out a young woman, when Cruise suddenly appeared. Stevens panicked. He believed that Cruise was about to shoot him so Stevens pulled out his own gun and opened fire. Cruise was killed instantly. Brown's rescue of these slaves was now a public event. Telegraphs were sent alerting Federal authorities along every one of the routes that Brown might take with orders to arrest him and recover the fugitives. Newspapers carried front page articles about the latest adventure of the notorious John Brown. The governor of Missouri offered a reward of $3,000 for the capture of Brown, dead or alive, while President Buchanan added his own personal reward of $250. State posses were also organized to join the manhunt to capture John Brown. Brown held an emergency meeting with the fugitives. He wanted to let them know how dangerous their flight to freedom had become, and gave each fugitive the choice of remaining with him or returning quickly to their plantations before their flight had been discovered.

Eleven fugitives chose to escape in spite of the danger. By sunrise the fugitives were in Kansas where they made camp in a deep ravine. It was the beginning of a 1,000 mile trek from Kansas to Canada. William Hutchinson was the Kansas correspondent for the *New York Times*. John Brown invited him to meet with the fugitives so that he could write a series of articles describing the escape. For the duration of the escape, *The New York Times* carried Hutchinson's sympathetic articles about the heroism and determination of the eleven fugitives to be free at any cost.

It was a bitterly cold winter. The snow was deep. The fugitives could not travel very fast because there were women and children in the party. Eager posses followed their tracks. It took a month to travel a mere 40 miles. This part of Kansas was filled with southern supporters, and hiding places were scant. The fugitives were able to hide for several days in an antislavery house near Topeka. This hiding place was discovered and the house was attacked by a United States marshal leading a posse of seventy five men. There were only fourteen people in the house at the time. Brown led the his men in an attack which successfully convinced the marshal into believing that they were facing a large body of defenders. The posse chose to retreat.

Finally, on February 4, 1859, the fugitives reached the free state of Iowa. By this time the "Great Escape" had electrified the entire North. When the fugitives reached Grinnell, the whole town turned out to greet them. They welcomed the exhausted travelers with gifts of money and supplies. On February 25, the fugitives stopped to rest in Springdale, Iowa where Jim Daniels's wife gave birth to a baby boy. Springdale citizens announced to the various posses that were still pursuing the fugitives that they would fight to the death against anyone who tried to seize the fugitives. On March 9, when the fugitives were ready to move out of Iowa, they were escorted to the train station by an honor guard. The fugitives were hidden in a box car which was on its way to Chicago.

John Jones, Source:
Chicago History Museum

John Brown arrived in Chicago ahead of his band of fugitives. He knew that the city would be one of the most hazardous stops for them. The city was flooded with posses eager to collect the many rewards that were being offered for the capture of the fugitives. Brown's first stop was the home of the black businessman John Jones, whose home was a major stop on Chicago's Underground Railroad. Brown had also brought to the meeting his white friend Alan Pinkerton, the man who would just two years later establish the United States Secret Service to protect the newly elected president, Abraham Lincoln.

Brown confided in the two men just how worried he was about the safety of his fugitives. Pinkerton assured Brown that the fugitives were quite safe in Chicago because people in the city were so outraged over the Fugitive Slave Act, as well as the Dred Scott decision, that the law could no longer be enforced in that city. What's more, John Brown himself had become such a hero that no public official dared arrest him. The two men were so confident that they urged Brown to keep the fugitives hidden in the city for one more day because Pinkerton had a plan.

The next morning Pinkerton held a secret meeting of prominent Chicago lawyers. First, Pinkerton softened up his audience by describing the suffering and dangers endured by the fugitives during their thousand mile exodus. His story so touched the hearts of these lawyers that they reached into their pockets and gave Pinkerton 600 dollars. Next, Pinkerton went to the home of Colonel O.G. Hammond, General Superintendent of the Michigan Central Railroad. Hammond told Pinkerton that he would supply the fugitives with a private car stocked with plenty of food and water. This car would travel non-stop to Detroit. No posse would dare interfere with his orders. In Detroit the Vigilance Committee had already made arrangements for a ferry to be waiting at the dock so that the fugitives would be able to board quickly and be whisked across the river to Canada and freedom. John Brown waved goodbye to his band of twelve fugitives in Detroit. His next stop would be Harpers Ferry.

CHAPTER

11

JOHN BROWN AT HARPERS FERRY

On October 17, 1859, telegraph wires hummed with the news that a band of antislavery zealots, led by John Brown, had taken over the Federal arsenal at Harpers Ferry, Virginia. When Brown left Kansas in 1858, he believed that the Federal government was now completely under the control of the slaveholders therefore he had to find a more radical way to end slavery in America.

For years John Brown had been studying the history of slavery in the Carribean, especially accounts of the successful slave revolt in Haiti, which resulted in the first black nation in the Americas. Brown had examined the military tactics of Haiti's great leader, Toussaint L' Ouverture. He was especially impressed by L'Ouverture's use of Haiti's vast mountain range as an impregnable base from which to launch multiple attacks on the French army. Toussaint knew that the French army was vastly superior to his guerilla bands in both manpower and military equipment, but the Haitian leader also knew that a European army could never penetrate his mountain strongholds.

Brown also learned about the existence of large fugitive settlements in the mountains of Jamaica, created by slaves who had revolted against British plantation owners and found freedom in these secure sanctuaries. These settlements had expanded over the years as thousands of other slaves escaped to the mountains. By 1830 Jamaican fugitive settlements had become quasi-independent states inside the mountain regions of the British colony.

Brown was fascinated by the possibility of turning the Allegheny Mountains, which ran through the key slaveholding states of Virginia, the Carolinas and Georgia, into similar fugitive settlements. John Brown knew that fugitive slaves had been living for generations in a group of settlements hidden deep within the Great Dismal Swamp.

Brown believed that it was possible to create similar settlements in the wilderness of the Allegheny Mountains, settlements which would be stations on the Underground Railroad. He began holding meetings with some of the most important leaders of the black Underground Railroad; men like William Still who controlled the vital Philadelphia terminal; William Lambert and George DeBaptiste, leaders of Detroit's Underground Railroad; John Jones, one of the most important black leaders in Chicago; Charles Langston who was now nationally famous for his role in the Oberlin rescue of John Price, and the most important leader of them all, Frederick Douglass, one of Brown's closest friends.

In April, 1858, Jermain Loguen escorted John Brown into Canada to meet with Harriet Tubman who lived in the town of St. Catherines between her forays into Maryland to rescue fugitive slaves. "Among the slaves" Loguen told Brown, "she is better known than the Bible for she circulates more freely." Brown was deeply impressed with Tubman. He wrote his son John Jr.: "Harriet Tubman hooked on his whole team at once. He, Harriet, is the most of a man naturally that I ever met with." [1]

In the spring of 1858, John Brown rode into Chatham, Ontario, which was the home of a sizable community of fugitive slaves. He had set up meetings with a number of black leaders to discuss his plan to set up Underground Railroad stations in the South's Allegheny Mountains. On May 8, John Brown assembled a convention of thirty-four blacks and ten white members of his Kansas band. He opened the first session by describing to the delegates his plan to carry the war against slavery into the South. Brown told the delegates that his first step would be to create a small military camp in the Virginia Mountains. From this stronghold, Brown would lead a small band of volunteer fighters in a series of lightening attacks on southern plantations to liberate slaves. Newly liberated slaves could choose to join the guerrillas or travel north on the Underground Railroad. Brown told the delegates that the guerrilla camp could easily be defended, because even a large military force would not be effective in this kind of mountainous terrain. Brown expected that the first guerilla camp would quickly expand into a series of settlements.

The delegates cheered when Brown described how the fugitive settlements would demonstrate to white America that American slaves could create an independent democratic society, its members living under the rules of a written constitution. He asked his audience

---

[1] Quarles, Benjamin. *Allies For Freedom; Blacks and John Brown.* New York: Oxford University Press, 1974. (Pg 42)

to take the first step in creating this new society by debating and voting on a model constitution for the first guerilla camp. It was a solemn moment when each delegate walked up to the table and signed the document.

Brown needed to raise a great deal of money if his plan was to succeed. It was vital that his army have enough weapons and supplies to maintain themselves during the initial raids on Virginia plantations. Brown had become a northern hero when reporters publicized some of his victories over pro-slavery militias in Kansas. Brown, although still a wanted man, was an honored guest in the homes of some of America's greatest intellectuals such as Ralph Waldo Emerson and Henry Thoreau.

Brown told some of his supporters about his plans. These supporters included prominent men like Samuel Howe, renowned as the first educator of the blind; Theodore Parker, one of the greatest Unitarian ministers in America; the radical minister Thomas Wentworth Higginson, who had led the rescue team that freed the fugitive Shadrack; and the wealthy Gerrit Smith, who had already raised hundreds of dollars to arm Brown's Kansas militia.

John Brown traveled to Cleveland for a meeting with Charles Langston, one of his most important black supporters. When abolitionists learned that Brown was in their city, they asked him to speak at a public meeting to talk about the situation in Kansas. Brown worried that he might be arrested, since the Federal government still considered him a fugitive. Langston assured him that the people of Cleveland, who were still incensed over the government's treatment of the Oberlin rescuers, would never allow John Brown to be arrested in their city. Langston also assured Brown that the various posses roaming the city would not dare to break into a public gathering no matter how tempting the reward money might be. They were right. Brown spoke to a large cheering crowd, but no government marshal or posse was brave enough to enter the auditorium.

The first attack on the South was planned for the summer of 1858, but, before Brown could gather his volunteers together, it was betrayed by one of his white recruits, Hugh Forbes. Forbes, an Englishman whom Brown had hired as a drillmaster, fancied himself as a great military leader. He had become very jealous of Brown. In the fall of 1857, just as Brown was completing his plans for the raid, Forbes wrote to a number of white abolitionist leaders, including three United States Senators, revealing details of Brown's planned raid on Virginia plantations. None of the senators took Forbes' revelations seriously, but Brown's supporters were frightened and insisted that the raid be postponed until the danger could be evaluated. Brown reluctantly agreed and hid his cache of arms. Not knowing when, or if, the attack on the South would ever be launched, the delegates to the Chatham Convention scattered while Brown sent the members of his Kansas militia back to Iowa to wait for further orders.

Sometime after the Chatham Convention, John Brown changed his plan to raid southern plantations. He decided instead to begin his campaign by attacking the government arsenal at Harpers Ferry, which stood on the borders of three states, Virginia, Maryland and Pennsylvania. There were some good reasons for this change of plan. Brown badly needed to seize the weapons kept in the Federal armory because his fund-raising had ground to a halt as a result of the Forbes betrayal. Harpers Ferry was only an hour's march to the mountains of Pennsylvania where, after the raid, his troops would be able to find temporary hiding places.

Brown sent his eldest son, John Brown Jr., to investigate the town of Chambersburgh, Pennsylvania. The town bordered both Virginia and Maryland and was the first town north of Harpers Ferry. Brown knew that the town had an active Underground Railroad. One of the most important black members of the Railroad in Chambersburgh was Henry Watson, a well- known black barber. It might have been John Brown Jr., who recruited Watson because, by the time Brown himself came to Chambersburgh, Watson had already become a valuable member of the team.

Brown also asked Kagi, one of the members of his Kansas militia, to move to Chambersburg and learn as much as he could about the geography and the people of the area. Brown told Kagi that he should rent a room in the boarding house of one of the town's most prominent citizens, a widow named Mary Ritner. Ritner's husband had been one of the most popular governors of Pennsylvania, the man who had organized the first public school system in the state. Governor Ritner, a close friend of the abolitionist United States

Senator Thadeus Stevens, shared the senator's hatred of slavery. Many townspeople suspected that Mary Ritner was also an active member of the Underground Railroad.[2]

On June 23, 1859, Brown traveled to Harpers Ferry, posing as a farmer who was interested in researching mining opportunities. Mining exploration would explain the reason for so many crates of heavy material (weapons and ammunition) that would soon be arriving. Brown began looking for a house that was both large enough and secluded enough to hide his band and, when he saw the Kennedy farm, knew that he had found his headquarters. He brought his teen-aged daughter Annie, and Martha, the seventeen-year-old bride of his son Oliver to the farm with him so that his neighbors would see only a picture of innocent domesticity. The Brown family attended services at the Samples Manor Church, but Brown was sometimes seen visiting other churches in the area, possibly so he could contact local black leaders without attracting attention.

In the summer of 1858, John Brown had also sent another member of his band to live in Harpers Ferry itself. John Cook moved into a boarding house operated by Mrs. Kennedy. He took a job as a lock tender on the canal, and peddled books on the side. This allowed him to scout the area and its population, and to send Brown information on various government installations. Cook was young and charming, and he quickly became a popular member of the community. He also fell in love with Mary, the daughter of his landlady; they were quickly married and, in 1859, Mary gave birth to a baby boy.

In September 1859, Brown was ready to launch his attack on Harper's Ferry and moved all his troops into the Kennedy farmhouse. On September 24, Osborn Anderson, one of the black delegates to the Chatham Convention, arrived. Because it was vital that he never be seen by the neighbors, Anderson was hidden in the attic and only went outdoors after dark. In spite of this hardship, Anderson describes the waiting period as a happy time because, "In John Brown's house and in John Brown's presence, men from widely different parts of the continent met and united into one company, wherein no cruel prejudice dared intrude its ugly self – no ghost of a distinction found space to enter."[3]

---

[2] Stake, Virginia Ott. *John Brown in Chambersburgh*. Chambersburgh Pennyslvania: Franklin County Heritage Inc., 1977. (Pg. 51)

[3] Anderson, Osborne P. *A Voice From Harper's Ferry*. Boston: Printed for the Author, 1861. (Pg. 58)

FrederickDouglass was one of John Brown's closest friends. Douglass had supported Brown's original plan to establish Underground Railroad stations in the mountains of Virginia. When Brown told Douglass about his new plan to attack a federal armory at Harpers Ferry, Douglass was strongly opposed. He told Brown that attacking the Federal government, rather than individual slaveholders, was a dangerous idea, which threatened to tear apart the growing antislavery movement.

Shields Green was a twenty four year old fugitive slave from Charleston, South Carolina when he met Brown for the first time at the home of Frederick Douglass. He was still grieving for his wife who had just died, and for his baby son whom he had been forced to leave when he fled north. Green listened raptly as Brown described his plan to establish armed fugitive camps in Virginia's Allegheny Mountains. Green immediately enlisted in Brown's band.

On August 19, Brown and Kagi met with Douglass and Green in an abandoned stone quarry in Chambersburg. The four men sat down among the rocks to talk about Brown's raid on Harpers Ferry. Douglass pleaded with Brown to abandon his plan. He pointed out to his friend that seizing a Federal arsenal would turn the whole country against them. Even many committed antislavery men might become angry at an attack on a United States government facility. Douglass told Brown that, "he was going into a perfect steel trap, and that once in he would never get out alive." [4]

For three days Douglass and Brown argued. Shields Green listened silently to the debate, which grew more impassioned each day. Finally Douglass realized that nothing he could say would convince Brown not to carry out the attack on Harpers Ferry and he decided to leave. Douglass then turned to Green and asked, "Are you coming with me?" Green was silent for a moment then announced "I b'leve I'll go wid de old man." Owen Brown, who had been at that last meeting, led Green out of the quarry. As the two men left Chambersburg, they saw a posse of men coming down the road after them. These men believed that Green was part of a fugitive slave escape plot. Owen finally had to fire his revolver in order to escape. Then the two men fled into the mountains where they finally shook off their pursuers. Exhausted, they reached the Kennedy farmhouse at dawn.

---

[1] Douglass, Frederick. *Life and Times of Frederick Douglass Written By Himself.* New York: Bonanza Books. Reprinted from the revised edition of 1892. (Pg. 319)

Dangerfield Newby was a forty-four-year-old freedman living on the Pennsylvania/Virginia border, who spent his days working in other men's fields. He was desperately trying to earn enough money to buy his wife, Harriet, and their seven children who were still slaves just over the border in Virginia. Newby had recently been freed under the terms of his white father's will but, since a new Virginia law ordered all freed slaves to leave the state immediately or face re-enslavement, he had been forced to abandon his family and move to Pennsylvania. As Newby struggled with his loneliness and the hopelessness of ever earning enough money to free his family, he received this heartbreaking letter from Harriet. "Dear Dangerfield, I want you to buy me as soon as possible for if you do not get me somebody else will. It is said Master is in want of money. If so I know not what time he may sell me and then all my bright hopes to cheer me in all my troubles will fade. If I thought I should never see you this earth would have no charms for me." [6]

John Brown's plan for the raid on Harpers Ferry was the only hope that Newby had of saving his family. Osborn Anderson remembered how Newby would slip quietly into the Kennedy farmhouse whenever he could. He would pore over the Provisional Constitution, especially Article XII which stated that, "The marriage relation shall be at all times respected." He would frequently ask Brown, "When can I answer Harriet?" Brown would pat him on the shoulder and declare, "Soon! Soon, Dangerfield." [7]

Newby was one of the few members of the band who could move freely about in the neighborhood because he lived near the Kennedy farm. In October, Newby reported that rumors were circulating that the Browns were hiding fugitive slaves. A citizens group was already demanding that the authorities search the Kennedy farm. Then Annie reported that one of the neighbors had wandered into the house and found Shields Green helping to clear the table. Brown decided that the mission was in danger. He decided to begin the raid as soon as possible without waiting for the rest of the recruits and weapons to arrive. Brown told the women to pack up immediately and get ready to leave for home. Brown and Watson escorted Mary Cook and her baby to Chambersburgh. Brown announced that the raid on Harpers Ferry would begin on Sunday, October 16.

---

[6] Carton, Evan. *Patriotic Treason: John Brown and the Soul of America.* New York: Free Press, 2006. (Pg. 285)

[7] Nelson, Truman John. *The Old Man: John Brown at Harper's Ferry.* New York: Holt, Rinehart & Winston, 1973. (Pg. 69-70)

On Saturday, October 15 three more recruits arrived at the farmhouse, Lewis Leary, John Copeland, and Francis Jackson Merriam. Copeland and Leary, two black men, had come from Oberlin. Both men had been leaders in rescuing John Price. They were sponsored by Charles Langston and other members of Oberlin's Vigilance Committee. Francis Merriam, a member of one of Boston's prominent abolitionist families, had traveled to Haiti and told Brown that he was eager to help in "stealing slaves down south" [8]

It was cold and dark that Sunday night when the twenty-two raiders began their five mile march over rolling hills and through deep woods. John Brown, driving an old farm wagon filled with weapons, led the way. Before dawn they crossed the bridge that led into the town of Harpers Ferry. Brown had left his son Owen, Francis Merriman, and Barclay Coppoc behind at the Kennedy farmhouse to guard the rest of the weapons and wait for the other volunteers who Brown believed were on their way.

Cook and Tibbs went ahead to cut the telegraph wires to Baltimore and Washington; the rest of the band entered Harpers Ferry. They easily occupied the Armory complex in the center of town, since each building was guarded by a single sentry. Brown then sent Kagi, and three other men to occupy the Halls Rifle Works, half a mile away, because he knew that thousands of guns were stored there.

After the Armory complex was secured, Brown sent a raiding party of six men who seized thirty of the town's prominent slaveholders. Brown planned to use these hostages as bargaining chips in case any of his men were captured. Ten slaves were also liberated by the raiding party. Anderson recalled that on the road, "We met some colored men, to whom we made known our purpose when they immediately agreed to join us." [9] The most important prisoner captured that night was Colonel Lewis Washington, great grand-nephew of the first President, George Washington.

So far the raid had been successful; but John Brown now made a serious mistake when he allowed an express train from Wheeling to continue on to Baltimore. When the train pulled into Baltimore, the

---

[8] Oates, Stephen. *To Purge This Land With Blood: A Biography of John Brown.* New York: Harper & Row, 1970. (Pg. 287)

[9] Anderson, Osborne P. *A Voice from Harper's Ferry.* Boston: Printed for the Author, 1861. (Pg. 94)

conductor shouted out the news that Harpers Ferry had been taken over by an abolitionist band.

Early Monday morning President James Buchanan was awakened by the frightening news that a massive slave revolt, led by wild-eyed abolitionists, had taken over the town of Harpers Ferry. He immediately called upon Colonel Robert E. Lee, the man who two years later would become the Commander In Chief of the Confederate army, to lead a band of ninety Marines to put down the rebellion. Meanwhile, small groups of armed locals had taken to the hills above the town and begun firing into the armory.

Brown, although he had never talked about it, must have been deeply affected by the massacre at Pottawatomie Creek, because, at Harpers Ferry he was very solicitous of all of his hostages. On Monday morning he sent some of the non-slaveholding hostages home and then wrote a note to the hotel, ordering breakfast for forty seven men. The hostages found themselves sitting side by side with the black liberators and some of their own slaves, eating a hearty meal of ham, hot cakes, potatoes, eggs and coffee

Brown desperately needed more arms, so he asked John Cook, Charles Tibbs, and a few of the liberated slaves to return to the Kennedy farm and load the rest of the arms into the wagon and transfer them to the schoolhouse building which was just outside Harpers Ferry.

By noon the small groups of locals had been joined by local militiamen from Charles Town. These troops stormed the two bridges that Anderson, Green, Hazlett, and Newby had been guarding. As the four men fled, a shot rang out and Newby was instantly killed. Shields Green quickly lifted his gun and killed the sniper.

John Brown had watched with dismay as local troops first attacked his men who were guarding the bridges, and then began moving into the town. He decided that the armory was too difficult to defend, so he moved his men and the hostages into the smaller engine house. Anderson and Hazlett had managed to escape from the hail of bullets and fled to the safety of the hills overlooking the town. Shields Green paused for a moment to see what Brown was doing. He saw Brown enter the engine house, then watched as militiamen began marching towards the building. Green decided that Brown was in trouble so, instead of joining Anderson and Hazlett, Green turned and walked back down into the engine house. Osborne Anderson remembers Green's last words to him, that "he must go down to de ole man."[10]

By one o'clock, Kagi, watching from inside the Halls Rifle Works, saw that hundreds of troops were getting ready to attack the building. Kagi immediately gave the order to his men to retreat through the back door and into the shallow waters of the Shenandoah River. The men began swimming towards a flat rock in the middle of the river. Kagi was hit by rifle fire and died in the river. Leary was shot climbing onto the rock. He survived for eight hours... The men who reached the rock fought desperately, trying to fight off the attackers and protect the mortally wounded Leary, but they were overpowered. The sight of the black Copeland seemed to especially infuriate the mob. The crowd shouted "lynch him" and they began tying scarves together to make a noose, when one gentleman, Dr. Stary, a respected member of the Harpers Ferry community, rode up and prevented the lynching. He managed to shield Copeland by holding back the mob long enough for a policeman to come forward and arrest Copeland.

Early in the afternoon the door of the engine house opened and one of the raiders, Will Thompson, walked out along with one of the hostages. Thompson was holding aloft a white flag and he had a note from John Brown asking for a truce. The letter asked that, in exchange for the hostages, his men be allowed safe passage out of Harpers Ferry. Ignoring the white flag, the furious mob arrested Thompson.

The battle between the raiders and the army troops continued all afternoon. Towards evening Brown again tried for a truce. He sent his son Watson, Aaron Stevens, and a hostage, the armory clerk, Archibald Kitzmiller. The militia's answer was a hail of bullets. Stevens was severely wounded and would have been killed except for the actions of Joseph Brua, one of the hostages who rushed out of the engine house and carried Stevens to the railroad station so that he could get medical attention. Then, surprisingly, Brua returned to the engine house.

---

[10] Libby, Jean. Editor *John Brown Mysteries*. Missoula, Montana: Pictorial Histories Publishing Company, 1999. (Pg. 97)

John Brown, engine house raid at Harpers Ferry.
Source: *Library of Congress, Prints and Photographs Division.*

Although seriously wounded, Watson managed to crawl back into the engine house. Later that afternoon, Oliver peered out of a crack in the engine room door. He saw a sniper pointing a rifle at the crack. Oliver lifted his own rifle but the sniper shot him first. It would take Oliver twelve agonizing hours before he died.

The hostages were terrified as they watched John Brown hovering over his dying sons. The prisoners were convinced that the grieving father might decide to wreak vengeance on at least a few of them. Brown, seeing the hostages' panic, tried to reassure them. He promised the prisoners that he was not going to kill anyone except those soldiers who were attacking his men. Brown, instead of using the hostages as a shield against the militia, who had begun trying to batter down the door, moved his prisoners away from the line of fire into the safest part of the engine room.

Some of the hostages were also very nervous about Shields Green, who had become Brown's chief lieutenant in the engine room. Green skillfully returned fire all night long, keeping the militia from invading the engine house.

By the next morning, when Robert E. Lee ordered the marines to break down the door of the engine house, they found only four raiders and their grieving captain, John Brown. As the marines entered the engine room, some of the liberated slaves were able to flee out the back door during the confusion. Those slaves that were captured by Lee claimed that they had been forced to work for Brown. Not every liberated slave in the engine room was able to make that claim. According to some hostages, Jim, Washington's coachman, fought like a tiger until the troops overran the engine house. Jim was one of the fugitives who escaped the engine house. He managed to reach the Shenandoah River, but angry troops caught him and bludgeoned him until he fell into the river and drowned.[11]

Phil Luchum, another liberated slave, enthusiastically knocked a hole in the engine house wall and thrust his rifle into the opening so he could fire upon the attacking militia. He kept on firing until he was mortally wounded.[12] Ben, another of the liberated slaves was arrested and thrown into jail where he died mysteriously. Osborn Anderson believed that Ben had died of his wounds; the official report stated that he had died of fright. A newspaper reporter heard a different story; a northern railroad executive briefly jailed on October 17 told that reporter that he believed that a black man had been lynched in the cell next to his.[13]

Marine Lieutenant Israel Green was the first soldier to enter the engine room. He was searching for John Brown. He found Brown bending over his dying son Watson, his dead son Oliver by his side. In a rage the officer sprang about twelve feet and thrust his sword into Brown's body almost killing him, then struck him several more times over his head. Brown was so severely wounded by this attack that he had to be carried out of the engine house on a stretcher.

Crowds of onlookers followed the marines into the engine house, shouting that Brown ought to be lynched. One of the hostages responded to the jeers of the mob," I would not go to see him hanged. He made me a prisoner but he spared my life and that of the other gentlemen. When his sons were shot down beside him, almost any other man would have taken a life for a life. I look on him as a prisoner of war who has fought fairly." [14]

[11] Libby Jean. *The Slaves Who Fought With John Brown*. Palo Alto, California: Jean Libby, 1988. (Pg. 10)

[12] Rosso, Peggy A. and Paul Finkelman Editors. *Terrible Swift Sword: the legacy of John Brown*. Athens: Ohio University Press, 2005. (Pg. 32)

[13] Libby, Jean. Ibid. (Pg. 11)

[14] Nelson, Truman. *The Old Man: John Brown At Harper's Ferry*. New York: Holt, Rinehart and Winston, 1973. (Pg. 151)

Following the raid on Harpers Ferry, the legend of John Brown began. Monday afternoon, Cook, who had been unloading stacks of arms in the schoolhouse, was told that Federal troops were attacking the engine house. He took off for Harpers Ferry to see for himself what was happening. A group of liberated slaves who had been helping Cook decided that the attack on Harper's Ferry had failed. They immediately left the schoolhouse. Cook reached the heights overlooking the town and scrambled up the rugged cliff. From this height Cook could see a group of men in front of the engine house firing rounds of bullets into the building. He climbed a tree and began firing in order to divert the troops. Shots were fired back and one of these shots cut the tree branch that Cook was clinging to. He fell about fifteen feet to the ground. Bruised and bleeding he made his way to the Kennedy farmhouse, but it was empty.

Back at the Kennedy farmhouse, Owen Brown waited for news of the Harpers Ferry raid. On Monday morning someone told Owen that they thought his father had been killed during the fighting. Owen ordered Merriman and Coppoc to follow him, and they all took off for Harpers Ferry. Before the men reached the town, they met Cook. Cook told Owen that his father and the rest of the band had taken refuge in the engine room, which was now surrounded by mobs of armed militiamen, and that, without more men, it would be impossible to mount a successful rescue. Owen agreed, so the four men left Harper's Ferry and began the difficult journey to Chambersburgh. Owen hoped that he could organize the rescue of his father, brothers, and band members with volunteers from the town's Underground Railroad.

Most of the fugitives helping Cook in the schoolhouse realized that John Brown's raid had failed and that they had to save themselves. They decided they must return to their plantations before their owners realized they had fled.

The fugitives used great ingenuity in protecting themselves from the wrath of slaveholders. One of Lewis Washington's slaves, a man called Mason, had come to the arsenal after his master was taken hostage. Later, Mason went with Cook to collect weapons from the Kennedy farmhouse. All day Monday, Mason, unsupervised, drove the wagon back and forth from the farmhouse to the schoolhouse until he heard the news that John Brown had been arrested. He managed to return to the Washington plantation and told such a pathetic story about how he had been forced to help John Brown, that Washington was touched. Mason then helped Washington find one of his favorite horses as well as a favorite shotgun taken by the raiders. Washington was so impressed that Mason was cited as the symbol of a faithful slave. During the Civil War, Mason, the "faithful slave" became a Union spy.[15]

There was so much confusion, it seemed that every observer told a different story about the events at Harpers Ferry. Most whites insisted that the slaves that Brown liberated refused to participate and fled the scene at their first opportunity, to return home to their masters. There were others who questioned just how faithful the slaves of Harpers Ferry really were.

Anthony Hunter had been a slave on a Harpers Ferry plantation. During the Civil War he fled his plantation and joined the Union Army. Hunter became an aid to Lieutenant Robert Copeland. One night Copeland asked Hunter to tell him about John Brown's raid. Copeland wondered if any of the slaves had supported the raid. Hunter told Copeland that there were many more slaves involved in the raid on Harpers Ferry than had ever been revealed. Hunter stated that the original plan was for these recruits to meet up with the Brown raiders, not in Harpers Ferry, but on Monday evening in the mountains. When these slaves saw that Brown had been defeated they quietly returned to their plantations.[16]

Meanwhile Owen led the four remaining band members into the Virginia mountains. They dared not use any roads, or even well worn pathways, for fear of being captured. Instead they had to force their way through the heavy undergrowth and up the steep slopes, hoping that they were traveling in the right direction. The night was freezing and the men had not eaten all day and they were extremely tired.

Cook was keeping his spirits up by talking about how wonderful it would be when he was finally re-united with his wife and baby, who he knew were waiting for him at Chambersburg. Now Cook was growing increasingly more fatigued. He found it difficult to walk because his ankle had been sprained when he fell from the tree. He told the others that he was unable to go on and would have to

[15] Libby Jean. *Slaves Who Fought With John Brown*. Palo Alto, California: Jean Libby, 1988. (Pg. 32)

[16] DeCaro, Louis. *John Brown: The Cost of Freedom*. New York: International Publishers, 2007. (Pg. 84-86)

rest. He knew the area well enough that he could find his own way into Chambersburgh, so he told the others to leave him and continue walking. Cook decided to risk walking on the road and he was arrested just a few miles outside Chambersburg.

The other men managed to reach Chambersburgh. They were exhausted and starving, so they headed for Mary Ritner's boarding house. They hid in the bushes surrounding the house, but Ritner told them to leave immediately. She was even afraid to bring them some food because Federal marshals were watching her house. The men slipped back into the woods. Owen was especially worried about Merriman. His feet were covered with infected blisters and he could no longer walk. Somehow the three men got him to the railroad station, Owen had to carry him part way on his back. His beard was shaved and Owen, using a needle and thread, repaired Merriman's clothes. Looking a bit more respectable, Merriman boarded the train to Philadelphia where he was met by an old Concord friend, James Redpath. Redpath found a temporary hiding place for Merriman where he could rest and restore himself. The other three men, possibly helped by members of Chambersburg's Underground Railroad, also somehow managed to escape the many U.S. marshals and local posses searching for them. The three men remained hidden for months until, when the Civil War began, the danger of being tried for treason had ended.

Osborne Anderson. Source: *Boyd B. Stutler Collection, West Virginia Archives.*

Osborn Anderson and Albert Hazlett were hiding in the hills overlooking Harpers Ferry trying to decide what their next move should be, when they saw Federal troops entering the engine house. They agreed that they must get help from Owen and the other men waiting at the farmhouse. Anderson and Hazlett, after an grueling night hiding in the mountains, finally reached the Kennedy farmhouse but the farmhouse was deserted. The two men decided to head for the mountains and Chambersburgh.

After another night on the mountain, with no food for 48 hours, Anderson and Hazlett finally found a few ears of corn to eat. The two men were just ten miles outside Chambersburgh when Hazlett announced that he could not go on. He told Anderson that he would rest for the remainder of the night in the mountains and try again in the morning. Anderson begged him to try and continue. He told Hazlett that it was too dangerous for him to travel by day because hundreds of troops were searching for them. Hazlett agreed it was dangerous, but he was unable to move. He told Anderson he would take the stage coach into town the next morning and hope he would not be recognized. Hazlett knew that Anderson was in much more danger than himself because, as a black man, he could only travel by foot, so he begged Anderson to go on without him. The two men embraced and Osborn Anderson continued on the road to Chambersburgh. Albert Hazlett was arrested as he walked down the road to Carlisle.

Hazlett was tried and convicted of treason. On March 15, 1860, on the eve of his execution, he wrote to a friend "I am willing to die in the cause of liberty. If I had ten thousand lives I would willingly lay them down for the same cause." [17]

Finally Anderson reached Chambersburgh and knocked on the door of an acquaintance. The man hustled him inside and told him he must leave immediately. Anderson's friend was suspected of being part of John Brown's raid and a United States marshal was watching his house. He told Anderson to eat quickly and leave. Just as Anderson was stuffing food into his pockets he heard a knock on the door and heard the voice of the marshal announcing that he had a warrant to search the house for any raiders. Anderson quickly slipped out the back door and fled.

Twenty-four hours after Anderson escaped from the trap at Chambersburgh, he arrived at the Pennsylvania town of York. In York, Anderson had a friend, William Goodridge, who could shelter him for a while and let him rest. Goodridge was a wealthy black merchant who had risen from apprentice barber to the owner of thirteen railroad cars. He was so respected in York that few townsmen realized that Goodridge was one of the most important station masters on the Underground Railroad. He used his cars to carry fugitive slaves arriving in York to other stations on the

---

[17] Villard, Oswald Garrison. *John Brown, 1800-1859: Fifty Years After.* New York: A. A. Knopf, 1943. (Pg. 682)

Underground Railroad. Goodridge was also a good friend of John Brown.

Anderson was able to stay at the Goodridge home until he was rested enough to travel again. When Anderson finally reached Canada, he decided, with the help of Mary Ann Shadd, editor of the *Provincial Freeman*, to write about his experiences at Harpers Ferry. It was called "A Voice From Harpers Ferry."

When the government searched the Kennedy farmhouse, they found a packet of letters from some of Brown's most important northern supporters, including Frederick Douglass. Douglass, although he had opposed the raid on Harpers Ferry, now found himself in grave danger. He was in Philadelphia when he was told that John Brown had been captured. Douglass learned that some of the letters found at the Kennedy farmhouse implicated him in the raid on Harpers Ferry. The nation was now in such a state of hysteria that Douglass was in danger of being arrested. His friends begged him to leave the city immediately, so Douglass fled to New York. They were right. John Hurn, a telegraph operator and an admirer of Douglass, suppressed for three hours a telegram from Virginia authorities to the sheriff of Philadelphia ordering him to arrest Frederick Douglass on charges of murder, robbery and inciting to servile insurrection. Even Douglass' home town of Rochester was no longer a safe haven for him. Abolitionist leaders learned that the Governor of New York was prepared to surrender Douglass to Virginia officials. Douglass decided to flee to Canada.

A wave of hysteria was sweeping the country. In the South, visions of mass slave revolts terrified slaveholders. In the North, Federal marshals were scouring the countryside, issuing subpoenas to everyone they believed was involved with John Brown. The charge of treason hovered in the air. Northern antislavery leaders, who had been treating Brown as the hero of the Kansas resistance, were terrified. Letters found in the Kennedy farmhouse, written by some of Brown's most successful fund raisers suggested that the writers knew about Brown's plans to raid Harpers Ferry. Five of these men, known as the "Secret Six" went into hiding. Gerit Smith had himself committed to the Utica Lunatic Asylum while Howe and Stearn fled the country. At the time of John Brown's raid, Theodore Parker was already in Europe. The youthful Frank Sandborn stayed hidden in

Concord, Massachusetts, which was so full of abolitionist supporters that it would be difficult for a Federal marshal to locate his hiding place. Only Thomas Higginson remained at home where anyone could find him if they wished. He was busy planning the rescue of John Brown and the other raiders.

John Brown refused to be rescued. He realized that, although he had lost the skirmish at Harpers Ferry, he now had the opportunity to win a major battle in the cause of abolition. He would use his trial to rally the country against slavery. Higginson and Mary Brown were already on their way to Charles Town where the trial was about to take place, when they received word from Brown not to come. He told his followers that it was vital that he stand trial so that his antislavery message would reach the world.

While fear overwhelmed most abolitionists and many of John Brown's friends were still in hiding, Henry David Thoreau, the great naturalist and philosopher, took a more courageous stand. As soon as he heard about the arrest of John Brown, he quickly organized a meeting of the citizens of Concord, Massachusetts. At this meeting Thoreau delivered an address called "A Plea for Captain Brown." In this address Thoreau publicly supported Brown and his attack on Harpers Ferry, even though the Federal government still had plans to put anyone who had some knowledge of the raid on trial for treason. Concord citizens cheered as Thoreau called Brown "an angel of light." Ralph Waldo Emerson, revered as one of America's most popular writers, stood up and declared that John Brown "would make the gallows as glorious as the cross." [18] The people of Concord were helping to change the way northerners viewed John Brown.

People all over the country had been eager to learn more about this antislavery fanatic. They wondered if his goal had been to launch a bloody slave revolt and kill off all the slaveholders in Virginia. This was certainly the belief of many southerners. Yet If John Brown wanted to kill all slaveholders, reporters wondered, why had Brown treated his slaveholder hostages so humanely, keeping them in a corner of the building so that they would be safe from the gun fire? Reporters who were busy interviewing many of the former hostages, were surprised to hear that John Brown made sure that his hostages were well fed and made as comfortable as possible. Reporters told

---

[18] Potter, David M. *The Impending Crisis 1848-1861*. New York: Harper & Row, Publishers, 1976. (Pg. 379)

their readers that when Federal troops began firing into the engine house, Brown immediately moved the captive slaveholders to a position of safety. These reports were published in newspapers throughout the nation and eagerly read by Americans of every political tenet. Northerners began to wonder what kind of a man John Brown really was.

John Brown's letters from jail to his friends and supporters, describing his commitment to liberating slaves, and combating the poisonous effect of slavery on the morality of America, were also published in various northern newspapers. These letters were so deeply moving that the picture of Brown as a vindictive madman began to change. His conduct deeply affected his jailers and the newspaper reporters who were hanging around the jail. Reporters began to write admiring stories about John Brown.

The other prisoners, Coppoc, Hazlett, Cook, and Stearns also impressed these reporters as they repeatedly proclaimed their pride in giving their lives to end slavery. The two black raiders, Shields Green and John Copeland amazed the country by the dignity and courage with which they faced death. Copeland wrote his parents, just before his execution, in a letter that was circulated throughout the North, "My fate as far as man can see is sealed, but let this not occasion you any misery... remember that if I must die, I die in trying to liberate a few of my oppressed people."

Judge Parker, the man who presided over Copeland's trial, was so impressed by John Copeland that he stated in an article in the *St Louis Globe* that "Copeland was the prisoner who impressed me best." [19]

Just one week after his capture, John Brown's trial began. He was still suffering from his wounds and during the entire week of the trial he was not able to sit on a chair; instead, he lay upon a pallet. As soon as the jury declared him guilty and the judge announced that he would be executed, John Brown, still unable to sit up, spoke from his cot. His speech would reverberate around the world.

I have that to have interfered as I have done, as I have always freely admitted I have done, in behalf of His despised poor, is no wrong, but right. Now, if it is deemed necessary that I should...

---

[19] Cheek, William and Aimee Lee Cheek. *John Mercer Langston and the Fight for Black Freedom 1829-65.* Urbana: University of Illinois Press, 1989. (Pg. 357)

John Brown's Trial. Source: *West Virginia State Archives.*

...forfeit my life for the furtherance of the ends of justice and mingle my blood further with the blood of my children and with the blood of millions in this slave country whose rights are disregarded by wicked, cruel and unjust enactments, I say let it be done.[20]

John Brown was hanged at Charlestown, Virginia on December 2, 1859. Church bells all over the North tolled in honor of the martyr. Many people in the North covered their homes and churches in black bunting. Thousands of people came together in memorial meetings in cities all over the North. Conservatives in the Massachusetts Legislature barely defeated a resolution to adjourn on the day of John Brown's execution. Southerners were horrified at these reactions. How could the South remain in a Union where so many northerners were proclaiming John Brown as a martyr to freedom?

The *Atlanta Confederacy* spoke for many southerners when it stated "We regard every man in our midst an enemy to the institutions of the South who does not boldly declare that he believes African slavery to be a social, moral, and political blessing." [21]

In 1861 Union soldiers would march into battle singing, "John Brown's body lies a moldering in his grave but his spirit marches on".

[20] Potter, David M. *The Impending Crisis 1848-1861.* (Pg. 377)
[21] Ibid (Pg. 383)

CHAPTER

12

THIS CIVIL WAR IS NOT A WAR ABOUT SLAVERY IT IS A WAR TO SAVE THE UNION.

The Confederate attack on Fort Sumpter radically changed public opinion throughout the North. Until the moment that the garrison was forced to surrender, the South had many supporters in the North. There had been a number of bills passed in Congress designed to placate southerners and preserve the Union. One particular bill, a Constitutional Amendment, would preserve slavery forever by forbidding Congress from passing any law abolishing slavery. To the horror of antislavery men, it passed Congress by a two-thirds vote. Even this measure did not appease the secessionist leaders of the South. Outrage in the North produced a huge outpouring of support for the Union. When Abraham Lincoln asked for volunteers to defend the Union, seventy five thousand men rushed to enlist. Frederick Douglass explained why the attack on Fort Sumpter had such a transforming effect on northerners. Slaveholders were not only demanding that their slave system had to be protected, but "It is not merely a war for slavery, but it is a war for slavery domination" [1]

In the beginning, both the North and the South believed the war would be over quickly and victory would be theirs. The North had almost three times more military-age white males than did the South, but the Confederacy had three and a half million slaves. "Our Negroes" exalted one Richmond newspaper, "will do the shoveling while our brave cavaliers will do the fighting".[2] The southern journalist J.D.B. DeBow predicted a Confederate victory in the summer of 1861 because he explained it would be able to "turn out every citizen as a soldier, with slaves to attend the camp and wait on the soldiery, yet leave slaves enough at home to carry on the ordinary

---

[1] Lockwood, John and Charles Lockwood. *The Siege of Washington: The Untold story of the Twelve Days That Shook the Union.* New York: Oxford University Press, 2011. (Pg. 9)

[2] Goodheart Adam. *1861 The Civil War Awakening.* New York: Vintage Books, 2012. (Pg. 297)

routine of industry." [3] The Confederate victory at the first battle of Bull Run only confirmed southern confidence. Thomas Cobb, a leading secessionist from Georgia, wrote his wife exulting that "[First Bull Run] has secured our Independence" [4]

While southerners counted on the loyalty of slaves to help win the war, their slaves had plans of their own. African Americans had watched the political conflict between the North and the South escalate into war and they realized that at last they had a real chance at freedom. With the southern branch of the Underground Railroad as its nucleus, African Americans created a new, broader organization called Lincoln's Legal Loyal League. By 1860 the South's Underground Railroad was a network which had spread throughout the slave states. It was primarily a black organization but, from the beginning, there were always a handful of white southern members dedicated to the abolition of slavery. The new Legal League began to reach out to white southern unionists, some of whom had no interest in abolition, but were dedicated to supporting the Union cause. These two diverse groups would find themselves working together to defeat the Confederacy. Legal League members would play a major role in transforming the Civil War from a war only to preserve the Union into a revolution that would finally destroy slavery in America.

In 1861 Abraham Lincoln's major concern was to prevent the border states of Maryland, Kentucky, and Missouri from joining the Confederacy. The President believed that if any one of these states seceded the Union cause would be lost. If Maryland seceded, Washington D.C. would be completely surrounded by Confederate states, Virginia to the south and Maryland to the north and west. Lincoln would be forced to abandon the capital. Kentucky, the reason that the President believed Kentucky was crucial to a Union victory was its strategic location. On its north flowed the Ohio River and to

[3] Levine, Bruce. *Confederate Emancipation: Southern Plans to Free and Arm Slaves During the Civil War.* New York: Oxford University Press, 2006. (Pg. 61)

[4] Robinson, Armstead L. *Bitter Fruits of Bondage: The Demise of Slavery and the Collapse of the Confederacy, 1861-1865.* Charlottesville: University of Virginia Press, 2005. (Pg 71)

its west was the Mississippi River. If the Confederacy won Kentucky it could use the rivers to invade Ohio, Indiana, and Illinois. Kentucky's port cities also gave the Union access to several major river systems including the Tennessee and Cumberland rivers that flowed into the South's heartland. Missouri was vital to the Union cause because it guarded the western shore of the Mississippi River and prevented the Confederacy from attacking Kansas and Illinois.

Lincoln began his campaign of wooing the slaveholders of the border states by assuring them that he was fighting the war only to save the Union and, therefore, the Federal government was no threat to their slave property. To prove to Union slaveholders how committed his government was to leaving their slave property untouched, Lincoln promised them that as long as they remained in the Union, his government would vigorously enforce the Fugitive Slave Law. In 1861 the President believed that many Confederate slaveholders who still cherished the Union could be won to the Union cause if they believed their slave property would be safe. Lincoln tried to appeal to these slaveholders by announcing that he was ordering the Union Army to return any escaping slaves, not only from Union states, but from any territory conquered by the Union army. The President also sent a message to Confederate slaveholders that he would allow them to cross over into Union lines in order to pick up their runaway slaves. It was a message that horrified abolitionists throughout the North.

Fortress Monroe, Virginia, was a Union military installation just south of Washington D.C. In May 1861 three fugitive slaves appeared at the headquarters of General Benjamin Butler, commander of the fortress. The three slaves, Frank Baker, Shepard Mallory, and James Townsend told General Butler that they had just

Stampede of Slaves to Fortess Monroe, 1861. From: *Harper's Pictorial History of the Great Rebellion.* Source: *New Hanover County Public Library, Wilmington, N.C.*

escaped from the Confederate front where they had been building fortifications. It could not have been an easy decision for the fugitives. Would Union officials return them to their masters, or would they be allowed to stay? The men did have some bargaining chips; they could give the new commander of the fort accurate information on Rebel operations. General Butler, who had just arrived at his post, was an unlikely challenger of the Fugitive Slave Law. He had never been in the army; he had received his commission because he was a prominent Democratic politician from the State of New York. Butler had been a delegate to the 1860 Democratic Party Convention and had actually supported Jefferson Davis as the Democratic presidential candidate. This was the man who would decide the fate of the three fugitives.

The next day, as Butler was still trying to decide what to do with the three runaways, their owner, a Confederate colonel, appeared at his headquarters under a flag of truce. The slaveholder demanded under the terms of the Fugitive Slave Law, which Lincoln had promised southerners he would enforce, that Butler return his slaves. General Butler listened to this demand with some astonishment. Then he informed the slaveholder that, since Virginia claimed to be out of the Union, the Fugitive Slave Law no longer applied to Virginia. Furthermore, Butler insisted that since Virginia and the Union were now at war, he had a right to confiscate all enemy property, which certainly would include fugitive slaves. The general announced that these fugitives were now contraband of the war and quickly put them to work in his camp. Even Lincoln was pleased that General Butler had a few more willing hands to help the army. He approved the idea of confiscating Confederate slaves who had been working for the Confederate army and putting them to work for the Union.

The news spread quickly that the Union army was protecting fugitives. General Butler was amazed that within three months, hundreds of black men, along with their families arrived at Fortress Monroe. Nobody in the Federal government knew what to do with this flood of fugitives. The labor of the adult men was badly needed by the Union army; even their wives could be put to work as nurses, cooks, laundresses, and seamstresses, but what was Butler to do about the children? Butler told Washington that it would be impossible to separate families and send tiny children back into slavery. Soon the land around the fortress was covered with the temporary camps of hundreds of fugitive families. Butler begged Washington for guidance. Henry Jarvis, one of the fugitives who had escaped to Fortress

Monroe, knew what he wanted to do; the ex-slave offered to enlist in the Union army. General Butler insultingly rejected his offer telling Jarvis that it wasn't a black man's war. Jarvis' retort was, "I told him that it would be a black man's war before they got through." [5]

Lincoln's policy was contradictory. On one hand the President was still trying to placate border slaveholders , yet, at the same time, Lincoln realized how dependent the army was on the labor of these fugitives. In August, 1861, the United States Congress recognized both the need to support Lincoln's border policy while acknowledging the value of these contraband fugitives to the Union army. They passed the First Confiscation Act which stated that all property, including slaves, used by the Confederate army against the Federal government could be confiscated by the Union army and used in the war effort. Only slaveholders from Union states could still use the Fugitive Slave Law to recapture their slaves. There were some Union soldiers who rebelled at returning fugitives to any slaveholders. In July 1861 an officer reported that one of his men refused an order to arrest a suspected fugitive. "I can obey no such order; it was not to put down [Negro] insurrection that I enlisted but to defend my country's flag! I am ready to bear the consequences, but never to have a hand in arresting slaves." [6]

Since cotton was the major cash crop of the southern economy, the Confederate government counted on the sale of raw cotton to England to purchase war supplies. In the summer of 1861, Abraham Lincoln issued orders to the Union Navy to begin a blockade of the Southern coast to prevent the Confederacy from selling their cotton abroad. To enforce a Union blockade, the navy first had to seize control of the sea islands, a vast chain of over 100 tidal and barrier islands off the coast of the Atlantic Ocean that stretched from Virginia down to Florida.

The battle for control of the sea islands began in October, 1861, when a vast flotilla of Union naval vessels and army transport ships set sail for Port Royal, one of the largest and most important of the sea islands. This island lay just off the coast of Georgia between Charleston and Savannah. When slaveholders first saw Union warships sailing towards their island, Port Royal planters panicked and fled to the mainland. As soon as the news spread that

[5] Foner Eric. *The Fiery Trial: Abraham Lincoln and American Slavery.* New York: W. W. Norton & Co. 2010. (Pg. 187)

[6] Goodheart, Adam. *1861: The Civil War Awakening.* New York: Alfred A. Knopf 2011, (Pg. 341-342)

the Yankees had been sighted and that freedom might be only a few days away, most of the island's slaves fled into the fields and swamps, forcing their masters to leave without them. The conquest of Port Royal was celebrated in the North as one of the first great Union victories. Thousands of fugitive slaves greeted the Union army when they landed on Port Royal. Union officers immediately put them to work fortifying the island.

The struggle of the sea island slave population to remain in their homes under the protection of the Union army was the first great victory of southern slaves against the Confederacy. This was not an easy victory. Some slaveholders fought to bring their slaves with them to the mainland and sometimes the battle turned bloody. There were stories that slaves who resisted removal were shot. There was one story that a group of slaves was locked in the cotton house by their owner because they refused to leave with him. In his fury the slaveholder set fire to the building and the slaves burned to death. On Edisto Island, when a Confederate raiding party tried to capture some of the male fugitives, the women of the island began firing at the soldiers. The surprised soldiers began shooting back, killing some of the women before the rest of the women drove the Rebels off the island.

Susannah, a skilled family seamstress, was considered by her owner to be a very devoted slave, but, to his great surprise, when her master ordered her to leave with him, she refused. Her master began telling her dire stories about what the Yankees would do to her when they arrived. Unmoved, Susannah refused to budge. Susannah's owner finally left without her. A few days later Susannah's master's son came back to the plantation. He had orders from the Confederate commander to burn all of the cotton crop to prevent the Yankees from harvesting it. When he ordered the slaves to begin the burning they refused. After all, these newly liberated slaves decided that the cotton crop now belonged to them and they were not going to allow the Rebels to destroy it. Frustrated slaveholders returned to the mainland to plan another attack on the cotton fields. Susannah and the other island women took turns guarding the fields both day and night, while the men of the island hid in the woods and swamps with their weapons ready to attack any *Planter* who tried to burn the cotton. Planters finally decided to abandon the cotton fields to their ex-slaves.

Beaufort was one of the most important ports on South Carolina's coast. On the night of April 22, 1862, Southerners on Beaufort still felt that they were safe from a Union attack because the cannon of neighboring Fort Macon were aimed at the narrow channel leading to the town's wharf. No Union vessel could enter the town without being observed. What the people of Beaufort did not know was that the Union army was going to use the expertise of a group of black watermen. These slave pilots knew the treacherous currents, shoals and tides of Beaufort, and they convinced Union officers that they could guide their troops into Beaufort without having to fight a bloody battle. The watermen were just waiting for a dark night to execute their daring plan. For days they had collected a flotilla of simple rowboats which they now filled with Federal soldiers. Lookouts within Fort Macon could not see the small boats as they quietly rowed through the channel, led by the black guides. These guides brought the boats quietly through the difficult waters of the sound and through a narrow channel across the mouth of the Newport River. Then they slipped their small boats just beneath the guns of Fort Macon, careful to make no noise. Without using an oar, they let the tide carry their vessels into Beaufort Harbor. The town guards never heard a sound, and when the people of Beaufort awoke that morning, they discovered that their town was now occupied by the Union army. Because of the skill of the black watermen, the key port of Beaufort had been taken without a shot being fired.

By the summer of 1862, the Federal government was in control of the sea islands along with some of the South's port cities. This news spread quickly into slave quarters all along the Southern coast. Hundreds of fugitives took off to find the Union army, joining the 10,000 sea island ex-slaves. One slave who had successfully escaped to the Union lines exulted that "it used to be five hundred miles to git to Canada from Lexington but now it's only eighteen miles! Camp Nelson is now our Canada." [7]

The deeper the Union army penetrated into Confederate territory, the more the army needed workers to provide support services. The only laborers they could depend on were the thousands of ex-slaves who were flooding every Union camp and installation. Happy Union soldiers were delighted to watch contraband workers building fortifications, clearing campgrounds, repairing roads, bridges

---

[7] Litwack, Leon F. *Been in the Storm So Long: The Aftermath of Slavery.* New York: Vintage Books, 1979. (Pg 51)

and railroad tracks. Union generals were especially pleased because every contraband who lifted a shovel meant that another white soldier could be sent onto the battlefield.

The flight of so many slaves to the Union was beginning to affect the Confederacy's war effort. Jefferson Davis, president of the Confederacy, had depended on slave labor to support his army. Now hundreds of slaves, who were working close to the front line, were fleeing to the Union lines. More and more Confederate soldiers were forced into guard duty just to prevent even more escapes. By the summer of 1862, so many slaves were escaping to Union lines that Confederate General John Pemberton issued an order that only white soldiers could work on the front line of the battlefield because slaves "could not be trusted to work so near the enemy." The general was also forced to divert troops to guard black laborers who were working miles away from the battlefield, " to prevent the escape of slaves and for the protection of persons and property against insubordination of negroes." [8] Even back home, runaways had become a serious problem for the Confederacy. Jefferson Davis had received reports suggesting that as many as 15,000 blacks from the interior of the state of Georgia, far from the front, had escaped to Union lines during the first nine months of the war.[9] State governors were rejecting Jefferson Davis' call for more volunteers to join the Confederate army because, they told the President, they needed more men in their own state militias to prevent increasing numbers of slaves from fleeing to the Federal lines.

The determination of some of these slaves to be free astonished Yankee officers. Running away was even more dangerous than it had been before the war, now that state militia and newly organized local home guard units were patrolling the southern countryside. Home guard units were especially vicious, using packs of well trained bloodhounds, running down fugitives with their horses, sometimes tying runaways to their horses as they dragged them off to jail.

Harry Smith, a young Virginia slave, recalled years later in his book, Fifty Years of Slavery in the United States of America, what slaves risked by supporting the Union army. In one case, when patrollers caught up with fifty fugitives on their way to join the Union army, all fifty of them were massacred.. In another case when

---

[8] Williams David. *Bitterly Divided: The South's Inner Civil War.* New York: New Press, 2008. (Pg. 191)

[9] Quarles, Benjamin *The Negro In the Civil War.* Boston: Little Brown and Company, 1953. (Pg. 71)

twelve men were caught "giving information to the Yankees about the whereabouts of pro Confederate guerillas, "The men were taken down to the salt river, a hole cut in the ice and they were singled out, shot and pushed under the ice".[10]

Yet in spite of all the increased military power used by Confederate state and local governments, slaves continued to escape by the thousands. As one fugitive explained, "Slavery is not so bad, but liberty is so good".[11]

Slaveholders hoped that terror tactics might keep their slaves from fleeing. When six South Carolina fugitives were caught returning to the plantation to rescue their families, a local court ordered them to be hanged that day. Plantation slaves were encouraged to watch the execution in the hope that the sight would discourage any thought of escaping.

The Millers were a slave family living on a plantation just outside Savannah who, when they heard the news that the Union army was close by immediately began planning their escape. The patriarch of the family tried the first escape but he was caught and dragged back to the plantation. His owner pulled Miller out to the middle of the slave quarters and began beating him while a group of white men looked on. They told each other that five hundred lashes across the back of this elderly man would certainly discourage other slaves from trying to reach the Union lines. But as the terrible beating proceeded, Mrs. Miller was already making her own escape plans. This seventy year- old woman had gathered her children and grandchildren together and hid them in a nearby swamp, deciding to escape that very night. Mrs. Miller had found a wooden flat boat, which was considered so dangerously unseaworthy that it had been left to rot in the swamp. She placed her family into this boat and they floated forty miles down the river to the Union lines. When Mrs. Miller finally reached a Union gunboat she stood up in the cramped boat, her youngest grandchild in her arms and cried out with joy, "My God! We are finally free!" Her grandsons enlisted in the army

---

[10] Oakes James. *Freedom National: The Destruction of Slavery in the United States,* 1861-1865. New York: W.W. Norton & Company, 2013. (Pg. 404)

[11] Williamson, Joel. *After Slavery: The Negro in South Carolina During Reconstruction, 1861-1877.* Chapel Hill: University of North Carolina Press, 1965. (Pg. 8)

work battalions. The rest of the family settled down near the camp and waited. A few months later an elderly black man with a terribly scarred back was seen floating down the river waving excitedly as he spotted a Union gunboat. Soldiers quickly rescued the man from the leaky boat. It was Mr. Miller, who had waited until his body healed before attempting another escape.[12]

The Union army soon recognized that African Americans made the best spies. Alan Pinkerton was the first Union official to recognize that fact. When the war began he was asked by his close friend George McClellan, newly appointed General of the Potomac Army, to establish a spy network in Virginia. Pinkerton began in a very traditional fashion by sending two of his most skilled operatives, Mrs. Hattie Lawton and Timothy Webster to the Confederate capital, Richmond where they soon became part of the social life of the city. Pinkerton, a member of the Underground Railroad, also understood the power of the slave grapevine. He begged Union officers to question fugitives as soon as they arrived at a Union campground. These officers were astonished at the wide ranging information fugitives had to give them on Confederate troop movements.

John Scobell was a Legal League member who had been freed just before the war. The moment war was declared, Scobell rushed over to volunteer his services to the Union army. The officer who first interviewed Scobell was so impressed by the black man's personality and extraordinary powers of observation that he decided to send the ex-slave directly to Alan Pinkerton.

Scobell's first assignment was to visit every Confederate camp in northern Virginia and collect as much information as he could about their army's military plans. Scobell had a wonderful cover; as a black man he was able to enter the camp without arousing suspicion. Sometimes he would have bags of produce to sell to the always hungry soldiers; other times he would be hired as a day laborer to dig ditches and fortifications. At least once Scobell presented himself as a cook. Scobell's most useful accomplishment was his ability to sing, and play his banjo. Rebel soldiers were bored and eager for entertainment.

---

[12] Higginson, Thomas Wentworth. *Army Life in a Black Regiment.* Boston Beacon Press, 1962. (Pg. 247)

Scobell's talent for singing Scotch ballads made him a popular visitor in every camp in northern Virginia.

Alan Pinkerton assigned Scobell to work with Mrs. Lawton and Timothy Webster When Pinkerton's white operatives were arrested in Richmond in 1862, Scobell, who played the role of Mrs. Lawton's coachman, was never even questioned because his ability to act the part of a humble, ignorant servant was so polished. Scobell and the Legal League remained part of the Union army spy network until the end of the war.

In early 1862, Vincent Colyer, Superintendent of the Poor for North Carolina, was stationed in New Bern, North Carolina. His official duties were to provide a variety of social services to the thousands of fugitives that had fled to the federally controlled islands and ports of North Carolina. Unofficially, Colyer was given the assignment of organizing some of the fugitives into a network of spies and sending them into Rebel- controlled areas to gather information for the Union army.

March Haynes was a Savannah river pilot who knew the waterways around the city intimately. One day he slipped into the Union camp and volunteered to help the Union. He became one of Colyer's most successful spies. Savannah officials finally began to suspect Haynes of working for the Yankees, but friends were able to warn him that he was in danger of being arrested. He and his wife fled the city, but Haynes continued to work for the Union. He used the homes of Savannah friends and Union supporters as his new base of operations. Haynes would spend several days in the city gathering information on the strength and location of Confederate defenses, then report back to Union officers. General Quincy Gillmore was so impressed by Haynes that he expanded his assignment. Gillmore gave Haynes a sturdy swift boat painted a drab color to blend in with the waters of the Savannah River. Haynes collected a crew, then sailed his boat into the marshes below Savannah. As soon as it was dark Haynes and his men would move swiftly throughout the city collecting information.

On one of Haynes expeditions, he was shot in the leg; but in spite of his wound, he returned safely to the Union lines. In April, 1863, Haynes was arrested and jailed by Savannah officials, but somehow talked the officers into releasing him. When the war ended in 1865, and the village of Mitchelville on the island of Port Royal held their first election, March Haynes was elected village marshal.

Furney Bryant headed another one of Colyer's bands of spies. When Colyer first met Bryant he had just escaped from slavery and he could neither read nor write. The fugitive eagerly accepted Colyer's invitation to join one of the literacy classes that he was teaching. Colyer was impressed by how quickly the young fugitive learned everything he was able to teach. Colyer recruited Bryant into his network of spies. Furney Bryant soon headed a band of fifty spies who sometimes traveled as much as three-hundred miles deep into Confederate territory to gather information for the Union army. It was a dangerous undertaking. From time to time Bryant and his men might be pursued by bloodhounds. In 1863, Bryant enlisted in the 1st North Carolina Colored Regiment where his gallantry and intelligence on the battlefield so impressed Union officers that he was promoted to the rank of sergeant.

Abraham Galloway, was a North Carolina fugitive slave who fled to Canada in 1857. The twenty-year-old Galloway was a dedicated antislavery man, committed to fighting slavery back in the United States. The fugitive was soon a featured speaker at abolitionist gatherings in New England and Ohio. Many believed that Galloway was also a conductor on the Underground Railroad. Sometime just after the war began, Galloway returned south. He carried letters of introduction from abolitionists to Generals Butler and Burnside. Galloway offered to do some spying for the Union; after all, he had friends everywhere. Galloway soon set up a network that included most of coastal North Carolina.

After the fall of Fort Sumpter, Confederate forces occupied all of the Union military outposts in the South including the navy shipyards in Norfolk, Virginia. In the shipyard harbor, the South had one of its most potent weapons to use against the Union blockade. This was the nine-gun ship, the *Merrimac* which had recently been converted into an ironclad. It was a new technique that allowed a ship builder to cover a wooden vessel with iron plating, thereby turning an ordinary sailing vessel into a formidable fighting ship. The Union navy at this time did not have the technique of converting their own ships into ironclads.

In the *Merrimac's* first appearance, it had shown just how dangerous such a ship could be. In the space of five hours the ironclad had managed to capture or incapacitate three ships and two Union frigates. Lincoln and his cabinet met to discuss just how the Union blockade could continue as long as the South had such a formidable weapon. Some cabinet members raised the possibility that the *Merrimac* might be able to sail up the Potomac and attack Washington itself.

The answer to their dilemma would not come from Northern shipbuilders, who were anxiously trying to develop their own ironclad design, but from a middle-aged African American woman, Mary Louvestre. She was a slave in the household of Simon Louvestre, the naval engineer who had designed and built the *Merrimac*. Louvestre was an extremely talented seamstress who created dresses not only for her own mistress, but for many other slaveholder's wives in Norfolk. Nobody ever questioned her comings and goings around the city.

One of her daily duties was to clean Simeon Louvestre's office. One day as she quietly polished the brass, she overheard her owner and a group of Confederates discussing the plans for creating their wonder ship, the *Merrimac*. As soon as the men left she began searching the shop until she found the vessel's plans. The next morning Mary Louvestre got up even earlier than usual. She gathered sheets of the tissue paper which she used for her dressmaking patterns and slipped them inside her dress. Then she left for the shop. It was too early for anyone else to be there. She took out the plans for the *Merrimac* and began tracing them onto the tissue paper. Every day for a week she left her room early until she had copied the entire set of plans for the ship.

Next, she asked her owner if she might visit her former owner, who still lived in the Shenandoah Valley. It would only take a week, she assured the Louvestres. They thought it was so charming and loyal of her to wish to visit her old master and mistress that they readily agreed to her request, and even wrote a note for her to carry stating that she had their permission for the trip so that she would not be stopped by the Rebel posses that were policing the Virginia countryside looking for escaping slaves

The first part of the trip was easy. Louvestre got rides with slaves who were hauling supplies for the Confederate army. But when she reached Fredericksburg she needed help to cross over to the Union side. Just outside of town she whispered to a black teamster that she had to cross the lines. He directed her to the headquarters of the Legal League. The League assigned a guide to lead her through the lines to the village of Centerville, which was occupied by the Union army. She arrived in Washington with her precious plans and put them in the hands of the Secretary of the Navy, Gideon Wells.

Louvestre quietly returned home to Norfolk and waited to see what would happen.

Now that they had the plans for the *Merrimac*, Union engineers were quickly able to convert one of their own wooden boats into an ironclad, which they called the *Monitor*. The battle of the Ironclads took place at Hampton Road, Virginia. The *Merrimac* was beginning a final attack on a badly damaged frigate called the Minnesota when suddenly a strange looking ship appeared, looking more like a cheese box on a raft than a fighting vessel. The *Merrimac* began confidently firing at this new enemy but its cannonballs just bounced off of the sides of the *Monitor*. The battle of the ironclads raged for hours; finally the *Merrimac* tried to ram the *Monitor* but it was the *Merrimac* itself that was damaged and had to sail away. The *Merrimac* was so badly damaged that the Confederate navy was forced to sink her themselves to prevent the ship from falling into Union hands. The victory of the *Monitor* meant that the Federal government's fleet stationed at the Union navel base at Hampton Roads had been saved. Without that base, Lincoln would never have been able to maintain the blockade of Southern ports.

July 1863 was the turning point of the Civil War. Two events, one on July 3rd, and the second on July 4th, were the decisive days. The first event was the fall of Vicksburg. President Lincoln knew that if the Union army was ever going to compel the Confederacy to surrender, it must first control the Mississippi River so that the Confederacy would be divided in half. The Union army had won a spectacular victory in occupying New Orleans in 1862, but the Union forces remained blocked because Confederates still occupied Vicksburg. This key city was midway between New Orleans and Memphis, and sat high on a chain of bluffs overlooking the Mississippi. It was surrounded by more than thirty miles of impassable water-logged swampland. General Grant had tried and failed three times to mount an attack on Vicksburg from the river itself. Now, in the late spring of 1863, Grant decided on a radical plan. He decided to surround the city by moving his entire army through the swampland and encircle Vicksburg. Grant could execute this dangerous maneuver because he now had the help of black and white

Union spies who were able to guide Union troops through some of the secret pathways that crisscrossed the swampland. Vicksburg was now under siege; the defenders were unable to get either food or supplies. On July 4th Vicksburg surrendered to General Grant.

The second key event was the Battle of Gettysburg, this victory was also aided by an ex-slave. In the late spring of 1863, flush with a series of victories against the Union army in Virginia, General Robert E. Lee decided to take the war into the Union itself. He believed that, if northerners were forced to experience the horrors of war, they would soon agree to allow the Confederate states to secede. In late June, Lee's troops began their historic march into Pennsylvania.

In 1863, General Hooker took command of the Army of the Potomac. One of his first acts was to create a centralized intelligence system. In June, one of his operatives, Capt. John McEntee, was approached by a young black man, Charlie Wright. Wright, a fugitive slave from Culpeper Virginia, had some valuable information for the Union army. He informed McEntee that a dozen separate Confederate regiments under the commands of General Ewell and General Longstreet had passed through Culpeper and were on their way to Maryland. The information was immediately passed on to General Hooker. Hooker ordered his army to shadow the movement of these Confederate troops. Thanks to Wright's alerting General Hooker, when Lee's troops reached Gettysburg, they discovered that the Union army had already secured three key ridges west of town. The Confederate army was never able to dislodge Union forces from these ridges. Lee's gamble had failed. From now on, all of the[13] battles would be fought on southern soil.

The most important battlefront during the Civil War was northern Virginia. If the Union army could capture Richmond, the capital of the Confederacy, they believed that the Confederacy would have to surrender. Even though Alan Pinkerton's operatives had been captured, there was another spy network in Richmond which the Confederates never uncovered. This network was the creation of an aristocratic Virginian woman, Elizabeth Van Lew. For years this intrepid lady operated a wide-ranging organization of spies and rescuers. Van Lew's network included men and women, patricians and workers, blacks and whites. Her network seemed to be everywhere in the city, from the depth of Richmond's notorious Libby Prison, where

---

[13] Rose P. K. *"Black Dispatches: Black American Contributions to Union Intelligence During the Civil War"*. Studies in Intelligence. March, 2007.

Union soldiers captured on the battlefields of Northern Virginia were held, to the homes of some of the most important Confederate leaders, including Jefferson Davis, President of the Confederacy.

Van Lew, along with her family, had always been against slavery, but it was not clear if the family had ever been part of Richmond's Underground Railroad. When Virginia joined the Confederacy, Van Lew's first concern was simply a charitable impulse to help the Union soldiers captured after the battle of Bull Run. That made her suddenly a suspicious character in Richmond, where every other aristocratic lady was busy nursing Confederate soldiers. Anyone interested in Yankees was obviously a secret Union supporter. Van Lew had to do something to divert suspicion. She and her mother began visiting some Confederate camps as well, bringing these soldiers food and other comforts. Then, in a stroke of genius, she and her mother invited Captain George Gibbs, new head of the Yankee prison complex, to make his home with them. Even that first year, Van Lew was aware of the fact that Yankee prisoners had valuable information on the battlefield strength of the Confederate army, which would be useful to the Federal government. She needed to find a way to send that information through the Confederate lines and into the hands of the Union army. Van Lew's servants introduced her to the members of Richmond's Legal League.

In the winter of 1862, the danger to Van Lew increased significantly when Pinkerton's network was betrayed. In spite of the danger, she decided to expand the network by reaching out to other secret Union supporters. Some of her new recruits were former Whig Party members, doctors, lawyers, businessmen, and ministers who, like Van Lew, were still considered pillars of Richmond society. Other secret Unionists were a group of shopkeepers, and workingmen including a group of German antislavery immigrants.

Van Lew and the network had already begun helping in the escape of Union soldiers. At first they merely assisted soldiers who had already escaped from jail, by providing safe houses and a way to reach the Union army. By the end of 1862, Van Lew and her associates had found ways of organizing escapes right out of Libby Prison, the largest jail in the Confederacy. Some members of the network had found ways of recruiting people who worked in Libby itself. One of the most important recruits was Erasmus Ross, clerk of Libby prison. While publicly he sounded like the most zealous of Rebels, privately he was a dedicated Union man. Van Lew also was able to recruit a few Rebel soldiers working as guards in the prison.

In April, 1862, the Confederate government realized that the war was not going to be over quickly. Jefferson Davis knew that if the Confederacy was going to be victorious he needed more troops, yet the number of new volunteers had radically dwindled . Davis decided on a revolutionary act; he asked his Congress to pass a law drafting all white males between the ages of eighteen and thirty five years of age. America had never had a draft, and it was one of the most unpopular laws ever passed by the Confederate Congress. Most draftees were poor farmers, and many of them were bitter because they were being forced to abandon their families, who would have to survive on the meager wages of a soldier in the Confederate army. Van Lew discovered that many times, even this pitiful wage had not been paid in months. By 1862, food prices began to escalate all through the south. Soldiers' families, who no longer had adult males to help grow food and the small cash crops that they needed to survive, were becoming desperate. When Van Lew learned about the dire straits of some of these families, she started to explore the possibility of recruiting these. She offered to pay a few of the prison guards simply to look the other way when an escape was in process. Van Lew also discovered that a handful of Rebel soldiers were secret Unionists. These guards volunteered to help in the escapes.

Black members of the Legal League were always the most crucial links in the Richmond network. Jail workers carried messages back and forth between the prisoners and the network. When an escape was planned, Van Lew would station a few black Legal Leaguers just outside the jail. They quickly whisked an escaped soldier to a safe house. We know very little about the black members of Van Lew's network, most of whom remained anonymous. We do know about two who managed to penetrate Jefferson Davis's own household. One was William A. Jackson, who became President Davis' coachman. Jackson eagerly listened to every bit of conversation that went on among passengers riding in his coach. When he thought the information was important enough, Jackson would sneak through Confederate lines to reach a Union army station, as he did not trust anyone else to deliver his reports.

Mary Elizabeth Bowser, one of Van Lew's most successful operators, had been a slave of the Van Lew family. Elizabeth and her mother were so impressed by Bowser's character and talent that they freed her and then sent Bowser to a Quaker school in Philadelphia

Mary Elizabeth Bowser. *Nanny in the Davis Household.* Source: *U.S. Army Military Intelegence Museum, Fort Huachuca, Arizona.*

so that she could receive a first-rate education. When the war began Bowser was recruited by Van Lew to play a key role in her network. Bowser returned to Richmond and, acting as a simple illiterate slave girl, she was sent into the home of Jefferson Davis, the new president of the Confederacy, as a household servant. As the seemingly ignorant slave waited at table, she was able to hear Confederate leaders discussing military strategy and other important issues, and she would send reports to Van Lew about these conversations. As she cleaned the rooms of the Confederate White House, Bowser would routinely check all the papers on the President's desk to see if there was any information that would be useful to the Union..

Bowser had a photographic memory, so, in the evenings, she would be able to write down the exact contents of these documents. For years her role in the Civil War was not acknowledged but, in 1995, Mary Elizabeth Bowser was inducted into the U. S Army Military Intelligence Corps Hall of Fame.

General Butler was increasingly impressed by the kinds of intelligence reports he was getting from Van Lew. Her next triumph overwhelmed the general. On the night of February 9, 1864, over one hundred Yankee soldiers escaped from Libby Prison. The next morning prison officials discovered the tunnel through which the men had achieved their freedom. Furious, they questioned everyone who might be responsible for the successful escape. Libby Commandant Thomas Pratt Turner decided that Robert Ford, one of the Black prison workers, was part of the plot and must know where the escapees were hiding. Turner was right – Ford was one of the chief organizers of the escape; he knew the identity of many of the Richmond network. He probably could have led Turner to most of the safe houses where the Yankee soldiers were hiding. Turner whipped Ford almost to death. He received 500 lashes but never said a word. In July, 1864, Ford himself escaped Libby Prison.

When General Grant took over command of the Union army in 1864, he sent a message to Van Lew asking that she report directly to General Sharpe, Chief of the Bureau of Military Intelligence, so he could receive her reports as quickly as possible. By August, 1864, Van Lew's network was sending General Sharpe an average of three intelligence reports a week. Ulysses Grant regarded the Van Lew network as one of the most effective spy operations of the entire Union army.

In the spring of 1862, the Federal government was in control of the more than 100 sea islands, but they did not have enough troops to establish permanent bases on most of them. Only the major islands like Fortress Monroe, Port Royal, Hilton Head and Beaufort had permanent Union bases. The rest of the islands were irregularly supervised by Union gunboats sailing up and down the coastal waterways. These unprotected islands were constantly attacked by bands of Confederate raiders. Union officers needed more soldiers to protect these smaller islands so they could remain in Federal hands The army begged the Federal government for troops to launch a series of raids against the Rebel forces, but the government had no troops to spare; Northern Virginia was, after all the major battlefield. The sea islands, although a very important part of the blockade, would have to fend for themselves.

General David Hunter, just appointed commander of the Department of the South, told his officers to recruit some of these self-emancipated black men into bands of guerilla raiders. Their assignment would be to launch a series of small attacks on the Confederate mainland. Hunter believed that even small raids might prevent the Confederate army from retaking any of the sea islands. These guerrilla raids forced the Confederate army to build forts and station hundreds of troops all along the waterways of the Carolinas and Georgia.

One band of fugitive raiders was organized by an ex-slave known only as Bob. Bob was a slave in the coastal town of Washington, North Carolina, when the Union gunboats began shelling the town. Bob and the rest of the town's slave population had been ordered by Confederate officers to dig fortifications. Bob, however, had other ideas. He decided to organize an escape because, as he told a Union officer, "there was no way that I was going to fight for the Rebels if I could help it." That night while they were being guarded by a single Rebel soldier, Bob whispered to the sixteen other captives that it was now or never if they wanted to escape. Quietly they sneaked up behind the guard and took him prisoner, then the fugitives took off to find the Union army.

Bob and his men were soon making regular raids on the mainland. On one assignment, the band was pursued by one hundred armed Confederate troops. The Rebels shouted out calls to surrender but Bob just laughed and sailed back to the Union base.

One day the band had an assignment, which took them to Rodman's Point. As soon as they landed, they were greeted with a hail of fire from a company of Rebel soldiers hiding in the bushes. The men ran back to the boat but the boat was stuck on a sand bar and could not be launched. Ordering his men to lie flat on the floor of the craft, Bob announced that, "Somebody's got to die to get us out of this and it may as well be me." He then deliberately got out of the boat, pushed the vessel off the sandbar, then fell into the boat, his body pierced by five bullets.[14]

St. Simon's Island was one of the most important of Georgia's sea islands; but in the summer of 1862, the Union army had suffered a series of battlefield defeats in northern Virginia. Troops were being transferred from the sea islands to the Virginia front. St Simon's Island was one of places that the Union army had to abandon. When General Hunter heard that the Confederates were about to raid the islands, the general ordered the evacuation of the fugitive settlers. Twenty-five fugitives refused to leave. They insisted that they had the right to fight any Rebel raiders in order to preserve their freedom on St. Simon. General Hunter agreed. He ordered the army to issue muskets to the settlers, so Union officers handed out the guns and hoped for the best.

The settler band elected the black ex-slave John Brown to be their leader. His first order was to break into all the deserted plantation houses and collect all the arms they could find. In August, 1862, the Confederates sent a raiding party to attack the island. When the Rebels landed, they were met by a hail of bullets and they fled into the swamp, John Brown and his men following closely behind. The swamp was so dense that the men had to walk single file down the narrow trail with John Brown leading the way. The

[14] Brown, William Wells. *The Negro In the American Rebellion.* New York: The Citadel Press, 1971. (Pg. 215)

Confederates found a spot where the swamp opened up a bit and, using a huge log as cover, managed to set a trap for their pursuers. When the fugitive band came into view the Rebels began firing. John Brown was killed and some of the other band members were wounded, but they continued fighting. When the Union army led by Sergeant Trowbridge finally landed on the island, they were met by the band of armed fugitives who triumphantly announced that they had already driven the Rebels off the island. Although Trowbridge and his men remained on the island for several weeks the Rebel guerrillas never returned. The sea islands remained under the control of the Union army until the end of the Civil War.

By 1862, many Union officers and men had become angry at having to enforce the Fugitive Slave Law. Jack Scroggins was a Maryland slave who knew nothing about Lincoln's border policy; he only knew that freedom was just over the border in Virginia where the Union army was camped. Scroggins planned his escape carefully. He waited until there was an especially dark night, slipped away from the slave quarters, and began walking toward the Union lines. When he finally arrived at the camp, exhausted but eager to volunteer his services to the Union army, Scroggins was arrested and thrown into jail while Union officers notified his owner, Samuel Cox, that the army had his fugitive slave in custody. Lincoln had promised that his army would vigorously enforce the Fugitive Slave Law, and the Union army's prompt return of Cox's fugitive slave was the proof of this promise.

Cox immediately set off for the Union lines to claim his property and dragged Scroggins back to his plantation. Cox promptly tied Scroggins to a post in the center of the slave quarters and forced all of his slaves to watch as he began flogging him. Cox was determined to show every one of his slaves the consequence of trying to escape to the Union army. Cox continued beating the fugitive until Scroggins was dead. When the report of Scroggins' murder reached the Union camp, Union soldiers were horrified. Other stories of runaways being returned to slaveholders helped trigger a small but significant revolt by Union soldiers who announced that they would no longer act as slave catchers, no matter what the President had promised loyal slaveholders.

Members of Congress were also listening. By the winter of 1862, many of them were voicing their objection to the Union army enforcing the Fugitive Slave Law. These Congressmen pointed out that fugitive slaves were beginning to play an important role in the ability of the Union army to fight effectively. In March, 1862, Congress passed the Second Confiscation Act. This act forbade members of the army or navy from returning any fugitive slave to a Rebel owner, and the new definition of a Rebel slave owner was living in a Confederate state. The Fugitive Slave Law would now only be enforced in the border states of Kentucky, and Maryland. (Missouri was in such a state of chaos and civil war that the Fugitive Slave Law could not be enforced) That spring, Congress also passed a law abolishing slavery in the District of Columbia. Almost immediately, between 100 and 200 fugitives poured into Washington every week, and it was impossible to distinguish if the fugitive was from the Rebel state of Virginia or the loyal state of Maryland, where Lincoln still insisted that the Federal government was enforcing the Fugitive Slave Law.

Kentucky slaveholders were especially angry at the new Confiscation Act and had begged Lincoln not to sign it. Slaveholders told the President that it would undermine slavery throughout their state. Kentucky slaveholders were right; slaves understood that they could use the Second Confiscation Act to help destroy slavery in the Union state of Kentucky as well as slavery in the Confederate states. One of the ways that self-emancipated slaves from Kentucky manipulated President Lincoln's conflicting orders was to insist, as did the ten fugitives who appeared at Camp Nevin, that "there masters are rank Secessionists, in some cases are in the rebel army." [15]

In November, 1862, Lyrus Moley, a Kentucky slave, organized the escape of fifteen other slaves. Their destination was the Union regiment of Colonel Smith Atkins, stationed on the border between Kentucky and Tennessee. When they arrived, a delighted Atkins put the fugitives to work building fortifications. Moley's owner led an angry group of planters into Atkins camp and demanded that the Colonel return these fugitives immediately. After all, he told Atkins, Kentucky was a Union state and Lincoln had promised to protect their slave property. Atkins, who was an ardent antislavery man, refused. He told the slaveholders that any fugitives working in his camp must be the slaves

---

[15] Oakes, James. *Freedom National: The Destruction of Slavery in the United States, 1861-1865.* New York: W.W. Norton & Company, 2013. (Pg. 167)

of Confederate officers, and he had confiscated them as contraband. The delegation of planters then rode on to Union headquarters to demand that Atkins obey the law. Atkins was ordered to return Lyrus Moley and the other fugitives to their owners immediately. Atkins still refused, even though he was now faced with a civil contempt citation. The next day an angry mob marched into town and tried to capture the runaways. There was a pitched battle between the mob and a group of Union soldiers, and the mob was driven off. Before the violence got any worse, the army received news that Rebel troops were moving north into Kentucky. Colonel Atkins' regiment was ordered to the front. Among the marching troops were Lyrus Morley and his band of self- emancipated black men.

In the spring of 1862, President Lincoln, while still committed to placating slaveholders in the border states and sending out confusing messages about enforcing the Fugitive Slave Law, began to doubt that any of the slaveholders of the Confederate states were ever going to rise up and force their state back into the Union. It was time to turn to the only reliable southerners in the Confederacy, African Americans.

The Union army was beginning to rely not only on the labor of these ex-slaves, but on their success in creating spy networks and military raids deep in Confederate territory. Lincoln now told General David Hunter that he could begin enlisting black men into a special unit to defend the endangered sea islands. A few months later, Lincoln, still conflicted about the role ex-slaves should play in the Civil War, ordered Hunter to disband the unit. The formal unit was disbanded, but many of Hunter's blacks unofficially continued raiding plantations, railroad lines, warehouses, and Confederate installations. In the North, a demand was growing to allow black men to fight in the Union army, but Lincoln was not ready for such a radical decision. The President still held the belief, shared by many white Americans, that black men could never fight on a battlefield. It would take a series of Union military disasters before Lincoln would finally turn to African Americans for help. When he did, it would change the meaning of the Civil War.

CHAPTER

13

YOU NEED US TO WIN THE WAR

In 1862, Lincoln was wrestling with another major problem, the possibility that England was about to recognize the Confederacy as an independent state. The British government had never forgiven their former colonies for establishing a new nation, especially now since America was beginning to challenge Britain's dominance as an economic world power. Some of Britain's most powerful leaders believed that, if the South became a separate nation, the American threat to English control would be over. Because Lincoln insisted that the Civil War was only a war to save the Union, the British government saw no reason not to recognize the Confederacy. Only the powerful British antislavery movement opposed their government's plan to recognize the Confederacy.

British government recognition of the Confederacy would have been a devastating blow to the Union cause. It would certainly have shattered the Federal government's blockade of the Southern coast because Britain had the most powerful navy in the world. Lincoln found himself facing an impossible task. Somehow he must continue to convince border state slaveholders that the Civil War was being fought only to preserve the Union and that the Federal government had no plans to end slavery, while at the same time suggesting to the British people that support of the Union did have something to do with slavery's abolition.

The South had the support of a powerful group, British mill owners. These textile magnates, hungry for Southern cotton, were demanding that Parliament break the Union blockade that was causing British workers to lose their jobs. The British Prime Minister, Lord Palmerston, told his countrymen that Britain could not allow some millions of its people to suffer in order to please the Northern states.

In this crisis, John Andrews, the governor of Massachusetts, made a suggestion to the President. He had been watching the career of a young African-American man who had just become the minister

John Sella Martin. Source:
*Black Past.org, from a report of the
Anti-Slavery Conference held in
Paris in August 1867*

of the Joy Street Baptist Church, one of Boston's most prestigious institutions.

The Reverend John Sella Martin had a spellbinding effect on audiences, both black and white. Governor Andrews thought that Martin's ability to inspire American audiences might work the same magic in Britain.

The 27-year-old Martin landed in England in September, 1861, knowing that he had a very difficult mission. British mills were beginning to close because of the shortage of cotton; many workers had already lost their jobs. Yet Martin also knew that many British workers were passionately dedicated to the cause of antislavery. The problem Martin faced was how to explain Lincoln's contradictory statement about slavery to British workers who wondered why they should fight to keep their country neutral if abolition was not the goal of the Federal government.

Martin had one powerful reply. The South, he reminded his audiences, was a slave society while the North represented free labor. If the North won the war, the South would no longer dominate the American Congress; therefore, a victorious Federal government would have the power and the duty to abolish slavery. For six months Martin toured England. His passionate belief that a Union victory would mean the end of slavery in America convinced audiences and persuaded British abolitionists to continue the fight for neutrality.

John Sella Martin's audiences were also profoundly moved by his own personal story. They were very concerned when they heard that Martin's sister and her two children were still slaves. Reverend John Curwen, a Congregationalist minister, organized a fund-raising committee to purchase Martin's entire family. Their response touched Martin's heart. Curwen's congregation was poor, yet they gladly reached into their own pockets to help liberate Martin's family. One woman told the congregation how she had saved a penny each week out of her meager salary for the Martin family collection. In August 1862, four hundred pounds had been raised, and Martin returned to Boston for a joyous reunion with his sister and her two children. He had not seen her for twenty years.

In 1863, Martin received a special invitation from his English friend Harper Twelvetrees, a leading British abolitionist. Twelvetrees was building a new church for his employees and he asked Martin to become its first minister. How could Martin refuse, since Twelvetrees had been one of the leaders who had helped raise money to free his family? There was another even more important reason for Martin to return to England. The South was beginning a new major campaign to gain British recognition. This time they counted on the fact that, because of the success of the Union blockade, so many British mills had closed and thousands of workers had lost their jobs. Many of these workers lived in London's East End and they would be part of Martin's new congregation. The workers had been some of the most active supporters of British neutrality. Now, Lincoln worried that, because so many British workers had been unemployed for so long, British laborers might insist that England recognize the Confederate government so that the cotton mills could reopen.

The battle for recognition of the Confederacy was led by Britain's mill owners. They organized Southern Clubs in every town in England. They paid unemployed workers to fill the halls every time Southern Clubs held a meeting. Attendees were paid to cheer every speaker who demanded that England recognize the Confederacy. British abolitionists mounted their own battle for the support of workers. The situation was a tense one. Would British workers remain committed to abolition, in spite of the fact that so many of them were facing destitution?

Many ex-slaves played a vital role in the struggle to keep England neutral. William and Ellen Craft, now living in England, spoke at abolitionist meetings all over England. Henry Box Brown drew large crowds wherever he spoke. Frederick Douglass, who had become the most important black leader in America, had a large and devoted following in England. His articles pleading for support for the Union cause were published in many of the most important British newspapers.

When John Sella Martin arrived back in England in January 1863, he brought with him a powerful new weapon for the Union cause; Lincoln had just issued the Emancipation Proclamation. Martin now began a strenuous schedule of lectures all over England.

Thousands of workers flocked to hear him and cheer the Union's new commitment to ending slavery. Hundreds of resolutions were passed urging Parliament to reject the proposal to recognize the South. John Bright, one of England's greatest working class leaders, claimed that John Sella Martin's influence on British workers was one of the reasons that recognition of the South went down to defeat.

At the same time, while President Lincoln had just ordered General David Hunter to disband his band of black raiders, another slave was making plans to escape. Robert Smalls was about to become one of the first black heroes of the Civil War. On May 13, 1862, Captain F. J. Nickols of the Union ship *Onward* spotted a Confederate ship sailing out of Charleston Harbor waving a white flag. Surprised, Nickols ordered his gunners to hold their fire. When the Confederate ship floated alongside the *Onward,* the captain was astonished to see that the ship was manned only by a black sailor. That sailor, Robert Smalls, gleefully announced that he had just confiscated the *Planter* from the Confederate government and wanted to contribute his prize to the United States.

Robert Smalls. Source: *Library of Congress, Prints and Photographs Division.*

Smalls was born a slave in 1839 on a plantation in Beaufort, South Carolina. In 1850, his master, Henry Mckee, moved to Charleston. To the eleven-year-old boy, the city was a revelation. For the first time in his life he met free blacks and slaves who were able to work for themselves by paying their masters a monthly stipend. Many of these black laborers had earned enough money to buy their own freedom. Smalls convinced Mckee to let him find a job.

Smalls loved everything about life alongside the ocean, especially the art of sailing. He quickly found jobs around the Charleston Harbor. By 1860, Smalls was an experienced sailor, and promptly hired on to the cotton steamer, *Planter.* It was a substantial ship, 150 feet long, and it could carry 1400 bales of cotton. Its route was the plantations and wharfs of the Pee Dee River. Smalls soon talked the captain of the *Planter* into letting him steer the ship. This was quite a triumph for Smalls since black men were never allowed to become ship pilots.

Smalls was anxious to earn as much money as possible, because he now had a wife and daughter. He vowed that he would free his family even before he himself was free. His family's purchase price was 800 dollars, a formidable sum of money to raise, as Smalls was making sixteen dollars a month, out of which he had to pay his master fifteen dollars.

Smalls hoped that, by studying the maps and charts of Charleston Harbor, he might command a larger salary. He soon became a master at locating every major channel that led out to sea, as well as every treacherous reef and shoal that made the harbor such a difficult waterway to navigate. Late in 1861, the Confederate government took over the *Planter* and converted it into a special dispatch boat. Smalls' expert navigation skills were recognized when he was promoted to wheel man. One of his new responsibilities was to sail the *Planter* down the coast to make a survey of Confederate forts and to help lay mines in the Edisto and Stono rivers. Smalls memorized everything, including the signals needed to pass the Confederate forts and batteries in the Charleston harbor.

In November 1861, Smalls watched as the Union fleet began the attack on Port Royal. At soon as Federal troops were in control of the key islands surrounding Charleston, Smalls began planning his escape. First he recruited the black crew of the *Planter*. On a Sunday afternoon in April, the crew met to hear Smalls' escape plan. First they would they gather up their families and bring them to an abandoned merchant ship anchored in the Cooper River. After darkness the crew would secretly sail the *Planter* to this ship, pick up the women and children, and set sail for the Union fleet that was blockading Charleston harbor. This plan would succeed only if Smalls was able to choose the right moment to launch the escape. That afternoon the men took a solemn pledge to follow Smalls' commands and be ready to escape at a moments notice.

Smalls chose the night of May 12th for the escape. The captain of the *Planter*, along with the entire white crew, decided to go into town, leaving Smalls and the black crew alone to guard the ship. Smalls was delighted. The night before, 200 pounds of ammunition and four guns had been loaded onto the ship, which was supposed to be delivered the next day to the Charleston battery. Smalls had deliberately slowed down loading the cargo so that it could not be delivered that day because, as he happily reported later to Union officials, he believed that the cargo might be useful to "Uncle Abe."

Now the *Planter* steamed quietly up to the wharf where Smalls' wife and daughter had been hidden along with four other women and two children. Smalls called a final meeting of the escapees and they all agreed that, if the ship were captured by the Rebels, they would blow up the *Planter* rather than return to slavery.

At three AM, the *Planter* cast off and began its risky journey. The ship had to pass five heavily fortified Rebel forts. Smalls began by hoisting the vessel's two Confederate flags, then he slowly eased the ship into the inner channel. Smalls sailed the *Planter* at its customary slow pace traveling right under the guns of each fort and coolly giving the appropriate signal. Wearing the Captain's hat and mimicking his gait, Smalls stood in the pilot house with the cord in his hand blowing the usual salute. Finally he passed the last fort, Fort Sumpter. Smalls then cut through the inland waters and into the open sea. Now Smalls sailed the *Planter* full speed ahead straight to the line of Federal ships blockading the harbor.

An observer aboard one of the Union ships blockading the harbor reported on what happened next. They saw a Confederate ship sailing towards them with a white flag of surrender waving in the wind. The captain ordered the crew to hold their fire. They looked in vain for some white man who might be in charge of the crew but all they saw was a group of joyous black men, women, and children dancing on the deck. Robert Smalls stepped forward and, taking off his hat, shouted, "Good morning sir! I've brought you some of the old United States guns sir." [1] A delighted Congress granted half the prize money to Smalls and his crew. The capture of the *Planter* was more than a symbolic victory. General Sherman had been complaining for months to Washington about the shortage of ships in his fleet.

As the war continued, the Legal League began opening new branches all over the South. The organization expanded the role of the Underground Railroad by helping the hundreds of Union soldiers trying to find a way back to the Union lines.

Many of the soldiers had escaped from Confederate jails; others had been left behind after a raid or battle.

---

[1] McPherson, James M. *The Negro's Civil War: How American Blacks Felt and Acted During the War For the Union.* New York: Vintage Books, 1965. (Pg. 159)

Nancy Johnson and her husband were slaves on a Georgia plantation far from the battlefield. Late one night a man stumbled into their cabin and begged them for help. He was an escaped Union soldier. She and her husband made the instant decision to hide the desperate man. The next day when their master, David Baggs, questioned the couple about the escaped Yankee, the Johnsons just looked confused and rather stupid.

Later that day a posse of whites rode into the slave quarters announcing prison or death to anyone hiding a Yankee. They searched every cabin but did not find the escaped soldier. The Johnsons had created a secret and very secure hiding place for their first Yankee soldier. At first the Legal League only helped Yankee soldiers or white Union men. Later they expanded their aid to Confederate deserters. Nancy Johnson explained to an interviewer how "some of the rebel soldiers deserted and came to our house and we fed them. They were opposed to the war and didn't own slaves and said they would die rather than fight. Those who were poor white people, who didn't own slaves, I befriended them because they were on our side." [2]

So many African Americans were helping rescue Union soldiers, that new recruits were told by their officers that if they were ever in trouble and needed help to trust only blacks. When a group of Union officers who were being held in the Charleston city jail were told they were going to be transferred to another prison, they realized this was an opportunity to escape. Somehow they had found some Rebel uniforms, which they put on under their uniforms. As the prisoners were marched out of the jail, with Confederate soldiers milling all about the courtyard, the officers managed to slip out of line and peel off their Yankee uniforms. Now, disguised as rebel soldiers, they slipped unnoticed out of the jail courtyard into the city of Charleston.

For a short time they were able to move freely around the city, but they had no idea how to find their way back to the Union lines. Strolling through the streets they saw the shop of Thomas Brown, a black barber. It was empty of customers. It was time to take a risk. The officers walked quietly into the shop and asked Brown for help. Unknowingly they had just reached one of the leaders of Charleston's Legal League. Brown acted quickly. He led the officers to the back of the shop. Then he summoned his son and told him that he must find permanent hiding places for the officers immediately, before the Confederates discovered that they had escaped. By evening Brown's

[2] Williams, David. *Bitterly Divided: The South's Inner Civil War.* New York: The New Press, 2008. (Pg. 185)

son reported that he had found enough black families to hide every one of the officers.

For two months the soldiers remained hidden while the Confederate army searched throughout Charleston for their escaped prisoners. While the officers remained hidden, Brown tried to figure out a way to move the men out of Charleston. Black guides, he believed, would be too conspicuous and would put the officers in great danger. Brown needed to find a group of white Unionists willing to help, a very difficult task in this most Confederate of all cities. Brown finally found a group of German Unionists who were willing to help, and the officers were able to reach the safety of the Union lines.[3]

When in 1864 Lieutenant Hanibal Johnson and three other prisoners escaped from a Confederate prison camp in South Carolina he remembered his commander's advice. Hesitantly he knocked on the door of a black cabin. The four escapees were welcomed and put into the capable hands of the Legal League. The soldiers were hidden in various slave cabins. One evening during a heavy snow storm the soldiers were forced to take refuge in an abandoned barn. The next day the men were surprised and grateful to see a few black men entering the barn carrying food. These men had traveled six miles in the heavy snow to make sure that the soldiers would not go hungry. It took Johnson and his comrades almost five weeks to finally reach Knoxville where there was a Union army base.[4]

There were men in almost every state in the Confederacy who remained loyal to the United States government. Some of these men felt so committed to the Union cause that they decided to enlist in the United States army. Reaching an army base was not always easy and white southern Unionists began to organize their own form of Underground Railroad. This Railroad set up a series of safe houses and found guides willing to help these men slip through Rebel lines and find the closest Union outpost.

Reverend John Aughey had been a delegate to the January 1861 Mississippi State Convention which voted to secede. Aughey was one of the few men to vote against secession. The minister was

[3] Berlin, Ira et al editors. *Free At Last: A Documentary History of Slavery, Freedom, and the Civil War.* New York: The New Press, 1992. (Pg. 161-163)

[4] McPherson, James. *The Negro's Civil War.* (Pg. 153-155)

such a devoted Union man that when the war broke out he organized
a guerilla band of Unionists to fight against the local Rebels. In July
1862 Aughey was arrested for treason and put into the Tupelo jail.
A few days before his scheduled execution his cellmates helped him
escape. He had been trying to find his way to a Union army base so
he could enlist but he had become hopelessly lost. Tired and hungry
Aughey realized he needed help. When he saw a simple farmhouse
and noticed that there were no slaves working in the field, he decided
to take a risk. He knocked on the door and discovered that he had
stumbled into a station of the new Underground Railroad. Aughey was
moved from station to station until he reached the Union lines. Over
one hundred thousand white southerners fought in the Union army.

Some of these white Unionists began to reach out to African
Americans. Harry Smith remembers how some whites would secretly
slip into slave cabins to read them the latest war news. William
Walters was a small child when his family fled the plantation during
the war, and it was a white family in Nashville who helped hide his
family and then direct them to a safe route to the Union camp.[5]

By the beginning of 1862, Jefferson Davis was facing another
problem. Some slaveholders, worried that that their plantations might
be in the path of the Union army, were determined to save their
investment in slaves. Many of them abandoned their plantations and
moved their slaves to areas that they hoped the Union army would
never reach. Even Jefferson Davis worried about keeping his slaves
from fleeing to the Union army. Davis and his brother Joseph owned
a plantation on the banks of the Mississippi River. It was called
Davis Bend and it was located twenty miles below Vicksburg. In May
1862, after the fall of New Orleans, Davis advised his brother that he
should gather up the plantation slaves and move them to the interior
of Mississippi far from any possibility of any Union army advances.
Joseph agreed with his brother and hastily collected a group of
household slaves and moved them to Vicksburg. (The Confederates
believed that the city could never be conquered by the Yankees.) Then
Joseph returned to Davis Bend to gather up the plantation slaves.
Davis was in for a surprise.

[5] Robinson, Armstead L. *Bitter Fruits of Bondage: the Demise of Slavery and the
Collapse of the Confederacy 1861-1865*. Charlottsville: University of Virginia Press,
2005. (Pg. 78)

No sooner had the slaves watched their owner's vessel leave the dock then they sprang into action. They understood that this was their chance for freedom. First they sacked the plantation house, destroyed the cotton crop, and took complete control of the plantation. When Joseph Davis returned he was met with the unheard of demand that his former slaves refused to work unless they were paid for their labor. Back in Richmond, Jefferson Davis received a series of lurid accounts about what was happening. One telegram claimed that Negroes were in a state of rebellion. Charles Mitchell, a relative of Davis, reported that the slaves refused to submit to the overseers or work in the fields and, when Joseph attempted to round them up so that he could carry them inland, Davis's original plan, the slaves simply refused to go. Other slaves, Joseph reported to his brother, fled to the Union army, "their departure was sudden and in the night." [6] After the Union

Slaves Fleeing to the Union. Source: *Library of Congress, Prints and Photographs Division.*

army captured Vicksburg, Davis Bend was occupied by a party of sixty armed African Americans who later successfully fought off a raiding party of Confederates.

Other slaveholders, trying to hold onto their slave property, were having similar problems. Many slaves resisted the move. Some ran away to find the Union army. Others fled into nearby wilderness areas until their owners were forced to leave without them. The resistance of southern slaves was creating major problems for the Confederate government. The government had counted on using the labor of area slaves to work on fortifications near the front, but so many slaveholders were running away that slave labor was becoming

[6] McCurry, Stephanie. *Confederate Reckoning: Power and Politics in the Civil War South.* Cambridge: Harvard University Press, 2010. (Pg. 256)

scarce. Plantations close to the battlefield had been abandoned and so could no longer supply the army with food. Hungry soldiers were beginning to complain to anyone who would listen. In late 1862 Davis was dealing with another problem; the roads the army needed to move troops and supplies to the front were clogged by fleeing slaveholders.

By early 1862 the Confederate government realized that the war could not be fought with volunteers alone because the number of these volunteers was decreasing dramatically. In April the government passed the first draft law in modern history. This conscription bill called for every white man between 18 and 36 to be drafted into the Confederate army. There were several exemptions that allowed men to remain at home, but two of the most important exemptions infuriated thousands of poor white southerners. One exemption allowed a man to pay for a substitute to take his place. The second exemption would allow an owner of twenty slaves or his overseer to remain at home to supervise these slaves. Non-slaveholding whites hated this new draft law, especially these two clauses which allowed rich men to stay at home while poor men were forced into the army. Who, they demanded of the Confederate government, would take care of their families, when poor farmers were forced to leave their land without any able bodied man left to plant the crops that poor families depended on? A new slogan swept through the South. This was a rich man's war and a poor man's fight. The explanation that the Confederate government gave to angry poor farmers was that allowing a white man to remain at home to control the slave population would benefit everyone, not just slaveholders. Slaves must be supervised in order to make sure that they continued to grow the foodstuffs that the South needed for both the military and the civilian population. To pacify angry draftees the Confederate government promised that planters would take some responsibility in caring for the families of the Confederate soldiers.

The Confederate government had negotiated agreements with local planters to provide food products to soldiers' families at a reduced rate. It did not take long before these agreements fell apart. Cotton had become so scarce on the world market that the price of a bale of cotton had skyrocketed. Many planters decided to grow cotton instead of food the Confederate army and the local communities needed. Many planters contracted with blockade runners to sell their cotton in Europe and share the profits. These planters were growing rich while most Southerners began to suffer from a growing food shortage. Food prices began to soar and many soldiers' families could not find enough food to feed their starving children.

Soldiers were receiving letters from their families describing conditions at home. Letters like the one that a Confederate deserter received from his wife, Mary.

"My Dear Edward...

I would not have you do anything wrong for the world, but before God, Edward, unless you come home we must die. Last night I was aroused by little Eddie's crying. I called "what's the matter, Eddie?" and he said, Oh mama, I'm so hungry." And Lucy, Edward, your darling Lucy, she never complains, but she is growing thinner and thinner, and Edward, unless you come home we must die."

Your Mary" [7]

By the end of 1862, Confederate generals were reporting mass desertions throughout the army, and recruiters were discovering that many hundreds of able-bodied men were evading the draft. By the time the war ended there was an estimate that over one thousand Confederate soldiers had deserted the army.

Another Underground Railroad was developing to help these Confederate deserters and draft dodgers. This was certainly not the old antislavery Underground Railroad. Most of these deserters were indifferent to the issue of slavery; they were simply opposed to fighting the war. They believed that it was the rich slaveholders who had started the war and then forced poor southerners to fight that war for them.

Deserters headed for the swamps, mountains and forest areas where they formed armed bands together with other southerners who were resisting the draft. Some deserters fled south to Florida and the swampland where the remnants of the Seminole Indian nation still ruled. The Seminoles, who had fought off every attempt by the American army to force them out of their ancestral home in

[7] Barret, John G. *The Civil War in North Carolina*. Chapel Hill: The University of North Carolina Press, 1963. (Pg. 191)

Florida, found that their support was sought by both Yankees and Confederates. They wisely remained neutral. Yankees left them alone and Confederate home guards could never penetrate the swampland. Throughout the war the land of the Seminoles remained a sanctuary for both Black and white refugees.

One of the areas where the resistance by bands of draft dodgers and Confederate deserters was intensifying was the Wiregrass country, a wild region which stretched from just below Macon, Georgia west though parts of Alabama and down into the Florida panhandle. What especially worried the local governments in the region was that the usual barriers between black and white southerners seemed to be breaking down. Local slaves acted as spies for many of these bands, letting them know when Confederate forces were in the area, as well as providing them with food and other supplies. Jeff Anderson's band even invited a group of fugitive slaves to join them.[8]

Some of the leaders of the Wiregrass bands met with a group of Union officers based on the Florida coast, who agreed to supply the bands with guns and ammunition.[9]

Many of the able-bodied men who had been allowed to remain at home under the twenty slave exemption were organized into local military units called Home Guards, whose main assignment was to prevent slaves from running away. It was an impossible task. Slaves were running away by the thousands, not only those close to the front line but from plantations all over the South. Slaves who were unable to flee to the Union army found sanctuaries in swamps, forests or mountains.

With so many slaves fleeing, the South's plantation economy was falling apart. By late 1862 the Confederate government was so desperate for food and supplies that the government passed a new law for a tax in kind. This gave Confederate officials the right to enter a farmer's storehouses and confiscate ten percent of their provisions to be sent to the front. Poor farmers faced an array of Confederate officials and home guards who had the right to seize food, livestock, horses, plows and even slaves. Rich men could buy off the raiders, but the poor were at their mercy. More and more Confederate soldiers hearing about their family's plight decided to desert.

---

[8] Weitz, Mark A. *More Damning Than Slaughter: Desertion in the Confederate Army.* Lincoln: University of Nebraska Press, 2005. (Pg. 212)

[9] Williams David. *A People's History of the Civil War: Struggles for the Meaning of Freedom.* New York; The New Press, 2005. (Pg. 323-4)

One stronghold for fleeing Confederate deserters was Jones County, Mississippi. The people of Jones County were not in favor of secession, but after Mississippi voted to join the Confederacy, many of their young men volunteered to fight for the southern cause. Then the Confederate Congress passed the "Twenty Negro Law" and later the "Ten Percent Law." Jones County volunteers were furious. Newton Knight was one of these infuriated soldiers. His grandfather and uncles were slaveholders, but his father hated slavery and so did Knight. He had reluctantly enlisted in the Confederate army, but in late 1862 Knight got a letter from his wife Serena describing just how the "Ten Percent Law" was being enforced. Serena told her husband how a Confederate cavalryman had burst into her barn and seized her one and only horse. Serena told her husband that without a horse she had no way to get into town in order to get the supplies she and the children desperately needed in order to survive. Knight decided it was time to go home.

In October, after the bloody battle of Corinth, seven thousand Confederate soldiers were reported absent without leave; Newton Knight, along with thirty nine of his neighbors from Jones County, were part of that group. It was two hundred miles from Corinth to Jones County. Along the way they found fugitive slaves hiding in the woods and swamps. These fugitives knew how to live in the inhospitable surroundings and were willing to help the Confederate deserters. It was the beginning of a unique alliance between the slaves and a handful of yeomen farmers in Jones County.

The escape was not successful. The Confederate army along with units of the home guard rounded up most of the deserters and sent them back into the army. Knight was singled out for special treatment; he was demoted from sergeant to private and thrown into jail until he agreed to return to Company F. In 1863 during the chaos following the Confederate defeat at Vicksburg, Knight led one hundred members of Company F back home to the piney hills of Jones County. There they created a safe haven that the Confederate army was never able to penetrate.

The summer of 1862 was a critical time for the Union cause. The North was reeling from a number of military defeats in northern Virginia. Casualties were high. The Union army needed fresh troops to continue fighting, but the number of new recruits was slowing down. General Rufus Saxton, the new commander of the sea islands, told President Lincoln that he might be forced to abandon many of the sea islands if he could not find a way to replenish his army. The general suggested that he be given the authority to enlist the services of the hundreds of fugitive slaves who had been clamoring for a chance to fight on the battlefield for their own freedom.

Lincoln hesitated to give Saxton the authority to begin recruiting ex-slaves because as he told friends, "It was hard to believe that men raised in fear and trembling could exhibit the courage and self confidence necessary for good soldiering." He also was afraid that if blacks were armed, "in a few weeks the arms would be in the hands of the rebels." [10]

General Saxton decided to send Robert Smalls to meet with President Lincoln in the hope that Smalls might convince Lincoln that black men were willing and able to fight. On August 16, 1862, Robert Smalls had a private meeting with President Lincoln. Lincoln was eager to hear from Smalls himself about the capture of the *Planter*. The President asked him whether black men on the battlefield would fight or flee. Smalls insisted that, like the black crew that he had led in the capture of the *Planter*, hundreds of other African Americans were eager to fight and die for their freedom. Smalls reminded Lincoln that some of these fugitives had already given their lives in the defense of the Union cause.

On Tuesday, September 23, 1862, Lincoln announced that he was planning on issuing an emancipation proclamation that would free all of the slaves living in Confederate occupied territory. In this preliminary draft of the proclamation, nothing at all was said about enlisting black men into the Union army. Yet when Smalls left Washington he carried with him a letter from Secretary of War Stanton authorizing General Rufus Saxton to arm 5,000 black men to defend the sea islands against Confederate attacks.

There was one place where African Americans were already battling the Confederate army. Roanoke Island was a swampy piece of North Carolina only ten miles long and two miles wide, but the island was the key to controlling the vital water routes between Chesapeake Bay and Albemarle Sound. On February 8, 1862, the Union General

[10] Oakes, James. *The Radical and the Republican: Frederick Douglass, Abraham Lincoln, and the Triumph of Antislavery Politics.* New York: W. W. Norton, 2008. (Pg. 203-204)

Ambrose Burnside, commanding sixteen gunboats and leading 7,500 soldiers, waded ashore. The general then marched his men through the waterlogged swampland to defeat Rebel forces and take control of the island. Abermarle Sound was now under Federal control.

By the spring of 1862, while many of the smaller southern Atlantic coast towns were under Union control, the two major cities of Wilmington and Charleston remained Confederate strongholds. Since the Confederates still controlled most of the towns that lined the rivers flowing between Roanoke Island and Norfolk, Virginia, North Carolina inland waterways were battlegrounds under constant attack. It was a continuous struggle for the Union army to keep North Carolina's vital waterway system under the control of the Federal government, as they did not have the manpower to keep the waterways free from Rebel raiders. Lincoln could not send the troops that they needed because the major battlefield was still northern Virginia. In desperation, Union officers turned for help to the maroon settlers living in the Great Dismal Swamp. A great number of fugitive slaves had joined other black settlers who had made their homes in the Swamp for generations. Union officers hoped that these black settlers would help protect the waterways. Union officers arranged to meet with leaders of the settlements to work out an agreement. These officers must have been surprised to discover that some of the settlement leaders, like Jack Ferelis, were white deserters from the Confederate army. Union officers asked the men if they would launch a series of raids against Rebel bases in the area if the Union army would supply them with weapons and even small boats.

Of course this agreement between the Union army and the guerrillas could never be made public. Lincoln was still committed to winning over slaveholders in North Carolina by returning fugitive slaves to any slaveholder who claimed to support the Union. Army officers had been ignoring these instructions ever since they invaded Roanoke Island, because they needed the help of every fugitive they could lay their hands on.

The guerillas, called Buffaloes by contemptuous Rebel soldiers, gloried in the name. "The Buffaloes are here", they shouted as they raided plantations or led Yankee soldiers on expeditions deep into Confederate territory, sometimes traveling three hundred miles to reach their target. During these raids the Buffaloes freed hundreds of slaves. They boasted that their goal was to free every slave in eastern North Carolina.

In the summer of 1862, the Buffaloes seized Wingate Plantation, home of Richard Dillard, an ardent secessionist and one of most prominent planters in the area. This plantation was located on the Chowan River, seventeen miles from the Great Dismal Swamp. The main house was perched on a high bluff overlooking the river, making it an ideal spot to build a fort. The buffaloes named their fort, Fort Ferelis, in honor of Jack Ferelis, who had been the Buffaloes' first military leader and had recently died in battle. The Union army considered Fort Ferelis so important that they ordered one of their gunboats to be permanently anchored in the river below the fort.

Fort Ferelis immediately attracted hundreds of fugitive slaves. There were fifty acres of flat open land where tents and huts could be erected, and the fugitives had enough land to grow food for their families. Here women and children would be safe and their men would be free to join the Buffalos; hundreds of fugitives volunteered to fight the Rebels.

In the spring of 1863, the North Carolina Home Guard decided to launch a series of major attacks against Fort Ferelis. The first assault began in March when one hundred and fifty members of the Guard tried to storm the fort, but were driven back across the river. In April while the Union gunboat had left Fort Ferelis on a special mission, a substantial Rebel force again attacked the fort. The women and children who had taken refuge inside the fort were warned about the Rebel attack and fled into the swamp. Most of the Buffalo bands who tried to re-enter the fort were driven away by the strength of the offensive. But twenty three Buffaloes managed to slip into the fort and creep up to the tower where they fought off the Rebel barrage until the Union gunboat sailed back up the river and forced the Confederates to retreat.

The Home Guards took their revenge for these Rebel defeats at the hands of the Buffaloes. Buffaloes were never treated as Union soldiers; when captured they were simply killed. The Home Guard also launched attacks against the families of the Buffaloes. They raided Culpeper Island, one of the oldest black settlements of the Great Dismal Swamp. They found nobody there but old people, women and children since most of the able bodied men were away fighting. The Home Guard massacred the entire population of the village.[11]

---

[11] Leaming, Hugo Prosper. *Hidden Americans: Maroons of Virginia and the Carolinas.* New York: Garland Press, 1995. (Pg. 295-312)

14

A NEW BIRTH OF FREEDOM; THE CIVIL WAR BECOMES A REVOLUTION

General Saxton at last had his orders and he began recruiting 5,000 black men to form the first black regiment of the Civil War. Saxton's regiment would not officially be part of the Union army, only an auxiliary regiment whose task would be limited to the protection of the sea islands from Confederate attacks. Back in April, 1862 when General David Hunter had gotten Lincoln's reluctant approval to begin recruiting an irregular fighting unit of ex-slaves, one of his first recruits had been a six-foot-tall coal-black man named Prince Rivers. Rivers had been owned by an aristocratic family in Beaufort. When the family, fearful of the Union army, fled inland, Rivers refused to leave and the Confederate government was offering a $2,000 reward for Rivers' capture. On first meeting Prince Rivers General Hunter told his friends that this ex-slave was the most impressive man, black or white, he had ever met. The general appointed Rivers to be sergeant of his new regiment, the first black sergeant in the Union army.

That spring Hunter decided to take Prince Rivers with him when he traveled to New York City. Maybe meeting the impressive Sergeant Rivers would convince some prominent New Yorkers that it was time to enlist black soldiers in the Union army. As Prince Rivers proudly walked down Broadway in his Union uniform, he was attacked by a mob infuriated at the sight of his sergeant stripes. Rivers managed to fight off his assailants until the police arrived. Just a month after the regiment had been organized in the fall of 1862, Lincoln was still worried about the angry response of slaveholders in Missouri, Kentucky, and Maryland so he ordered the regiment disbanded.

On the evening of January 1, 1863, Abraham Lincoln signed the Emancipation Proclamation. Huge crowds of African Americans gathered in churches, meeting halls and even on street corners to await with eager anticipation the announcement that the Proclamation had actually been signed. One of the largest of these celebrations was held in Boston. At the Tremont Temple, an

Emancipation Day in South Carolina. Source: *Frank Leslie's Illustrated Newspaper.*

audience of 3,000 blacks and whites waited all evening while they were entertained by brief speeches, choruses and other musical entertainment. A line of messengers was stationed between the telegraph office and the speaker's platform. Frederick Douglass remembered how tortuous the waiting was that evening. "Eight, nine, ten o'clock came and went and still no word... suspense was becoming agony"... suddenly a man rushed to the podium with the joyous news " 'It is coming! It is on the wires!' People exploded into expressions of wild joy. Some voices cried out in shouts of praise while others began to sob with tears of relief" [1]

In the Union-occupied territories of the South, the celebrations were even more exuberant. In Norfolk, Virginia, 2,000 black people marched joyously through the streets of the city while 10,000 others watched and shouted their exultation. In Beaufort thousands gathered and listened in hushed silence as the Proclamation was read aloud. Then spontaneously the assembled crowd of African Americans began singing "My Country Tis of Thee." News of the Emancipation Proclamation sped quickly through the grapevine reaching slave quarters deep in the heart of Dixie. To the joy of abolitionists and

---

[1] Franklin, John Hope. *The Emancipation Proclamation.* New York: Doubleday, 1963. (Pg. 112)

African Americans throughout the nation, the final Proclamation
included the statement that the government would begin enlisting
black men into the Union army.

Even before the final Proclamation had become the law of
the land, General Saxton needed to find an officer to command his
promised new regiment. Most white men were still aghast at the very
idea of allowing black men into the army, but John Andrews, Governor
of Massachusetts, told General Saxton there might be one man who
would welcome the chance to lead the Union's first black regiment,
Thomas Wentworth Higginson. Higginson was a member of Boston's
Vigilance Committee and had been a close friend of John Brown.
He had been advocating the enlistment of black men into the Union
army since the war began. In November 1862 Higginson set sail for
Beaufort, South Carolina to launch his historic mission.

General Saxton next task was to find the men to fill the
regiment. He began by trying to recruit the members of General
Hunter's volunteer raiders. The General discovered he had a problem
with these former guerrillas; they were very angry at the fact that
the Union army had discarded them before they had a chance to
fight. Saxton turned to Prince Rivers for help, and Rivers did not fail
him. Prince Rivers quickly announced that he was going to reenlist;
then he explained: " This is our time. If our fathers had had such a
chance as this we should not have been slaves now." And if he and his
comrades did not make the most of this chance "another one will not
come and our children will be slaves always." [2] He then set out on a
one-man recruiting drive.

When Higginson arrived in Beaufort he looked around at
the milling crowd of disorganized black men overflowing the newly
created army camp and knew he needed help if he were going to
establish military discipline. He turned to Prince Rivers for help. As
the new sergeant of the regiment, Rivers moved among the raw troops
and quickly established order. He was soon adding to his duties by
helping to write regimental reports. Higginson believed that Rivers
was a better administrator than any of his white officers, and once
remarked that if Sergeant Rivers had been given a formal education
he would be qualified to command an army. After the war Prince
Rivers was elected by the voters of Edgefield to the state legislature
three times.

Saxton realized how vital these new recruits were to the Union

---

[2] Levine, Bruce. *The Fall of the House of Dixie: The Civil War and the Social
Revolution That Transformed the South.* New York: Random House, 2013. (Pg. 134)

cause. If these ex-slaves finally proved to President Lincoln that black men were willing to fight and die for their freedom the same as white men were, they would change the nature of the Civil War. Even though the South Carolina First Regiment's assignment was limited to the defense of the sea islands, General Saxton decided to test his regiment on a real battlefield. On January 23, 1863, the South Carolina First Regiment got their first assignment – a week-long raid along the coast of Georgia and Florida. The troops traveled on a captured Confederate steamer. Their first target was a valuable Confederate salt mine. The men rushed off the boat, attacked the Rebel pickets guarding the mine, overwhelmed them and destroyed the mine. That week the regiment destroyed $20,000 of Confederate property and liberated one hundred and fifty slaves, many of whom decided to join the regiment. There were so many volunteers that Saxton was able to form a second regiment led by Colonel James Montgomery, a man who had fought beside John Brown in Kansas.

General Saxton, with the agreement of General Hunter who had just been commissioned head of the Union Army's Department of the South, decided that his two new black regiments were ready for a greater challenge. On the morning of March 10, 1863, Colonel Thomas Higginson, leading the two regiments, sailed up the St. John River. Their destination was Jacksonville, Florida. The expedition was carried out with such secrecy and skill that the town was surrounded by Union soldiers before the people even knew that the army had arrived. The city was occupied without a shot being fired. Citizens of Jacksonville were horrified when they awoke to discover black soldiers patrolling their streets.

Skirmishes between Union and Rebel forces were a daily occurrence. Confederate officers wanted to mount a campaign to retake the city, but Confederate General Beauregard told them he could not spare the soldiers. Of course, the general did not realize that only a small force of 900 men held the city. Colonel Higginson disguised his troops' weakness by all sorts of devices. He set up empty tents all over town and never let his troops parade as a group. He was also aided in his deception by local blacks who, when questioned by Rebel scouts who regularly sneaked into the city, would exaggerate the number of troops stationed in Jacksonville.

Unknown to the Rebel scouts, the Second South Carolina regiment led by Colonel Montgomery had left the city and traveled seventy-five miles up the river to the town of Palatka. The regiment returned in triumph, their boats filled with supplies and fugitive slaves. General Saxton wrote Secretary of War Stanton that, "It is my belief that scarcely an incident in this war has caused a greater panic throughout the whole Southern coast than this raid of the colored troops in Florida" [3]

Confederate Brigadier General Joseph Finegan, commanding the District of Florida, wrote a letter in which he stated, "That the entire negro population of East Florida will be lost and the country ruined there cannot be a doubt, unless the means of holding the St. John's River are immediately supplied." [4] General Beauregard regretfully informed Richmond that he could spare neither men nor guns from Charleston or Savannah. Unfortunately the Union army was also unable to send reinforcements to hold Jacksonville permanently, so after ten days, Colonel Higginson was ordered to leave Jacksonville. Nevertheless, the success of the South Carolina 1st and 2nd regiments had begun to dispel President Lincoln's concern that black men were not capable of fighting.

The leaders of the Confederacy had no doubt that black men would fight. The fear of slave revolts had haunted southerners since the first slaves had been brought to the colonies. Southern life was filled with tales of the hanging or burning of hundreds of slaves only suspected of leading slave revolts. The Confederate government announced that Generals Hunter and Saxton, if they were captured, would not be treated as enemy officers. Instead, they would be treated like leaders of a slave revolt and their sentence would be hanging.

By late spring of 1863, the Union army had suffered a series of disastrous military defeats and casualties were high. The northern recruiting drives had produced only a trickle of new men. President Lincoln was desperate to find more men to fill the depleted Union ranks. There was only one place left where he might find a fresh source of fighting men, black recruits. The President told General Grant that he expected him to enlist 100,000 black soldiers as soon as possible for the Union army.

When Edward Kinsley, a new Union army recruiter, arrived

[3] Cornish, Dudley Taylor. *The Sable Arm: Black Troops In the Union Army, 1861-1865.* Lawrence, Kansas: University Press of Kansas, 1987. (Pg. 139)
[4] Ibid.

in New Bern, North Carolina in the spring of 1863 he expected to find hundreds of black men ready to enlist. He had received reports that "as many as 1,000 African Americans had been drilling in New Bern on their own eager for a chance to join the fray."[5] However every time he tried to approach a group of black men about enlisting they turned away and refused to talk to him. Why, he wondered were the black people of New Bern suddenly so antagonistic to the Union army. It did not take him long to discover that the reason for this surprising hostility was the man that Lincoln had appointed as the military governor of North Carolina, Edward Stanley. The President had selected Stanley because he was one of the few North Carolina politicians who had remained loyal to the Union. But although Stanley was a Union man, he was also a passionate supporter of slavery.

When Stanley first arrived in New Bern he was dismayed to discover that the Union army was paying ex-slaves wages of eight dollars a month. The governor tried without success to convince the army to cancel all wages for New Bern blacks. Stanley immediately closed every school that Vincent Coyler had created for the black population of Union-controlled North Carolina citing the old state law that forbade anyone from teaching reading to black people. Coyler was so outraged that he immediately took off for Washington to protest the governor's action. It took an order from the President himself before the schools were reopened.

Another disturbing action of the new governor was, even after Congress had passed the Second Confiscation Act forbidding the Union army to return slaves to their owners, Stanley was still returning fugitive slaves to their masters. He based his behavior on the fact that every one of these slaveholders insisted that they supported the Union. Under Stanley's new rules the entire black population of Union controlled North Carolina was in danger of re-enslavement.

New Bern blacks were even more upset at the treatment that William Henry Singleton had received from some Union army officers. Singleton had organized one of the most effective black scouting bands in New Bern. As soon as Singleton had heard that blacks were about to be enlisted into the Union army, he began to prepare himself and his scouts to serve. Singleton immediately began organizing freedmen into a black militia group and began drilling them. He wanted them

---

[5] Cecelski, David S. *The Fire of Freedom: Abraham Galloway & The Slaves' Civil War.* Chapel Hill: The University of North Carolina Press, 2012. (Pg. xiv)

to be ready to enlist the moment North Carolina organized a black regiment. Instead of an invitation to be a part of the Union army, Singleton and his men were ordered to report to the army's work gangs. Singleton and his militiamen indignantly refused; this order was too much like a return to slavery. After all, the Confederacy had been using slave work gangs since the war began. The army's provost marshal was so angry at Singleton's response that he ordered the arrest of one hundred of the militiamen.

If recruiter Edward Kinsley could not break through the mistrust of New Bern blacks his mission would certainly fail. He asked everyone in town, black and white for help. He was told the only way to win back the support of blacks was to convince Abraham Galloway that the Union cause was still worth fighting for.

Who, Kinsley wondered, was Galloway?

Abraham Galloway was born into slavery in New Bern. He was very happy when his master moved to Wilmington. The twenty year old had dreamed of escaping and he knew that there was a branch of the Underground Railroad in that port city. When he and another slave decided to escape the Railroad put them in touch with a friendly ship's captain who hid them aboard his vessel and carried them to Philadelphia.

Galloway's first stop after slipping ashore was the office of Philadelphia's Vigilance Committee. The year was 1857 and Philadelphia was no longer a safe place for fugitive slaves. William Still suggested to the two runaways that they travel on to Canada. Officially Galloway lived in Kingston, Ontario for three years. There are also unconfirmed reports that during this time Galloway was also a conductor on the Underground Railroad slipping down into the New Bern, Wilmington area from time to time and guiding other slaves to freedom. It would certainly explain why as soon as Galloway returned to New Bern in 1861 he had become the most trusted black man in town.

Abraham Galloway.
Source: *North Carolina Museum of History, Dept. of Cultural Resources.*

Galloway agreed to meet with Kinsley but he insisted that the meeting must be held in secret. Blacks in New Bern had not forgotten the treatment that William Singleton had been given by the Union army. Kinsley was told to come to the boarding house of Mary Ann Starkey, one of the most trusted black leaders in the town. The time was midnight and the Union officer was led up the stairs to the attic. Kinsley describes what happened next. He saw "by the dim light of the candle that the room was filled with blacks, and right in front of him stood Abraham Galloway and another huge negro both armed with revolvers." [6]

Galloway told Kinsley that he was speaking for everyone in New Bern when he said that; "if the Union intended to make the war a crusade for black freedom, then Kinsley would find no shortage of recruits in New Bern, but if the Federal army planned to use black men like chattel and wage a war merely for the preservation of the Union, that was another story." [7]

The men presented Kinsley with their other list of demands. They wanted the same pay as white soldiers. They needed to know what kind of protection their families would receive if they enlisted. If husbands and fathers were off fighting, would the army make sure that the women and children had food and other provisions? They also wanted to make sure that the Union army would keep open the schools that Vincent Coyler had established, so that their children would be educated. Galloway then took out a pistol and aimed it at Kinsley's head and forced the recruiter to swear that the Federal army would meet these conditions. "The next day the word went forth and the blacks came to the recruiting station by [the] hundreds and a Brigade was soon formed." [8] More than 5,000 African Americans were recruited in New Bern.

There was one place where black men had been fighting as Union soldiers since the summer of 1862, in spite of Lincoln's ban on black enlistment. This was in Kansas. James Lane was not a man to wait for presidential approval. Lane had been a member of John Brown's militia band and was now a United States Senator. In 1861 Lane volunteered to become an officer in the Union army. Lincoln sent him to the volatile Kansas-Missouri border, which was under constant attack by Rebel guerillas. Lane knew it was vital that Missouri remain in the Union, but he also knew that Washington could not

[6] Cecelski, David S. *The Fire of Freedom: Abraham Galloway & the Slaves' Civil War.* Chapel Hill: The University of North Carolina Press, 2012 (Pg. xv)

[7] Glisson, Susan, M. editor. *The Human Tradition in the Civil Rights Movement.* New York: Rowman and Littlefield Publishers, 2006. (Pg. 5)

[8] Ibid (Pg. 6)

send enough troops to secure the area.

The President was so worried about Missouri remaining in the Union that, when General Fremont issued an unauthorized emancipation proclamation, Lincoln quickly cancelled the order and relieved Fremont of his command. Lane issued his own orders a bit more subtly. On August 6, 1862, Lane sent a letter to Secretary of War, Edwin Stanton, announcing that, "I am receiving Negroes under the late act of Congress."[9] Although Congress had passed an act on July 17 allowing the army to receive persons of African descent into military service, Lincoln still had not put this law into operation because he was still waiting for the right political moment. Stanton immediately wrote Lane back reminding him that only the President had the authority to enlist black troops. Lane blithely ignored Stanton's orders. He took out advertisements in all of the local newspapers urging African Americans to come to Leavenworth and join the Union army. By October, Lane had organized two regiments of the Kansas Colored volunteers and this maverick officer did not hesitate to use black men on the battlefield.

The Kansas Volunteers, during the battle of Island Mounds, were the first group of black soldiers to prove conclusively the determination of African Americans to fight for their liberty. On October 27, 1862, the regiment was ordered to attack the stronghold of a Rebel band on a well-fortified Missouri island in the Osage River. It was a bloody battle between these new Yankee soldiers and the six hundred Rebels, but in the end the black regiment was victorious. The Rebel band was forced to retreat. William Truman, one of the Rebel leaders, reported that "the black devils fought like tigers... not one would surrender."[10] The Colored Kansas regiment had never been officially mustered into the Union army; therefore the fact that it had won a small battle against Rebel forces was not widely reported in the North. It was in Louisiana that black soldiers would begin to convince the North that they were as willing to fight for their freedom as any white man.

[9] Quarles, Benjamin. *The Negro in the Civil War*. Boston: Little Brown and Company, 1953. (Pg. 114-115)

[10] Ibid (Pg. 115)

New Orleans, sitting at the mouth of the Mississippi River, was the South's most important port. Over half of all the cotton grown in the South passed through its port. If Lincoln's blockade were to be successful, New Orleans must be conquered. It was a formidable task. Guarding the southern approach to the city were two heavily armed fortresses, Fort Jackson and Fort St. Philip. Between these two fortresses the Confederate navy had fastened two heavy iron chains that completely blocked the mouth of the Mississippi River. Confederate generals believed that this defense was so powerful that Union forces would never attack New Orleans from the south. They concentrated all of their military force at the northern entrance to the city.

Captain David Farragut of the United States Navy had a plan that would allow him to attack the city from the south. On the night of April 20, 1862 a small group of seamen sailed quietly under Fort Jackson and, with sledge hammers and chisels, cut the chains and cleared the river. Then the navy flotilla sailed up the river and the surprised Rebel forces began firing. The battle lasted for just an hour, then the Union ships sped up the river to New Orleans. On April 29 the American flag was raised over the New Orleans City Hall.

The capture of New Orleans was a great victory for the Union, but the rest of Louisiana was still solidly Confederate. Rebel control of Louisiana was a constant danger to Federal control of New Orleans. Union officers cabled Washington that they urgently needed more troops to preserve their victory. The Union army had hoped that they could recruit enough white troops from within the city to fill their ranks, but there were few volunteers.

Brigadier General John Phelps was camped four miles above the city. His mission was to protect the city against any attacks. Phelps was dangerously short of troops and he knew that he could not expect any help from the Union army. Phelps decided to turn to the slaves for help. The General sent out an announcement that offered freedom to any slave belonging to a Rebel, who wanted to join the Union army as a laborer. Fugitives began streaming towards Phelps' camp. One of the men heading for the Union camp was Octave Johnson.

Johnson had been a slave on a sugar plantation in St James Parrish when, in 1861, the overseer threatened him with a beating if he did not work harder. Johnson's answer was to escape, along with thirty other fugitives. They established a rough maroon camp in one of the nearby swamps. It was a harsh existence. The fugitives slept on logs and burned cypress leaves to keep away the thick clouds of mosquitoes that hovered over the camp. They lived by stealing chickens, turkeys and pigs from local plantations, and shared their booty with plantation slaves. In return the fugitives received corn meal, salt, and other staples.

When, in September, 1862, General Phelps issued his offer of freedom, Octave Johnson and his band left their swamp hideout and made their way to the Union camp to receive their precious certificates of freedom.[11] They then waited along with hundreds of other fugitives for the Federal government to allow them to fight the Rebels. Phelps begged General Benjamin Butler to allow him to arm these volunteers so they could help him defend New Orleans. Butler refused. He told Phelps that the hundreds of fugitives filling his camp could only be used as laborers. Phelps replied that he didn't need laborers, he needed fighting men if he were to protect the city, and the only fighting men around were the fugitives. Butler was adamant there would be no black fighting men in his army. Not only was it against Federal policy, it was also a waste of weaponry. The general believed that "Blacks were horrified of fire arms and it would be ludicrous in the extreme to put weapons in their hands." [12]

General Butler needed to enlist hundreds of new troops. He hoped to find these fresh troops among those city leaders who had tried to keep Louisiana from seceding. Butler had also been wooing Louisiana planters by returning their fugitive slaves in hopes that they would at least remain neutral in the struggle. White New Orleans, however, remained defiantly Rebel. Black New Orleans had already volunteered to raise thousands of troops for the Union, but Butler rejected their offer. On August 5th Confederate troops attacked Baton Rouge, and the Union occupation of New Orleans was in danger. The Federal government informed General Butler that they were unable to send any additional troops to defend the city. In desperation Butler turned to black New Orleans citizens for help, the same people he had just so arrogantly rejected. They agreed to organize a black regiment to defend the city.

The Creole community of New Orleans had a tradition of military service that went back to the time when Louisiana was first a French and later a Spanish colony. Black Creoles had come to the

---

[11] Berlin, Ira et al editors. *Free At Last: A Documentary History of Slavery, Freedom, and the Civil War.* New York, New Press, 1992. (Pg. 51-52)

[12] Hollandsworth, James G. *The Louisiana Native Guards: The Black Military Experience During the Civil War.* Baton Rouge: Louisiana State University Press, 1995. (Pg. 13)

aid of Andrew Jackson during the war of 1812 when Jackson saved
the city from the British attack. Black New Orleans leaders began
recruiting immediately and in just a few weeks had enlisted enough
soldiers to fill two regiments. General Butler was astonished by the
patriotism of these free blacks. He was even more surprised by some of
the leaders of the Native Guard. One volunteer Francis E. Dumas was
a distant relative of the French poet and writer Alexandre Dumas.
He was the son of a wealthy white sugar *Planter* and a beautiful
mulatto woman. His father sent him to Paris to be educated and,
when he returned to New Orleans, Dumas took his place as a member
of the Black elite of the city. Dumas was the wealthiest black man in
Louisiana.

Andre Cailloux, one of the chief recruiters for the new black
regiments, upset the General's racist view of African Americans even
more forcefully. He was a successful businessman whose cigars were
one of the most popular brands in the city. He was also admired as
a great sportsman, one of the best boxers in the city, as well as an
accomplished horseman. He was fluent in both English and French.
Skeptical whites could not explain his talent and abilities on the basis
of any white blood he might possess because Cailloux proudly boasted
that he was the blackest man in New Orleans.

There was tremendous white opposition to General Butler's use
of black troops especially because these regiments had black officers.
When the First Regiment of the Louisiana Native Guard marched
through the city, they were hooted and jeered by New Orleans
whites. Louisiana slaveholders were even more disturbed by the
sight of armed blacks patrolling just outside their plantations in full
view of their slaves. Even though Lincoln had promised Louisiana
slaveholders that, if they took the Union oath, they would be able
to keep their slaves, slaveholders realized that slavery was already
falling apart. So many slaves had fled and had become members of the
Native Guards that there were three full regiments now in the field.
Other slaves had simply gone on strike and refused to work unless the
slaveholders paid them some form of wage.

For months General Butler refused to send the black Regiments
into battle because of his belief that black men were incapable of
fighting. Instead they were assigned to guard and repair the railroad
lines around the city. It seemed that even though African Americans
had finally been allowed to join the army they would not get the
chance to prove that they could fight. When Butler was replaced in
December of 1862 by General Banks, that hope became even dimmer

278

as Banks set out to replace every black line officer with a white one. Captain Andre Cailloux remained the only black officer in the Louisiana Native Guard.

Then in May, 1863, General Ulysses Grant began his siege of Vicksburg, Mississippi. The occupation of Vicksburg would split the Confederacy in half and make the entire Mississippi River a Union river. Before Grant could capture Vicksburg, the strategic town of Port Hudson must be taken. The town was located on a bend in the Mississippi River just twenty miles north of Baton Rouge, giving the Rebels control of the two hundred mile stretch of the river between Vicksburg in the north and Port Hudson in the south.

The town of Port Hudson was a formidable target. The town stretched three miles along the river protected by an eighty foot bluff. From the rear the Confederates had built a twenty foot thick parapet which was pierced by rifle pits and sharpened tree branches. Around this parapet was a fifteen foot ditch filled with water. On top of the parapet was a battery of guns. General Banks knew that he would need more than the 30,000 white troops that he had available to capture Port Hudson. Reluctantly he ordered Andre Cailloux's Native Guards to join in the attack.

On the morning of May 27, the Union army began the attack. General Banks' strategy was to bombard the fort until the Rebel army was exhausted. Then the entire Union line was to rush in and attack. The 1,080 members of the Native Guard were placed on the extreme right front of the battle line. Their assignment was to advance along Telegraph Road which ran through a thick forest then emerged into an unprotected flood plain. This flood plain had no cover and the Native Guard would be exposed to the full force of Confederate fire. As the moment of the attack grew near, Captain Cailloux walked up and down the line encouraging his company of untried troops. He told the men how much confidence he had in them and how well he expected them to do in this their first battle. Cailloux understood that General Banks had given his company an almost suicidal mission against sharpshooting Confederate troops, but he also knew that his soldiers must prove to Union doubters that black troops would fight and die if necessary for their liberty.

At ten o'clock the bugle sounded, followed by the sharp command "Charge!" The First Native Guards emerged from the sheltering cover of the woods to storm the fort. The rebels began firing. Sheets of flame flashed from the six gun battery. Soldiers began falling from the deadly fire, but the troops continued their advance. Captain Cailloux, at the head of company E called out words of encouragement as the men raced towards the fort. A shot rang out and Cailloux's left arm was shattered, but he continued to lead his men forward, his arm hanging uselessly by his side. At one o'clock Cailloux finally led his men to the fifteen foot ditch that they had to cross in order to begin the deadly climb up the parapet. "Follow me!' he cried out as a shell ripped through his body and he fell down dead.[13]

His men followed Cailloux's last command. They attempted to ford the ditch but it was impossible. Rebel soldiers on top of the parapet fired an unceasing battery of gunfire at the black troops. Cailloux's men managed to reach a point only fifty yards from Rebel batteries, but the firepower was so intense that they were forced back again and again. The fighting finally ended at four o'clock when the order to retreat was finally sounded. The casualties for the Native Guard were high; thirty seven members of the Guard were killed, 155 were wounded and 116 were missing in action.

On July 9, Port Hudson finally surrendered to General Banks and Andre Cailloux's body was brought home to New Orleans. Captain Cailloux's funeral profoundly affected the city. For Black Creoles, one of their greatest heroes was about to be buried, and they were determined to honor him. On July 25 his body was brought to the Urquhart Street Hall where it lay in state for four days, his casket covered with flowers and draped with the American flag.

The hall where Cailloux lay in state was filled with hundreds of mourners, while outside hundreds more made the streets leading to the hall impassible. His flag draped casket moved through the streets until it reached the cemetery where he was buried with full military honors. His funeral was attended by thousands, and it was said to have been one of the most magnificent ceremonies in the city's history.

The assault by the Louisiana Black Native Guard on Port Hudson had an electrifying effect on Northern opinion. The *New York Times* had been very skeptical about the ability of blacks to fight, but Port Hudson changed the paper's opinion. On June 11, 1863, the newspaper declared in an editorial that the time for accepting blacks into the Union Army had arrived.

In the spring of 1862, Harriet Tubman heard the news that the Union army had captured Port Royal. She immediately packed her bags and set sail for South Carolina. General Hunter,

---

[13] Ibid (Pg. 54-55)

Commander of the Army of the South who knew her reputation as an Underground Railroad conductor, was delighted to see her. He needed her services both as a nurse and as a Union scout, so Hunter offered her a small stipend. Tubman moved from camp to camp throughout the Department of the South wherever there was a call for her services. Tubman was widely known among Maryland slaves but, in South Carolina, blacks had never heard of her. They simply saw her as another northerner paid by the Yankees and, therefore, they did not trust her. Tubman decided to reject her small stipend. She supported herself by baking and selling pies and root beer. Later she also operated a small wash house. By day she nursed soldiers and the ex-slaves, who arrived in the camps ill, starved, and destitute. At night she baked her pies and washed clothes. Soon Tubman became as much of a beloved figure among the black population of the sea islands as she was in Maryland.

When Generals Hunter and Saxton asked Tubman if she could undertake a scouting mission for them, she was ready. Tubman picked nine black men who had lived in the area all their lives. These men were trusted by local slaves and a few of them were also river pilots. Under Tubman's command the men set out to discover the location of the Rebel forces in the area, report on their movements, and discover their strengths and weaknesses.

The Department of the South had a dual mission to keep the sea islands under Union control and enforce the blockade. The second was to harass the Confederate army from Jacksonville, Florida in the south to Charleston in the north, so that they would be unable to divert part of their forces into the battlefields of northern Virginia. Generals Hunter and Saxton's area of command included a coastline that was extremely jagged, marked by countless islands and rivers that ran deep into the South's interior. The most effective way to tie down the Confederate army without depending on fresh troops was for the Union army to use the tactic of guerrilla warfare. For this, black soldiers were ideal.

Colonel Montgomery was put in charge of organizing forays into enemy territory. His assignment was simple; seize and destroy all property that could be used to support and sustain the Confederate war effort. The Rebels' most important resources were their slaves who formed the basis of the plantation economy; they grew the food and other products the Confederacy relied on. Slaves were also essential in the construction and preservation of rebel forts, railroad tracks, bridges and roads. Montgomery was ordered to bring out as many slaves as possible on each one of his raids. The colonel knew that the perfect leader to lead his guerilla raids was Harriet Tubman and her band of scouts.

The most extraordinary expedition organized by the Department of the South was a raid up the Combahee River. The nominal commander of the expedition was Colonel Montgomery, but the real organizer and leader of the campaign was Harriet Tubman. In the spring of 1863, Tubman informed Montgomery that the countryside was ripe for an attack. Tubman and her small band began by making an exhaustive study of the territory: every torpedo placed in the river by the Rebels, the size and location of every Rebel fort and encampment. Each bridge and railroad was carefully mapped by Tubman's scouts. Her scouts had also infiltrated the slave quarters of every plantation on the bank of the river, and recruited men and women to help in the campaign.

It began during the night of June 2, 1863, as Tubman and Montgomery led three gunboats holding 300 Black troops up the Combahee River. Confederate pickets along the river spotted the boats but, since they did not have the manpower to fight the invasion, most of them fled inland. The Union gunboats were able to put ashore small groups of soldiers to secure the Confederate posts without any casualties. As the boats continued up the river, soldiers dismantled the torpedoes that the Confederates had placed in the river to prevent just such a raid. Railroad tracks and bridges were destroyed. Cotton, rice and other products were loaded onto the ships. What the ships could not carry they burned. Seven hundred and fifty six liberated slaves filled the gunboats as they steamed back to Beaufort. Many of the fugitives immediately enlisted in the Union army.

The *Commonwealth,* a Boston newspaper, announced that for the first time in history a black woman led American troops into battle. The newspaper reported to an astonished nation that this black woman, Harriet Tubman, had been such a brilliant leader that her troops managed to destroy a million dollars worth of Confederate property without the Union army losing a single man or even suffering a single casualty.[14]

---

[11] Conrad, Earl. *General Harriet Tubman. Washington D.C.:* The Associated Press 1943. (Pg. 169-171)

The devastating defeats and terrible casualties that the Union experienced during the summer and fall of 1862 had seriously depleted the army and there were very few new recruits to replace them. Reluctantly, in March, 1863, Lincoln initiated a conscription law. The draft was even more unpopular in the North than Jefferson Davis' draft law of 1862 had been in the South.

On July 13 in New York City, as the government began drawing names for the first inductees, a riot broke out. The draft office was set on fire; mobs began roaming the streets of the city, setting fire to buildings, attacking police stations, looting stores, and assaulting every government building in their path. A special target of the rioters was the black community. Black homes and boarding houses were burned to the ground. Several blacks were hanged or burned to death. The worst attack was leveled at the Colored Orphan Asylum where a crowd gathered and shouted "Kill all the niggers," then, as 237 children were hustled out the back door, the rioters set fire to the building and it burned to the ground. For four days mobs roamed unchecked throughout the streets of the city, the police unwilling or unable to control the rioters. President Lincoln was forced to send 800 Federal troops into the city before order was finally established. It remains the worst riot in American history.[15] There were anti draft riots in other cities throughout the North. The draft had become a serious political problem for the Republican Party.

The President was becoming more impressed every day about the fighting ability of African Americans as he read reports about their performances on the battlefields of Kansas, the sea islands and Louisiana. Then came Fort Wagner.

Massachusetts was the first state to organize a black regiment. By March, 1863, 1,100 men had enlisted in the 54th Massachusetts Regiment. Robert Shaw, the son of a prominent white abolitionist, became its first commander. President Lincoln was anxious to recapture the city of Charleston, birthplace of the Confederacy. It was a formidable task since the city was protected by a series of barrier islands, which guarded the harbor. The Confederate army had built

---

[15] Smith, Page. *Trial By Fire: A People's History of the Civil War and Reconstruction.* New York; McGraw-Hill Book Company, 1982. (Pg. 478)

a series of forts on these islands to protect the city against a Union invasion. One of these forts was Fort Wagner, located at the summit of Morris Island. The island itself had been captured by the Union army, but Fort Wagner was still in enemy hands. On July 18 the men of the 54th Regiment were proud to be selected to lead the first attack against Fort Wagner. They vowed to show the world that they were as willing to fight and die for their county as any white man.

Sergeant William Carney was one of those soldiers. Carney, born a slave in Norfolk, Virginia, had used the Underground Railroad to escape. He found his father living in Boston and sometime before the Civil War the two men returned to Norfolk and rescued the rest of their family.

These soldiers faced a formidable task. Fort Wagner was one of the strongest single earthworks ever constructed. Its walls were huge, made of sand held together with grass cover, earth and logs. Inside the fort there were 1,700 armed Confederate soldiers waiting for the Union attack, an attack that seemed suicidal. Sitting just above Charleston Harbor, Fort Wagner was the last great Confederate fortification blocking a Union attack on the city.

Colonel Robert Shaw gave the command to charge and the men began climbing the steep hill that led to the entrance to Fort Wagner while a barrage of shots and shells exploded around them. Many of the regiment were killed or wounded but those who remained fought their way to the parapet. Only a dozen men, along with Colonel Shaw managed to reach the top of the parapet. Then Shaw was shot his body falling into the fort.

William Carney seized the regimental flag and moved toward the entrance to the fort. He looked around and discovered that he was all alone. Around him lay the bodies of the dead and wounded. Carney dared not enter the fort alone so, for thirty minutes, he flattened himself against its outer slope waiting for reinforcements. When other Union regiments began a second assault the remnants of Carney's regiment were finally able to retreat.

By the time Carney had traveled halfway down the slope he had been shot in both of his legs, in one arm and in his breast. He finished his descent, creeping on one knee, exhausted by the pain and loss of blood. Finally another Union soldier saw Carney and ran to help him. The soldier offered to carry the flag but Carney refused, stating

---

[16] Logan, Rayford and Michael R. Winston editors. *Dictionary of American Negro Biography*. New York: W. W. Norton & Company, 1982. (Pg. 90)

that "No one but a member of the 54th should carry the colors." [16] When Carney finally reached the Union lines he received emergency treatment and was sent back to the Regimental encampment still clutching the flag. Carney announced to his cheering comrades that, "The old flag never touched the ground."[17] For his bravery at Fort Wagner, Sergeant William Carney became the first African American to be awarded the Congressional Medal of Honor.

The story of the 54th regiment's brave assault on Fort Wagner convinced Lincoln along with most northerners, that black men could fight. The President ordered his generals to put their black regiments side by side with white troops on the battlefield.

The Union Army's Department of the South was never designated a major battlefield but Generals Hunter and Saxton had been given the responsibility of maintaining a tight blockade of the southern coast. The two generals told Washington that they needed more fighting men in order for them to maintain the blockade. The answer was always no. The battlefields in Virginia had become a bloodbath with Union casualties mounting every day. The army could not spare any troops for the Department of the South. The generals were forced to rely on the ex-slaves of coastal South to increase their fighting power. One of their most important resources was Robert Smalls.

Smalls was now in the Union navy. His knowledge of Confederate fortifications was vital to Generals Hunter and Saxton. Smalls fought in seventeen battles. When the Union forces attacked Charleston in 1863, Smalls was piloting the ship, Keokuk, commanded by Captain Rhind. The fleet was caught unaware by a rain of Confederate cannonballs, as they rounded Morris Island. The *Keokuk* was struck ninety-six times before finally sinking. Smalls was one of the few survivors of that battle.

In another battle Smalls was piloting the *Planter* through the mouth of the Stono River when Rebel forces tried to recapture the ship. The Rebels began shelling the vessel, striking the smoke stack, the lookout tower, and the roof of the wheel house where Smalls was sitting. Captain Nickerson, believing that there was no chance of escape, ordered Smalls to beach the ship and surrender. Smalls

[17] Ibid (Pg. 91)

refused, saying "A white man is regarded by Confederate soldiers as a prisoner of war, but all of this crew are run-away slaves. No quarter will be shown us." [18] Smalls then tried to speed up the ship, but a rain of shells poured down upon him. The panicked captain left the pilot house. Smalls immediately took control of the ship and steered the boat safely out of reach of the guns. Captain Nickerson resigned as captain of the *Planter*. General Saxton was unable to find another naval officer willing to command a black crew. Saxton made a radical decision and promoted Robert Smalls to the position of captain of the *Planter*; Smalls became the first black naval captain in American history.

The Fort Pillow Massacre. Source: *Library of Congress, Prints and Photographs Division.*

Smalls was certainly right about the danger that black Union soldiers faced if they were caught by the Confederates. Every black soldier had already heard what happened to their fellow soldiers during the battle of Fort Pillow, Kentucky. On April 12, 1863, General Nathan Forest led a Confederate battalion up to the gates of the fort. His soldiers encircled the garrison and demanded that the Union army surrender. There were only 557 soldiers inside the fort, which included 262 new black recruits. At first the defenders of Fort Pillow, although badly outnumbered, refused to surrender. They answered General Forest's ultimatum with a blast of gunfire. The battle did not last

---

[18] Uya, Okon Edet. *Robert Smalls: From Slavery to Public Service 1839-1915.* New York: Oxford University Press. 1971 (Pg. 23).

long because the inexperienced soldiers were overwhelmed by Rebel fire. They raised the white flag of surrender and Confederate soldiers swarmed into the Fort.

What happened next was a horror story. Some Rebel soldiers shot black soldiers as their hands were raised in surrender. Other Confederates shot into groups of wounded soldiers as they lay on the ground pleading for help. One group of Union soldiers was ordered into the barracks house and then the building was set on fire. The screams of the men could be heard for miles. One report, states that 360 blacks were massacred that day, many of whom were not even soldiers. Two hundred white Union soldiers were killed that day as well, simply because they chose to fight alongside black troops. The news of this, the worst slaughter of the Civil War, spread throughout the north only because there were a few survivors. From that moment on, black soldiers would raise the cry, "Remember Fort Pillow" whenever they went into battle.

15

THE END OF SLAVERY

In the fall of 1863 the Confederate government was once more faced with the problem of needing new troops to fill their regiments The government decided that the answer to their problem was to launch a series of military campaigns against army deserters and draft dodgers in order to force them back into the army. One of the most concentrated attacks was directed at the 300 members of Newton Knight's band. When Confederate soldiers marched into Jones County, they discovered that the Knight band had the support of most of the local farmers. The band had raided warehouses filled with confiscated food and other items collected by the tax collector, and passed them out to the hungry people of the county. They had also attacked Confederate raiders and members of the Home Guard as they burst into people's homes trying to confiscate food and goods. In return, farming families alerted Knight and his followers whenever Confederate soldiers were in the neighborhood. Generations later Jones County natives still talked about how Newton Knight had saved their families from starvation.

Knight found another group of supporters when Rachel Knight joined the band . Rachel Knight was a slave woman and one of the most important leaders within the plantation slave community, when she decided to become a courier between the slaves of Jones County and Newton Knight. It was a unusual alliance. Rachel Knight was owned by Newton's uncle, David Knight, a man who had fathered two of Rachel's children. She certainly had no reason to trust any member of the white Knight family. Yet for some reason Rachel decided to trust Newton Knight. This alliance was vital in protecting the Knight band.

Some of the slaves on Jones County plantations were members of the Legal League. George Washington Albright was only fifteen years old when Lincoln signed the Emancipation Proclamation. His father had already fled the plantation to join the Union army. When Albright heard that his father had died during the battle of Vicksburg, he became a runner for the Legal League. His job was to travel from plantation to plantation spreading the news about the historic Proclamation and recruiting groups of slaves to help the Union cause. Rachel convinced Legal League members to support the Knight band. She moved secretly between the various deserter camps and the slave cabins in Jones County. In addition to spying for the Union army, Legal League members also collected food and supplies, stolen from their masters, for the Knight band.[1] When Confederate raiders began marching into the Piney Woods, Newton was warned by Rachel's network and the band was able to fight off the attack.

In October, after defeating the Confederate raid, sixty members of Knight's band held a secret meeting inside an old trading post called Smith's Store. The men declared their independence from the Confederacy and pledged their alliance to the Union cause. They called themselves the Jones County Scouts and they elected Newton Knight their captain. They then began a recruiting drive to enlist white deserters and fugitives slaves into the Scouts. Knight also linked his Scouts up with other deserter bands throughout the region. There were reports that these loosely organized bands had made contact with the Union army in Florida. By the spring of 1864, the Confederacy seemed to have lost control of southeast Mississippi. There was even a report that the Union flag was now flying over the Jones County Courthouse.

By 1863, Lumpkin County in North Georgia had collapsed into its own internal Civil War. Many of the people living in this non-slaveholding Appalachian community had not voted for secession, but they were not anti-Confederacy; they just wanted to live their lives as they had always done. After the Confederate government passed the Conscription Act, angry mountaineers retreated into the mountains to avoid the army. By 1863 the men of Lumpkin County were joined by thousands of draft dodgers, Confederate deserters, and fugitive slaves. By October 1864, the Union army had managed to organize some of

---

[1] Jenkins, Sally and John Stauffer. *The State of Jones: The Small Southern Town That Seceded From the Confederacy.* New York: Doubleday, 2009. (Pg. 42)

the anti-Confederate bands hiding out all over Appalachian Georgia into an armed revolt against the Confederacy which lasted until peace was declared.[2]

In 1864 both the Union and Confederate armies had abandoned the towns bordering the Great Dismal Swamp; they were preparing for the final critical battles of the Civil War in Northern Virginia. Members of the North Carolina Home Guard were left alone to carry out the ongoing battles against the Buffaloes and their deserter allies. These Home Guard members believed that most of the townspeople, because they did not own slaves, were secret Union supporters. They suspected that some of them were surreptitiously helping the deserter bands. Home Guard members were passionately committed to the Confederate cause, and they vowed they would win the war against the Buffaloes and deserters. Home Guard leaders believed that the only way to end local support for the Dismal Swamp bands was by terrorizing the people living along the Albermarle Sound.

Even people who tried to remain neutral in the ongoing battles between Home Guards and Buffaloes might be attacked by members of the Home Guard. Finally, in desperation, even Confederate supporters tried to withdraw from the battle. The governing bodies of five counties passed resolutions addressed to the Confederate States of America asking that their government do one of two things, "either send enough regular army troops to hold and pacify the countryside, or cease aid and encouragement to the Confederate Home Guard and to order the same to cease its operation." [3]

By the fall of 1863 the Buffaloes had expanded the guerilla war into central Virginia. Buffaloes organized massive and continuous raids in the lush pastures. On January 14, 1864, The *Richmond Examiner* reported that,"... it is so difficult to find words of description ...of the wild and terrible consequences of the negro raids in this obscure theater of the war." [4] Food was becoming so scarce in Richmond by the beginning of 1864 that food riots led by women, desperate to find enough food to feed their families, were becoming a regular event.

[2] Sutherland, Daniel editor. *Guerillas, Unionists, and Violence on the Confederate Home Front.* Fayetteville: University of Arkansas Press, 1990. (Pg. 37)

[3] Leaming, Hugo Prosper. *Hidden Americans: Maroons of Virginia and the Carolinas.* New York: Garland Publishing Inc., 1995. (Pg. 318-319)

[4] Ibid (Pg. 322)

In January, 1865 President Jefferson Davis was facing the worst crisis of the war. Abraham Lincoln had won re-election. The Confederate army was only one fourth the size of the Union army and more troops were deserting every month. Davis knew that he had exhausted every possible source that could supply his army with fresh troops. There was no place left to look. The President remembered a suggestion sent to him in December 1863 by General Patrick Cleburne, a hero of the Confederate Army of Tennessee. This memorandum suggested that the Confederacy immediately begin training the "most courageous of our slaves to become soldiers." [5] Jefferson Davis was so shocked by this suggestion that he immediately banned any further discussion of using slaves in the army even within his own Cabinet. If Cleburne had not been a Confederate hero he might have been tried for treason.

Cleburne in his notorious memorandum also pointed out the fact that slavery, which had been the major source of strength in the beginning days of the war, was now the source of its greatest weaknesses. The general pointed out that the Confederacy could no longer count on using slaves on or even near the battlefield because so many of them were fleeing towards the Union lines.

Confederate leaders were learning other bitter lessons about their slaves. General Francis Shoup informed a senator that, "it is by no means certain that the negro is so deficient in courage as is generally believed." In fact Shoup stated that, "Lincoln had induced blacks to fight as well if not better than have his white troops." [6]

In January, 1865, a handful of Confederate leaders began thinking the unthinkable; they might have to abolish slavery in order to save the Confederacy. One of those leaders was Judah Benjamin, the Confederate Secretary of State. On February 9, Benjamin told a disbelieving crowd in Richmond, "I came here to say disagreeable things. I tell you there are not enough able bodied white men in the country ...But war is a game that cannot be played without men," he went on, "so where are the men to come from?" He told the crowd that there were some 680,000 military age black men. "Let us say to every negro who wishes to go into the ranks on condition of being made free – Go and fight; you are free." [7]

---

[5] Levine, Bruce. *Confederate Emancipation: Southern Plans to Free and Arm Slaves During the Civil War.* New York: Oxford University Press, 2006. (Pg. 2)

[6] Ibid (Pg. 85)

[7] Ibid (Pg. 35)

Benjamin made his speech to support Jefferson Davis, who had just suggested that the Confederate government purchase 40,000 slaves to serve as front-line military laborers. In order to guarantee that these slaves remain loyal to the South, Davis insisted that such slave labor should be promised eventual freedom. Many southerners correctly viewed this proposal as the first step in the destruction of slavery itself. As the *Lynchburg Republican* pointed out, "if 250 negro men are entitled to their freedom because they fight for it, then their wives, children and families are also entitled to the same boon ...soon nothing at all would remain of the South's peculiar institution." [8]

Jefferson Davis's proposal produced an angry uproar that could be heard throughout the entire South. "Was it not to prevent the destruction of slavery ...that the South had opted first for secession and then for war?" asked the *Macon Telegraph* and Confederate newspaper. Charleston's principal newspaper editors were appalled. *The Courier* insisted that, "Slavery, Gods institution of labor and the primary political element of our Confederation... must stand or fall together," while the Mercury's editor thundered that, "We want no Confederate Government without our institutions." Texas' Caleb Cutwell spoke for a majority of southerners when he claimed that, "Independence without slavery, would be valueless because the South without slavery would not be worth a mess of pottage." [9]

Jefferson Davis realized he would have to get the support of the South's most revered leader if he was going to be able to use slaves in the Confederate army. On February 18, 1865 General Robert E. Lee wrote to Mississippi Congressman Barksdale in a letter that the general expected to be printed, that arming slaves was, "not only expedient but necessary." [10]

On March 4th, 1865, the Confederate Congress passed a bill to allow the recruitment of slaves into the army. Why did Jefferson Davis and the Confederate Congress decide that they had to ignore public outrage in order to use slaves in the army? They had no choice

---

[8] Ibid (pg. 52), [9] Ibid (pg. 55-57), [10] Ibid (pg. 36)

if they wanted to stave off defeat. The slave population of the South had become a vast underground network working diligently to defeat the Confederacy. Black soldiers, mostly ex-slaves were now ten percent of the Union army, and these black soldiers could fight. One third of black Union soldiers were listed as dead or missing in action.[11] The Confederate government urgently needed to win at least some of their slaves to fight for the southern cause. They hoped that slaves would respond to this modest offer of a partial emancipation.

Martin Delany. Source: Wikipedia

When Martin Delany heard that the Confederate government had begun talking about limited emancipation he acted quickly. He remembered that in the summer of 1864, President Lincoln and Frederick Douglass had begun talks about sending a band of black scouts into the Rebel states to spread the news about the Emancipation Proclamation and recruit troops for the Union army. Delany decided that now was the time to put that plan into action. He took off for Washington determined to meet with the President. His friends told him that such a meeting would be impossible to arrange. Delany insisted that it was urgent that the Federal government present a counter- offer to southern slaves. To his surprise, Lincoln agreed to meet with Delany the next morning. Delany proposed that Lincoln send an army of blacks, commanded by black officers deep into the heart of Dixie where slaves had never heard about Lincoln's Emancipation Proclamation. The sight of black officers leading black soldiers would deliver the most powerful kind of freedom message. These troops would be able to recruit black men who could attack the Confederate army from the rear. Delany convinced the President that the only equipment that his black phalanx would need would be some light artillery. Lincoln was impressed and agreed to the plan. Martin Delany was inducted into the Union army with the rank of Major, the first black officer in the history of the United States army. He had just begun recruiting volunteers to march south when General Lee surrendered at Appomattox.

---

[11] Litwack, Leon F. *Been in the Storm So Long: The Aftermath of Slavery.* New York: Vintage Books, 1979. (Pg. 97-98)

On April 2, 1865, General Robert E. Lee abandoned Richmond and moved his army south. The next day a triumphant Union army entered the Confederate capital. At the head of one of the columns was Major Charles Francis Adams, grandson of John Quincy Adams, hero of the Gag Rule campaign, leading his regiment of black cavalry.

Garland White, a former fugitive slave, now a Union chaplain, left a vivid description of this historic day. "From a Richmond jail imprisoned slaves could be chanting 'slavery chains broke at last;' next, the doors of all the slave pens were thrown open and thousands came out shouting and praising God and Father or master Abe." Garland was resting in camp when he was told that a black lady was looking for him. Surprised that anyone in that teeming crown might know him, he went back into the street. His arm was seized by an elderly woman who hesitantly asked what his mother's name was. "Nancy," Garland responded. He was then bombarded by more questions about his life as a slave and his escape to freedom. Finally the woman announced in a voice trembling with emotion, "This is your mother, Garland, whom you are now talking to, who has spent twenty years of grief about her son." [12]

On April 14, Robert Smalls sailed the *Planter* into Charleston Harbor. He had been invited as a guest of the government to salute the Stars and Stripes as it was raised again over Fort Sumter. When the people along the wharf caught sight of Smalls, guns began to boom, bells rang, and the band started playing as the crowd cheered their favorite hero. At the stroke of noon the battle-scarred United States flag which had waved over Fort Sumpter until the final surrender was handed to the fort's old commander Robert Anderson for him to raise again. As the old flag reached its apex, cannons roared, drums beat, bells pealed, and the crowd roared. Then came the singing of the Star Spangled Banner and many in the crowd began to weep.

[12] Winik, Jay. *April 1865: The Month That Saved America.* New York; Harper Collins Publisher, 2001. (Pg. 117)

On January 31, 1865, even before Lee's Surrender, the US Congress voted to pass the 13th amendment to the United States Constitution, prohibiting slavery anywhere in the United States. When the vote was announced, the galleries, filled to overflowing with people wanting to witness this historic event, began to cheer wildly. Congressmen embraced one another, some members even wept. The capital cannons boomed a 100 gun salute. Then by acclamation, the House of Representatives voted to adjourn, "in honor of this immortal and sublime event." It was the end of slavery in America.

Scene in the House on the passage of the 13th amendment proposition to the Constitution. January 31, 1865.
Source: *The Library of Congress Prints and Photographs Division.*

BIBLIOGRAPHY

Anderson, Osborne P. *A Voice From Harper's Ferry*. Boston: Printed for the author, 1861.

Andrews, William L. and Henry Louis Gates Jr., Editors: *Slave Narratives*. New York: Library of America, 2000.

Andrews William L. *To Tell A Free Story: The First Century of Afro-American Autobiography 1760-1865*. Urbana: University of Illinois Press, 1986.

Aptheker, Herbert. *To Be Free; Studies in American Negro History*. New York: International Publishers, 1948.

----------. *Towards Negro Freedom*. New York: New Century Publishers, 1965.

Ash, Stephen V. *Firebrand of Liberty: The Story of Two Black Regiments That Changed the Course of the Civil War*. New York: W. W. Norton & Company, 2008.

Bacon, Margaret Hope. *Rebellion at Christiana* New York: Crown Publishers, Inc. 1975.

----------. *But One Race: A Life of Robert Purvis*. Albany: State University of New York Press, 2007.

Baker, H. Robert. *The Rescue of Joshua Glover a Fugitive Slave; The Constitution and the Coming of the Civil War*. Athens, Ohio: Ohio University Press, 2006.

Barrett, John G. *The Civil War in North Carolina*. Chapel Hill: The University of North Carolina Press, 1963.

Berlin, Ira. *The Making of African America: The Four Great Migrations*. New York: Viking,2010.

----------. *Many Thousands Gone: The First Two Centuries of Slavery in America*. Cambridge: Harvard University Press, 1998.

----------. *Slaves Without Masters: The Free Negro in the Antebellum South*. New York: Vintage Press, 1976.

Berlin, Ira et al. *Slaves No More: Three Essays on Emancipation and the Civil War*. New York: Cambridge University Press, 1992.

----------. *Free At Last: A Documentary History of Slavery,Freedom, and the Civil War*. New York: The New Press, 1992.

Berlin, Ira and Ronald Hoffman editors. *Slavery and Freedom in the Age of the American Revolution*. Urbana and Chicago: University of Illinois Press, 1986.

Blackett, R. J. M. *Beating Against the Barriers: The Lives of Six Nineteenth-Century Afro-Americans*. Ithaca: Cornell University Press, 1986.

Blight, David W. *Beyond the Battlefield: Race, Memory & the American Civil War*. Amherst: University of Massachusetts Press, 2002.

----------. *Passages To Freedom: The Underground Railroad in History and Memory*. Smithsonian Books in association with the National Underground Railroad Freedom Center, 2006

----------. *Race and Reunion: The Civil War in American Memory*. Cambridge: Harvard University Press, 2001.

Blockson, Charles L. *Hippocrene Guide to the Underground Railroad*. New York: Hippocrene Books, 1995.

----------. *The Underground Railroad: Dramatic Firsthand Accounts of Daring Escapes to Freedom*. New York: Berkley Books, 1994.

Blumrosen, Alfred W. and Ruth G. Blumrosen. *Slave Nation: How Slavery United the Colonies and Sparked the American Revolution*. Naperville, Illinois: Sourcebooks, Inc. 2005.

Bolster, W. Jeffrey. *Black Jacks: African American Seamen in the Age of Sail*. Cambridge, Massachusetts: Harvard University Press, 1997.

Bontemps, Arna. *Great Slave Narratives: Selected and Introduced by Arna Botemps*. Boston: Beacon Press, 1969.

Bordewich, Fergus M. *Bound for Canaan: The Underground Railroad and the War for the Soul of America*. New York: Harper Collins Publishers, 2005.

Borone, Joseph. *"The Vigilant Committee of Philadelphia."* The Pennsylvania Magazine of History and Biography, July 1968, No 3.

Boyer, Richard Owen. *The Legend of John Brown: A Biography and a History*. New York: Knopf, 1972.

Bradford, Sarah. *Harriet Tubman: The Moses of Her People*: New York: Citadel Press, 1961.

Brandt, Nat. *The Town That Started the Civil War*. Syracuse, New York: Syracuse University Press, 1990.

Brefogle, William. *Make Free: The Story of the Underground Railroad.* Philadelphia: J.B. Lippincott Co., 1958

Brown, Henry Box. *Narrative of the Life of Henry Box Brown: Written by Himself.* New York: Oxford University Press, 2002.

Brown, William Wells. *The Negro in the American Rebellion: His Heroism and His Fidelity.* Introduced and annotated by William Edward Farrison. New York: The Citadel Press, 1971.

Buckmaster, Henrietta. *Let My People Go: The Story of the Underground Railroad and the Growth of the Abolition Movement.* Boston: Beacon Press, 1941.

Burchard, Peter. *One Gallant Rush: Robert Gould Shaw and His Brave Black Regiment.* New York: St. Martin's Press, 1965.

Bynum, Victoria. *The Long Shadow of the Civil War: Southern Dissent and its Legacies.* Chapel Hill: The University of North Carolina Press, 2010.

Campbell, Stanley W. *The Slave Catchers: Enforcement of the Fugitive Slave Law 1850-1860.* New York: W. W. Norton & Company, 1968.

Carton Evan. *Patriotic Treason: John Brown and the Soul of America.* New York: Free Press, 2006.

Cecelske, David. *The Fire of Freedom: Abraham Galloway and the Slaves Civil War.* Chapel Hill: The University of North Carolina Press, 2012.
--------. *The Waterman's Song: Slavery and Freedom in Maritime North Carolina.* Chapel Hill: University of North Carolina, 2001.

Cheek, William and Aimee Cheek. *John Mercer Langston and the Fight for Black Freedom.1829-65.* Urbana: University of Illinois Press, 1989.

Claxton, Melvin and Mark Puls. *Uncommon Valor: A Story of Race, Patriotism, and Glory in the Final Battles of the Civil War.* Hoboken, New Jersey: John Wiley and Sons, Inc., 2006.

Clinton, Catherine. *Harriet Tubman: The Road to Freedom.* New York: Little Brown and Co.,2004

Coffin, Levi. *Reminiscences.* Cincinnati: Western Tract Society,1879.

Collison, Gary. *Shadrack Minkins: From Fugitive Slave To Citizen.* Cambridge: Harvard University Press, 1997.

Conrad, Earl. *General Harriet Tubman.* Washington D.C.: Associated Press,1943.

Cornish, Dudley Taylor. *The Sable Arm: Black Troops in the Union Army,1861-1865.* Lawrence, Kansas: The University Press of Kansas, 1987.

Craft, William and Ellen Craft. *Running a Thousand Miles for Freedom.* Baton Rouge, Louisiana: Louisiana State University Press, 1999.

Crow, Jeffrey J. *The Black Experience in Revolutionary North Carolina.* Raleigh: Department of Cultural Resources, Division of Archives and History, 1977.

DeCaro, Louis. *John Brown: The Cost of Freedom.* New York: International Publishers, 2007.

Deyle, Steven. *Carry Me Back: The Domestic Slave Trade in American Life.* New York: Oxford University Press, 2005.

Dillon, Merton L. *Slavery Attacked: Southern Slaves and Their Allies 1619-1865,* Baton Rouge: Louisiana State University,1990.

Donald, David. *Charles Sumner and the Coming of the Civil War.* New York: Alfred A. Knopf, 1965.

Douglass, Frederick. *Life and Times of Frederick Douglass: Written by Himself. His Early Life as a Slave, His Escape, and His Complete History.* With a New Introduction by Rayford W. Logan. Reprinted from the revised edition of 1892. New York: Bonanza Books, 1962.

Drayton, Daniel. *Personal Memoir of Daniel Drayton, for Four Years and Four Months a Prisoner (for Charity's Sake) in Washington Jail.* New York: Negro Universities Press,1969.

Du Bois, W. E. Burghardt. *John Brown.* Centennial Edition. New York: International Publishers, 1962.

Egerton, Douglas R. *Death or Liberty: African Americans and Revolutionary America.* New York: Oxford University Press, 2009.

Emilio, Luis F. *A Brave Black Regiment: The History of the 54th Regiment of Massachuusetts Volunteer Infantry 1863-1865.* New York: Da Capo Press 1995.

Fairbank, Calvin. Rev. *Calvin Fairbank During Slavery Times.* New York: Negro University Press, 1969.

Fehrenbacher, Don E. *The Dred Scott Case: Its Significance in American Law and Politics.* New York: Oxford University Press, 1978.

Finkelman, Paul Editor. *Antislavery.* New York: Garland Publishing, Inc. 1989.

---------. *Rebellions, Resistance and Runaways Within the Slave South.* New York: Garland Publishing, Inc. 1989

Fogel, Robert William. *Without Consent Or Contract: The Rise and Fall of American Slavery.* New York: W.W. Norton Co. 1989.

Foner, Eric. *The Fiery Trial: Abraham Lincoln and American Slavery.* New York: W.W. Norton & Company, 2010.

---------. *Free Soil, Free Labor, Free Men: The Ideology of the Republican Party Before the Civil War.* New York: Oxford University Press, 1970.

Foner, Philip S. Editor *The Life and Writings of Frederick Douglass.* New York: International Publishers, 1950.

Forbes, Ella. *But We Have No Country: The 1851 Christiana Resistance.* Cherry Hill, New Jersey: Africana Homestead Legacy Publishers, 1998.

Franklin, John Hope. *The Emancipation Proclamation.* New York: Doubleday, 1963.

Franklin, John Hope, and Loren Schweninger. *Runaway Slaves: Rebels on the Plantation.* New York: Oxford University Press, 1999.

Freehling, William W. *The South Vs. The South: How Anti-Confederate Southerners Shaped the Course of the Civil War.* New York: Oxford University Press, 2001.

Frey, Sylvia R. *"Between Slavery and Freedom: Virginia Blacks in the American Revolution."* The Journal of Southern History. V. 49 # 3 August 1983.

Frey, Sylvia R. *Water From the Rock: Black Resistance in a Revolutionary Age.* Princeton, New Jersey: Princeton University Press,1991.

Frost, Karolyn Smardz. *I've Got A Home In Glory Land: A Lost Tale of the Underground Railroad.* New York: Farrar, Straus and Giroux, 2007.

Galpin, W. Freeman. *"The Jerry Rescue."* New York History: Proceedings of the New York State Historical Association vol. 43, 1945.

Gara, Larry. *The Liberty Line: The Legend of the Underground Railroad.* Lexington; University Press of Kentucky, 1996.

----------. *"William Still and the Underground Railroad."* Pennsylvania History 28 1996.

----------. *"Fugitive Slave Law: a Double Paradox,"* Civil War History 10 (1964) pg 229-40.

Gates, Henry Louis, editor. *The Classic Slave Narratives.* New York: Mentor, 1987.

George, Carol V. R. *Segregated Sabbaths: Richard Allen and the Rise of Independent Black Churches 1760-1840.* New York: Oxford University Press, 1973.

Giddings, Joshua R. *The Exiles of Florida.* New York: Arno Press, 1969.

Glatthaar, Joseph T. *Forged in Battle: The Civil War Alliance of Black Soldiers and White Officers.* New York: Free Press, 1990

Goodheart, Lawrence B. *"The Chronicles of Kidnapping in New York: Resistance to the Fugitive Slave Law, 1834-1835."* Afro-Americans in New York Life and History 8, January 1984.

----------. *1861: The Civil War Awakening.* New York: Alfred A. Knopf, 2011.

Goodrich, Thomas. *War to the Knife: Bleeding Kansas 1854-1861.* Mechanicsburg, Pennsylvania: Stackpole Books, 1998.

Green, Lorenzo. *"Some Observations on the Black Regiment of Rhode Island in the American Revolution."* The Journal of Negro History. V. 37 April 1952.

Grover, Kathryn. *The Fugitive's Gibraltar: Escaping Slaves and Abolitionism in New Bedford, Massachusetts.* Amherst: University of Massachusetts Press, 2001.

Guin, Jeff. *Our Land Before We Die: The Proud Story of the Seminole Negro.* New York: Jeremy P. Tarcher/ Putnam Inc, 2002.

Hadden, Sally E. *Slave Patrols: Law and Violence in Virginia and the Carolinas.* Cambridge: Harvard University Press, 2001.

Hagedorn, Ann. *Beyond The River: The Untold Story of the Heroes of the Underground Railroad.* New York: Simon & Schuster, 2002.

Harrold, Stanley. *The Abolitionists and the South 1831-1861*. Lexington: University Press of Kentucky, 1995.

----------. *Gamalied Bailey and Antislavery Union*. Kent, Ohio: Kent State University Press, 1986.

----------. *Subversives : Antislavery Community in Washington D.C.* Baton Rouge: Louisiana State University Press, 2003.

Henson Josiah. *An Autobiography of the Reverend Josiah Henson*. Reading, Massachusetts: Addison Wesley Press, 1969.

Higginson, Thomas Wentworth. *Army Life in a Black Regiment*. Boston: Beacon Press, 1962.

Hilty, Hiram H. *By Land and By Sea: Quakers Confront Slavery and its Aftermath in North Carolina*. Greensboro, North Carolina: North Carolina Friends Historical Society, 1993.

Hinks, Peter P. *To Awaken My Afflicted Brethren: David Walker and the Problem of Antebellum Slave Resistance*. University Park, Pennsylvania: The Pennsylvania State University Press, 1997.

Hinton, Richard J. *John Brown and His Men*. New York: Arno Press and the New York Times, 1968.

Hodges, Graham Russell Gao. *David Ruggles: A Radical Black Abolitionist and the Underground Railroad in New York City*. Chapel Hill: The University of North Carolina Press, 2010.

Hodges, Willis Augustus. *Free Man of Color: The Autobiography of Willis Augustus Hodges*. Edited, with an Introduction, by Willard B. Gatewood Jr. Knoxville: University of Tennessee Press, 1982.

Hollandsworth, James G. *The Union Native Guards: The Black Military Experience During the Civil War*. Baton Rouge: Louisiana State University Press, 1995.

Horton, James Oliver. *Free People of Color: Inside the African American Community*. Washington: Smithsonian Institute Press, 1993.

Horton, James and Lois E. Horton. *Black Bostonians: Family Life and Community Struggles in the Antebellum North*. New York: Holmes and Meier Publishers, 1979.

----------. *In Hope of Liberty: Culture Community and Protest Among Northern Free Blacks 1700-1860*. New York: Oxford University Press, 1997.

Hudson, J. Blaine. *Encyclopedia of the Underground Railroad.* North Carolina: McFarland & Co, Inc., 2006.

----------. *Fugitive Slaves and the Underground Railroad in the Kentucky Borderland.* Jefferson, North Carolina: McFarland & Company, Publishers, 2002.

Hunter, Carol. *To Set the Captives Free: Reverend Jermain Westley Loguen and the Struggle For Freedom in Central New York 1835-1872.* New York: Garland Publishing, Inc., 1993.

Huston, James L. *Calculating the Value of the Union: Slavery, Property Rights, and the Economic Origins of the Civil War.* Chapel Hill: The University of North Carolina Press: 2003

Jacobs, Donald M. editor. *Courage and Conscience: Blacks & White Abolitionists in Boston.* Bloomington: Indiana University Press, 1993.

Jacobs, Harriet. *Incidents in the Life of a Slave Girl:* Written By Herself. Boston: 1861.

Jenkins, Sally and John Stauffer. *The State of Jones: The Small Southern County That Seceded From the Confederacy.* New York: Doubleday, 2009.

Jones, Norrece T. *Born a Child of Freedom, Yet a Slave: Mechanisms of Control and Strategies of Resistance in Antebellum South Carolina.* Hanover and London: Wesleyan University Press, 1990.

Jordan, Ervin L. *Black Confederates and Afro-Yankees in Civil War Virginia.* Charlottesville: University Press of Virginia, 1995.

Kaplan, Sidney and Emma Kaplan. *The Black Presence in the Era of the American Revolution.* Revised Edition. Amherst: University of Massachusetts Press, 1989.

Katzman, David K. *Before the Ghetto: Black Detroit in the Nineteenth Century.* Urbana: University of Illinois Press, 1973.

Landers, Jane. *Black Society in Spanish Florida.* Urbana: University of Illinois Press, 1999.

Langston, John Mercer. *From the Virginia Plantation to the National Capital.* New York: Arno Press, 1969.

Larson, Kate Clifford. *Bound for the Promised Land: Harriet Tubman, Portrait of an American Hero.* New York: Ballantine Books, 2004.

Leaming, Hugo Prosper. *Hidden Americans: Maroons of Virginia and the Carolinas.* New York: Garland publishing Inc. 1995.

Lemisch, Jesse. *"Jack Tar in the Streets: Merchant Seamen in the Politics of Revolutionary America."* William and Mary Quarterly. V. XXX, # 3 July 1968.

---------. *Jack Tar vs John Bull: The Role of New York's Seamen in Precipitating the Revolution.* New York: Garland Pub, 1997.

Levine, Bruce. *Confederate Emancipation: Southern Plans to Free and Arm Slaves During the Civil War.* New York: Oxford University Press, 2006.

---------. *The Fall of the House of Dixie: The Civil War and the Social Revolution That Transformed the South.* New York: Random House, 2013.

Levy, Leonard. *"The "Abolitionist Riot": Boston's First Slave Rescue."* The New England Quarterly 1952.

---------. *" Sim's Case: The Fugitive Slave Law in Boston."* The Journal of Negro History. January 1950.

Libby, Jean Editor. *John Brown Mysteries.* Missoula, Montana: Pictorial Histories Publishing Company 1999.

---------. *The Slaves Who Fought With John Brown.* Palo Alto, California: Jean Libby, 1988.

Lindquest, Charles. *The Antislavery Underground Railroad in Lenawee County, Michigan 1830-1860.* Lenawee, Michigan: Lenawee County Historical Society, 1999.

Linebaugh, Peter and Marcus Rediker. *The Many Headed Hydra: Sailors, Slaves, Commoners, and the Hidden History of the Revolutionary Atlantic.* Boston: Beacon Press 2000.

Litwack, Leon F. *Been in the Storm So Long: The Aftermath of Slavery.* New York: Vintage Books, 1979.

Logan, Rayford and Michael R. Winston ed. *Dictionary of American Negro Biography.* New York: W.W. Norton, 1982.

Loguen, Jermain W. *The Rev. J.W. Loguen as a Slave and as A Freeman.: A Narrative of Real Life.* New York: Negro University Press, 1968.

Lovejoy, J. C. *Memoir of Rev. Charles T. Torrey.* New York: Negro University Press, 1969.

MacDougall, Marion G. *Fugitive Slaves 1619-1865.* Boston: Ginn & Co., 1891.

MacLeod, Duncan. *Slavery, Race, and the American Revolution.* Cambridge, U.K.: Cambridge University Press, 1974.

Markle, Donald. *Spies & Spymasters of the Civil War*. Revised Edition. New York: Hippocrene Books, 2000.

Martin, Waldo E. *The Mind of Frederick Douglass*. Chapel Hill: The University of North Carolina Press, 1984.

Mayer, Henry. *All On Fire: William Lloyd Garrison and the Abolition of Slavery*. New York: St. Martin's Press, 1998.

Mcfeely, William S. *Frederick Douglass*. New York: W. W. Norton & Company, 1991.

McGlone, Robert. *John Brown and the War Against Slavery*. Boston; Cambridge University Press., 2009.

McGowan, James A. *Station Master on the Underground Railroad: The Life and Letters of Thomas Garrett*. Moylan, Pa.: Whitsie Press, 1977.

McPherson, James M. *Battle Cry of Freedom: The Civil War Era*. New York: Oxford University Press, 1988.
----------. *The Negro's Civil War: How American Blacks Felt and Acted During the War For the Union*. New York: Vintage Books, 2003.

Miller, William Lee. *Arguing About Slavery: The Great Battle in the United States Congress*. New York: Alfred A. Knopf, 1996.

Missall, John and Mary Lou Missell. *The Seminole Wars: America's Longest Indian Conflict*. Gainesville: University Press of Florida, 2004.

Mohr, Clarence. *On the Threshold of Freedom: Masters and Slaves in Civil War Georgia*. Athens: The University of Georgia Press, 1986.

Morris, Thomas D. *Free Men All: The Personal Liberty Laws of the North 1780-1861*. Baltimore: The John's Hopkins University Press, 1974.

Morrison, Michael A. *Slavery and the American West: The Eclipse of Manifest Destiny and the Coming of The Civil War*. Chapel Hill: The University of North Carolina Press, 1997.

Mull, Carol. *The Underground Railroad in Michigan*. Jefferson, North Carolina: McFarland & Co. Inc. 2010.

Mulroy, Kevin. *Freedom on the Border: The Seminole Maroons in Florida, the Indian Territory, Coahuila, and Texas*. Lubbock, Texas: Texas Tech. University Press, 1993.

Nash, Gary B. *Forging Freedom: The Formation of Philadelphia's Black Community 1720-1840.* Cambridge, Massachusetts: Harvard University Press, 1988.

Nash, Gary. *The Unknown American Revolution: The Unruly Birth of Democracy and the Struggle to Create America.* New York: Viking, 2005.

Nelson, Truman. T*he Old Man: John Brown at Harper's Ferry.* New York: Holt, Rinehart, and Winston, 1973.

Nevins, Allan. *Ordeal of the Union Volume 1&2.* New York: Charles Scribner's Sons., 1947.

----------. *Emergence of Lincoln Volume 1&2.* New York: Charles Scribner's Sons, 1950.

Nye, Russel B. *Fettered Freedom: Civil Liberties and the Slavery Controversy 1830-1860.* Lansing Michigan; Michigan State University Press, 1963.

Oates Stephen B. *Freedom National: The Destruction of Slavery in the United States 1861-1865.* New York: W.W. Norton & Company, 2013.

----------. *The Radical and the Republican: Frederick Douglass, Abraham Lincoln and the Triumph of Antislavery Politics.* New York: W.W. Norton, 2008.

----------. *To Purge This Land With Blood; A Biography of John Brown.* Amherst: University of Massachusetts Press,1970.

Oickle, Alvin F. *Jonathan Walker: The Man With the Branded Hand.* Everett: Lorelli Slater, 1998.

Parker, John P. *His Promised Land: The Autobiography of John P. Parker.* New York: W.W. Norton, 1996.

Pease, Jane H. And William H. Pease. *They Who Would Be Free: Blacks' Search for Freedom, 1830-1861.* Urbana: University of Illinois Press, 1974.

Petit, Eber. *Sketches in the History of the Underground Railroad.* Westfield, New York: Chautauqua Regional Press, 1999.

Porter, Dorothy B. *"David Ruggles, An Apostle of Human Rights."* Journal of Negro History 28(1), 1943.

Porter, Kenneth W. *The Black Seminoles: History of a Freedom Seeking People* . Gainesville, Florida: University Press of Florida, 1996.

----------. *The Negro On the American Frontier.* New York: Arno Press, 1971.

Potter, David M. *The Impending Crisis 1848-1861.* New York: Harper & Row, 1976.

Quarles, Benjamin. *Allies for Freedom: Blacks and John Brown*. New York: Oxford University Press. 1974.

----------. *The Negro In the American Revolution*. Chapel Hill: University of North Carolina Press, 1961.

----------. *The Negro In the Civil War*. Boston, Little, Brown and Company, 1953.

Raphael, Ray. *A Peoples History of the American Revolution: How Common People Shaped the Fight for Independence*. New York: The New Press, 2001.

Redkey, Edwin S. Editor. *A Grand Army of Black Men: Letters from African-American Soldiers in the Union Army, 1861-1865*. New York: Cambridge University Press, 1992.

Redpath, James. *The Public Life of Captain John Brown: With an Autobiograpy of His Childhood and Youth*. London: Thayer & Eldridge, 1860.

Reneham, Edward J. *The Secret Six: The True Tale of the Men Who Conspired With John Brown*. New York: Crown Publishers, 1995.

Reynolds, David S. *John Brown Abolitionist: The Man Who Killed Slavery, Sparked the Civil War and Seeded Civil Rights*. New York: Alfred A. Knopf, 2005.

----------. *Mightier Than the Sword: Uncle Tom's Cabin and the Battle for America*. New York; W.W. Norton & Company, 2011.

Ricks, Mary Kay. *Escape on the Pearl*. New York: Harper Collins, 2007.

Richards, Leonard L. *The California Gold Rush and the Coming of the Civil War*. New York: Alfred A. Knope, 2007.

Robinson, Armstead L. *Bitter Fruits of Bondage: The Demise of Slavery and the Collapse of the Confederacy, 1861-1865*. Charlottesville: University of Virginia Press, 2005.

Robinson, Donald L. *Slavery in the Structure of American Politics 1765-1820*. New York: Harcourt Brace Jovanovich, Inc.1971.

Robinson, William H. *From a Log Cabin to the Pulpit, Or Fifteen Years in Slavery*. Eau Claire: James H. Tifft, 1913.

Rose, P.K. *"Black Dispatches: Black American Contributions to Union Intelligence During the Civil War."* Studies in Intelligence. March 2007.

Runyon, Randolph Paul. *Delia Webster and the Underground Railroad*. Lexington: University Press of Kentucky, 1996.

Russo, Peggy A. And Paul Finkelman Editors. *Terrible Swift Sword: The Legacy of John Brown*. Athens: Ohio University Press, 2005.

Sanborn, F. B. Editor. *The Life and Letters of John Brown: Liberator of Kansas and Martyr of Virginia*. New York: New American Library, 1969.

Scott, Otto J. *The Secret Six: John Brown and the Abolitionist Movement*. New York: NYT Times Books, 1979.

Siebert, Wilbur H. *The Underground Railroad From Slavery to Freedom*. New York: The Macmillan Company, 1898.

Slaughter, Thomas P. *Bloody Dawn: The Christiana Riot and Racial Violence in the Antebellum North*. New York: Oxford University Press, 1991.

Smedley, R.C. *History of the Underground Railroad*. New York: Arno Press and the New York Times, 1969.

Smith, Page. *Trial By Fire: A People's History of the Civil War and Reconstruction*. New York: McGraw-Hill Book Company, 1982.

Sokolow, Jayme A. *" The Jerry McHenry Rescue and the Growth of Northern Antislavery Sentiment During the 1850's"* Journal of American Studies. December 1982.

Stake, Virginia Ott. *John Brown in Chambersburgh*. Chambersburgh, Pennsylvania: Franklin County Heritage, Inc. 1977.

Stamp, Kenneth M. *America in 1857: A Nation on the Brink*. New York; Oxford University Press, 1990.

---------. *The Peculiar Institution: Slavery in the Ante-Bellum South*. New York: Vintage Books,1956.

Sterling, Dorothy. *Black Foremothers: Three Lives*. New York: The Feminist Press, 1988.

Stewart James Brewer. *Abolitionist Politics and the Coming of the Civil War*. Amherst: University of Massachusetts Press, 2008

---------. *Holy Warriors: The Abolitionists and American Slavery*. Revised Edition. New York: Hill and Wang, 1996.

---------. *Joshua R Giddings and the Tactics of Radical Politics*. Cleveland: The Press of Case Western Reserve University, 1970.

Still, William. *The Underground Railroad*. Chicago: Johnson Publishing Co., 1970.

309

Stowe, Harriet Beecher. *A Key to Uncle Tom's Cabin*. Boston: John P Jewett & Co. 1853.

---------. *Uncle Tom's Cabin*. New York: Bantam Books, 1981.

Strangis, Joel. *Lewis Hayden and the War Against Slavery*. North Haven, CT: The Shoe String Press.1999.

Sterling, Dorothy. *The Making of an Afro-American: Martin Robison Delany 1812-1885*. New York:Doubleday & Company, 1971.

Strother, Horatio T. *The Underground Railroad in Connecticut*. Middletown, Connecticut: Wesleyan University Press. 1962.

Sutherland, Daniel E. Editor. *Guerillas, Unionists, and Violence on the Confederate Home Front*. Fayetteville: University of Arkansas Press, 1999.

Tadman, Michael. *Speculators and Slaves: Masters, Traders and Slaves in the Old South*. Madison: University of Wisconsin Press, 1996.

Tatum, Georgia Lee. *Disloyalty in the Confederacy*. Lincoln: University of Nebraska Press, 2000.

Taylor, Nikki M. *Frontiers of Freedom: Cincinnati's Black Community 1802-1868*. Athens, Ohio: Ohio University Press, 2005.

Twyman, Bruce Edward. *The Black Seminole Legacy and North American Politics 1693-1845*. Washington D.C.: Howard University Press, 2001.

Ullman, Victor. *Martin Delany and the Beginning of Black Nationalism*. Boston Beacon Press, 1971

Uya, Olkon Edet. *Robert Smalls: From Slavery to Public Service, 1839-1915*. New York: Oxford University Press. 1971.

Villard, Oswald Garrison. *John Brown, 1800-1859: A Biography Fifty Years After*. New York: A. A. Knopf, 1943.

Von Frank, Albert J. *The Trials of Anthony Burns: Freedom and Slavery in Emerson's Boston*. Cambridge: Harvard University Press, 1998.

Walker, David. *Walkers Appeal with a new preface by William Loren Katz*. New York: Arno and the New York Times, 1969.

Walker, Jonathan. *The Trial and Imprisonment of Johnathan Walker*. Gainsville: University Press of Florida, 1974.

Weitz, Mark A. *More Damning Than Slaughter; Desertion in the Confederate Army.* Lincoln: University of Nebraska Press, 2005.

Weld, Theodore Dwight. *American Slavery As It Is: Testimony of a Thousand Witnesses.* New York: Arno Press, 1968.

Whitman, T. Stephen. *Challenging Slavery in the Chesapeake: Black and White Resistance to Human Bondage,1775-1865.* Baltimore: Maryland Historical Society,2007.

Williams, David. *A Peoples History of the Civil War: Struggles for the Meaning of Freedom.* New York: The New Press, 2005.

----------. *Bitterly Divided; The South's Inner Civil War.* New York: The New Press, 2008.

Williams, David et al. *Plain Folk in a Rich Man's War: Class and Dissent In Confederate Georgia.* Gainesville: University Press of Florida, 2002.

Wilson, Joseph T. *The Black Phalanx: African American Soldiers in the War of Independence, the War of 1812 & the Civil War.* New York: Da Capo Press, 1994.

Wilson, Ellen Gibson. *Loyal Blacks.* New York: Capricorn Books, 1976.

Winch, Julie. *A Gentleman of Color: The Life of James Forten.* New York: Oxford University Press, 2002.

----------. *Philadelphia's Black Elite: Activism, Accommodation, and the Struggle for Autonomy,1787-1848.* Philadelphia: Temple University Press, 1988.

Winik, Jay. *April 1865: The Month That Saved America.* New York: HarperCollins Publishers, 2001.

Wood, Gordon S. *Empire of Liberty: A History of the Early Republic, 1789-1815.* New York: Oxford University Press, 2009.

Yellin, Jean Fagan. *Harriet Jacobs: A Life.* New York: Basic Civitas Books, 2004.

Yetman, Norman R. *Life Under the "Peculiar Institution": Selections From the Slave Narrative Collections.* Huntington, New York: Krieger Publishing Co. 1976.

END

INDEX

Army of the Potomac, 241
Articles of Confederation, iv, 20, 145
Atkins, Smith (Colonel), 248–49
Atlanta Confederacy (1861-1865), 226
Atlas (Whig newspaper), 186
Attucks, Crispus (Massachusetts fugitive slave), 2, 4, 8–11, 9f, 10f, 42
Attucks, John (Wampanoag Indian), 8
Aughey, John (Reverend), 257–58
Auld, Captain (Douglass' church-going master), 126
Austin, Elbridge (Grey's Boston lawyer), 46

B

Baggs, David (Johnsons slavemaster), 256
Bailey, Gamalied (New Era editor), 68, 71
Bailey, Margaret, 71
Baines, Eliza (Norfolk, Virginia slave), 60
Baker, Frank (slave), 229
Baltimore (Maryland)
    about, 51, 61, 67, 135
    harbor, 45
    jail, 113
    market women, 61
    train, 214–15
Baltimore American (newspaper), 55
Banks, General, 278–80
Barksdale (Mississippi Congressman), 292
Bates, Polly Ann (black woman), 42
Baton Rouge (Louisiana), 48, 277, 279
Battle Creek (town), 105
battle in Boston (1747), 3–4
battle of
    Bull Run, 228, 242
    Bunker Hill, 11
    Christiana, 179f, 180
    Concord, 11
    Corinth, 263
    Fort Wagner, x, 283–85
    the Ironclads, 238–40
    Island Mounds (Missouri), 275
    Lexington, 11
    Saratoga, 14
    Vicksburg (Mississippi), 240–41, 259, 263, 279
    Yorktown, 16–17
Battle of
    Gettysburg (1863), 241
Bayliss, William D. (Kesiah captain), 59
Beaufort (South Carolina port), 232–33, 245, 268–69, 282

Beaufort aristocratic family (South Carolina), 267
Beaufort Harbor (North Carolina), 233
Beaufort island, 245
Beaufort plantation (South Carolina), 253
Beauregard (Confederate General), 270–71
Belden, George (US Attorney), 199–200
Benjamin, Judah (Confederate Secretary of State), 291–92
Benton, Thomas Hart (Missouri Senator), 196
Bethel AME Church (Cincinnati), 89
Bibb, Henry (abolitionist lecturer), 128, 153–55
Bibb, Malinda, 153–55
Bibb, Mary (wife of Henry Bibb), 154–55
Bible of America's anti-slavery movement.
    See Uncle Tom's Cabin
Birchtown (Nova Scotia), 144, 146
Birney, James (abolitionist), 91
black
    Canadian settlements, 66
    Creoles, 277, 280, 288
    Detroiters, 103–4
    dockworkers and boatmen, 89
    Loyalists in Nova Scotia, 144–48
    maroons, 56
    men, self-emancipated, 245, 249
    militia group of freedmen, 272–73
    New Orleans, 277–78
    New Yorkers, 40–41
    Nova Scotia settlers, 144–46
    Philadelphians, 28, 111
    pilot, 59
    Pittsburgh, 100
    sailors' extradition (1839), 117
    seamen, 63–64
    seamen's law (Southern States), 64
    Seminoles, 75, 77, 81–82, 84–85, 87, 167–68
    teamsters, 51
    watermen (Underground Railroad conductors), 32, 57–58, 233
Black Codes, 90
black community
    in Boston, 42–43, 113–14, 170
    in Cincinnati, 89–92
    in Columbia, 35
    in Elgin County (Ontario, Canada), 156
    in Ohio, 88 *(See also Cincinnati (Ohio)* in
        Philadelphia, 108–9, 111
    in Pittsburgh, 100
    in Toronto (Ontario, Canada), 152, 157

315

Ironclads, battle of, 238–40

Union Navy blockade of Southern coast, 231
volunteers to defend the Union, 75,000, 227
Whig, 194
Lincoln, Levi (Quock Walker's lawyer), 17
Lincoln's Legal Loyal League (Legal League), 228, 236. *See also* Legal League
Little Charles (Fox's slave), 48–49
local military units (Home Guards), 234, 262, 266, 288, 290
Lockley, Jock (free man), 40
Loguen, Jermain W. (Syracuse black minister), 175–78, 208
Long, Henry (fugitive slave), 166, 182
Longstreet, General, 241
Louisiana (territories), 15, 24–26, 64, 275–80, 283
Louisiana black soldiers, 275
Louisiana Native Guard, 278–80
Louisiana Purchase (1803), 24
Louisiana slaveholders, 278
Louvestre, Mary (African American woman), 239–40
Louvestre, Simon (slaveholder, *Merrimac* designer), 239
Lovejoy, Elijah (white abolitionist martyr), v, 115–17
Lovejoy's warehouse (Alton, Illinois), 116
Lowe, Jacob (US Marshal), 199
Lowell, Massachusetts, 26–27
Lower Neuse River, 52
Luchum, Phil (liberated slave), 218
Lumpkin County (North Georgia), 289
Lundy, Benjamin (antislavery newspaper editor), 113
Lynchburg Republican, 292

M

Macon (Georgia), 133, 164, 262
Macon Telegraph, 292
Madison (Cincinnati), 90
Madison, James (President), 75–77
Madison Underground Railroad station, 90
Mahan, Asa (abolitionist), 98
Mahan, John Bennington, 94–95
Mahan, William, 95
Maitland, Sir Peregrine (Lieutenant Governor of Canada), 150, 152
Mallory, Shepard (slave), 229–30
maroon camps, 19
maroon colonies, 19
maroon settlers (Great Dismal Swamp), 265
Martin, John Sella (Reverend), 251–53, 251f

Maryland (slaveholding state)
about, 45, 51, 54, 67, 142, 208, 210, 228
courts, 74
government, 33
grand jury (1892), 113
jail, 69
plantations, 51, 64
slaveholders, 64–65, 67, 141 (*See also* Prigg, Edward)
slaveholders convention (1842), 67 (*See also* Torrey, Charles)
slaves, 55, 65, 67, 134 (*See also* Norton, Jo)
Maryland Underground Railroad, 55. (*See also* Predo, Henry)
Mason (Lewis Washington's slave), 219–20
Mason County Kentucky, grand jury in, 95
Mason-Dixon line (1820), vii, 161, 183
Massachusetts, 3, 8, 17–18, 26–27, 29, 31, 46, 119, 143
Massachusetts Constitution (1780), 17
Massachusetts Court, 142
Massachusetts Declaration of Rights, 17
Massachusetts law (1837), 46
Massachusetts Legislature, 47, 226
Massachusetts militia, 11
Massachusetts Personal Liberty Laws, 143
Massachusetts ship owner, 113. (*See also* Todd, Francis)
Massachusetts slaveholders, 18
Massachusetts State Legislature, 8, 143
Matilda (young Missouri slave woman), 91
May, Samuel (white abolitionist, New York), 177–78
McCarty, US Marshal, 190
McClellan, George (Pinkerton's friend), 236
McClintock, Dr. (Pittsburgh mayor), 100
McEntee, John (Captain), 241
McHenry, Jerry (fugitive), 177–78
McIntosh, Ebenezer (shoemaker), 5–6
Mckee, Henry (Smalls slavemaster), 253
McKim, James (Brown's recruit), 132
McKinseyites (criminal gang), 104
Merchant's Exchange (Boston), 186–87
Mercury (newspaper), 292
Merriam, Francis Jackson (Brown's recruit), 214
Merrimac (Confederate nine-gun ship), 238–40
Merriman, Francis (Brown's recruit), 214, 219, 221
Messinger, John (Milwaukee businessman), 190
Methodist church (Philadelphia), 109–10
Mexican anti-slavery law, 72

New York City
about, 7, 38–41, 50, 114, 166
port, 40
raid by Royal Navy (1757), 3
riot (1863), 283
New York City Underground Railroad, 39, 41.
See also Garnet, George; Ruggles, David;
Williams, Peter; Wright, Elizur
New York City Vigilance Committee, 30, 38, 40–41
New York Governor, 223
New York legislature (1857), 196
New York Supreme Court, 202
New York Times, 280
New York Tribune, 156, 199
New Yorkers, upper class, 39
Newly, Dangerfield (freedman), 213
Newly, Harriet, 213
Nickerson, Captain, 285–86
Nickols, F. J. (Captain of Union ship Onward), 253
Nicolls, Edward (British Lieutenant Colonel), 78
"Non Importation" pact, 7, 9
Norfolk (Virginia), 32, 45, 49, 55, 60, 169, 238–40,
265, 268, 284
Norfolk American Beacon (newspaper), 58
Norfolk mayor, 62–63, 63f
Norfolk navy shipyards, 238
Norfolk Underground Railroad, 284
North Carolina
Home Guard, 266, 290
Quakers, 54
slave trader, 189
slaveholders, 109, 131
Underground Railroad, 54
North Star Journal (newspaper), 46, 143
Northampton Committee of Safety (Virginia), 13
Northern abolitionist leaders, 113
Northern antislavery leaders, 223
northern industrialists, 27
Northern shipbuilders, 239
Northern states
antislavery communities of, 74
black men or women in a free state were
presumed to be citizens of that state, 107
Dred Scott decision (1857), 195–96, 206
ex-slaves became lecturers on the antislavery
circuit, 129
freedom to any slave enlisting in Continental
Army, 12–13
Fugitive Slave Law, mass protests, 166, 183

horror of slavery became a reality (1845),
128–29
laws to protect free black citizens from being
kidnapped and sold into slavery, 45
Personal Liberty Laws, 191
political battle between North and South
(1849), vii
religious revival movement, 99
Republican Party (1856), 194, 196, 283
slave hunters invaded searching for
fugitive slaves and freedmen, 22
slavery abolished (1812), 51, 57
slavery was illegal (1830), 21
slavery was immoral, 99
stories from abolitionist circuit, 127–28
Supreme Court and laws protecting free black
citizens were unconstitutional (1842), 45
Whig Party, 124, 162, 193, 242
Northern Virginia battlefields, 236–37, 241–42,
245–46, 263, 265, 281, 290
Northwest Ordinance (outlawed slavery), 195
Northwest Territory, 145
Norton, Jo (Maryland slave), 134–35, 176–78
Notes of Canada West (Shadd), 158
Nova Scotia (Canada), 144

O

Oberlin, Ohio (abolitionist town)
about, 97–98, 197–201
antislavery commitment, 98
black community leaders, 198
charity funds, 198
rescuers (1851), 198, 198f, 199, 201, 203,
208–9
Underground Railroad, 198
Vigilance Committee, 214
Wellington rescuers, 198–201
Oberlin College, 136–37, 198. See also
antislavery rebels of Lane College
Oberlin Institute's Board of Trustees, 98
Oconchattemicco (Seminole Chief), 82
Ohio, 90–91, 93
Ohio (steamboat), 102
Ohio Antislavery Society, 97
Ohio legislature, 88
Ohio River (slavery–freedom dividing line), 23, 44,
88–89, 93, 136, 138–39, 228
Ohio State Supreme Court, 201
Ohio Supreme Court ruling (1841), 91

ABOUT THE AUTHOR

Throughout her career and following her retirement as a librarian, Evelyn Millstein, researched and taught African American history, with particular emphasis on the unground railroad. She found that her audiences were enchanted with the underground railroad story, a saga not about important national leaders but about people like themselves. They loved stories about heroic fugitives, brave rescuers, and entire communities fighting for the right of men and women to be free. As an educator, she helped teachers integrate black history into the regular American history curriculum. She had long regarded the Underground Railroad crusade to be one of the most important movements in American history – our first interracial movement led by African Americans – that had an impact on our nation's history never truly appreciated by scholars. Evelyn Millstein lives in Royal Oak, Michigan with her husband of 65 years, Al Millstein, a retired lawyer.

Made in the USA
Lexington, KY
05 June 2018